The Hajj

Every year hundreds of thousands of pilgrims from all over the world converge on Mecca and its precincts to perform the rituals associated with the Hajj, which Muslims have been doing since the seventh century. In this volume, scholars from a range of fields – including history, religion, anthropology, and literature – together tell the story of the Hajj and explain its significance as one of the key events in the Muslim religious calendar. By outlining the parameters of the Hajj from its beginnings to the present day, the contributors have produced a global study that takes in the vast geographies of belief in the world of Islam. This volume pays attention to the diverse aspects of the Hajj, as lived every year by hundreds of millions of Muslims, touching on its rituals, its regional forms, the role of gender, its representation in art, and its organization on a global scale.

Eric Tagliacozzo is Professor of History at Cornell University. He is the author of *Secret Trades, Porous Borders: Smuggling and States along a Southeast Asian Frontier, 1865–1915* (2005), which won the Harry J. Benda Prize from the Association of Asian Studies, and of *The Longest Journey: Southeast Asians and the Pilgrimage to Mecca* (2013). He is the Director of the Comparative Muslim Societies Program at Cornell, the Director of the Cornell Modern Indonesia Project, and the editor of the journal *Indonesia*, and has recently served on the Southeast Asia Council of the Association of Asian Studies (AAS).

Shawkat M. Toorawa is Associate Professor of Arabic Literature and Islamic Studies at Cornell University. He is the author of *Ibn Abi Tahir Tayfur and Arabic Writerly Culture: A Ninth Century Bookman in Baghdad* (2005), and the editor and coeditor of several collections, including *The Western Indian Ocean: Essays on Islands and Islanders* (2007) and *Islam: A Short Guide to the Faith* (2011). He is a Mellon Foundation New Directions Fellow, an executive editor of the Library of Arabic Literature, and serves on the editorial boards of *Middle Eastern Literatures* and the *Journal of Abbasid Studies*.

FIGURE 1 Pilgrims Camped on the outskirts of Mecca, 1880s

Call people to the pilgrimage! They will come to you on foot, on every lean camel, and by every distant pass, and will see its benefits for themselves. (Q Ḥajj 22: 27–28)

The Hajj

Pilgrimage in Islam

Edited by
ERIC TAGLIACOZZO
Cornell University

SHAWKAT M. TOORAWA
Cornell University

CAMBRIDGE
UNIVERSITY PRESS

CAMBRIDGE
UNIVERSITY PRESS

One Liberty Plaza, 20th floor, New York, NY 10006, USA

Cambridge University Press is part of the University of Cambridge.

It furthers the University's mission by disseminating knowledge in the pursuit of education, learning, and research at the highest international levels of excellence.

www.cambridge.org
Information on this title: www.cambridge.org/9781107612808

First published 2016
Reprinted 2020

Printed in the United Kingdom by TJ International Ltd. Padstow Cornwall

A catalog record for this publication is available from the British Library.

Library of Congress Cataloging in Publication Data
Tagliacozzo, Eric, editor. | Toorawa, Shawkat M., editor.
The Hajj : pilgrimage in Islam / edited by Eric Tagliacozzo, Shawkat Toorawa.
New York : Cambridge University Press, 2015. | Includes bibliographical references and index.
LCCN 2015040729 | ISBN 9781107030510 (hardback)
LCSH: Muslim pilgrims and pilgrimages – Saudi Arabia – Mecca.
LCC BP187.3 .H2433 2015 | DDC 297.3/524–dc23
LC record available at http://lccn.loc.gov/2015040729

ISBN 978-1-107-03051-0 Hardback
ISBN 978-1-107-61280-8 Paperback

Contents

The colour plate section appears between pages 146 and 147.

List of Maps, Charts, and Figures

MAPS

CHART

FIGURES

PLATES

Contributors

Saud al-Sarhan is Director of Research at the King Faisal Center for Research and Islamic Studies in Riyadh.

Robert R. Bianchi is Lecturer in Law at the University of Chicago Law School and is an attorney-at-law in private practice.

Benjamin Claude Brower is Associate Professor of History at the University of Texas at Austin.

Gary R. Bunt is Reader in Islamic Studies at the University of Wales Trinity Saint David.

Juan E. Campo is Associate Professor of Religious Studies at the University of California, Santa Barbara.

Sylvia Chiffoleau is a Researcher at the Laboratoire de Recherche Historique Rhône-Alpes in Lyon.

Valeska Huber is a research fellow in Colonial History at the German Historical Institute London.

Fareeha Khan is an independent scholar affiliated with Willamette University and currently resides in Jeddah.

Harry Munt is Lecturer in Medieval History at the University of York.

Asma Sayeed is Associate Professor of Islamic Studies at the University of California, Los Angeles.

Eric Tagliacozzo is Professor of History at Cornell University.

Shawkat M. Toorawa is Associate Professor of Arabic Literature and Islamic Studies at Cornell University.

Michael Wolfe is President and Co-Executive Producer of Unity Productions Foundation and Co-Director of Muslims on Television and Screen.

Travis Zadeh is Associate Professor of Religion at Haverford College.

Preface

We both arrived at Cornell in 2000 in the departments of History and Near Eastern Studies, respectively. Over the years, the Hajj came up again and again as a topic of common interest, discussed over countless coffees and teas. Finally, at some point forgotten by us both, we endeavored to turn this shared interest into something more concrete and discussed getting a small group of scholars together to explore different aspects of the pilgrimage to Mecca. We approached Marigold Acland at Cambridge University Press with our idea, and she was very supportive. It has taken us a few years to bring the volume into the form it is in now, but slowly and surely the manuscript has taken shape. We owe Marigold and her generosity of spirit a great debt. We are grateful also to Will Hammell, Sarika Narula, Maria Marsh, Joshua Penney, Emma Collison, Mary Bongiovi, Sarah Green, Suzette Costello, Sathish Kumar, Holly Johnson, and especially Kate Gavino, who was a wonderful steward of the project.

We wish to thank our contributors, who all worked hard to meet the various deadlines we set them; Joe Lowry for vetting the glossary; Nij Tontisirin for designing the map of the world Muslim population; and Juan Campo, Faheem Moheed, and Saud al-Sarhan for making available photographs from personal and private collections. Most importantly, we wish to thank our families, who put up with literally years of the two of us disappearing haphazardly to the Ithaca Bakery, where we would sit and work on this volume. The spirit of all of these people – near and far – is in this book.

Abbreviations

Ar.	Arabic
BCE	before Common Era
ca.	approximately (*circa*)
CE	Common Era
d.	died
EI2	*Encyclopaedia of Islam*, New [2nd] ed. (Leiden: Brill, 1954–2009)
EI3	*Encyclopaedia of Islam Three*, 3rd ed. (Leiden: Brill, 2007–)
lit.	literally
pl.	plural
Q	Qur'ān
r.	ruled
s.v.	see entry under the word (*sub verbo*)

Note on Dates and Transliteration

DATES

Dates are typically CE unless otherwise noted. Where appropriate or informative, the Gregorian date is separated from the Islamic date by a slash (e.g., 204/820).

TRANSLITERATION

We have endeavored to standardize transliteration of Arabic, and followed as transparent a system as possible for the benefit of non-specialists. We retain the ʿayn (ʿ), and the hamza (ʾ) where appropriate. As there is no standard regarding the final (often silent) feminine marker in Arabic, readers may encounter, for example, both Jedda and Jeddah. As for the recurring words "Hajj" and "ʿUmra," which appear in English dictionaries, we have treated them as English words and capitalized them.

Note on Dates and Transliteration

TRANSLITERATION

Introduction

Eric Tagliacozzo and Shawkat M. Toorawa

The Hajj (Ar. *ḥajj*) is one of the largest gatherings of human beings on the planet; it is also one of the oldest. Every year millions of Muslims from around the world head to the city of Mecca and its environs to perform the Hajj during the month allocated for this ritual, or to perform the ʿUmra, the so-called minor pilgrimage, which can be done at any time of year. They come from all over the Middle East, but from much further afield as well – Africa, Asia, and increasingly from Europe, the Americas, and Australia. It is no exaggeration to say that the Hajj is the most important annual event in the world involving the transnational movement of human beings. The present book attempts to describe the various aspects and facets of the Muslim pilgrimage, with contributions ranging from discussions of the localized rituals of the Hajj itself to the building of a modern global infrastructure. Politics, economics, religion, global health, and transport are all part of the fabric of this volume, as is the lived experience of the pilgrimage as expressed in the literature and art of its practitioners.

We have asked specialists to weigh in with their own perspectives on how the Hajj works, so that the book can be greater than the sum of its parts. It is no doubt beyond any one person's expertise to write comprehensively about the global pilgrimage to Mecca, taking into account its many aspects and given the complexity of global connectivities – no one scholar has the languages, archival reach, or ethnographic experience to craft such a narrative. There is a long history to the pilgrimage to Mecca, but it can also be viewed through anthropological, sociological, and other disciplinary lenses. We have endeavored here to bring many of these approaches into one volume, so as to give a multivalent and multifaceted account of this enormous, international enterprise. We hope that as a collective we have succeeded in saying something cohesive and important about the Hajj as a religious, cultural, and sociopolitical phenomenon.

The Muslim Hajj has existed for nearly fourteen hundred years and has recognizable precursors. The Hijaz was an important crossroads for trans-Arabian caravans, and Mecca was already a pre-Islamic pilgrimage site at an early date. As Islam spread after Muhammad's death in the seventh century CE, Muslims traveled to Mecca and its environs to fulfill one of Islam's fundamental injunctions, to "make the annual pilgrimage to the House [i.e., the Kaʿba at Mecca] if one is able." What is more, Mecca, Medina, and other sites associated with the life and message of the Prophet became incorporated into the life-ways of Islam and began to attract year-round visitors and scholars. This process started in the seventh century but quickly gained momentum as Islam spread throughout the world through trade, conquest, and migration. Within a few generations after the life of Muhammad, Muslims could be found across nearly the entire breadth of the Old World, from Morocco to China. This history, in other words, became an increasingly global one from a very early date.

Many Muslims heed the call to perform the Hajj or the impulse to visit the sacred precincts. Yet the vast majority of pilgrims are by no means wealthy or able to take the time off from work and other daily, local responsibilities in order to do so. In pre-modern times, the trip could take many months; today, it takes thousands of dollars to undertake the journey. Yet, despite these concerns of both distance and expense, the number of pilgrims rises year after year, with around three million attending the annual Hajj at present, all arriving in the holy cities at approximately the same time. Some eleven million perform ʿUmra year-round, including more than a million during the fasting month of Ramaḍān alone. These figures show no signs of diminishing. On the contrary, the willingness and desire to make the Hajj is clearly increasing in numerous societies across the globe. The pilgrimage is a way for Muslims to get in touch not only with the history of their faith, but also with themselves – it is a communal journey, but also at the same time a deeply personal one. For this reason, our volume describes and discusses the Hajj from a number of different, yet interlocking, vantages. No single book can capture all of the ritual, historical, and geographical aspects of the Hajj, but we hope that our contributors have succeeded in evoking many, if not most, of the salient issues around the pilgrimage to Mecca. Indeed, we hope that this book will be profitably read side by side with its predecessors,[1] including several excellent volumes that have appeared in the past few years.[2] We have accordingly divided the chapters into four rubrics that we feel showcase the ways that the Hajj can and has been actualized: (1) Evolution, on the ways in which the Hajj originated and evolved; (2) Journey, which describes the history of the movement of pilgrims and proceeds more or less chronologically through time; (3) Infrastructure, which looks at the way that the Hajj is managed, by focusing on economics, health, and the welfare of pilgrims; and (4) Performance, where perspective shifts to the ways in which the pilgrimage is performed, how it is entering the "modern age," and how it is represented in travel accounts, and folk, popular, and elite art forms. The Hajj is triangulated therefore over time and distance, across customs and modes of organization, and as a religious obligation, as well as an aesthetic.

Part I, "Evolution" opens with Harry Munt's "Pilgrimage in pre-Islamic Arabia and Late Antiquity" which provides the historical and geographical context for the Hajj. Specifically, by relying on inscriptions and other relatively sparse sources, Munt situates pilgrimage in the Arabian Peninsula within the wider ambit of the late antique eastern Mediterranean. The Hajj, for all its specificities, has antecedents in local and interregional pilgrimages, both to the north and also in South Arabia. Munt notes that there is no evidence that pilgrimage in Arabia was interregional before the advent of Islam (properly, the Prophet

[1] Notably M. Gaudefroy-Demombynes, *Le pèlerinage à la Mekke* (Paris: P. Geuthner, 1923); F. E. Peters, *The Hajj: The Muslim Pilgrimage to Mecca and the Holy Places* (Princeton University Press, 1994); F. E. Peters, *A Literary History of the Muslim Holy Land* (Princeton University Press, 1994); R. R. Bianchi, *Guests of God: Pilgrimage and Politics in the Islamic World* (New York: Oxford University Press, 2004). The following collection is indispensable: *Records of the Hajj*, ed. A. Rush, 10 vols. ([Slough:] Archive Editions, 1993): I: *Pilgrim Prayers, Invocations and Rites*. II: *The Early Caliphal, Mamluk and Ottoman Periods, 630–1814*. III: *The Ottoman Period, 1814–1887*. IV: *The Ottoman Period, 1888–1915*. V: *The Hashimite Period, 1916–1925*. VI: *The Saudi Period, 1926–1935*. VII: *The Saudi Period, 1935–1951*. VIII: *The Saudi Period, 1951–*. IX: *Health Affairs and the Hajj*. X: *Documents and Maps*.

[2] M. E. McMillan, *The Meaning of Mecca: The Politics of Pilgrimage in Early Islam* (London: Saqi Books, 2011); A. I. al-Ghabbân, *Les deux routes syrienne et égyptienne de pèlerinage au nord-ouest de l'Arabie Saoudite*, 2 vols. (Cairo: Institut français d'archéologie orientale, 2011); V. Porter, *The Art of Hajj* (Northampton, MA: Interlink Books, 2012); V. Porter, with M. A. S. Abdel Haleem et al., *Hajj: Journey to the Heart of Islam* (Cambridge, MA: Harvard University Press, 2012); A. Petersen, *The Medieval and Ottoman Hajj Route in Jordan: An Archaeological and Historical Study* (Oxford: Oxbow, 2012); M. Chekhab-Abudaya and Cécile Bresc (eds.), *Hajj: The Journey through Art* (Milan: Skira, 2013); L. Mols and M. Buitelaar (eds.), *Hajj: Global Interactions through Pilgrimage* (Leiden: Sidestone Press, 2014).

Muhammad), but there is sufficient evidence to suggest that it was popular.[3] What sets the Hajj apart, in the Muslim telling, is the role of Abraham and before him Adam, both of whom are believed to have built the "House of God" at the site on which the city of Mecca then, and now, stands. Fareeha Khan takes up this sacred history in "Why Mecca? Abraham and the Hajj in the Islamic Tradition."[4] Drawing on the Qur'an, the Prophet's attested practice (as described in the Hadith corpus), and elaborations in classical Muslim sources, Khan shows how central the story of Abraham, Hagar, and Ishmael is to the Hajj, and to its meaning as a ritual of obedience and worship. Indeed, the centrality of Abraham to Muslim worship generally can be seen from the fact that, as Khan notes, "every day, Muslims remember the blessings bestowed by God on the biblical figure Abraham when they recite ... their five daily prayers."

Although Mecca is the Islamic *axis mundi* and the prime focus (literally) of ritual attention, as Travis Zadeh shows in "The Early Hajj, Seventh–Eighth Centuries CE," much was in flux in the two centuries following the death of Muhammad.[5] This led to lasting and profound transformations, especially in terms of the relationship of those in political power to the protection of the sanctuary, and of the routes leading to it. Those transformations, as Zadeh demonstrates, are captured in competing architectural expressions and "various discursive efforts that turned to the mythopoeic power of narrative to mold and reimagine the significance of the Kaʿba." Zadeh discusses the fact that women in political authority, or women allied to those in power, were a significant source of patronage, largesse, and decision making. Asma Sayeed makes that the focus of her chapter, "Women and the Hajj."[6] She does not confine herself to this, however, and also broaches such questions as the juridical and social factors affecting women's ability to embark on the Hajj, the specific ritual demands made on women pilgrims – for whom it has been described as a kind of jihad – and the complementarity of women's religious education

[3] For a study of the city of Medina, where the Prophet Muhammad is buried, see H. Munt, *The Holy City of Medina: Sacred Space in Early Arabia* (Cambridge University Press, 2014).

[4] Khan's *The Ethical Contours of a Fatwa: Women, Sufism and Islamic Law in Late Colonial India*, forthcoming.

[5] Zadeh is the author of *Mapping Frontiers across Medieval Islam: Geography, Translation and the ʿAbbāsid Empire* (London and New York: I. B. Tauris, 2011).

[6] Cf. A. Sayeed, *Women and the Transmission of Religious Knowledge in Islam* (Cambridge University Press, 2013).

and the Hajj. She concludes her chapter with a discussion of two memoirs by women in order to give direct voice to women pilgrims and their experience of their voyages.

Part II, "Journey," is organized according to the means of transport used by pilgrims to reach Mecca, namely, land, sea, and air. Inevitably, and predictably, there is temporal overlap – even in the age of air travel, millions still also make the trip by sea or land – but this seemed to us a productive way of thinking about the nature and modalities of the journey. In "Hajj by Land," Benjamin Brower shows that "[o]verland travel was and remains at the heart of every Hajj," not only because the Hajj itself consists in movement from one location to another over land, but also because the Qur'an implies a preference for land travel in its injunction, "Proclaim the Pilgrimage to the people. Let them come to you on foot and on every lean camel" (Q Ḥajj 22:27). Brower describes the road-building projects of the Umayyad–Abbasid era (seventh–thirteenth centuries), the caravans of the Mamluk era (thirteenth–sixteenth centuries), and those of the Ottoman period as well (sixteenth–nineteenth centuries). When he discusses the twentieth-century Hijaz Railway, Brower is able to show the intensification, and effect, of state control over the Hajj.[7]

In "Hajj by Sea," Eric Tagliacozzo explores the maritime dimensions of the historical transit to the Hijaz.[8] Whereas those crossing the seas might have constituted a small percentage of hajjis in earlier centuries, by the nineteenth and twentieth centuries they often accounted for half of all pilgrims, often from very far away. Indeed, as Tagliacozzo notes, "over time the pilgrimage to Mecca gradually became more and more of an oceanic venture, and remained thus into the middle decades of the twentieth century." He focuses on three distinct regions: the long coast stretching from the Maghreb all the way to Egypt, the Indian subcontinent and Arabian Sea, and maritime Southeast Asia. He notes that "the sea allowed for the pilgrimage to Mecca to take place as part of the global project of modernity, as this project was enacted and evolved in the later nineteenth century. Crucial here was the development of the steamship, a Western invention, but one that was quickly adopted both by Muslim powers and also by Muslim populations."

[7] Brower takes up questions he raises in *A Desert Named Peace: The Violence of France's Empire in the Algerian Sahara* (New York: Columbia University Press, 2009) and in the forthcoming *The Colonial Hajj, 1798–1962*.

[8] For a detailed discussion of Southeast Asian pilgrims, see E. Tagliacozzo, *The Longest Journey: Southeast Asians and the Pilgrimage to Mecca* (New York: Oxford University Press, 2013).

If the steamship meant a shorter, less expensive journey, then air travel brought exceptional speed and affordable travel, and resulted in what Robert Bianchi identifies as explosive growth in his chapter, "Hajj by Air." Yet, he points out also that this explosion, coupled with economic success, has also wreaked havoc, bringing overcrowding, stampedes, commercialization, monopoly, and a host of other problems and challenges. The unprecedented numbers have resulted in the instituting of quotas, imposed both by Saudi Arabia and by other nations. Bianchi looks in particular at the following countries, some of which send large numbers of pilgrims, others of which have had contested relationships with the Saudi Hajj authorities – Indonesia, Pakistan, India, Bangladesh, Nigeria, Turkey, Russia, and China.[9]

Part III, "Infrastructure," opens with Sylvia Chiffoleau's "Economics: Agents, Pilgrims, and Profits," which looks at the economic stakes in the transportation of pilgrims, especially the transition from what was in the main a Muslim economic activity to one of concern – and profit – to the colonial powers of the nineteenth and twentieth centuries. Chiffoleau describes the competition between the various actors, and also the economic dependence of the Hijaz on the Hajj. Her chapter also highlights economic and fiscal aspects of the Hajj that are often neglected, such as the levying of taxes and subsidies on pilgrims.[10]

In "The Pilgrimage to Mecca and International Health Regulations," Valeska Huber broaches the question of global health, notably the intersection of contagious diseases and mass pilgrimage. She approaches the question by juxtaposing two types of bodies, international organizations on the one hand and the pilgrims themselves on the other. Science and statistics are enlisted to show the ways in which sanitation, disease control, quarantine, and enforcement were deployed as strategies of containment and technologies of control. As Huber shows, although increasingly effective organization and communication appeared to lead to a reduction in health issues, globalization has actually lead to a resurgence of epidemics – witness the presence of MERS (Middle East Respiratory Syndrome) in Saudi Arabia, even as we write this introduction.[11]

9 See also R. R. Bianchi, *Guests of God: Pilgrimage and Politics in the Islamic World* (New York: Oxford University Press, 2004).

10 See also S. Chiffoleau and A. Madoeuf (eds.), *Les pèlerinages au Maghreb et au Moyen-Orient: espaces publics, espaces de public* (Beirut: Institut français du Proche-Orient, 2005).

11 On the question of people on the move, see V. Huber, *Channeling Mobilities: Migration and Globalisation in the Suez Canal Region and Beyond, 1869–1914* (Cambridge University Press, 2013).

Next, Saud al-Sarhan's "The Saudis as Managers of the Hajj" addresses the role of the Saudi Arabian government in directly administering the pilgrimage. Al-Sarhan looks at the "international conflicts over banned or circumscribed cultural practices" associated with the pilgrimage to Mecca. These practices, he notes, are incompatible with the conservative Salafi ideology espoused by the Holy Cities' custodians. In spite of that espousal, the government maintains that the Hajj is apolitical, even while it uses the Hajj to promote a positive image for itself. Al-Sarhan shows that in spite of the pressures that they face, the Saudis have been largely successful in keeping pilgrims safe and secure.[12]

The four chapters that comprise Part IV, "Performance," look at the different ways in which the Hajj is performed and in which that performance is manifested and represented. In "Performing the Hajj," Shawkat Toorawa describes the rituals of the ʿUmra and of the Hajj, notably the acts required of pilgrims during the several hours of the former or the five days of the latter in Mecca and its precincts. He also gives examples of the ceremonies that take place before pilgrims leave for Mecca, and when they return home. He proposes that the pilgrimage be understood as a metaphor of return, and as a reenactment of the Prophet Muhammad's actions.[13] In "Decoding the Hajj in Cyberspace," Gary Bunt emphasizes the fact that "understanding technological interfaces is increasingly important in developing a comprehension of contemporary Islamic issues and their dissemination," and that the Hajj is no exception to this. The growth of cyber Islamic environments has been exponential in the past fifteen years or so – the Hajj, initially only represented online, can now even be performed "digitally." One can "access" Mecca on the net, "enter" Hajj portals, and be guided by Hajj apps, equipped with GPS, during the course of the whole pilgrimage. Statistically most people will never perform the Hajj, but as Bunt notes, in the digital age, "there is no need for those staying at home to not feel part of the Hajj" any longer.[14]

Everyone who goes on Hajj has stories to tell; some will write these down in travel accounts and memoirs. In "The Pilgrim's Complaint: Five Accounts of the Hajj," Michael Wolfe looks at five critical Hajj accounts,

[12] Al-Sarhan is preparing a monograph based on his "Early Muslim Traditionalism: A Critical Study of the Works and Political Theology of Ahmad Ibn Hanbal" (unpublished thesis, University of Exeter, 2011).

[13] Toorawa has co-edited (with Roger Allen), *Islam: A Short Guide to the Faith* (Grand Rapids, MI: William B. Eerdmans Pub., 2011).

[14] Bunt is the author of *iMuslims: Rewiring the House of Islam* (Chapel Hill: University of North Carolina Press; London: C. Hurst & Co, 2009).

one from the early 1960s, and four much more recent ones. Three are by men: Jalal Al-e Ahmad's *Lost in the Crowd* (1964), Abdellah Hammoudi's *A Season in Mecca* (2005), and Michael Muhammad Knight's *Journey to the End of Islam* (2009). Two are by women: Asra Nomani's *Standing Alone in Mecca* (2005) and Qanta Ahmed's *In the Land of Invisible Women* (2008). These accounts – the direct result of personal experiences of performing the Hajj – all critique the apparatus of the Hajj. They also sometimes critique the transformed raison d'être of performing it, providing a very instructive counterpoint to descriptions that are more devotional and pious.[15] Juan Campo's "Visualizing the Hajj: Imagining a Sacred Landscape, Past and Present" looks at the history of the representation of the Hajj. This representation has encompassed such diverse media and genres as manuscripts, certificates, paintings, pamphlets, periodicals, books, calendars, pictures, postcards, signboards, films and videos, television broadcasts, web sites, and social media. Campo tells us that written accounts and Hajj certificates were significant in the pre-modern period, whereas in the modern period, visual media have become more prominent, especially with the advent of printing and photography.[16] Indeed, how the Hajj will be performed in the future, and how that will look (and also be represented) has yet to be determined.

As we hope the foregoing makes clear, we have endeavored in the present volume to sketch out a vision of the Hajj that is both historical and contemporary, one that takes into account elite and folk modes of practice, and that is sensitive to the breathtaking geographic diversity of the pilgrimage, now a truly global phenomenon. Although the Hajj started some fourteen centuries ago, it has evolved and undergone trans-valuations and shifts in mode and execution over time. Camel caravans gave way to Hajj by sail, and pilgrims are now primarily conveyed by air, jets hurtling aspirants over vast distances. It once took pilgrims from Indonesia, the world's largest Muslim polity, months if not years to perform the Hajj. It now takes the descendants of those same people only hours to fly across the ocean, and the entire experience can be completed in a few weeks. Banditry at the sacred sites by tribesmen eager to capitalize on the flow of visitors to the holy cities has now been replaced by a modern infrastructure and state-based security that has to be seen to be believed. The pages that follow impart some sense

[15] Cf. M. Wolfe, *One Thousand Roads to Mecca: Ten Centuries of Travelers Writing about the Muslim Pilgrimage*, revised and expanded (New York: Grove Press, 2015).

[16] Cf. J. Campo, *The Other Sides of Paradise: Explorations into the Religious Meanings of Domestic Space in Islam* (Columbia: University of South Carolina Press, 1991).

of the evolution of the Hajj as it has developed over the centuries as a common endeavor for many millions of people.

The Hajj is of course also – some would say primarily – an inner journey, a voyage toward God and toward an understanding of oneself. That dynamic is also broached in this volume. Taken together, the chapters answer such questions as: How has the meaning of the Hajj changed for pilgrims over time? What position does it occupy in the mental field of believers, and has this always been constant, or has the significance of the ritual changed over the centuries? Does the Hajj mean the same thing to women as it does to men, and how do its practices differ across the gender divide, in terms of the lived experience of the trip, and its many daily dimensions of practice? How does the pilgrimage look to different traditions within Islam, when the members of so many divergent "streams" of the religion (Sunni, Shiʿite, progressive, Salafi, and so on) all come to the holy cities at the same time? The book attempts to explore some of these more inwardly focused dimensions of the Hajj as well, laying out a cross-section of the ritual's meanings to the various adherents of the faith who all perform its outlines together.

In sum, we hope to be able to give a sense of the Muslim pilgrimage as a "total experience." There is of course no "model Hajj," no template of unitary experience for how a single Hajj must be undertaken. Rather, as is clear from the contributions collected here, the pilgrimage to Mecca is as varied as its practitioners, a diffuse yet coordinated mode of religious praxis that has taken on many colors over the centuries. Trying to understand the Hajj as a phenomenon forces one to confront religiosity, of course, but also sociology, the anthropology of belief, history writ large across huge spaces of both geography and time, and politics, all at once. The complexity of the Hajj is daunting, yet it is an institution and a practice that allows itself to be studied. It is, in fact, now being examined more and more by scholars in different academic bailiwicks wearing different academic lenses. We offer the present volume as an extension of this process of analysis, though it is of necessity only one of many such works that attempt to shine light on this fascinating topic. If we succeed in stimulating further conversation and analysis of the Hajj as a subject of discourse by scholars and believers alike, then we will know that our own endeavor in assembling this volume has been a worthwhile project indeed.

PART ONE

EVOLUTION

MAP 1 Arabian Peninsula

1

Pilgrimage in Pre-Islamic Arabia and Late Antiquity

Harry Munt*

In the first century BCE, a monumental inscription was erected in the kingdom of Saba' at Itwat – today Jabal Riyām, approximately thirty miles north of Ṣanʿāʾ in Yemen – in the local prestige language, Sabaic; it outlined a number of ordinances prescribed by the god Ta'lab for his people Samʿay. The first of these stated "that Samʿay should not fail in [the month] Dhū Abhay to go on pilgrimage (*hḥḏrn*) to [the shrine of the god] Almaqah in Mārib."[1] More than a thousand miles north of Jabal Riyām, near Bi'r al-Ruṣayʿī in southern Syria, at some point between the first century BCE and the early fourth century CE, a (semi)nomadic inhabitant of the desert steppe on the fringes of the Roman Empire inscribed a graffito upon an available rock in the language of the nomads of that area, which today we call Safaitic. He dated his short text with reference to "the year the pilgrimage to Sīʿ was in vain/suspended" (*s¹nt bṭl ḥg s¹ʿʿ*).[2] At these two extremities of the Arabian Peninsula, practices of

* I am very grateful to Robert Hoyland for his comments on an earlier draft of this chapter. I also wish to acknowledge the generous funding my research has received from the British Academy.

1 R 4176, ll. 1–2; translation (slightly modified) from M. A. Ghul and A. F. L. Beeston, "The Pilgrimage at Itwat," *Proceedings of the Seminar for Arabian Studies*, 14 (1984), 33. For more background information on the inscription, see K. A. Kitchen, *Documentation for Ancient Arabia*, 2 vols. (Liverpool: Liverpool University Press, 1994–2000), II, 530. [Kitchen's work should be consulted for full references for all the abbreviated sigla for South Arabian texts used in this chapter.]

2 BREnv.A.1. This text is currently unpublished, but it is referred to in M. C. A. Macdonald, "References to Sīʿ in the Safaitic inscriptions," in J. Dentzer-Feydy et al. (eds.), *Hauran II. Les installations de Sīʿ 8: du sanctuaire à l'établissement viticole* (Beirut: Institut Français d'Archéologie du Proche-Orient, 2003), I, 278.

pilgrimage were current in the centuries preceding the start of the prophetic career of Muhammad in Mecca, loosely halfway between the sites of our two texts and the location of another shrine, the Kaʿba, already associated with practices of pilgrimage for those who lived in the surrounding areas.

This prevalence of pilgrimages, in some parts of the Arabian Peninsula at least, should not really come as any surprise. Pilgrimage was certainly popular in the late antique eastern Mediterranean. The most famous center of such practices in this period was, of course, Palestine and in particular Jerusalem. Ever since the reign of Herod the Great (r. 37–4 BCE), Jerusalem had been a center of interregional pilgrimage for Jews, albeit that various Roman emperors had at certain times attempted to restrict their right of access to the city.[3] Jerusalem and the other biblical sites of Palestine were then taken up enthusiastically by Christians as places for pious visitation, in spite of the opposition to such practices from a theologian as prominent as Gregory of Nyssa, and the indifference of others, such as Augustine.[4] The earliest Christian personal narrative of a pilgrimage to Palestine and Jerusalem records a journey made by an anonymous traveler from Bordeaux in 333 CE, already during the lifetime of the emperor Constantine (r. 306–337 CE), and several other late antique examples followed this precedent.[5] In the face of his contemporaries who disparaged such journeys, Jerome, himself an immigrant to Palestine, declared in a letter to an old friend from Rome, Desiderius, written in 393 CE, "To worship on the spot where the feet of the Lord once stood is part of the faith."[6]

Compared to the long and eloquent testimonies to the magnetic attraction of Jerusalem and Palestine for Jewish and Christian pilgrims from within the Roman Empire, however, there is far less material about the pilgrimage practices performed by the inhabitants of the pre-Islamic

[3] M. Goodman, "The Pilgrimage Economy of Jerusalem in the Second Temple Period," in L. I. Levine (ed.), *Jerusalem: Its Sanctity and Centrality to Judaism, Christianity, and Islam* (New York: Continuum, 1999), 69–76.

[4] For Gregory's and Augustine's views on pilgrimage, see B. Bitton-Ashkelony, *Encountering the Sacred: The Debate on Christian Pilgrimage in Late Antiquity* (Berkeley: University of California Press, 2005), 30–64, 106–139.

[5] J. Elsner, "The *Itinerarium Burdigalense*: Politics and Salvation in the Geography of Constantine's Empire," *Journal of Roman Studies*, 90 (2000), 181–195. For other late antique examples, see J. Wilkinson, *Egeria's Travels*, 3rd ed. (Oxford: Aris & Phillips, 1999), and J. Wilkinson, *Jerusalem Pilgrims before the Crusades* (Warminster: Aris & Phillips, 1977).

[6] From letter 47, cited by Bitton-Ashkelony, *Encountering the Sacred*, 71.

Arabian Peninsula.[7] What was the nature of these pre-Islamic Arabian practices of pilgrimage? Was pilgrimage a phenomenon found only in certain regions of the peninsula, or was it practiced ubiquitously? Who undertook these pre-Islamic Arabian pilgrimages and for what purposes? We are far from possessing full answers to these and similar questions, but this chapter will seek some tentative responses.

PRE-ISLAMIC PILGRIMAGE TO MECCA AND ITS HINTERLAND

By far the most famous pre-Islamic Arabian pilgrimage practices known today are those to the Kaʿba in Mecca and to sites in its hinterland, especially Mina and ʿArafat. There is a rather large amount of material on these sites and pilgrimages in Islamic-era Arabic works; the best known are Ibn Hishām's (d. ca. 218/833–834) redaction of Ibn Isḥāq's (d. ca. 150/767–768) biography (*sīra*) of Muhammad, the local histories of Mecca by al-Azraqī (d. ca. 250/864–865) and al-Fākihī (d. ca. 279/892–893), and the *Kitāb al-Aṣnām*, the "Book of Idols," by Ibn al-Kalbī (d. ca. 204/819–820). The information offered by sources such as these on pre-Islamic pilgrimage in the Ḥijāz is extremely problematic, since they were written by Muslim scholars who heavily reshaped the history of the pre-Islamic Hijaz through a filter of early Islamic concerns, not in the least by tending to exaggerate the significance of Mecca – the Prophet's hometown – and its sanctuaries in the period before and during Muhammad's career. However, it is worth offering here a summary of the information available in these sources, albeit one that largely ignores the various controversies and debates which surrounded almost every part of the history of pre-Islamic Mecca and the Hajj offered by the later Arabic accounts.[8]

[7] For a general history of pre-Islamic Arabia, see R. G. Hoyland, *Arabia and the Arabs from the Bronze Age to the Coming of Islam* (London: Routledge, 2001).

[8] The bibliography on pre-Islamic Mecca and its pilgrimages is quite large. There are two relatively accessible surveys, with some further references, in F. E. Peters, *Mecca: A Literary History of the Muslim Holy Land* (Princeton, NJ: Princeton University Press, 1994), especially 3–56, and F. E. Peters, *The Hajj: The Muslim Pilgrimage to Mecca and the Holy Places* (Princeton, NJ: Princeton University Press, 1994), especially 3–59. Unless otherwise stated, the material for the following is drawn principally from Peters' works. For two important studies among several which raise fundamental problems with any attempt to consider the Arabic sources' depiction of pre-Islamic Arabian religion, see P. Crone, *Meccan Trade and the Rise of Islam* (Oxford: Blackwell, 1987); G. R. Hawting, *The Idea of Idolatry and the Emergence of Islam: From Polemic to History* (Cambridge: Cambridge University Press, 1999).

The most common interpretation of the relevant passages in the Qur'an has it that Abraham, the father of Isaac and Ishmael, built the first sanctuary at Mecca, known as God's house or the Ka'ba (Q Baqara 2: 125–127), although some Muslim accounts suggest rather that Adam first erected the Ka'ba, but that Abraham re-founded it after the Flood had destroyed Adam's construction. According to the Qur'an, it was Abraham who, having (re)constructed God's house, first proclaimed to people that they perform pilgrimage (Ar. *ḥajj*) to it (Q Ḥajj 22: 27).[9] At some point after the lifetime of Abraham, for one reason or another, the inhabitants of the Hijaz – the area of the western Arabian Peninsula that includes Mecca – gradually abandoned their Abrahamic monotheism and moved toward the worship of a number of idols. This is apparently one of the fundamental developments that led Muslim scholars to refer to the pre-Islamic period of Arabia's history as the *jāhiliyya*, an age of "ignorance" and/or "barbarism."

Within and around Mecca itself, control of the sanctuaries moved periodically from one tribe to another – the two most commonly mentioned are Jurhum and Khuzāʿa – until one Quṣayy ibn Kilāb led his tribe of Quraysh (the tribe into which Muhammad was born in the late sixth century CE) to supremacy in the area.[10] Quṣayy established a loose system of government in Mecca, creating "offices" to oversee certain rights claimed by Quraysh and apportioning those offices to his sons. These display the twin importance attached by Quṣayy to control of both local trade and pilgrimage: they included, for example, the guardianship of the Kaʿba (*ḥijāba*), the provision of water for pilgrims (*siqāya*), and the provision of food for pilgrims (*rifāda*).[11] In the period following Quṣayy's consolidation of his power, roughly during the fifth and sixth centuries CE, Quraysh supposedly came to attain considerable regional power for themselves by consolidating their control of local trade and of the pilgrimage to the sacred shrine at the heart of Mecca, the Kaʿba. Sura 106 of the Qur'an famously refers to the "*īlāf*" of Quraysh in their winter and summer journeys; there was and is considerable debate over what this enigmatic term actually means, but a very common explanation

[9] There is also a much more vague account of the foundation of God's house and the proclamation to people to perform pilgrimage to it at Q Āl ʿImrān 3: 96–97.

[10] Peters (*Mecca*, 10) estimates that if Quṣayy was a historical personality, he would have been born in the late fourth century CE.

[11] For a much more detailed discussion of the Arabic narratives about these offices, see G. R. Hawting, "The 'Sacred Offices' of Mecca from Jāhiliyya to Islam," *Jerusalem Studies in Arabic and Islam*, 13 (1990), 62–84.

FIGURE 2 Mural of the Kaʿba, Gurna, Upper Egypt

is that it was a series of pacts arranged by Quṣayy's grandson, Hāshim ibn ʿAbd Manāf, with the tribes surrounding Mecca so that Quraysh traders could pass through those tribes' territories in complete safety.[12] The prestige of Quraysh's association with the Kaʿba and surrounding *ḥaram* (loosely "sacred enclave") at Mecca, not to mention their control of many of the rites of pilgrimage to the settlement, is reportedly what led the tribes to consider it in their best interests to come to a mutual understanding.

There were at least two different pilgrimage practices involving Mecca and its hinterland. First, there was the Hajj, which took place in the month of Dhū al-Ḥijja and chiefly involved sites outside of Mecca, at Mina and ʿArafat. Second, there was the ʿUmra, which took place in the month of Rajab and primarily centered around sites within Mecca, principally the Kaʿba and the two hillocks, al-Ṣafā and al-Marwa. It was this latter pilgrimage that was chiefly under the control and supervision of

[12] For a modern skeptical discussion of this understanding, see Crone, *Meccan Trade*, 204–214.

Quraysh; they had many fewer rights at the sites involved in the Hajj to Mina and ʿArafat. (It was only in Islamic times that these two practices of pilgrimage were combined into the Hajj that we know today.[13]) The Quraysh, who were seemingly not happy with the existence of these Hajj rites, over which they had little control, apparently founded an association known as the *ḥums* to counter them. They were known for their observance of stricter ritual regulations, including the stipulation that they would not leave Mecca's haram during the Hajj to participate in the rites at ʿArafat. One of the principal aims of the *ḥums*-association, therefore, seems to have been to promote the sanctity of Mecca's Kaʿba – over which Quraysh exercised full control – at the expense of the Hajj sites outside Mecca's haram.

Among the various rites involved, sacrifice played an important role in both pilgrimages, at Mina in the Hajj and at al-Marwa during the ʿUmra. There was also a very close link between the Hajj and a handful of market fairs which took place at nearby sites; Mecca's local historian Abū al-Walīd al-Azraqī explains how a market would be held at ʿUkāẓ for the first twenty days of Dhū al-Qaʿda, then would move to Majanna for the remaining days of Dhū al-Qaʿda, and would then proceed to Dhū al-Majāz for the first eight days of Dhū al-Ḥijja before everyone then started the Hajj.[14] Quraysh and the various sacred sites and shrines in and around Mecca were associated with the worship of many deities, among whom Allah was but one, albeit maybe a rather important one. The Kaʿba in particular was associated with a god called Hubal, who is said to have played an important role overseeing the practice of casting lots using arrows and who also turns up (probably: the name is spelled *hblw*) in a Nabataean inscription, datable to 1 BCE/CE, from Hegra/Madāʾin Ṣāliḥ in the northern Hijaz.[15]

Such is an overview of some of the Arabic material on pre-Islamic pilgrimages to Mecca and its hinterland. There is, however, as implied earlier, a serious catch to the picture as summarized here: none of this

[13] There is still an Islamic ʿUmra, which can be performed at any time during the year, though many recommend the month of Rajab; see further M. J. Kister, "'Rajab is the month of God ...' A Study in the Persistence of an Early Tradition," *Israel Oriental Studies*, 1 (1971), especially 219–220.

[14] Al-Azraqī, *Akhbār Makka wa-mā jāʾa fīhā min al-āthār*, ed. R. Malḥas, 2 vols. (Beirut: Dār al-Andalus, n.d.), I, 187–188; Peters, *Hajj*, 34.

[15] J. F. Healey, *The Religion of the Nabataeans: A Conspectus* (Leiden: Brill, 2001), 127–132.

information has come from contemporary sources. To date, no one has published a pre-Islamic text, document, inscription, or anything else with an incontrovertible reference either to Mecca, the Hajj there, or the ʿUmra. The earliest references to these pilgrimages come in the Qurʾan itself and, in the published documentary record, in two dated Arabic graffiti of the first Islamic century which ask God to accept their inscribers' pilgrimages (in both cases, the word used is *ḥijja*): the earliest of these is dated to 82/701–702 and was found near Fayd, in Najd on the Kufa–Mecca road; the other is dated to Dhū al-Qaʿda 91/August–September 710 and was found on the Syria–Medina road, roughly seventeen miles southeast of Tabūk.[16] Now this does not mean that there were no pre-Islamic shrines in and around Mecca, nor that the inhabitants of the region did not undertake pilgrimages to them at specified times. It does, however, make it hard for historians today to verify the material provided in the later Arabic narratives and, consequently, to learn much from them about pre-Islamic Arabian pilgrimage practices. Instead, we have to turn to what contemporary evidence there is from the peninsula.

Such evidence concerns mostly the southwest and northwest edges of the Arabian Peninsula. This is roughly the area of modern Yemen and southwest Oman on the one hand, and Jordan, southern and eastern Syria, and northwest Saudi Arabia on the other. Just as for Mecca, the major evidence for shrines and pilgrimage practices for the rest of the Hijaz and central Arabia (the region known in Arabic as Najd) survives only in the later Arabic sources, with Ibn al-Kalbī's *Kitāb al-Aṣnām* (*Book of Idols*) being a mine of information. Since the scale of the problems associated with using these texts for the history of pre-Islamic Arabia requires treating them at considerably greater length than can be done here, it seems most appropriate to restrict ourselves to the testimony of contemporary evidence. Given the availability of such evidence, the focus of what follows will be on the evidence for pilgrimages in South Arabia and northwest Arabia, respectively. At the end of the chapter, we will return to the question of what conclusions we can draw about pilgrimage in pre-Islamic Arabia more generally.

[16] See, respectively, F. al-Hawas et al., "Taqrīr awwalī ʿan aʿmāl al-tanqībāt al-athariyya bi-madīnat Fayd al-taʾrīkhiyya bi-minṭaqat Ḥāʾil (al-mawsim al-awwal 1427h. – 2006m.)," *al-Aṭlāl*, 20 (1431/2010), 35; A. I. al-Ghabbân, *Les deux routes syrienne et égyptienne de pèlerinage au nord-ouest de l'Arabie Saoudite*, 2 vols. (Cairo: Institut Français d'Archéologie Orientale, 2011), II, 499–501 (no. 1).

PILGRIMAGE IN PRE-ISLAMIC SOUTH ARABIA

Practices of pilgrimage certainly have a long pedigree in South Arabia. In a recent book, Joy McCorriston has even referred to pilgrimage as "Arabia's oldest and certainly most important meta-structure," meta-structures being "core cultural ideas that endure over extremely long time frames."[17] In one chapter of her book, McCorriston uses an investigation of a cattle skull ring found at Kheshiya in Hadramawt to argue that the "distinctly Arabian habitus of pilgrimage" was already in place for millennia. She suggests, "From 4500 BC, pastoralists traveled to a sacred site for ritual purposes, including cattle sacrifice, communal feast, and a seasonal, temporary community whose cosmic beliefs were constructed out of a system of structured and structuring dispositions."[18]

There is a decent amount of documentary evidence for pilgrimage in South Arabia thanks to the large number of inscriptions that have survived from the first millennium BCE and first six centuries CE. At least four texts actually refer to pilgrimages using the root *ḥ-g-g*, whose Arabic cognate is the word *ḥajj*. Three of these texts – all in Sabaic, two datable to the seventh or sixth century BCE and one to the second century CE – are from the area of Haram, in the Yemeni Jawf northwest of Maʿīn/Qarnaw.[19] They associate a pilgrimage with the deity Dhū Samawī, and the text from the second century CE (*CIH* 533) provides evidence of some of the ritual regulations surrounding the rites:

> Amat Abīhā has confessed and made penitence to Dhū Samawī, the lord of Bayyin, because a man approached her [for sex] on the third day of the pilgrimage (*qrbh mr' ywm ṯlṯ ḥgtn*) while she was menstruating, and he left without performing ablutions.

The fourth is from Shabwa in Hadramawt, in a dialect of the local language, Hadramitic, with many features reminiscent of Sabaic. It is a graffito in which one Ḥgr b. Slmt invoked the monotheistic deity Rḥmnn (Ar. *al-Raḥmān*, "the Compassionate") and his brother, Mrṯdm, noting that he had made a pilgrimage (*ḥg*).[20]

[17] J. McCorriston, *Pilgrimage and Household in the Ancient Near East* (New York: Cambridge University Press, 2011), 1, xvii, respectively.

[18] Ibid., 85–134, quotations from 132–133.

[19] They are *CIH* 533, 547, and 548, on which see C. Robin, *Inventaire des inscriptions sudarabiques, tome 1: Inabba', Haram, al-Kāfir, Kamna et al-Ḥarāshif* (Paris: De Boccard, 1992), 74–76, 78–81, 102–103; Kitchen, *Documentation*, II, 122, 124.

[20] Hamilton, 11; see W. L. Brown and A. F. L. Beeston, "Sculptures and Inscriptions from Shabwa," *Journal of the Royal Asiatic Society*, 86, 1–2 (1954), 60–62; J. Pirenne, *Les*

Now, *ḥ-g-g* was not the only root that provided words for pilgrimage in South Arabian texts; other roots commonly used include *w-f-r* and *ḥ-ḍ-r*, and the texts which employ these can tell us more about pre-Islamic pilgrimage practices.[21] One of the most important such texts is R 4176, the inscription with which this chapter opened. After the start of the text, in which the god Taʾlab ordered his people Samʿay to go on pilgrimage to the shrine of Almaqah in Mārib in the month of Dhū Abhay,[22] there follows a whole series of regulations governing worship in and pilgrimage to the temple of Taʾlab in Riyām.[23] This pre-Islamic pilgrimage was actually mentioned by the early fourth-/tenth-century Yemeni antiquarian Abū Muḥammad al-Hamdānī. In book 8 of his *Iklīl* (*The Crown*), for example, he noted: "As for Riʾām/Riyām, it is a temple (*bayt*) by which an ascetic had lived and to which pilgrimage was made. It is atop Jabal Itwa in the land of Hamdān."[24] Among the regulations and ordinances mentioned in the first-century BCE text R 4176 are some that govern similar topics to the regulations surrounding the Islamic Hajj to Mecca including, for example, hunting, sexual relations, cutting of hair (perhaps), arguments and disputes, and more besides. The text also refers to the pilgrims "while in sacral state" (*kḥrm*).[25] Finally, it is worth mentioning that this text also refers to banqueting in connection

témoins écrits de la région de Shabwa et l'histoire (Paris: Paul Geuthner, 1990), 86; Kitchen, *Documentation*, II, 235. On the remarkably successful promulgation of monotheism – now known to be Judaism – in South Arabia from the late fourth century CE, see C.-J. Robin, "Ḥimyar et Israël," *Comptes rendus des séances de l'année: académie des inscriptions et belles-lettres* (2004), 831–906.

21 On the use of these roots in texts to denote pilgrimage, see further A. F. L. Beeston et al., *Sabaic Dictionary (English-French-Arabic)* (Leuven: Peeters, 1982), 66, 157–158; J. C. Biella, *Dictionary of Old South Arabic: Sabaean Dialect* (Chico, CA: Scholars Press, 1982), 139–140, 184–185.

22 Pilgrimage to Almaqah at Mārib during the month of Dhū Abhay is also reported in other texts; see J. Ryckmans, "Himyaritica (5)," *Le muséon*, 88 (1975), 218–219; J. Ryckmans, "Les inscriptions sud-arabes anciennes et les études arabes," *Annali dell'Istituto Orientale di Napoli*, 35 (1975), 452.

23 Ghul and Beeston, "Pilgrimage to Itwat." Pilgrimage to the god Taʾlab is also seemingly referred to (*lhḥḍrn tʾlb*) in a first-century CE Sabaic inscription from Riyām (Gl. 1361), regarding which see J. M. Solá Solé, *Sammlung Eduard Glaser IV: Inschriften aus Riyām* (Vienna: Harmann Böhlaus, 1964), 36–38; Kitchen, *Documentation*, II, 200.

24 Al-Hamdānī, *al-Iklīl*, book 8, ed. N. A. Faris (Beirut: Dār al-ʿAwda, n.d. [repr.]), 66; see also book 10, ed. M.-D. al-Khaṭīb (Cairo: al-Maṭbaʿa al-Salafiyya, 1368/1949), 17.

25 For further discussion of the similarity between the interdictions governing pilgrimage and sacred spaces reported for pre-Islamic South Arabia and those for other pre-Islamic Arabian pilgrimages elsewhere, as well as the Islamic hajj, see Ryckmans, "Inscriptions sud-arabes," 453–457.

with pilgrimage, which seems to have been a relatively common South Arabian practice.[26]

A brief discussion of two further examples of pre-Islamic South Arabian pilgrimage can help expand our picture a little. One site where a politically significant ritual banquet connected to pilgrimage seems to have been practiced is Shabwa, the capital of the South Arabian kingdom of Hadramawt before the latter was brought to an end by the Himyarites in the early fourth century CE.[27] At least two texts refer explicitly to a pilgrimage there. One of these is Hamilton 11 (discussed earlier). The other is Iryānī 37/B.3, a Sabaic text from Mārib datable to ca. 290 CE.[28] Lines 11–12 of this text make reference to a pilgrimage to the deity Sīn/Siyān (*ḥḏr s¹yn*) in Shabwa (*s²bwt*). There is also a very famous passage by the Latin author Pliny (d. 79 CE), in which he notes how a tithe on the frankincense brought to Shabwa was taken by the priests of a temple there and used to pay for a banquet which the god "Sabis" had to put on for a fixed number of days.[29]

The final South Arabian site to be discussed here is Jabal al-Lawdh, northeast of Ṣanʿāʾ on a promontory overlooking the Jawf.[30] Inscriptions from the site (there are around 150 in total) can be dated to two distinct periods, roughly the fifth–fourth centuries BCE and the first century CE. There were two cultic sites here, a lower and an upper, each closely associated in both periods with the rulers of Sabaʾ. Inscriptions

[26] See especially J. Ryckmans, "Le repas rituel dans la religion sud-arabe," in M. A. Beek et al. (eds.), *Symbolae biblicae et mesopotamicae Francisco Mario Theodoro de Liagre Böhl dedicatae* (Leiden: Brill, 1973), 327–334; C.-J. Robin and J.-F. Breton, "Le sanctuaire préislamique du Ǧabal al-Lawḏ (Nord-Yémen)," *Comptes rendus des séances de l'année: académie des inscriptions et belles-lettres* (1982), 610–616. The word used in Sabaic for such banquets is *ʾlm*. Banquet halls are also fairly common features of Palmyrene and Nabataean towns and shrines, although there appear to be no texts that explicitly connect such a practice with pilgrimage; see especially D. Tarrier, "Banquets rituels en Palmyrène et en Nabatène," *ARAM* 7 (1995), 165–182, but also T. Kaizer, *The Religious Life of Palmyra: A Study of the Social Patterns of Worship in the Roman Period* (Stuttgart: Franz Steiner, 2002), 220–229; Healey, *Religion of the Nabataeans*, 165–169; P. Alpass, *The Religious Life of Nabataea* (Leiden: Brill, 2013), 77–79, 232–233.

[27] On this town in general, see J.-F. Breton, "Shabwa, capitale antique du Ḥaḍramawt," *Journal Asiatique*, 275 (1987), 13–34; Pirenne, *Témoins écrits*. On the pilgrimage there, see also Ryckmans, "Himyaritica (5)," 217–219; Ryckmans, "Repas rituel," 332; A. Korotayev, "Religion and Society in Southern Arabia and among the Arabs," *Arabia*, 1 (2003), 69–70.

[28] M. ʿA. al-Iryānī, *Fī taʾrīkh al-Yaman* (Cairo: Dār al-Hanā, 1973), 184–88; Kitchen, *Documentation*, II, 246.

[29] Pliny, *Naturalis Historia*, ed. and trans. H. Rackham et al., 10 vols. (London: William Heinemann, 1938–1963), XII.32.63.

[30] For a general discussion of the site, see Robin and Breton, "Sanctuaire préislamique."

demonstrate that the lower site was certainly connected with banqueting (Sabaic *ʾlm*) and also, interestingly, with a variety of deities, including *ʿṯtr ḏḎbn*, *ʿṯtr ws*^{1}*mʿ ʿdy kwrn*, and Almaqah; a similar situation applied to the upper site.[31] A number of other deities are also attested in other texts from the site outside the two cultic centers.[32] That said, apparently at Jabal al-Lawdh, the only deity specifically connected with ritual banqueting is *ʿṯtr ḏḎbn*.[33] The important point for us, in any case, is that ritual banqueting clearly took place at the site, and, since it is a fairly remote site, it is a plausible assumption that here, too, the banqueting was associated with pilgrimage. The remoteness of the site and the wide variety of deities commemorated in the inscriptions found there also suggest that it was used as a place for gathering by a number of different tribes in the area.

For South Arabia, it is apparent that there were a number of holy sites associated with pre-Islamic practices of pilgrimage, at least some of which took place at well-defined times of year and were associated with a number of ritual regulations that governed pilgrims for the duration of their pilgrimages. The other part of Arabia for which we have some contemporary evidence is the northwest.

PRE-ISLAMIC PILGRIMAGE IN NORTHWEST ARABIA

There is some epigraphic evidence for practices of pilgrimage among those (semi)nomadic groups who inhabited the northwest fringes of the Arabian Peninsula, albeit much less than can be found for South Arabia. The North Arabian texts are also of a rather different nature to their South Arabian counterparts; whereas the latter were mostly dedicatory or monumental texts, the former are almost exclusively graffiti. There are at least four graffiti, inscribed in a pre-Islamic North Arabian language known today as Safaitic, which employ a word derived from the root *ḥ-g-g* to denote the performance of a pilgrimage. In total, more than 20,000 Safaitic texts have been discovered in southern Syria, northeast Jordan, and northern Saudi Arabia, mostly written by nomads, probably between the first century BCE and the early fourth century CE.[34]

[31] Robin and Breton, "Sanctuaire préislamique," 601, 604–608.

[32] Robin and Breton, "Sanctuaire préislamique," 603.

[33] Robin and Breton, "Sanctuaire préislamique," 610, 613.

[34] See especially M. C. A. Macdonald, "Reflections on the Linguistic Map of Pre-Islamic Arabia," *Arabian Archaeology and Epigraphy*, 11 (2000), 35, 45–46; M. C. A. Macdonald, "Nomads and the Ḥawrān in the Late Hellenistic and Roman Periods: A Reassessment of the Epigraphic Evidence," *Syria*, 70 (1993), 303–403.

Two of the *ḥ-g-g* texts, both found in northern Jordan, simply record that their named inscriber had performed a pilgrimage without offering any more specific data.[35] The other two, however, offer a little more insight. The first of these is the unpublished text BREnv.A.1, which has already been mentioned. The author of this text employed as a dating formula the phrase, "the year the pilgrimage to Sīʿ was in vain/suspended." Sīʿ, in the Ḥawrān, was the location of a famous temple to the deity Baʿal-Shamīn, which was connected by a processional way to the city of Canatha two miles away.[36] Inscriptional and archaeological evidence dates the construction of the temples at the site – there were three – to the late first century BCE and during the first and second centuries CE. Several modern scholars have noted that the temple complex at Sīʿ does not appear to have been a royal creation of any sort, but rather was a point at which the (semi)nomadic groups of the area interacted with the settled communities.[37] The possible interpretation that the pilgrimage to Baʿal-Shamīn at Sīʿ could be "in vain" is an interesting one. Michael Macdonald has suggested that one of the purposes of many pilgrims traveling to Baʿal-Shamīn at Sīʿ may have been to help ensure a decent rainfall for the coming year and that the pilgrimage might have been "in vain" because that rainfall did not arrive.[38] This seems plausible: Baʿal-Shamīn was long associated with agricultural fertility, and prayers for rain (in Arabic the practice is called *istisqāʾ*) are well known

35 G. L. Harding, "The Cairn of Haniʾ," *Annual of the Department of Antiquities of Jordan*, 2 (1953), 46 (no. 184); E. A. Knauf, "More Notes on *Ǧabal Qurma*, Minaeans and Safaites," *Zeitschrift des deutschen Palästina-Vereins*, 107 (1991), 96 (no. 4).

36 On Baʿal-Shamīn, see Healey, *Religion of the Nabataeans*, 124–126; H. Niehr, *Baʿalšamen: Studien zu Herkunft, Geschichte und Rezeptionsgeschichte eines phönizischen Gottes* (Leuven: Peeters, 2003). On the shrine of Baʿal-Shamīn at Sīʿ and the question of pilgrimage there, see J.-M. Dentzer, "Développement et culture de la Syrie du sud dans la période préprovinciale (1er s. avant J.-C. – 1er s. après J.-C.)," in J.-M. Dentzer (ed.), *Hauran I: recherches archéologiques sur la Syrie du sud à l'époque hellénistique et romaine* (Paris: Paul Geuthner, 1986), especially 405–406; F. Millar, *The Roman Near East, 31 BC–AD 337* (Cambridge, MA: Harvard University Press, 1993), 394–396; Healey, *Religion of the Nabataeans*, 65–67; Niehr, *Baʿalšamen*, 248–251; several papers in Dentzer-Feydy, ed., *Hauran II*, including Macdonald, "References to Sīʿ"; Alpass, *Religious Life of Nabataea*, 181–185.

37 Dentzer, "Développement et culture," 405; Millar, *Roman Near East*, 395; Alpass, *Religious Life of Nabataea*, 184.

38 Macdonald, "References to Sīʿ," 278. Elsewhere, Macdonald has suggested that another Safaitic text (that published in E. Littmann, *Syria: Publications of the Princeton University Archaeological Expeditions to Syria in 1904–5 and 1909, Division IV, Semitic Inscriptions, Section C, Safaïtic Inscriptions* [Leiden: Brill, 1943], 90–91 [no. 350]) refers to "the year of the withholding of Baʿal-Shamīn" (*s¹nt ḥgzt bʿls¹mn*), which he interprets as referring to a year in which the god withheld rain; see Macdonald, "Nomads and the Ḥawrān," 366, n. 414 (translation slightly adapted).

from discussions in Islamic Arabic texts and from a handful of pre-Islamic South Arabian inscriptions.[39] Nonetheless, it is perhaps unlikely that every pilgrim traveling to Sīʿ would have had this intention in mind, and it is also possible that the brief Safaitic formula used in this text may simply refer to a year in which the pilgrimage to Sīʿ had to be suspended for one reason or another.

The final Safaitic text which needs to be discussed here was also found by a cairn in northern Jordan. It is particularly interesting since, according to the rather tentative interpretation of its editors, it records some of the ritual requirements associated with undertaking a pilgrimage:[40]

By Duʾayy b. Nashshāl. He washed [his clothes] [and] he curbed sexual intercourse in order to go on pilgrimage (*ldʾy bn ns² l wrḥḍ bḥ lgm lyḥg*).

We do not know the place to which Duʾayy b. Nashshāl wanted to travel on pilgrimage – it may just as well not have been the temple of Baʿal-Shamīn at Sīʿ – but, if this interpretation is correct, this is the only North Arabian text to give any indication of the possible ritual taboos associated with pilgrimage. It is worth noting in passing that they resemble Islamic rules concerning the Hajj to Mecca as well as some of those mentioned in the South Arabian texts discussed earlier.

That is about it for North Arabian epigraphic evidence for pilgrimage, although archaeological evidence may suggest one or two further examples of pilgrimage sites. The famous Nabataean city of Petra, for example, was filled with temples, tombs, high-places and processional ways, and it is entirely possible, albeit as yet undocumented, that some of these were foci for pilgrimages.[41] More solid archaeological evidence for pilgrimage may come from Khirbat al-Tannūr and Khirbat al-Dharīḥ, two relatively small sites to the north of Petra.[42] Khirbat al-Tannūr was an isolated high place with no settlement nearby, which suggests it was attended by pilgrims. Khirbat al-Dharīḥ, approximately five miles to the south, is known to have been important from the first century BCE to the fourth century CE, and may have been a stopping place for pilgrims on the way to

[39] *EI2*, s.v. "Istiskāʾ", 269–271; Ryckmans, "Inscriptions sud-arabes," 457–458 (where two third-century CE Sabaic texts are presented).

[40] F. V. Winnett and G. L. Harding, *Inscriptions from Fifty Safaitic Cairns* (University of Toronto Press, 1978), 437 (no. 3053).

[41] See the surveys of Petra's sacred landscape in Healey, *Religion of the Nabataeans*, especially 39–52; Alpass, *Religious Life of Nabataea*, 37–109.

[42] Healey, *Religion of the Nabataeans*, 59–62; Alpass, *Religious Life of Nabataea*, 202–214.

Khirbat al-Tannūr, although it is just as likely that it was used by traders and others traveling between Petra and Bostra or the cities of the Decapolis.

Those Arabians who lived on the fringes of the Roman and Sasanian empires were understandably relatively well known to the late antique inhabitants of those empires, who sometimes mentioned them and purported to describe some of their customs in works written in Latin, Greek, and Syriac. (The words most commonly used to refer to these northern Arabians were "Saracens" in Latin and Greek, and *ṭayyāyē* in Syriac.[43]) A number of these customs involve pilgrimages of one sort or another. Although we must remember, of course, that the authors of these texts were "outsiders" to the communities and practices they describe, and that a host of pejorative stereotypes govern their descriptions, it is nevertheless worth looking at a handful of the possible examples in brief.[44]

The first-century BCE Greek historian Diodorus Siculus records that "the Arabs who are called Nabataeans" had a "national gathering" at specific times at a place by a "certain rock" which was two days' journey from the settled lands. Diodorus' discussion of this gathering makes it clear that it was a time for buying and selling, but he provides little evidence for any religious nature to the meeting.[45] Two fourth-century CE Christian authors – the heresiologist Epiphanius of Salamis and also Jerome – mention an annual gathering which included "Saracens" at the temple of Venus/Aphrodite in Elusa, an ancient city in the Negev approximately twelve miles southwest of Beersheba.[46] It has been suggested that the shrine at Elusa was actually dedicated to the Arabian goddess al-ʿUzzā, largely on the basis of a bilingual Greek-Nabataean inscription from Cos, in which the Nabataean al-ʿUzzā is rendered in the Greek as Aphrodite,

[43] I have been careful to refer to the inhabitants of the Arabian Peninsula as "Arabians" rather than "Arabs," since the latter carries much more specific connotations and there is much debate among modern scholars as to what those connotations were; for a recent contribution to the debate, see M. C. A. Macdonald, "Arabs, Arabias, and Arabic before Late Antiquity," *Topoi*, 16 (2009), 277–332. When I use "Arabs," it is because that is the specific term used in the source(s) I am discussing.

[44] On the situation of these groups on the fringe of the Roman Empire and their interactions with the latter, see now G. Fisher, *Between Empires: Arabs, Romans, and Sasanians in Late Antiquity* (Oxford University Press, 2011).

[45] Diodorus Siculus, *Bibliotheca Historica*, ed. and tr. C.H. Oldfather et al., 12 vols. (London: William Heinemann, 1933–67), XIX.95.1–2.

[46] Epiphanius, *Panarion*, tr. F. Williams, 2 vols. (Leiden: Brill, 1987–94), LI.22.11; Jerome, *Life of Hilarion*, tr. C. White in *Early Christian Lives* (London: Penguin, 1998), §25. For a modern discussion, see Healey, *Religion of the Nabataeans*, 67–68; Alpass, *Religious Life of Nabataea*, 160–163.

but really this is only speculation.[47] There is no evidence from Nabataean or North Arabian texts of any pilgrimage to a shrine dedicated to al-ʿUzzā in the Negev. The so-called Piacenza Pilgrim, who traveled to Palestine in the mid-to-late sixth century CE, also mentioned that near Mount Sinai the "Saracens" had erected an idol of white marble where they had a festival at a specified time.[48]

One final example of a Greek discussion of a pilgrimage involving "Saracens" can shed a little more light on pre-Islamic Arabian pilgrimage practices. It concerns those who inhabited the area around the so-called Palm Grove (*phoinikĀn*), referred to by several Greek authors and which was probably somewhere near Tabūk.[49] In approximately 530–531 CE, the Roman official Nonnosus participated in an embassy on behalf of the emperor Justinian I (r. 527–565 CE) to South Arabia and Axum, and a part of his account of this journey was preserved by the Byzantine bibliophile Photius (d. *ca.* 893 CE) in his *Bibliotheca*. Nonnosus observed that the "Saracens" met twice a year at a sacred site, during which "they observe a complete peace, not only towards each other, but also towards all men living in their country"; furthermore, at these times, "wild animals are at peace with man."[50] Nonnosus' observation on this biannual pilgrimage festival of the inhabitants of the northern Hijaz is strongly reminiscent of the prohibitions on fighting and hunting that are also prescribed during the Islamic Hajj and in some South Arabian inscriptions.

CONCLUSIONS

The evidence is patchy, but it is reasonable to assume that there were a significant number of relatively localized pilgrimage sites and practices at the southwest and northwest corners, at least, of the Arabian Peninsula in

[47] M.-J. Roche, "Remarques sur les Nabatéens en Méditerranée," *Semitica*, 45 (1996), 78–80; Healey, *Religion of the Nabataeans*, 117.

[48] Piacenza Pilgrim, *Itinerarium*, §38; translated in Wilkinson, *Jerusalem Pilgrims*, 87.

[49] Strabo, *Geography*, ed. and tr. H. L. Jones, 8 vols. (London: William Heinemann, 1917–32), XVI.4.18, 21; Diodorus, *Bib. Hist.*, III.42–43; Procopius, *History of the Wars*, ed. and tr. H. B. Dewing, 5 vols. (London: William Heinemann, 1914–28), I.19.7–13; II.3.41. Modern discussion in I. Shahîd, *Byzantium and the Arabs in the Sixth Century*, 2 vols. (Washington DC: Dumbarton Oaks, 1995–2009), I/i, 124–130.

[50] Photius, *Bibliotheca*, ed. and tr. R. Henry, 9 vols. (Paris: Société d'Édition « Les Belles Lettres », 1959–91), 2b, ll. 28–32; translation from *Bibliotheca: A Selection*, tr. N. G. Wilson (London: Duckworth, 1994), 28. For more on Nonnosus and his mission, see G. W. Bowersock, "Nonnosus and Byzantine diplomacy in Arabia," *Rivista storica italiana*, 124 (2012), 282–290.

pre-Islamic times. These are witnessed in surviving epigraphic texts from both regions and in the testimonies of authors active within the Roman Empire. Arabic works of the second/eighth century and later mention a handful of pre-Islamic pilgrimage practices in the central Hijaz and Najd, but contemporary evidence for them is almost entirely lacking. We can assume that pilgrimages such as the Hajj and ʿUmra to Mecca were being undertaken by the inhabitants of that region, at least during the sixth and early seventh centuries CE, but since there is no evidence in the documentary record for any large, interregional Arabian pilgrimage customs it is unwise to consider pre-Islamic Mecca and its hinterland as a center for any such practice. It has been suggested by several scholars now that as the traditional power structures in the Arabian Peninsula collapsed over the course of the sixth century CE – virtually all of the powerful groups in Arabian politics in late antiquity, including the Jafnids/Ghassanids in the northwest, the Nasrids/Lakhmids in the northeast, and the Himyarites in the south, disappear from the record during this century – Quraysh of Mecca were able to increase their standing and authority and take on more of an interregional role, largely thanks to their control of the Meccan sanctuary and its pilgrimage.[51] As plausible as this suggestion might be, however, while the presentation of the collapse of the traditional Arabian powers at this time is based on contemporary evidence, that concerning Mecca's and Quraysh's subsequent accumulation of power is not.

Given the lack of contemporary evidence for pre-Islamic pilgrimage to Mecca or anywhere else in the central Hijaz and Najd, it is important to ask whether pilgrimage in pre-Islamic Arabia was restricted to the settled areas of the peninsula (such as South Arabia) and zones on the fringes of those settled areas and the Roman and Sasanian empires. There is no easy answer to this question, although I think it would be foolish to assume that there were no pilgrimages undertaken by the nomadic inhabitants of central Arabia. Several of the sanctuaries previously discussed seem to have drawn nomadic and semi-nomadic pilgrims from neighboring areas (Jabal al-Lawdh, Sīʿ, Sinai), and one pilgrimage practice – that observed by Nonnosus – may well have involved primarily nomadic participants.

[51] A. Korotayev [Korotaev], V. Kilmenko and D. Proussakov, "Origins of Islam: Political-Anthropological and Environmental Context," *Acta Orientalia Academiae Scientiarum Hungaricae*, 52 (1999), 243–276; C.-J. Robin, "Arabia and Ethiopia," in S. F. Johnson (ed.), *The Oxford Handbook of Late Antiquity* (Oxford University Press, 2012), 297–306.

Any pilgrimages to Mecca and its hinterland would also presumably have seen a large number of nomadic participants. Pilgrimage may not, therefore, have been a ubiquitous part of pre-Islamic Arabian life, but it does not seem unreasonable to suggest that it was more widespread than the contemporary evidence can precisely demonstrate. That said, we must be aware that the precise religious and ritual practices adhered to were not uniform across the peninsula. Patricia Crone, for example, has pointed out that the phenomenon of living "holy men" establishing and perpetuating sacred enclaves as documented for the twentieth-century Hadramawt by Serjeant, a phenomenon which he assumed to be a continuation of pre-Islamic practice, is not observable in the northern areas of the Arabian Peninsula.[52] If the practices of establishing sacred spaces differ across Arabia, we should probably expect many of the rites involved in any pilgrimages to them to have differed as well.

There may have been a number of reasons why pilgrimage was popular, at least in parts of pre-Islamic Arabia. Several of the examples discussed in this chapter (Mamre, Shabwa, the later accounts about Mecca) certainly highlight the important economic role played by pilgrimage and specifically the connection with trade; others (Jabal al-Lawdh, Sīʿ, perhaps Khirbat al-Tannūr) indicate the usefulness of pilgrimage sites on the frontiers between settled and (semi-)nomadic societies as places where various groups could interact with one another. There is also little doubt that political rulers – especially in South Arabia – sought to patronize certain pilgrimage practices and utilize them for their own ends, just as certain church leaders did with the late antique Christian pilgrimages to Palestine and Jerusalem.[53] It is possible that some participants in these pilgrimages had expectations of ritual efficacy: think, for example, of the possible comment in a Safaitic text that the pilgrimage to Sīʿ one year had been "in vain," perhaps because Baʿal-Shamīn had not seen to it that his worshippers received their due of rain. Anthropologists, such as Victor Turner and Bonnie Wheeler, have stressed a number of both communal and private social roles played by

52 R. B. Serjeant, "Haram and hawtah: The Sacred Enclave in Arabia," in A. Badawi (ed.), *Mélanges Taha Husain: offerts par ses amis et disciples à l'occasion de son 70ième anniversaire* (Cairo: Dār al-Maʿārif, 1962), 41–58; Crone, *Meccan Trade*, 184, n. 81.

53 For an overview of the relationships between rulers and sacred spaces in South Arabia, see further Korotayev, "Religion and Society"; McCorriston, *Pilgrimage and Household*, 12–13, 42, 59, 66, 76–77. On church leaders and Palestine/Jerusalem, see Bitton-Ashkelony, *Encountering the Sacred*.

the various customs of pilgrimage throughout history.[54] Although we can say with confidence that pilgrimage in pre-Islamic Arabia played a number of necessary social, political, and economic roles among the various communities of the peninsula, without further, more precise evidence about the nature of the various associated rituals and regulations, it is extremely difficult to say anything more certain.

[54] V. Turner, "The Center Out There: Pilgrims' Goals," *History of Religions*, 12 (1973), 191–230; B. Wheeler, "Models of Pilgrimage: From Communitas to Confluence," *Journal of Ritual Studies*, 13 (1999), 26–41.

2

Why Mecca?

Abraham and the Hajj in the Islamic Tradition[1]

Fareeha Khan

Every day, Muslims remember the blessings bestowed by God on the biblical figure Abraham when they recite the following in their five daily prayers:

> O Allah, bless Muhammad and the folk of Muhammad as You blessed Ibrahim and the folk of Ibrahim. And show grace to Muhammad and the folk of Muhammad as you did to Ibrahim and the folk of Ibrahim . . . for You are truly the Most Praiseworthy and Noble.[2]

Numerous reasons are given to explain why Muslims are asked to recognize and pray for Abraham daily in this way. One of the reasons, discussed further in this chapter, is the belief that Abraham himself had prayed for Muhammad and his followers. Another more foundational reason is that the sharia of the prophet Muhammad and that of the prophet Abraham are said to have had a special link and resemblance.[3]

According to Islamic theology, God created human beings so that they would know and worship Him. He created the universe as an arena full of signs (*āyāt*) that point to His existence, and gave the human being the unique capacity to choose to submit to Him and worship Him. However, while these signs provide general direction toward the existence of a higher power, an interpreter – or prophet – is needed to help truly interpret and explicate the meaning of these signs. Ever since the creation of the human being and his placement on earth, prophets and messengers (that

[1] For *haaji baaba*.

[2] As translated in Ibn al-Naqīb, *Reliance of the Traveller: The Classic Manual of Islamic Sacred Law*, tr. N. H. Keller (Beltsville, MD: Amana Publications, 1994), 143.

[3] A. A. Thānawī, *Zād al-Sa'īd* (Lahore: Ummi Press, n.d.), 29–30.

subset of prophets sent with a unique "message," i.e., a unique set of laws [*sharīʿa*]) were sent to each people, in order to call them to God, to warn them against corrupt and immoral behavior, and to remind them of the coming Judgment.

All of the prophets are believed to have been sent with the mission of teaching the same theological principles – the main one being the absolute oneness of God (*tawḥīd*). But not all shared the same detailed legal and ritual rulings required of them by God. According to Muslim belief, one reason for the special connection between Abraham and Muhammad was that they not only shared theological principles (*uṣūl*), but also detailed legal matters (*furūʿ*), such as circumcision, ritual animal sacrifice, the direction of prayer (toward Mecca and the Kaʿba[4]), and the performance of the pilgrimage to Mecca (*ḥajj*).[5]

The Hajj makes apparent more than any other ritual the connection between Islam and the religion of the prophets who came before Muhammad. At the center of the Hajj (and the religious life of Muslims in general) is the cubelike structure of the Kaʿba. Today it stands some fifty feet in height, along the same dimensions given to it during the life of the prophet Muhammad. But Muslims believe that the Kaʿba was designated as a center of worship from even before human existence. According to Islamic tradition, the first thing God created was His Throne (*al-ʿarsh*), after which he created water. "When the Throne was still over water,"[6] God commanded that a spot be designated below His Throne called ("the much-frequented house," *al-bayt al-maʿmūr*), which the angels circumambulated. The site of Mecca, and the Kaʿba, is said to be directly below this much-frequented house, such that if one were to ascend vertically from the Kaʿba, one would directly encounter it.[7] The much-frequented house is thus the "celestial Kaʿba."[8]

In Muslim tradition, it is from Mecca that the "earth was rolled forth," "and the first to circumambulate [the Kaʿba] were the angels."[9] According

[4] Muhammad first prayed toward Jerusalem; some seventeen months after his migration to Medina, revelation changed the direction back to Mecca, the *qibla* of his forefather, Abraham. See M. M. Shafiʿ Usmānī, *Maʿāriful-Qur'ān*, tr. M. H. Askari and M. Shamim, rev. M. Taqi Usmani, 6 vols. (Karachi: Maktabe-e Darul-Uloom, 1996–2005), I: 375–383.

[5] Al-Qurṭubī, *Tafsīr al-Qurṭubī al-jāmiʿ 'li-aḥkām al-Qur'ān* (Cairo: Dār al-Shaʿb, 1961), II: 1351.

[6] Q Hūd 11: 7.

[7] B. Z. A. Thānawī, *Taskīn-i Hajj-o 'Umra ma'a khawātin ke khususi masa'il* (Karachi: Kutubkhana Mazhari, n.d.), 39.

[8] Usmānī *Ma'āriful-Qur'ān*, VIII: 191.

[9] Al-Kharkūshī, *Sharaf al-Muṣṭafā* (Mecca: Dār al-Bashar al-Islāmiyya, 2003), II: 203.

to these and other Prophetic traditions,[10] the angels were the first to build a structure of worship at the site where the earthly Kaʿba now stands. When Adam, the first human and also the first prophet, was sent down to earth and came to this spot in Mecca to circumambulate, the angels informed him that they had already been doing so for "two thousand years."[11] Other traditions relate that it was with the help of the angels and their knowledge of its dimensions that Adam built the Kaʿba, the very first built structure on the earth. Like the one in the heavens, this Kaʿba became the designated center of worship on earth.

This Kaʿba is said to have remained standing until the Flood, at which time it was raised up into the heavens.[12] When Abraham reached the future site of Mecca, there was nothing there to mark the location of the Kaʿba except a mound of earth.[13] Abraham had been living in Syria,[14] but had been commanded to bring his first-born child Ishmael and his wife Hagar to the valley of Mecca. He left them near the ancient site of the Kaʿba, in the middle of the uninhabited desert, in God's care. Qurʾan commentators mention that this was not easy for Abraham. Even though Hagar agreed to remain there with her baby in accordance with God's command, Abraham was still very concerned. When he was some distance from them, he made the following prayer:

O my Lord! make this city one of peace and security: and preserve me and my sons from worshipping idols. (Q Ibrāhīm 14:35)

O our Lord! I have made some of my offspring to dwell in a valley without cultivation, by Thy Sacred House; in order, O our Lord, that they may establish regular Prayer: so fill the hearts of some among men with love towards them, and feed them with fruits: so that they may give thanks. (Q Ibrāhīm 14:37)[15]

10 Although the Prophetic traditions relating to the building of the Kaʿba by the angels and by Adam are not considered "strongly authenticated," Muslim scholars are in agreement that the Kaʿba existed before the time of Abraham. The scholarly disagreement centers on whether Adam or the angels first built it. M. Z. Kandahlawi, *Faḍāʾil-e Hajj* (Karachi: Maktaba al-Bushra, 2011), 10.

11 Al-Kharkūshī, *Sharaf al-Muṣṭafā*, II: 204.

12 Usmānī, *Maʿāriful Qurʾān*, II: 321.

13 Usmānī, *Maʿāriful Qurʾān*, I: 319.

14 According to the contemporary Syrian scholar Samīra Zāyid, Abraham was originally from a region near the western banks of the Euphrates, then migrated to Greater Syria-Palestine. He would go out on missions, calling people to worship God. On one such trip to Egypt, the pharaoh had designs on Abraham's wife, Sarah. He was thwarted through divine intervention, and in recognition of Sarah's piety, the pharaoh gifted her a bondsmaid, Hagar, whom Abraham would later marry at the suggestion of Sarah, who was childless at that point. S. Zāyid, *Mukhtaṣar al-Jāmiʿ fī al-sīra al-nabawiyya* 6 vols. (Damascus: al-Maṭbaʿa al-ʿIlmiyya, 1995), I: 41.

15 All Qurʾan translations are from Yusuf Ali unless otherwise specified.

Muslims scholars point out that this prayer was accepted on all counts. Mecca became a place of sanctuary, where battling tribes would call a truce, and the weak and forsaken could find refuge.[16] Abraham's sons remained firm in monotheistic faith and became the forefathers of two major monotheistic communities – the Children of Israel (*Banī Isrāʾīl*) in the case of Isaac (Abraham's younger son), and Muhammad's followers in the case of Ishmael.[17] Immediately after the prayer was made, Hagar and Ishmael were provided for through a miraculous wellspring of fresh water, Zamzam, still running and still visited by pilgrims to this day. Hagar and her son became the caretakers of the well, which gave them authority over the various tribes that began settling near this water. Over time, pilgrimage caravans and trade brought produce and goods from distant lands to what had once been a barren valley.

After leaving Hagar and Ishmael in the valley of Mecca, Abraham would return to visit them between his preaching missions.[18] On one such visit, when Ishmael was a grown and married man, God commanded the rebuilding of the Kaʿba. God's command to Abraham is related in the Qurʾan:

> Remember We made the House a place of assembly for men and a place of safety; and take ye the station of Abraham as a place of prayer; and We covenanted with Abraham and Ismaʿil, that they should sanctify My House[19] for those who compass it round, or use it as a retreat, or bow, or prostrate themselves (therein in prayer). (Q Baqara 2:125)

With the help of Ishmael, Abraham is said to have built the Kaʿba on its old foundations. To reach the upper heights of the Kaʿba, Abraham stood on a large levitating stone to help him with the building. The stone is said to have acquired the footprints of Abraham and is housed in a glass and gold encasement several feet from the door of the Kaʿba. Muslims consider the location of this stone, "the Station of Abraham" (*maqām*

[16] M. Lings, *Muhammad: His Life Based on the Earliest Sources* (Rochester, VT: Inner Traditions International, 1983), 3–4.

[17] Some Qur'an commentators held that all of the children of Isaac and Ishmael were protected from polytheism, while others held that only the sons of Abraham were protected (not his later descendants). See the commentaries on Q 14:35, e.g., Usmānī, *Maʿāriful-Qurʾān*, V: 275; al-Qurṭubī, *Tafsīr* V: 3597; al-Ālūsī, *Rūḥ al-maʿanī* XIII: 294–295.

[18] Zāyid, *Mukhtaṣar*, I: 41.

[19] Muslims do not believe that God resides within the Kaʿba. Rather, they see this as an indication of how God has honored the site. "The ascription of the House to Himself is an ascription of ennoblement and honoring (*iḍāfat tashrīf wa-takrīm*). It is the ascribing of a created thing to a creator, and a thing owned to an owner." Al-Qurṭubī, *Tafsīr*, I: 499.

Ibrāhīm), a place of blessing (*baraka*) and aim to pray as near to it as possible after circumambulating the Kaʿba.

After (re)building the Kaʿba, Abraham was asked by God to "proclaim the *ḥajj*" so that people would make pilgrimage to it (Q Ḥajj 22:27–28). When Abraham wondered aloud, "How will my voice reach them?" God answered saying that while it was Abraham's task to make the call, it was God who would have it be heard.[20] So Abraham proclaimed the Hajj, "and everything between the heavens and the earth heard his call,"[21] including "the souls of human beings still in the loins of their forefathers and the wombs of their mothers."[22] According to some Prophetic traditions, those destined to perform the Hajj called out, "*Labbayk*," "At your service!"[23] as many times as the number of times they would actually perform the Hajj.

After the Hajj had been proclaimed, Ishmael remained the caretaker of the Kaʿba and the sacred precincts (*ḥaram*) around it. He had married the daughter of the chief of the Jurhum, an Arab tribe that had come and settled in Mecca. After his death, two of his sons became the caretakers. This honor and responsibility carried on through Ishmael's descendants in the Jurhum tribe, until the third century CE, when a rival Arab tribe, the Khuzāʿa, managed to seize this powerful position thanks to infighting among the Jurhum. When the Jurhumites lost control of the Kaʿba, they placed the Black Stone[24] inside the well of Zamzam, blocked it, and covered it up. They wiped away any trace of the well's location and then fled to Yemen, leaving behind only a few branches of their tribe, who continued to live on the outskirts of Mecca but without any say over the sacred precincts.[25]

It was another three hundred years before control of the sacred precincts returned to the descendants of Ishmael. Quṣayy ibn Kilāb, a member of the tribe of Quraysh (one of the branches of Jurhum that had remained in Mecca), was married to the daughter of the chief of the Khuzāʿa. Quṣayy had many sons, much wealth, and the respect of the people of Mecca. According to one report, he joined forces with related tribesmen to oust the Khuzāʿa after the death of his father-in-law. According to another

[20] Kandahlawi, *Faḍā'il*, 11–12.
[21] Kandahlawi, *Faḍā'il*, 11–12.
[22] Al-Qurṭubī, *Tafsīr*, V: 4430.
[23] Hajj pilgrims chant the *talbiya*, which begins with this phrase.
[24] A stone fixed into the southeast corner of the Kaʿba, which Muslims believe to have been sent down from heaven.
[25] Zāyid, *Mukhtaṣar*, I: 53.

report, it was Quṣayy's father-in-law himself who wrote in his bequest that leadership of Mecca be restored to the children of Ishmael by naming his son-in-law as his heir (that is, instead of one of his own sons).

By the time of the birth of the Prophet Muhammad in the late sixth century, control of the sacred precincts and the Ka'ba had returned to the descendants of Abraham and Ishmael. The Quraysh, Quṣayy's tribe – and also Muhammad's – acquired esteem in the eyes of Meccans and the surrounding tribes, possibly because they were seen as the rightfully restored heirs of Abraham.[26]

However, claims to the contrary notwithstanding,[27] the spiritual legacy of Abraham and the Hajj appears to have been lost by this time. Even before the Khuzā'a had gained control, the Jurhumites, though monotheistic and clinging to the Hajj and a few Abrahamic rituals, are believed to have begun to lose sight of Abraham's mission. During the period of Khuzā'a leadership, one of the particularly charismatic Khuzā'a chieftains, 'Amr ibn Luhayy, changed the religious direction of the Meccan pilgrimage dramatically.[28] On a trip to greater Syria-Palestine, 'Amr had seen the people of that region engaged in idol worship. He brought back to Mecca a large stone idol called Hubal, which he placed at the Ka'ba and called people to worship it alongside God. Other tribes soon began to bring their own representative idols to be placed along the Ka'ba. By the time of Muhammad's birth, some three hundred idols are said to have been housed within the sacred precincts.[29]

By Muhammad's time, the Arabs had developed a system of polytheistic belief and ritual. Although they worshipped a deity named "Allāh" as God of the universe, they also believed that the idols could intercede on their behalf and could be a means thereby of reaching God.[30] The polytheists would take refuge with the idols, seek help from them in times of distress, and believed them not only capable of intercession with God, but also able to help and harm others individually, of their own accord. The tradition of the pilgrimage to the Ka'ba continued, but the focus and objects of prayer, prostration, and sacrifice were the idols in and around it.[31]

[26] Zāyid, *Mukhtaṣar*, I: 53.

[27] Ibn 'Āshūr, *al-Taḥrīr* (commentary on Q Naḥl 16:123).

[28] Zāyid, *Mukhtaṣar*, I: 56.

[29] Al-Būṭī, *Fiqh al-Sīra*, 37–38.

[30] Cf. Q Zumar 39:3: "Is it not to Allah that sincere devotion is due? But those who take for protectors other than Allah (say): 'We only serve them in order that they may bring us nearer to Allah.'"

[31] Zāyid, *Mukhtaṣar*, I: 59.

In the midst of this polytheism, a few scattered individuals appear to have remained attached to the idea of the oneness of God. Among the Arabs they were known as *ḥunafāʾ* (sing. *ḥanīf*). A hanif remained firmly on the Abrahamic path and "believed in the oneness of God; performed the Hajj; sacrificed [an animal in the name of God]; practiced circumcision; and faced the direction of prayer [toward the Kaʿba]."[32] It was hanifs who first recognized the truth of Muhammad's prophethood and message: they saw him as the messenger Abraham had prayed for, from the children of Ishmael, one who would again call people to worship and submission to God alone.[33]

When Muhammad first received revelation from God at the age of forty, it was the cousin of his wife Khadīja who confirmed the vision and experience he had. Khadīja's cousin, Waraqa ibn Nawfal, was a pious Christian scholar well versed in the scriptures. Waraqa had noticed signs of Muhammad being the awaited prophet some fifteen years earlier, when Muhammad and Khadīja had married. When Muhammad had his first revelatory experience, he was confused and overwhelmed by what he had experienced. To ease his worry, his wife took him to Waraqa, who confirmed that what Muhammad had seen was none other than the "greatest spirit," namely the Angel Gabriel, who had visited other prophets of the past. Waraqa told Muhammad that he was the prophet that God had promised to send to mankind before the end of time, and that he should be careful because "Thou wilt be called a liar, and ill-treated, and they will cast thee out and make war upon thee; and if I live to see that day, God knoweth I will help His cause."[34]

The Meccans did eventually force Muhammad out of Mecca, some thirteen years into his mission. People from every house, high and low, had started to accept his message, and the Meccans, and especially the Quraysh, felt threatened by the Prophet's influence and his teachings. They no longer recognized the idea of a prophet as Muhammad taught it; in their belief system, a prophet was now seen as a mythical holy figure who neither ate, nor drank, nor wed.[35] The central teaching of the oneness of God (*tawḥīd*) was also threatening, not only because it too now seemed foreign, but also because the entire tribal system of Arabia was built on

32 Al-Qurṭubī, *Tafsīr*, II: 1351.

33 See Q Baqara 2:127: "Our Lord! send amongst them [our progeny] a Messenger of their own, who shall rehearse Thy Signs to them and instruct them in scripture and wisdom, and sanctify them: For Thou art the Exalted in Might, the Wise."

34 Lings, *Muhammad*, 44.

35 Zāyid, *Mukhtaṣar*, I: 61.

polytheistic foundations, with Mecca, the Haram, and the Quraysh at its center. They did not want anything or anyone to disrupt this balance.

When the situation became too hostile in Mecca, the Prophet chose to move to a city some 400 km to the north. Yathrib – later renamed Medina after the Prophet moved there (from *Madīnat al-Nabī*, "City of the Prophet") – had a number of followers from both of its major tribes who had become Muslim and who had pledged their allegiance to the Prophet. They welcomed him to their city and provided a refuge and a base for the growth of Islam. For this reason, Medina came to be highly esteemed. Like the mosques in Mecca and Jerusalem, the Prophet's Mosque in Medina was also divinely decreed as a sacred precinct, or Haram. Within the carefully defined boundaries of all three holy sites, Muslims forbade hunting, the uprooting of trees, harvesting, and violence.[36] The medieval Muslim scholar al-Ghazālī instructs pilgrims on why Medina is so sacred, and the reason why visiting it is encouraged:

> As for the visit to Madina: when your eyes alight on the city walls, remember that this is the town which God, Great and Glorious is He, selected for His Prophet, on him be peace, that he made it the goal of his migration, that this was his home where he promulgated the binding decrees of his Lord, Great and Glorious is He, established his own exemplary precedents, strove against his foes and proclaimed his religion until God, Great and Glorious is He, took him to Himself. It then came to house his tomb.[37]

However beloved Medina was in the eyes of the Prophet thereafter, Mecca always held a special place. When leaving it, he had bade it farewell with the following words: "Of all God's earth, thou art the dearest place unto me and the dearest unto God,[38] and had not my people driven me out from thee I would not have left thee."[39] In response, during that very migration from Mecca to Medina, God revealed the following: "Verily He who hath made binding upon thee the Koran will bring thee home once more."[40] The Prophet left for Medina in order to build and establish a strong religious edifice, and over time, his influence extended well beyond

[36] R. K. Reinhart, "*Haram*," *Oxford Encyclopedia of the Islamic World*, II: 379.

[37] Al-Ghazālī, *Inner Dimensions of Islamic Worship*, tr. Muhtar Holland (Leicester: The Islamic Foundation, 1983), 117.

[38] A majority holds that Mecca is of higher rank than Medina. But as Aḥmad notes, "There is consensus that that portion of the earth where lies the pure body of the [Prophet], peace and blessings of God be upon him, is more excellent (*afḍal*) than all else in creation; it is even more excellent than the Mosque of the *Ḥaram*, the Kaʿba, God's Footstool (*ʿarsh*) and His Throne." S. Aḥmad, *Muʿallim al-ḥujjāj* (Karachi: Maktaba al-Bushra, 2011), 332.

[39] Lings, *Muhammad*, 118.

[40] Q Qaṣaṣ 28:85, as quoted in Lings, *Muhammad*, 120.

the vicinity of Mecca and Medina. After years of patiently calling others to believe, he was finally able to return to Mecca in a position of strength.

The return occurred after a long series of battles and negotiations. The main event that set the terms for the return to Mecca was the Treaty of Hudaybiyya, which took place six years after the migration to Medina. Its terms were in some ways humiliating to Muslims; for example, they were required to return any converts from Mecca who had fled to Medina to escape persecution, but no one who came back as an apostate from Medina to Mecca would have to be returned to the Muslims. The Prophet agreed to all of the terms, however, because he received a promise of ten years of peace in return, during which he could teach and call people to Allah without fear of being molested or harmed by the Meccans. This also allowed tribes who may have heretofore been reluctant to proclaim their faith (due to preexisting treaties with the Quraysh) to begin making alliances with Muhammad, since the treaty stated, "[W]hoso wisheth to enter into the bond and pact of Muhammad may do so; and whoso wisheth to enter the bond and pact of Quraysh may do so."[41]

The Companions of the Prophet were initially disappointed with this treaty, and could not understand why he had agreed to its humiliating terms. But God sent down a revelation after the treaty was signed, declaring it a "clear victory."[42] Soon they began to see its benefits, such that within a couple of years, the Prophet was in a position to march upon Mecca and face no resistance. The Prophet's followers and alliances had greatly increased, and when the Meccans violated the treaty, the Prophet gathered his Companions, some ten thousand strong, and entered Mecca unchallenged. The Meccans expected the worst for the years they had persecuted and challenged the Prophet, but instead they were granted pardon and forgiveness. The Prophet spent some days among the people, receiving those who had hidden their conversion from the hostile Meccans, and others who now had decided to accept the faith.

Before returning to Medina, the Prophet circumambulated the Kaʿba. He made his circuit between the Kaʿba and the 360 idols that surrounded it. As he did so, he repeated the verse "Truth has come, and Falsehood has perished, for Falsehood is (by its nature) bound to perish" (Q Isrāʾ 17:81).[43] While reciting, he pointed "at the idols, one by one, with his

[41] Lings, *Muhammad*, 253.
[42] Q Fatḥ 48:1 (my translation).
[43] My translation.

staff; and each idol, as he pointed at it, fell forward on its face."[44] Twenty years after the first revelation, and many centuries after ʿAmr ibn Luhayy, the Kaʿba was restored to its Adamic and Abrahamic purpose, namely the worship of the one God.

The Prophet made his one and only Hajj after the conquest of Mecca, after all of the idols had been removed from the Haram. During his Hajj, which took place eighty days before his death, the following verse was revealed:

> This day have those who reject faith given up all hope of your religion: yet fear them not but fear Me. This day have I perfected your religion for you, completed My favour upon you, and have chosen for you Islam as your religion. (Q Māʾida 5:3)

Muhammad recited the verse to the thousands of pilgrims gathered before him on the Day of ʿArafat, the culminating point of the Hajj. They rejoiced at the honor of being present at the occasion when God declared the completion of His favor upon the Muslims. But, as one Qurʾanic commentator points out, the "favor" and "completion of faith" referred to here are not addressed just to the monotheist Muslim followers of Arabia:

> In a nutshell, the message [of this verse] is that the ultimate standard of True Faith and Divine Blessing which was to be bequeathed to human beings in this world has reached its perfection on that great day. This is, so to say, the climax of the divine blessings in the shape of a True Faith which began with our Master Adam peace be upon him and continued in later times when the children of Adam in every period and every area kept receiving a part of this blessing in proportion to their prevailing conditions. Today, that faith and that Blessing in its final form has been bestowed upon the Last of the Prophets, the Messenger of Allah, God's peace and blessings be upon him, and to his community.[45]

When God promised Abraham in the Bible that He would bring forth "a great nation"[46] from the progeny of his first-born son Ishmael, Muslims interpret this nation to be the followers of the Prophet Muhammad. They see his mission as the continuation and culmination of the mission of all the prophets and messengers sent by God to mankind. In one Prophetic tradition, Muhammad said that he had been raised up as a prophet on the tolerant way of the hanifs (*al-ḥanafiyya al-samḥa*). In another hadith, he is

[44] Lings, *Muhammad*, 300.

[45] Usmānī, *Maʿāriful Qurʾān*, III: 46.

[46] "And as for Ishmael, I have heard you: I will surely bless him; I will make him fruitful and will greatly increase his numbers. He will be the father of twelve rulers, and I will make him into a great nation." Gen. 17:20 (NIV).

reported to have said, "I am the [answer to the] prayer of my father Abraham, and the 'good tidings' (*bushrā*) of Jesus."[47] Muhammad was a messenger, and so brought a new religious law, with some similarities shared with the Sharia of Abraham, and in some ways more "tolerant" (*samha*) than the laws of Moses.[48] He taught the same theological principles as the prophets who came before him, calling people to recognize God and submit to Him.

Muslims believe that submission (*islām*) to the one God was a teaching given to every human community on earth, since God says in the Qur'an, "And indeed, within every community have We raised up a messenger" (Q Naḥl 16:36). However, Abraham's position among these messengers is believed to have been special, since from him would come the greatest communities of *muslims* (believers or literally, "those who submit [to God]"): the community of Moses, the community of Jesus, and the community of Muhammad (since Moses and Jesus were Jewish prophets descended from Isaac's line, and Muhammad a non-Jewish prophet descended from the line of Ishmael). Among these, Muhammad also has a uniquely special honor, since Muslims believe the message of Moses and Jesus to have been changed and lost (through tribal exceptionalism in the case of the former and the divinification of Jesus in the case of the latter), while God promises to preserve the religion as revealed to Muhammad till the end of time.

Thus it comes as no surprise that Muslims remember Abraham every day in their prayers, or that, in the great pilgrimage they are called on to perform at least once in their lives, what they commemorate is the submission of Abraham, his wife Hagar, and their son Ishmael. As the spiritual forefather of the Prophet Muhammad, Abraham's acceptance of divine will is a reminder for Muslims that submission to God lies at the very core of human existence. The rites of the Hajj are intimately tied to the Abrahamic story, and thereby emphasize to the followers of Muhammad the timeliness of his prophetic message.

[47] As cited in al-Qurṭubī, *Tafsīr*, I: 516.
[48] Al-Būṭī, 34–35.

3

The Early Hajj

Seventh–Eighth Centuries CE

Travis Zadeh

BY FOOT OR BY DONKEY

Queen Zubayda (d. 216/831) and her husband (and first cousin), the famed Abbasid caliph Hārūn al-Rashīd (r. 170–193/786–809), are two of the most iconic figures associated with the early Meccan pilgrimage. Zubayda performed the Hajj on at least five occasions, and Hārūn nine times. They would travel to the Meccan sanctuary from the palatine city of Baghdad, which Zubayda's paternal grandfather, the caliph al-Manṣūr (r. 136–158/754–775), had founded. From the many public works that Zubayda sponsored along the route, the desert path from Iraq through the Arabian Peninsula came to bear her name, known popularly as the way or path (*darb*) of Zubayda. While the journey was no doubt arduous, the royal family was joined by a large entourage of high-ranking administrators, court companions, military officials, and servants.

Hārūn is famously said to have once performed the pilgrimage on foot, accompanied by Zubayda, in fulfillment of a vow. The story of carpets unfurled beneath their feet as they made their journey across the desert appears in medieval Arabic belletristic sources. It also features prominently in nineteenth-century European accounts of the Hajj as an expression of the costly extravagance of oriental despotism. As with much of the material on the early Abbasid pilgrimage, this particular event is enmeshed in the courtly imagination of later generations. First, there is some confusion over the date of the pilgrimage in question, though 173/790 appears to be most likely. According to the historian al-Ṭabarī (d. 310/923), Hārūn is said to have led the pilgrimage that year, having

FIGURE 3 Milestone from Darb Zubayda in the National Museum, Riyadh

left Baghdad in a state of ritual consecration.[1] This may well have been the germ for later anecdotes, which offer differing explanations for the oath, ranging from a vow uttered on the deathbed of a beloved concubine[2] to a humorous account of a promise the caliph made to one of his ministers.[3]

[1] Al-Ṭabarī, *Tārīkh al-rusul wa-l-mulūk = Annales quos scripsit Abu Djafar Mohammed ibn Djarir at-Tabari*, ed. M. J. de Goeje et al., 15 vols. in 3 vols. (Leiden: E. J. Brill, 1879–1901), III: 609.

[2] Ibn al-Sāʿī, *Nisāʾ al-khulafāʾ*, ed. M. Jawād (Cairo: Dār al-Maʿārif, 1968), 45–46.

[3] Ibn Qutayba (pseudo-), *Kitāb al-Imāma wa-l-siyāsa*, ed. ʿA. Shayrī, 2 vols. (Beirut: Dār al-Aḍwāʾ, 1990), II: 212–219.

This literary tapestry of telling and retelling is ripe for further expansion. Such is the case with the anecdote preserved by the Andalusi courtier Ibn ʿAbd Rabbih (d. 328/940): as carpets were unfurled before the pair day after day, Hārūn grew increasingly fatigued. Calling out for the arm of one of his servants, he exclaimed, "By God! Riding a boney donkey would better than walking on fine carpets!" Ibn ʿAbd Rabbih then uses this colorful turn of phrase as a gloss on the poetic proverb, "there is no pleasure in having an ass as my mount, but he who has had to walk will be pleased by whatever he rides."[4] While such material complicates any strict historicization, it also emphasizes that the imperial history of the pilgrimage forms part of a broad courtly process of memorialization. It is precisely because the Hajj held such profound political and religious significance for the ruling elite that these examples of discursive expansion took hold in the literary imagination.

The symbolic importance of the Meccan shrine as a caliphal prerogative is memorialized in a wide range of early Arabic materials, from official records and state chronicles, to literary anecdotes and courtly poetry. The pattern of articulating caliphal authority through the leadership of the pilgrimage and control over the Meccan sanctuary was set in motion during the Umayyad dynasty (41–132/661–750), which was based in Damascus. The Umayyad elite met a bloody end with the Abbasid revolt, which ultimately moved the political center of power to Iraq. In the very nascence of the Abbasid state, however, the new rulers also staked their claim to power through the Meccan sanctuary complex.

The early Abbasids located their authority as members of the *Ahl al-Bayt*, which in this period still retained a double meaning, as it signified both "people of the sanctuary," as well as descendants of the family of the Prophet.[5] This coalesces in their direct ancestor al-ʿAbbās (d. ca. 32/653), the paternal uncle of the Prophet, who according to the early historiographical material was responsible for preparing and distributing drink (*siqāya*) to pilgrims, as the custodian of the Zamzam well.[6] This is

[4] Ibn ʿAbd Rabbih, *al-ʿIqd al-farīd*, ed. M. M. Qumayḥa, 9 vols. (Beirut: Dār al-Kutub al-ʿIlmiyya, 1983), VII: 254; see S. Rāshid, *Darb Zubayda: The Pilgrim Road from Kufa to Mecca* (Riyadh University Libraries, 1980), 20 n. 20.

[5] See M. Sharon, "*Ahl al-Bayt*, People of the House: A Study of the Transformation of a Term from *Jāhiliyyah* to Islam," *Jerusalem Studies in Arabic and Islam*, 8 (1986): 169–184; cf. M. Sharon, "The Umayyads as *Ahl al-Bayt*," *Jerusalem Studies in Arabic and Islam*, 14 (1991): 115–149.

[6] See G. Hawting, "The 'Sacred Offices' of Mecca from Jāhiliyya to Islam," *Jerusalem Studies in Arabic and Islam*, 13 (1990): 62–63, 67; G. Hawting, "The Disappearance

a right that al-ʿAbbās inherited from his father, ʿAbd al-Muṭṭalib, the paternal grandfather of the Prophet Muhammad, who a generation before is famously said to have discovered the sacred well through a providential dream. The distribution of drink took place in a building generally known as the siqaya of al-ʿAbbās, located within the sacred precincts (*ḥaram*). The early Abbasid caliphs promoted themselves as the rightful leaders of the pilgrimage through their hereditary control over the Zamzam well and the office of the siqaya. This was expressed in the water works in and around the Meccan sanctuary, and in the development and maintenance of a network of wells, cisterns, and reservoirs dotting the Iraqi pilgrimage route through the desert. Over the course of yearly pilgrimages led either directly by the caliphs or by close relatives, the Abbasid elite fortified the Iraqi pilgrimage route by supplying it with wells, way stations, and castles that benefited the caliphs and their family, as well as ordinary pilgrims. Under the caliph al-Mahdī (r. 158–169/775–785), the political center of the empire was connected to the sacred precincts of Mecca and Medina through the extensive communications network of the imperial postal service (*barīd*).

Zubayda's celebrated charities included both the pilgrimage route and the Meccan shrine, which fit into a larger pattern of pious endowments. As with other leading members of the Abbasid ruling circle, Zubayda's patronage features prominently in the panegyric poetry produced by court poets. The world of verse on the Mecca shrine and the Hajj offers insight into a broad discursive regime that fused religious and political legitimacy in the providential power of sacred history and geography. When read against the historical backdrop of the period, this poetic material reveals how the early Abbasid elite affirmed their authority as the rightful guardians of the sacred shrine in symbolical terms.

POETRY, POLITICS, AND THE PILGRIMAGE

Three examples taken from the courtly panegyrics on Zubayda and the Meccan pilgrimage illuminate this process of dynastic self-fashioning. The first comes from the Baghdadi bookseller and transmitter of anecdotes and other belletristic material, Ibn Abī Saʿd (d. 274/887), who relates that during one of Zubayda's pilgrimages, Nuṣayb, a court poet from Yemen, sang a poem in her honor that began:

and Rediscovery of Zamzam and the 'Well of the Kaʿba,'" *Bulletin of the School of Oriental and African Studies*, 43,1 (1980): 44–54.

> The holy sanctuary and the Zamzam will greet
> the mother of the crown prince, the ornament of the pilgrimage rituals.
> Whoever reaches the station for casting stones will know that
> she will carry the burden of debt for every debtor.
> The tribe of Hāshim is the ornament of all creation
> and the mother of the crown prince is the ornament for the Hāshim ...[7]

In return, Zubayda granted Nuṣayb a hefty reward. Apart from the lavish praise that points to the interconnection between literary patronage and courtly self-fashioning, we can deduce several pieces of information from this anecdote. The reference to Zubayda as the mother of the heir apparent alludes to the caliphal election of her five-year-old son Muḥammad, who would succeed the throne after his father's death with the regnal title al-Amīn (r. 193–198/809–813) – the only Abbasid caliph whose parents were both from the Prophet's clan, the Hāshimīs. This pronouncement of succession took place in 175/792, when Muḥammad was barely five years old.[8] Thus, the pilgrimage in question most likely occurred the following year, when Zubayda traveled on the Hajj with her uncle and brother.[9] These verses also imagine the pilgrimage as a form of heraldry that grants legitimacy to the caliphal succession, which is confirmed here by the sacred landscape of the Meccan shrine. Similarly, the poem locates the Abbasid family in the heights of a cosmic hierarchy, as chief members of the Hāshimīs.

Nuṣayb's eulogy most likely precedes the ill-fated double succession announced in 183/799, when Hārūn declared that his eldest son ʿAbd Allāh, the future al-Ma'mūn (r. 198–218/813–833), would succeed al-Amīn as caliph. The terms of succession were famously instituted during the pilgrimage of 186/802, when Hārūn and his two heirs swore in the Kaʿba to the orderly transfer of power before an entourage of dignitaries and officials. Both brothers signed documents pledging their commitment to the pact and to a litany of severe privations should they break their oaths. These documents were in turn hung in the inner sanctum of the Kaʿba, an axis mundi that symbolically, at least, was designed to grant a sacred legitimacy to the entire affair. The oaths ultimately did not avert the civil war that soon ensued between the half-brothers.[10] Two other

[7] See Al-Iṣfahānī, *Kitāb al-Aghānī*, 24 vols. (Cairo: Dār al-Kutub al-Miṣriyya, 1927–61), XXIII: 14–15.
[8] Al-Ṭabarī, *Tārīkh*, III: 610–611.
[9] See Al-Ṭabarī, *Tārīkh*, III: 628–629.
[10] See T. El-Hibri, "Harun al-Rashid and the Mecca Protocol of 802: A Plan for Division or Succession?" *International Journal of Middle Eastern Studies*, 24, 3 (1992): 461–480;

important features of the encomium are the emphasis on caliphal charity and the reference to the Zamzam spring as a central location within the shrine complex. Indeed, both the charitable water works established along the route and the Zamzam well are consistent sites of poetic attention, as they foreground Abbasid piety in terms of hereditary rights over the sacred shrine.

The second example highlighting the poetic memory of Zubayda and the Meccan shrine underscores this very issue. Ibn Abī Saʿd also records the following verses by the Yemeni poet Ashjaʿ ibn ʿAmr al-Sulamī, who was originally in the service of Zubayda's father and went on to have an illustrious career as a panegyrist during the reign of Hārūn. At the end of an hour-long learning assembly, held for the four-year-old al-Amīn, Ashjaʿ recited the following two verses:

> His father is a king and his mother is of noble stock,
> from her emanates a blazing lamp for the faithful,
> she drank in Mecca's noble ground
> the unadulterated water of prophecy[11]

Zubayda gifted Ashjaʿ 100,000 dirhams for these verses, which celebrate al-Amīn's unique status as the son of two Abbasid royals and promote Zubayda as a sacred figure for the faithful through her connection to the water of prophecy, in a direct allusion to the Zamzam well. These verses also promote Zubayda as a spiritual guide.

The poetic portrayal of Zubayda as a leader features most prominently in an *urjūza*, a lengthy poem in the *rajaz* meter, composed by Ashjaʿ's lesser well known brother, Aḥmad ibn ʿAmr al-Sulamī, also a court poet. According to the poem's framing conceit, Aḥmad joined the entourage accompanying Zubayda during one of her pilgrimages. The driving rhythm of the *rajaz* meter is particularly conducive to movement and is the quintessential meter of the camel-driver urging his camels through the desert and to water. Following well-established motifs in the Arabic classical ode, the imagery of the urjuza opens up a vast and forbidding desert tableau. As the party moves away from civilization into the desert landscape, the shrubs and palm trees recede from view and the sources for water grow further apart. Through it all, Zubayda figures as a salvific guide, a saintly patroness of the pilgrimage; she unleashes torrents of water for the pilgrims through her charity and compassion.

R. A. Kimber, "Hārūn al-Rashīd's Meccan Settlement of AH 186/AD 802," *School of ʿAbbāsid Studies, Occasional Papers*, 1 (1986): 55–79.

[11] Al-Iṣfahānī, *Aghānī*, XVIII: 226.

The poem follows a basic pattern that serves to enumerate the halting grounds (*manāzil*) along the route from Baghdad to Mecca. The poet dedicates a stanza of five verses to each of over fifty halting grounds. In this poem (called a *mukhammasa*), the rhyme scheme for the strophic groupings is taken from the name of each station, as in the following strophe, rhyming in *-īla*, on the halting ground al-Salīla, whose well water is known to have been particularly bitter:

> [*thumma taraḥḥalnā ilā l-Salīla / marḥalatun miyāhuhā qalīla* ...]
> Then we journeyed on to Salīla / a station whose water was so scarce
> her group was unable to alight / so, elegant handed, she assisted
> giving of her flowing wealth / for water to be drawn by every means
> as a grace to the pilgrims and the local tribe / the sublime sovereign lent
> a hand to the graceful daughter of Abū al-Faḍl / for her, the sky is always ready to burst[12]

The rhyme scheme is well suited for the mnemonic purpose of recalling the names of the halting stations along the pilgrimage route. While Zubayda's father, Abū al-Faḍl, and husband, Hārūn al-Rashīd, are both alluded to, these two male authority figures remain in the background. In contrast, the verses celebrate Zubayda as the primary agent of generosity, which is here measured in water given for pilgrims. She took a direct, hands-on role in the improvement of the pilgrimage.

The poem notes that although the path is marked with milestones and postal route markers, it is rough going and strewn with rocks, a common trope in Arabic desert poetry. We are assured, however, that God lessens these difficulties through Zubayda's grace. Her charity is framed repeatedly in soteriological terms, as the poet affirms that "on the Day of Return she will have the greatest blessings," and exclaims, "blessings, blessings are upon you, O Zubayda!" This expression carries both the sense of blessings and joy, as well as eternal life, directly echoing the Qurʾanic promise that at journey's end, blessings await those who believe and do righteous deeds (Q Raʿd 13:29).[13]

On this journey, Zubayda, who is known to have preferred riding camels to asses,[14] is portrayed, both on foot and seated in her palanquin atop camels as a radiant sun illuminating everything in her path; she is more powerful than the Queen of Sheba, just as she outshines all other

[12] *Kitāb al-Manāsik wa-amākin ṭuruq al-ḥajj*, ed. Ḥ. al-Jāsir (Riyadh: Dār al-Yamāma 1969), 553, cf. 331. On Salīla, see Yāqūt, *Muʿjam al-buldān*, 5 vols. (Beirut: Dār al-Ṣādir, 1955–1957), III: 243.

[13] *Manāsik*, 550–551.

[14] Ibn Rusta, *Al-aʿlāq al-nafīsa*, ed. M. J. de Goeje (Leiden: E. J. Brill, 1882), 197.

women of the Hāshimī clan.[15] The poet characterizes Zubayda's works of public piety in the following terms, "the cupbearer of the pilgrims, the source of pride, she improved the path with silver and gems."[16] The improvement of the route reflects an Abbasid charitable tradition of supporting the pilgrimage. Similarly, the identification of Zubayda as giving drink to pilgrims fits into a well-worn motif of Abbasid religious and political legitimacy.

For instance, the anonymous and fragmentary history documenting the early formation of the Abbasid state, known by its modern title as the *Akhbār al-dawla al-ʿAbbāsiyya* ("Accounts of the Abbasid State") alludes to an association between the progenitors of the Abbasid caliphs, the Zamzam well, and the right to give pilgrims drink. This is represented in the figure of ʿAlī ibn ʿAbd Allāh (d. ca. 118/736), the paternal grandson of al-ʿAbbās and celebrated forefather of the Abbasids. He is portrayed as a particularly pious man who earned the sobriquet al-Sajjād, the worshiper or prostrator, for his continuous prayer;[17] while living in Damascus each day he would perform a thousand prostrations in the mosque over a tablet or board (*lawḥ*), which was taken from the Zamzam well.[18] The chronicle recounts a poem in praise of ʿAlī ibn ʿAbd Allāh, composed by al-Faḍl al-Lahabī (d. ca. 95/713), a Hāshimī poet and maternal grandson of al-ʿAbbās. The poem was delivered within the Meccan sanctuary while ʿAlī ibn ʿAbd Allāh was on pilgrimage. Al-Faḍl posed his verses as a rebuttal to a poet who had just sung the praises of the Umayyad caliph al-Walīd I (r. 88–98/705–715), while leading the caliph's mount by the halter. In response, al-Faḍl took the halter of ʿAlī ibn ʿAbd Allāh's mount and retorted with his own panegyric, which lists among ʿAlī's honors the distribution of drink to pilgrims:

> O Zamzam you are blessed by a stone-lined well
> Blessed for the one who gives water and for the thirsty
> The cupbearer gives drink to them[19]

[15] *Manāsik*, 545, 550.

[16] *Manāsik*, 551.

[17] See Al-Ṭabarī, *Tārīkh*, III: 2497.

[18] *Akhbār al-dawla al-ʿAbbāsiyya*, ed. ʿA. al-Dūrī and ʿA. al-Muṭṭalibī (Beirut: Dār al-Ṭalīʿa 1971), 145.

[19] *Akhbār al-dawla al-ʿAbbāsiyya*, 152–153; cf. Iṣfahānī, *Aghānī*, XVI: 183–184. Al-Faḍl returns to Zamzam and the right to provide drink to pilgrims elsewhere in his poetic corpus: see al-Fākihī, *Akhbār Makka*, ed. ʿA. b. ʿA. b. Duhaysh, 6 vols. (Beirut: Dār Khiḍr, 1994), II: 60–61.

One can find similar allusions to the hereditary claim over the Zamzam well and control of the siqaya in Abbasid court poetry. For instance, in a poem honoring the first Abbasid caliph, al-Saffāḥ (r. 132–136/749–754), the Persian court poet Bashshār ibn Burd (d. ca. 167/784) praises the Abbasid family in the following terms:

You are the cupbearers of the pilgrimage and without your cisterns and your buckets, people would not praise the station where they arrive[20]

Bashshār continues, "You have inherited from the Prophet of God the house of the caliphate." In the poetry of Bashshār during the caliphates of al-Manṣūr and al-Mahdī one can trace an ideological movement identifying the Abbasids as the *Ahl al-Bayt* ("family of the [Prophet's] house") an affiliation that is strongly associated with al-ʿAbbās and the right of the siqaya.[21] By the time Aḥmad al-Sulamī composed his urjuza in honor of Zubayda, there was an established discursive tradition that closely identified the Abbasids with the water rights of the pilgrimage.

As for the composition of the poem, there is no explicit indication of its particular historical context. However, given the absence of any reference to Zubayda's son al-Amīn, or the pressing question of caliphal succession, we have reason to suspect that the journey occurred after the Hajj of 186/802, when the oaths of succession were taken at the Kaʿba. This would suggest one of Zubayda's two last documented pilgrimages, both of which are associated with improving water for pilgrims. According to the Abbasid administrator al-Yaʿqūbī (fl. 278/891), Zubayda undertook the pilgrimage in 190/805, during a severe drought in Mecca, when the water of the Zamzam had all but dried up. At this point, Zubayda was said to have overseen an extensive excavation of the sacred well.[22] This event was also an impetus for the great water works she sponsored throughout the sacred city. According to an inscription preserved in the history of the shrine city by the Meccan historian al-Fākihī (fl. 272/885), one of the major cisterns which Zubayda constructed at the heights of the city was completed in 194/809–810. The inscription, written on marble and gypsum, remained visible in al-Fākihī's own day. It noted that Zubayda had

[20] Bashshār ibn Burd, *Dīwān*, ed. M. Ṭ. b. ʿĀshūr, 4 vols. (Cairo: Lajnat al-Taʾlīf wa-l-Tarjama wa-l-Nashr, 1950), III: 39, ll. 6–7.

[21] See M. Sharon, *Black Banners from the East: The Establishment of the ʿAbbāsid State: Incubation of a Revolt* (Leiden: Brill, 1983), 77, n. 8; idem, "*Ahl al-Bayt*," 177–178.

[22] See al-Yaʿqūbī, ed. M. T. Houstma, 2 vols. (Leiden: E. J. Brill, 1883); *Tārīkh*, II: 519; al-Azraqī, *Akhbār Makka*, ed. ʿA. b. ʿA. b. Duhaysh, 2 vols. (Mecca: Maktabat al-Asadī, 2003), I: 580; al-Fākihī, *Akhbār*, II: 74–75; Ibn Rusta, *Aʿlāq*, 42.

ordered the construction of the cistern to serve as a watering station for the pilgrims to God's shrine and for the people of His sanctuary.[23]

Turning to her final pilgrimage in 211/827, al-Fākihī depicts Zubayda as particularly keen on protecting her legacy as a patroness of the Meccan sanctuary and its water supply. Upon reaching the sacred city, Zubayda sharply rebuked the governor of the city for writing to the caliph al-Ma'mūn and not directly to her with a request for financial support to fund the construction and maintenance of cisterns.[24] At this point, Zubayda very much held a détente with al-Ma'mūn, who had deposed her son, the caliph al-Amīn, during the course of the bitter civil war. Her role and influence in the court was no longer as great as it had been during the caliphal reign of al-Amīn, when she had dirhams minted in her name.[25] The urjuza with its final prayer for her well-being may well fit into this later period in Zubayda's life and form part of a concerted effort to affirm her legacy as a patroness of the pilgrimage. Yet, efforts to historicize such material may risk obscuring how the Abbasid patronage of the Meccan pilgrimage served as part of a literary canvas for later generations to draw upon and configure.

While this tapestry preserves a profound historical value, it also maintains a very vibrant literary color. For instance, the Persian courtier and man of letters Ibn Khurdādhbih (fl. 269/882) recounts that the poet Abū al-Muhannā Mukhāriq fell madly in love with one of Zubayda's handmaids. In order to be closer to her, Mukhāriq followed Zubayda's entourage to Mecca. The anecdote ends with the poetic witticism that "while most people perform the Hajj out of piety and forbearance, Abū Muhannā's pilgrimage was all in the purist of a lady."[26] When reading such material, it is thus important to consider how a literary imagination animates the diverse historical contexts of the Meccan pilgrimage, while also serving as a model for it.

SOURCES FOR THE EARLY PILGRIMAGE

The majority of our knowledge on the early pilgrimage comes through source material from the Abbasid era, some fragmentary, and offering

[23] Al-Fākihī, *Akhbār*, III: 155.

[24] Al-Fākihī, *Akhbār*, III: 153–154; cf. Al-Azraqī, *Akhbār*, II: 856–857. See N. Abbott, *Two Queens of Baghdad: Mother and Wife of Hārūn al-Rashīd* (University of Chicago Press, 1942), 246–247.

[25] See L. Ilisch, "Münzgeschenke und Geschenkmünzen in der mittelalterlichen islamischen Welt," *Münstersche Numismatische Zeitung*, 14, 3 (1984): 15.

[26] Al-Iṣfahānī, *Aghānī*, XVIII: 370.

only a composite picture – for instance, the urjuza cited earlier exists only in a single acephalous manuscript that lacks the author's name and the title of the work. There are strong indications, however, that this work is the otherwise lost *Kitāb al-Ṭarīq* ("Book of the Route"), an incomplete geographical work by the Baghdadi historian and littérateur Wakīʿ (d. 306/918).[27] The manuscript describes in great detail the major pilgrimage routes through the Arabian Peninsula and is one of the most valuable sources for documenting the Abbasid patronage of the pilgrimage through the establishment and maintenance of water works and way stations across the Hijaz. This geographical work interrupts the dry list of stations and halting grounds with vivid verse citations and colorful anecdotes. As such, the text overlaps in important ways with imperial road books and administrative works, generally known as "routes and realms" (*al-masālik wa-l-mamālik*), which are peppered with belletristic attention to narratives and poetry. One of the earliest and most famous texts to bear the title *Kitāb al-Masālik wa-l-mamālik* (*Book of Routes and Realms*) is the geographical compendium by Ibn Khurdādhbih, which also preserves, though in a more truncated form, an account of the pilgrimage itinerary through the Hijaz.[28] The historical transmission of Ibn Khurdādhbih's road book is, to say the least, also rather messy; despite this, here too a clear outline emerges that promotes both Mecca and the seats of Abbasid power in Iraq as the central nodes of an expansive sacred geography.[29]

In terms of major compendiums, the histories of Mecca by Abū al-Walīd al-Azraqī (fl. 250/865), and by Abū ʿAbd Allāh al-Fākihī (who copies extensively from al-Azraqī's collection), are also among the most important primary sources for documenting the early pilgrimage. Similarly, Ibn Isḥāq's (d. 150/767) biography of the Prophet and history of the early community, as preserved by Ibn Hishām (d. 218/833), and al-Wāqidī's (d. 207/822) compendium on the early military

[27] See Ibn al-Nadīm, *al-Fihrist* ed. A. F. Sayyid, 2 vols. in 4 vols. (London: Al-Furqan Islamic Heritage Foundation, 2009), I: 352 253. On the question of authorship, see ʿA. al-Wuhaybī, "Hal huwa *al-Manāsik* am *Manāzil al-ṭarīq*? Wa-hal huwa li-Imām al-Ḥarbī am li-l-Qāḍī Wakīʿ?" *Majallat al-ʿArab*, 7/8, s. 23 (1409/1988): 433–441.

[28] Ibn Khurdādhbih, *al-Masālik wa-l-mamālik*, ed. M. J. de Goeje (Leiden: E. J. Brill, 1889), 125–128, 131–132; cf. al-Yaʿqūbī, *Kitāb al-Buldān*, ed. M. J. de Goeje (Leiden: E. J. Brill, 1892), 311–312.

[29] See Zadeh, "Of Mummies, Poets, and Water Nymphs: Tracing the Codicological Limits of Ibn Khurradādhbih's Geography," in M. Bernards (ed.), *ʿAbbāsid Studies IV* (Warminster: Gibb Memorial Trust, 2013), 8–75.

campaigns, offer valuable insight into how the pilgrimage and the shrine were envisioned by the early community. Although the historical writings of al-Balādhurī (d. 279/892) and al-Ṭabarī (d. 310/923) are of great importance, other collections, such as those by al-Khalīfa ibn Khayyāṭ (d. 240/854), Ibn Ḥabīb (d. 245/860), and al-Yaʿqūbī, also shed much light on the political history of Mecca and the pilgrimage. Many of these authorities were connected, in some fashion, to the imperial administration, and taken in the aggregate they form part of a particular Abbasid literary milieu. Nonetheless, they also draw extensively from earlier materials that were clearly in circulation during the Umayyad period.

Accessing the authenticity of this discursive stratum of Umayyad material has been a thorny issue for modern historians; even more challenging is the effort to separate the mythopoeic elements on the formation of the Meccan sanctuary from the historical record. A good example of these challenges can be found in an epistle, preserved by the Meccan historian al-Fākihī, ascribed to the ascetic al-Ḥasan al-Baṣrī (d. 110/728), who is known to have performed the pilgrimage at least twice. The letter celebrates the virtues (*faḍāʾil*) of Mecca and the Hajj rite through a collection of reports and sayings ascribed to the Prophet and the early community.[30] The material is designed to sanctify the various elements of the Kaʿba and the ritual stations of the pilgrimage. The letter also features a saying, ascribed to the Prophet Muhammad in some other sources, that "No prophet has fled his own people save that he went to Mecca and remained there worshiping God Almighty until he died." The letter continues by stating that around the Kaʿba are located the tombs of three hundred prophets, including the tombs of Noah, and the Arab prophets Hūd, Shuʿayb, and Ṣāliḥ.[31]

While the ascription is certainly open to question, there is good reason to believe that the text forms part of an early discourse on the sanctuary. For instance, the chief Abbasid judge Abū Yūsuf (d. 182/798) relates a nearly identical report on the tombs of the prophets; this may lend credence to the antiquity of the epistle. The epistlary genre is not only strongly associated with Ḥasan al-Baṣrī, but is a notable feature of Umayyad belletristic

[30] For a treatment of the expiating logic of the *faḍāʾil* discourse on the Meccan pilgrimage, see M. Katz, "The Ḥajj and the Study of Islamic Ritual," *Studia Islamica*, 98/99 (2004): 103–105.

[31] See Al-Fākihī, *Akhbār*, II: 291; see al-Ḥasan al-Baṣrī (attrib.), *Faḍāʾil Makka* ed. M. Z. M. ʿAzab (Cairo: Maktabat al-Thaqāfa al-Dīniyya, 1995), 63.

conventions.[32] Likewise, considering the date of Abū Yūsuf's collection, the dissemination of atomized material taken from the epistle could well have followed a movement from *narratio* to *exemplum*, with the epigraphic account ascribed to al-Ḥasan al-Baṣrī circulating in the Umayyad period and beyond in a piecemeal fashion.

PATRONS AND VILLAINS

As custodians of the Meccan sanctuary, the Abbasid caliphs appointed leaders of the annual pilgrimage, usually from within their own family – a practice that follows an established Umayyad precedent.[33] The first to be organized by the early Abbasid elite marked the culmination of their uprising against the Umayyad state in 132/750. The powerful general Dāwūd ibn ʿAlī (d. 133/750), uncle to the first two caliphs and short-lived governor of Mecca, led the pilgrimage that year in a procession with both religious and military significance.[34] In 136/753, the caliph al-Saffāḥ (d. 136/753) appointed his brother, the future caliph al-Manṣūr, to lead the pilgrimage, outwitting one of the most prominent military leaders of the Abbasid revolution, Abū Muslim al-Khurāsānī (d. 137/754), who sought the position.[35] In an attempt to win over the support of the Bedouins, Abū Muslim dug wells, leveled the road, and distributed head wraps and cloaks to the local Arabs on his own way to Mecca.[36] It was during this pilgrimage that, while in Mecca, al-Manṣūr learned of his brother's death, whereupon he assumed the title of caliph.[37] As caliph, al-Manṣūr also led the pilgrimage in the year 147/765; however, he did not make it far past Kufa, evidently for lack of water on the

[32] Abū Yūsuf, *Kitāb al-Āthār*, ed. A. al-Afghānī (Hyderabad: Lajnat Iḥyāʾ al-Maʿārif al-NuʿMāniyya, 1355/1936–1937), 117, § 545. See S. Mourad, *Early Islam between Myth and History: Al-Ḥasan al-Baṣrī (d. 110H/728CE) and the Formation of his Legacy in Classical Islamic Scholarship* (Leiden: Brill, 2006), 52, cf. 140–158. See also more broadly, D. J. Latham, "The Beginnings of Arabic Prose Literature: The Epistolary Genre," in A. F. L. Beeston et al. (eds.), *Arabic Literature to the End of the Umayyad Period* (Cambridge University Press, 1983), 154–179.

[33] On the Umayyad pilgrimage, see M. E. McMillan, *The Meaning of Mecca: The Politics of Pilgrimage in Early Islam* (London: Saqi Books, 2011).

[34] Ibn Saʿd, *Kitāb al-Ṭabaqāt al-kabīr*, ed. ʿA. M. ʿUmar, 11 vols. (Cairo: Maktabat al-Khānjī, 2001), VII: 471, §1950.

[35] Al-Ṭabarī, *Tārīkh*, III: 85; Al-Dīnawarī, *Akhbār al-ṭiwāl*, ed. ʿU. F. al-Ṭabbāʿ (Beirut: Sharikat Dār al-Arqam ibn al-Arqam, 1995), 345.

[36] Al-Ṭabarī, *Tārīkh*, III: 99.

[37] Al-Yaʿqūbī, *Tārīkh*, II: 437; Al-Ṭabarī, *Tārīkh*, III: 88.

route.[38] Nearly ten years later, al-Manṣūr set out on pilgrimage but died before reaching Mecca, possibly from a stomach ulcer aggravated by dysentery; his bier was carried to Mecca, where he was ultimately interred.[39]

Leading the community in pilgrimage was a caliphal prerogative explicitly based on the Prophet's precedent. In his history, al-Yaʿqūbī generally notes who led the pilgrimage each year. This is often followed by a chronological account of the various military campaigns undertaken, and the prominent jurists active during the caliphate in question. Al-Yaʿqūbī parallels a pattern set by al-Khalīfa ibn Khayyāṭ and others. This is a historiographical tradition kept alive by al-Ṭabarī in his universal history, and it appears to build upon actual lists, as preserved, for instance, by Ibn Ḥabīb (d. 245/860) and al-Masʿūdī (d. 345/956), likely kept as part of the state administration.[40] These records demonstrate that the early Abbasid caliphs followed an Umayyad practice of either personally leading the annual pilgrimage or delegating close relatives – particularly sons, cousins, and uncles – to do so.

Over the course of twenty-two years, al-Manṣūr led the pilgrimage six times. He charged his son and then heir apparent, Jaʿfar (d. 150/768) with the position in 148/766. In 153/770, the honor in turn fell to another of al-Manṣūr's sons, Muḥammad, who took the regnal name al-Mahdī upon assuming the caliphate.[41] Similarly, al-Mahdī honored his son and heir apparent, Mūsā al-Hadī (r. 169–170/785–786), with the post in 161/778.[42]

While later caliphs, particularly al-Mutawakkil (r. 232–247/847–861), invested hefty sums in renovating the Iraqi pilgrimage route and the Meccan sanctuary, the caliphate of Hārūn al-Rashīd is a high-water mark for direct caliphal presence in the region. The course of the following centuries witnessed a noticeable distancing between Baghdad and Mecca; as the central authority of the Abbasid empire weakened, large areas of the Hijaz fell into the hands of nomadic bandits outside of direct imperial control. While other caliphs sent representatives, Hārūn is generally

[38] Al-Ṭabarī, *Tārīkh*, III: 334, 429. This appears to be the same pilgrimage that al-Yaʿqūbī places in the year 142/760 (Al-Yaʿqūbī, *Tārīkh*, II: 447).

[39] Al-Ṭabarī, *Tārīkh*, III: 455.

[40] Ibn Ḥabīb, *Kitāb al-Muḥabbar*, ed. I. Lichtenstadter (Hyderabad: Dāʾirat al-Maʿārif al-ʿUthmāniyya, 1942), 11–44; Masʿūdī, *Murūj al-dhahab wa-maʿādin al-jawhar*, ed. Ch. Pellat, 7 vols. (Beirut: al-Jāmiʿa al-Lubnāniyya, 1966–1979), §§3630–3656.

[41] Al-Yaʿqūbī, *Tārīkh*, II: 469–470.

[42] Al-Yaʿqūbī, *Tārīkh*, II: 485.

credited as the last Abbasid caliph to personally make the pilgrimage to the sanctuary.[43]

The pilgrimage ceremony represented a significant undertaking, involving large caravans with vast retinues, which resembled, and at times indeed served as, military campaigns. Included were the royal family, elite military leaders, court companions, judges, the secretariat, and numerous attendants.[44] Travel through the desert necessitated protection from marauding Bedouins and a secure and steady supply of water. The lack of reliable water on the route from Iraq was a perennial problem, and ensuring that there was a sufficient amount for pilgrims was a caliphal responsibility. Al-Saffāḥ undertook a campaign to erect fortifications, al-Manṣūr established way stations (*manāzil*), and his son al-Mahdī ordered the construction of rainwater reservoirs at each watering hole, the establishment of wells, the restoration of cisterns, and the placement of milestones marking the route. This public project began in 161/777–778 and was still ongoing ten years later.[45] The high-ranking general Yaqṭīn ibn Mūsā, who oversaw the expansion of the Meccan sanctuary under al-Mahdī, was placed in charge of the project. Much work clearly remained, for when al-Mahdī set out for the pilgrimage of 164/781, he and his entourage had to abandon the enterprise due to a lack of water on the route.[46]

Hārūn continued this same work of fortifying the Iraqi pilgrimage route with castles, reservoirs, wells, and cisterns, which he also established in Mecca, Mina, ʿArafat, and Medina. Hārūn paralleled this building enterprise with fortifications along the Byzantine frontier, highlighting a broader imperial venture of controlling and demarcating territory.[47] In terms of water management, however, the extensive public works carried out by Hārūn's favorite wife, Zubayda, are far better known. She is said to have undertaken a massive irrigation project that cost over 1.5 million dinars and routed water through a series of canals, some twelve miles away from the holy city. The system of irrigation required the leveling of a vast amount of land. The project was mounted in response to the perpetual water shortages in Mecca and exorbitant inflation in the prices water-sellers were charging, particularly during the pilgrimage season.

[43] Al-Yaʿqūbī, *Tārīkh*, II: 505, 509, 521.
[44] See, e.g., al-Ṭabarī, *Tārīkh*, III: 665.
[45] Al-Ṭabarī, *Tārīkh*, III: 486.
[46] Al-Ṭabarī, *Tārīkh*, III: 502.
[47] Al-Masʿūdī, *Murūj*, §3449, cf. al-Azraqī, *Akhbār*, II: 845.

Al-Ya'qūbī relates that pilgrims and locals would drink water from Zubayda's cistern in the city.[48] In Mecca, Zubayda also built lodgings for travelers, and aided in ongoing efforts to dig wells and build cisterns along the desert pilgrimage route through Iraq and along the western frontiers. She supported these projects with charitable endowments designed to ensure their ongoing maintenance.

The Iraqi Hajj itineraries also formed the basis for the imperial postal network first established between Iraq and the cities of the Hijaz during the reign of al-Mahdī; according to al-Ṭabarī the network was completed in the year 166/781–782.[49] The efficiency and speed of the communication network famously made it possible for al-Mahdī to have ice imported to him while in Mecca.[50] Along the routes from Iraq through the Hijaz all sorts of exotica traveled, often as imperial booty donated to the sanctuary city.[51]

In addition to pious endowment of physical buildings in the form of mosques, forts, and palaces, the foundation and maintenance of wells and reservoirs along the route served as a form of charitable donation. Notable among the early leading members of the Abbasid ruling family to construct wells and other public works along the route are 'Īsā ibn 'Alī (d. 163/780) and 'Abd al-Ṣamad (d. 185/801), both of whom were uncles of al-Saffāḥ and al-Manṣūr, and were prominent leaders and governors with strong connections to the sanctuary complex.[52] The *Kitāb al-Ṭarīq* ascribed to Wakī' also credits the Barmakids, the powerful family of viziers during the reigns of the early Abbasid caliphs, with establishing several wells and watering stations.[53] Another notable contributor to the maintenance of the route through the foundation of wells is Yaqṭīn ibn Mūsā (d. 185/801), the famed general and promoter of the Abbasid cause, who held vast estates in Mesopotamia.[54] Yaqṭīn also served as the superintendent of the pilgrimage route.[55] This same road book illustrates that

48 Al-Ya'qūbī, *Buldān*, 316.

49 Al-Ṭabarī, *Tārīkh*, III: 517; see A. Silverstein, *Postal Systems in the Pre-Modern Islamic World* (Cambridge University Press, 2007), 61–62.

50 See al-Maqrīzī, *al-Dhahab al-masbūk fī dhikr man ḥajja min al-khulafā' wa-l-mulūk*, ed. J. al-Shayyāl (Cairo: Maktabat al-Thaqāfa al-Dīniyya, 2000), 76.

51 See S. Avinoam, "Made for Show: The Medieval Treasury of the Ka'ba in Mecca," in B. O'Kane (ed.), *The Iconography of Islamic Art: Studies in Honour of Robert Hillenbrand* (Edinburgh University Press, 2005), 269–283.

52 See *Manāsik*, 309, 344, 346, 347, 421.

53 See *Manāsik*, 285, 298, 303, 304, 332.

54 See Ibn Khurdādhbih, *Masālik*, 11.

55 *Manāsik*, 333.

the digging of wells served as a form of pious charity that extended beyond the Abbasid elite to include a range of other patrons. This is further supported by the archeological record which preserves a foundation inscription for two wells dug in the precinct of Mecca. The inscription perserves the name of the patron as Sulaymān ibn Mihrān, that is the famed Kufan traditionist and Qur'an reciter of Persian origin known as al-Aʿmash (d. 148/765). The foundation stone also records that the two wells were established as a form of public charity (*ṣadaqa*) for travelers.[56]

The vast majority of travelers to Mecca could not emulate the Basran traditionist al-Aswad ibn Shaybān (d. 165/781–782), a pious ascetic who left Basra on pilgrimage, taking with him as provision only a single female camel, which subsisted off the earth and which he milked in order to survive.[57] Even with reliable sources of water, the overland journey through the desert presented obvious physical difficulties for the pilgrims. The large caravans supporting the caliphs and their delegates would have also put pressure on the water supply. The sources make repeated reference to the problem of water shortages on the route.

The archeological evidence along the Darb Zubayda corroborates the textual sources documenting the great effort that the early Abbasids dedicated to the maintenance and construction of wells, cisterns, and rainwater reservoirs along the desert route. While the record is much less substantial, it is also clear that the Umayyads similarly maintained a pilgrimage route from Damascus.[58] Al-Masʿūdī recounts that the Umayyad caliph Hishām ibn ʿAbd al-Malik (r. 105–125/724–743) fortified the frontiers while also establishing waterways and cisterns along the road to Mecca, in a process that speaks both to the imperial definition of external boundaries and the internal demarcation of religious authority. Here al-Masʿūdī also alludes to the famed account of how the Abbasid general Dāwūd ibn ʿAlī destroyed the Umayyad waterworks in Mecca during the conquest of the city.[59] Archeological evidence of the early Umayyad caliphal sponsorship of wells can be seen in a

[56] Recorded in S. Rāshid et al., *Silsilat āthār al-Mamlaka al-ʿArabiyya al-Saʿūdiyya*, 13 vols. (Riyadh: Wizārat al-Maʿārif, 2003), II: 148–149.

[57] *Manāsik*, 594; Ibn Ḥajar, *Tahdhīb al-tahdhīb*, ed. I. al-Zaybaq and ʿĀ. Murshid, 4 vols. (Beirut: Mu'assasat al-Risāla, 1996), I: 171–172.

[58] For an epigraphic study of the archeological evidence, see Ḥ al-Kilābī, *al-Nuqūsh al-islāmiyya ʿalā ṭarīq al-ḥajj al-shāmī: min al-qarn al-awwal ilā l-qarn al-khāmis al-hijrī* (Riyadh: Maktabat al-Malik Fahd al-Waṭaniyya, 2009).

[59] Masʿūdī, *Murūj*, § 2219

fragmentary foundation inscription on a water tank established by Hishām ibn ʿAbd al-Malik (r. 65–86/685–705) outside the city of Suwayda, in the southeast of Syria.[60]

The historical sources also suggest that among the many points of conflict between the Umayyads and the Abbasids was the correct administration of water within the Meccan sanctuary. Several sources identify members of the Abbasid elite as custodians of the Zamzam well and the siqaya in the Umayyad period. This material intersects with a series of cynical reports concerning the depravity associated with the Umayyad governor of Mecca, Khālid ibn ʿAbd Allāh al-Qasrī (d. 126/743–744), who in one such report is said to have constructed an aqueduct to bring potable water into the holy sanctuary on the order of the caliph Sulaymān ibn ʿAbd al-Malik (r. 96–99/715–717).[61] Upon the completion of the aqueduct, Khālid slaughtered camels, distributed the meat, and then ascended a pulpit (*minbar*) he had placed next to the Kaʿba, whereupon he addressed the inhabitants of Mecca and encouraged them to drink the pure, cool water he had brought to the sanctuary, rather than the bitter salty water of the Zamzam. The residents refused the piped-in water, preferring the Zamzam, much to Khālid's consternation. The anecdote concludes with Dāwūd ibn ʿAlī's triumphant entrance into the city and his destruction of Khālid's aqueduct, whereupon the people of the city rejoiced. This would have taken place when Dāwūd led the first Abbasid pilgrimage to the Kaʿba in 132/749, which marked the beginning of his short tenure as governor of Mecca. In addition to extirpating the Umayyad waterworks within the sanctuary, Dāwūd is also known to have slaughtered all the members of the Umayyad royal family imprisoned in the holy city. There is every reason to believe that the revolutionary violence against the Umayyad ruling elite also extended to their architectural legacy within the sanctuary.[62] The fact that the destruction focused on the Umayyad distribution of water within the sanctuary sheds further light on the importance of the siqaya and the Zamzam well for the early Abbasid movement.

Marshall Hodgson took the account of Khālid's aqueduct as proof of the decadence and impiety of the Umayyad ruling elite.[63] While the aqueduct

[60] A. Rihaoui, "Découverte de deux inscriptions arabes," *Les Annales archéologiques de syrie*, 11/12 (1961–1962), 208, figs. 1–2; cited in Rāshid, *Darb*, 10.

[61] Al-Azraqī, *Akhbār*, II: 647–649; al-Fākihī, *Akhbār*, II: 82; III: 149–151.

[62] Al-Ṭabarī, *Tārīkh*, III: 72–73.

[63] Hodgson, *The Venture of Islam: Conscience and History in a World Civilization*, 3 vols. (University of Chicago Press, 1974), I: 267.

may very well have been a historical edifice erected by the Umayyads within Mecca, the extent to which it was designed as an act of impious desacralization remains to be seen. As noted previously, the early Abbasid caliphs responded to perennial water shortages both in Mecca and in the sanctuary itself with various public works. The Umayyad water project may well have addressed a similar challenge, only to be reshaped later into an act of sacrilege. Rather, this particular portrayal of the Umayyad aqueduct appears to reflect a broader Abbasid program of vilifying the Umayyads. Several accounts depict Khālid's activities in Mecca in extremely offensive terms. He is said, for instance, to have been willing to tear down the Kaʿba stone by stone and transport the dismantled edifice to Damascus, if the caliph so ordered, and to have boasted of the superiority of the piped water, describing the Zamzam as a filthy well where dung-beetles bred.[64]

OPENING UP THE KAʿBA

The historical record also documents that various state officials sought to shape the meaning of the Meccan sanctuary in terms that bolstered their own interests and authority. For instance, ʿUmar ibn al-Khaṭṭāb (r. 13–23/634–644) is said to have redrawn the boundary markers of the complex. Ibn al-Zubayr (d. 73/692), who declared himself caliph and mounted a revolt against the Umayyads, for his part took over the sanctuary and rebuilt the entire Kaʿba, giving the sanctuary two doors. Ibn al-Zubayr reportedly did this in an effort to reconstruct the edifice upon its original Abrahamic foundations, which the Quraysh had failed to do prior to the advent of Islam. He is also said to have expanded the Kaʿba to include the semicircular enclosure space (*ḥijr*) on the northwest side, thereby including within the walls of the Kaʿba the tomb of Ishmael, thought to have been buried in the sanctuary's walls. Additionally, Ibn al-Zubayr attempted to remove the siqaya watering station from the sanctuary complex, but demurred in the face of Ibn al-ʿAbbās's protests.[65] After the Umayyad general al-Ḥajjāj ibn Yūsuf defeated and executed Ibn al-Zubayr, he received orders from the caliph ʿAbd al-Mālik to destroy

[64] Al-Iṣfahānī, *Aghānī*, xxii, 16–18; cf. al-Khalīl b. Aḥmad, *Kitāb al-ʿAyn*, ed. M. al-Makhzūmī and I. al-Sāmarrāʾī, 8 vols. (Baghdad: Dār al-Rashīd, 1980–1985), I: 231.

[65] ʿAbd al-Razzāq, *al-Muṣannaf*, ed. Ḥ. al-Aʿẓamī, 11 vols. (Beirut: al-Maktab al-Islāmī, 1970–1972), V: 126, §9126.

Ibn al-Zubayr's structure, remove the second door added to the back, and restore the Kaʿba to its previous size.[66]

Non-Arab clients (*mawālī*) of Ibn al-Zubayr are said to have participated in the reconstruction. Some sources assert that Ibn al-Zubayr brought from Iraq Persian architects and craftsman to rebuild the Kaʿba.[67] A trace of this legacy may well linger in the Persian word *shādhurwān* used to describe the marble base of the Kaʿba.[68] Ibn al-Faqīh (fl. 289/902) reports that Ibn al-Zubayr had originally asked the Arabs how to go about rebuilding the Kaʿba. When he was unable to find a satisfactory answer, he sought help from the Persians, for he claimed that "they are descendants of Abraham and the sanctuary can only be raised up by Abraham's descendants."[69]

This move to graft Persians into the sanctuary is itself part of a larger socio-historical process of accommodating new converts in an ever-broadening fabric of Islamic religious identity. To a similar effect, Ibn al-Faqīh quotes the Qurʾanic verse (Q Baqara 2:125), "We have made the sanctuary a place of return for humanity." He explains this verse by citing the Khurasani exegete Muqātil (d. 150/767), who claimed that God did not limit the sanctuary to either Arabs or the Persians, but rather opened it up as a place of worship for all.[70] A similar sentiment is found in earlier Abbasid geographical literature, expressed, for instance, by Ibn Khurdādhbih, who relates that after Adam originally built the Kaʿba, people from all the nations of the world came on pilgrimage to honor the sanctuary.[71]

The very form of the Hajj is designed to bring Muslims from disparate lands together in the performance of a common sacred ritual. There is a tradition ascribed to the Prophet during the famed farewell sermon delivered on his pilgrimage to Mecca in 10/632. In it, the Prophet speaks of a society in which hierarchy is not based on ethnicity but on piety. According to a version of the sermon related by several transmitters, including notable Abbasid courtiers, the Prophet posed the following questions to the congregation of pilgrims:

66 See, e.g., ʿAbd al-Razzāq, *Muṣannaf*, V: 103–104; al-Ṭabarī, *Tārīkh*, II: 427, 854; al-Iṣfahānī, *Aghānī*, XVIII: 323–324; *Manāsik*, 488–492.

67 Al-Iṣfahānī, *Aghānī*, I: 250; Ibn al-Faqīh, *Kitāb al-Buldān*, ed. Y. Hād⊠ (Beirut: ʿĀlam al-Kutub, 1996), 403.

68 See al-Azraqī, *Akhbār*, I: 427–428; Al-Shāfiʿī, *Umm*, III: 450, Abū Bakr al-Bayhaqī (d. 458/1066), *Maʿrifat al-sunan*, VII: 240, §9927.

69 Ibn al-Faqīh, *Kitāb al-Buldān*, 403.

70 Ibn al-Faqīh, *Kitāb al-Buldān*, 75. Cf. al-Thaʿlabī, *al-Kashf wa-l-bayān*, ed. A. M. ibnʿĀshūr, 10 vols. (Beirut: Dār Iḥyāʾ al-Turāth al-ʿArabī, 2002): I: 269.

71 Ibn Khurdādhbih, *Masālik*, 133.

O people! Is your Lord not one? Is your father not one? Is it not so that there is no superiority of Arab over non-Arab nor non-Arab over Arab, nor of White over Black, nor Black over White, except in righteousness (*taqwā*)?[72]

In this famed account, the Hajj serves as an occasion to replace ethnic divisions with a hierarchy based on piety. The carefully selected language functions as a gloss on the following Qur'anic verse: "O People, We have made you men and women and made you nations (*shuʿūb*) and tribes (*qabāʾil*) so that you may know each other and that the most noble of you before God are the most righteous among you" (Q Ḥujurāt 49:13). The pairing of the Prophet's sermon with the Qurʾan passage is found in an array of early exegetical literature.[73] From this particular Qurʾan verse is derived the name '*shuʿūbiyya*', a cultural and literary movement that gained prominence in the early Abbasid period by offering a largely discursive form of resistance to the putative supremacy of Arabic culture and language. The *shuʿūbī* movement emerged from a social context in which the rigid ethnic divisions between the Arabs and their clients, characteristic of the earlier Umayyad social order, had been slowly dissipating. The movement, often known for advocating equality (*taswiyya*) between Arabs and Persians, was also strongly associated with arguments favoring Persian history and culture.[74]

The following account is particularly insightful in this regard. The Abbasid courtier of Arab descent Ibn al-Kalbī (d. 206/821) records a tradition from his renowned teacher al-Sharqī ibn al-Quṭāmī (d. ca. 150/767), who relates that the Zamzam took its name from the Sasanian period, when the Persian king Bābak set out for Yemen.[75] On his journey, Bābak made a pilgrimage to Mecca, where at the spot of the Zamzam he buried Qalʿī swords and jewels of the *zamāzima* (i.e., Zoroastrian priests, who were so named in Arabic for the whispering prayers associated with them, known onomatopoetically as *zamzama* prayers) as an offering. Ibn

[72] Ibn Ḥanbal, *al-Musnad*, ed. Sh. al-Arnāʾūṭ and ʿĀ. Murshid, 52 vols. (Beirut: Muʾassasat al-Risāla, 1993–2001), XXXVIII: 474, §23489. On the sermon, see L. Marlow, *Hierarchy and Egalitarianism in Islamic Thought* (Cambridge University Press, 1997), 22–28.

[73] See, e.g., al-Jaṣṣāṣ, *Aḥkām al-Qurʾān*, ed. by ʿA. M. ʿA. Shāhīn, 3 vols. (Beirut: Dār al-Kutub al-ʿIlmiyya, 1415/1994), I: 382.

[74] On the *shuʿūbiyya*, see I. Goldziher, *Muslim Studies*, tr. C. R. Barber and S. M. Stern, 2 vols. (Chicago: Aldine, 1966–1971), I: 137–198; R. Mottahedeh, "The Shuʿūbīyah Controversy and the Social History of Early Islamic Iran," *International Journal of Middle East Studies*, 7, 2 (1976): 161–182.

[75] Cited in Al-Bakjarī, *al-Zahr al-bāsim fī siyar Abī l-Qāsim*, ed. A. A. ʿAbd al-Shakūr, 2 vols. (Beirut: Dār al-Salām, 2012), I: 320.

al-Quṭāmī then alludes to the famous story of how, generations later, ʿAbd al-Muṭṭalib, paternal grandfather of the Prophet, had a vision that led him to discover the Zamzam. The well had long been hidden by the Jurhum tribe, who buried it when the rival Khuzāʿa attacked them and pushed them out of Mecca.[76] When ʿAbd al-Muṭṭalib unearthed the well, he found these votive offerings, and thus the well took its name from the jewelry of the Zoroastrian priests.

Ibn al-Quṭāmī's report presents an important variation on the discovery of the well, the reconstitution of the Meccan shrine, and the various offices associated with it. The earliest sources make no reference to the presence of a Persian king at the sanctuary.[77] For instance, Ibn Isḥāq reports that the Jurhum buried the treasure before fleeing Mecca.[78] The etiology of the Zamzam well, which links royal Sasanian votive offerings with the sanctuary, weaves Persian pre-Islamic history directly into the mythic landscape of Mecca and the Hajj. Al-Masʿūdī's report takes the association proposed by Ibn al-Quṭāmī even further, and relates that many Persians considered themselves descendants of Abraham and claimed that their ancestors traveled to the sanctuary and circumambulated the Kaʿba in veneration of their forefather, Abraham, who had originally built the shrine. According to al-Masʿūdī, the last of the ancient Persians to have performed the pilgrimage was Sāsān ibn Bābak, the Zoroastrian high priest and eponymous founder of the Sasanian empire. Al-Masʿūdī pauses to explain the importance of this Persian king by noting that the Sasanians traced their ancestry back to Sāsān ibn Bābak, "just as the Marwānids trace their ancestry back to Marwān ibn al-Ḥakam and the Abbasid caliphs back to al-ʿAbbās ibn ʿAbd al-Muṭṭalib. No other Persian king ruled who was not descended from [Sāsān]."[79]

The story of ancient Persians at the shrine serves to promote the Abbasids as the inheritors of an imperial Sasanian legacy of pilgrimages from Mesopotamia to the Kaʿba. Also advanced in this narrative complex is the idea that the Abbasids had a rightful claim to Mecca, as they were

[76] See al-Balādhurī, *Ansāb al-ashrāf*, ed. S. Zakkār and R. Ziriklī, 13 vols. (Beirut: Dār al-Fikr, 1996), I: 86.

[77] See, e.g., ʿAbd al-Razzāq, *Muṣannaf*, V: 313–319; al-Azraqī, *Akhbār*, II: 548–558.

[78] Ibn Hishām, *al-Sīra al-nabawiyya*, ed. M. al-Saqqā, I. al-Ibyārī, and ʿA. Shalabī, 2nd ed., 2 vols. (Cairo: Maṭbaʿat al-Bābī al-Ḥalabī, 1955), I: 154–155; see al-Azraqī, *Akhbār*, I: 155, 547–548.

[79] Al-Masʿūdī, *Murūj*, §573. See also S. Savant, "Isaac as the Persian Ishmael: Pride and the Pre-Islamic Past in Ninth and Tenth-Century Islam," in *Comparative Islamic Studies*, 2, 1 (2006): 14–15.

direct relatives of al-ʿAbbās, whose father, ʿAbd al-Muṭṭalib, rediscovered the Zamzam well. Admittedly, these claims are almost baroque in their articulation of linguistic, ethnic, and religious legitimacy: not only were ancient Persians genealogically related to Abraham, but they were also among the first to perform the pilgrimage to the Meccan shrine, and the founder of the Sasanian empire gave Zamzam its name, from a Persian word based on a Zoroastrian liturgical prayer (which evidently would have been recited in Persian).

In the course of the first two centuries of the Islamic era, both Mecca and the pilgrimage to it underwent profound and lasting transformations. The broad ritual contours of the Hajj and the monotheistic associations binding Abraham and Ishmael to the Meccan sanctuary can be traced back to the Qurʾan and the early Hadith corpus.[80] However, sweeping shifts in religious and political power came to define the meaning of the sanctuary and the pilgrimage rite in significantly new terms. These changes are reflected not only in the face of the ruling elite, but also in the expanding community of believers. This process of transformation is articulated in a series of often competing architectural expressions, as well as in various discursive efforts that turned to the mythopoeic power of narrative to mold and reimagine the significance of the Kaʿba.

[80] See R. Firestone, *Journeys in Holy Lands: The Evolution of the Abraham-Ishmael Legends in Islamic Exegesis* (Albany: State University of New York Press, 1990); see also U. Rubin, "Ḥanīfiyya and Kaʿba: An Inquiry into the Arabian Pre-Islamic Background of Dīn Ibrāhīm," *Jerusalem Studies in Arabic and Islam*, 13 (1990): 85–112; cf. G. Hawting, "The Origins of the Muslim Sanctuary at Mecca," in G. H. A. Juynboll (ed.), *Studies on the First Century of Islamic Society* (Carbondale: Southern Illinois University Press, 1982), 23–48.

4

Women and the Hajj

Asma Sayeed

> It is reported on the authority of ʿĀʾisha bint Abī Bakr that she asked, "O Prophet, shouldn't we (women) go out for *jihād* with you? Indeed, I don't think any deed in the Qurʾan is preferable to *jihād*." "No," he replied, "the best and most beautiful *jihād* is pilgrimage (*ḥajj*) to the House, [that is] the *ḥajj* which has been accepted by God."[1]

The hadith report above equates the challenges and rewards of a woman's Hajj with that of jihad, a struggle in the way of God which may entail a spiritual struggle or the taking up of arms. The metaphor explicitly highlights the rigors of the Hajj, one of the most perilous journeys a believer is obliged to take at least once in a lifetime. The challenges women face in fulfilling this ritual are arguably greater than those that men encounter. In spite of the hurdles, women's participation in the annual Hajj has persisted since the rise of Islam and is increasing significantly in the modern period. This chapter provides a legal and historical overview of women's Hajj and explores the ways in which this ritual creates a unique space for the expression of women's spirituality in the arenas of religious education and charity. The chapter also considers the genre of women's Hajj memoirs, a relatively recent development, and how historical and local contexts shape the ways women record their Hajj experiences for posterity. This topic is taken up also in Chapter 13 in this volume.

[1] Al-Nasāʾī, *Sunan al-Kubrā*, 12 vols. (Beirut: Muʾassasat al-Risāla, 2001), IV: 8, #3594. Abū Hurayra relates a similar hadith: "The jihad of the one who is elderly, the young, and the weak, and the woman is the hajj and the ʿumrah." Al-Nasāʾī, *Sunan al-Kubrā*, IV: 9 #3592. There are several other variants with similar import. See, e.g., Al-Bukhārī, *al-Jāmiʿ al-Ṣaḥīḥ*, 4 vols. (Cairo: al-Maṭbaʿat al-Salafiyya wa-Maktabatuhā, 1403 AH/1982–1983), II: 325, *bāb* #62 *Jihād al-Nisāʾ*.

LEGAL DISCOURSE

According to the Qur'an (notably Q Āl ʿImrān 3:97), Hajj is obligatory for men and women when certain minimal conditions are met.[2] Jurists elaborated on Qur'anic dictates and specified the five conditions that apply to both sexes: being Muslim, being sane, reaching the age of legal majority (*bulūgh*), being free from bondage, and possessing the financial means and physical ability to travel.[3] A majority of classical Sunni jurists stipulated additional conditions, as detailed in the following paragraphs, with respect to women. These gender-based preconditions and other women-specific rules and norms have significantly shaped how women fulfill this obligation and the opportunities that the Hajj has presented for their religious participation.

Jurists discussed two issues specific to women. One consideration was whether a woman was in observance of the legally mandated waiting period (*ʿidda*) after the death of her husband or after an irrevocable divorce.[4] This issue arises from a Qur'anic verse (Q Ṭalāq 65:1) which mandates that women should not leave their homes voluntarily or under duress when they are observing their waiting periods from divorce. Although this verse does not mention widows, jurists extended this restriction to widows observing their waiting periods. Because the waiting period can only be observed at a specific time (immediately following the death of her spouse or a divorce) and the Hajj can be undertaken in subsequent years, jurists agreed that observance of the waiting period particularly after the death of a spouse should take priority.[5] Ḥanbalī jurists, however, dissented from the majority of Sunnis and maintained that the ruling only applies to widows.[6] For them, an irrevocably divorced woman could go out to perform the Hajj, as could a woman whose divorce was not finalized (i.e., a revocable divorce, in Islamic legal terms).[7]

[2] For verses outlining Hajj rituals and etiquette, see, e.g., Q Baqara 2:158, 196, and Chapter 11 in this volume.

[3] For a detailed discussion of legal prescriptions regarding women's Hajj, see ʿA. Zaydān, *Mufaṣṣal fī aḥkām al-marʾa wa-l-bayt al-muslim*, 11 vols. (Beirut: Mu'assasat al-Risāla, 1993), II: 147–385.

[4] Jurists distinguish between irrevocable divorce (*ṭalāq bāʾin*) and one in which reconciliation is possible (*ṭalāq rajʿī*) with respect to when women can go out during their waiting periods. For the majority of Sunnī jurists, the waiting period for a divorce in which reconciliation is possible does not bar a woman from undertaking the Hajj. See Zaydān, *Mufaṣṣal*, II: 180–181.

[5] Zaydān, *Mufaṣṣal*, II: 180–181.

[6] The four surviving Sunni legal schools of thought are Ḥanafī, Ḥanbalī, Mālikī, and Shāfiʿī; the Ẓāhirī school, as will be mentioned, does not survive.

[7] Ibn Qudāma, *Mughnī*, 9 vols. (Beirut: Dār al-Kutub al-ʿIlmiyya, 1996), II: 170–171.

The second issue concerns a woman's safety during pilgrimage travel. For many jurists, this could be ensured only through the presence of a guardian; if the woman did not have one, she was required to travel in a company of women.[8] The complexity of the issue of women's safety (for both the Hajj and the 'Umra) in turn generated marked disagreements about the conditions that render the Hajj mandatory for women. Juristic recommendations, in turn, had significant implications not just for women's autonomy with respect to the Hajj but also in the very determination of its obligatoriness. I summarize in the following paragraphs the views of the major Sunni and Shi'ite schools of legal thought on this point.

A majority of jurists conceived of a woman's safety primarily in terms of the presence of a *male* guardian who could accompany the woman on her journey. The guardian could be her husband or a male with whom she could not legally contract marriage (*maḥram*), such as her son, her father, or her uncle.[9] Jurists also considered whether a woman could find the requisite security with a female companion or in a company of women. While many conceded that a group of women could ensure safety, only some felt that a single female companion was sufficient.[10] Over time, the prevailing opinion among the four major Sunni schools came to be that the Hajj is obligatory for a woman *only if and when* she has a male guardian (a mahram or a husband) or a company of women (or a mixed group) with whom she could travel. In the absence of such a guarantee of security, the very obligation of Hajj is not in force.

Ultimately, because this legal discourse mandates the presence of a guardian, it subsumes the fulfillment of a central pillar of practice to happenstance. That this outcome was flawed was recognized early on, and a dissenting view on the matter is attributed to none other than 'Ā'isha bint Abī Bakr, who upon hearing Muḥammad's Companions affirm that women needed a mahram to undertake the Hajj reportedly averred that "not every woman has one (i.e. a mahram)."[11] In a similar vein, and several centuries later, Ibn Ḥazm (d. 456/1064) the major exponent of the now defunct Ẓāhirī

[8] For an overview of Muslim women's travel, more generally, in the medieval period, see M. Tolmacheva, "Medieval Muslim Women's Travel: Defying Distance and Danger," *World History Connected*, June 2013. Retrieved from worldhistoryconnected.press.illinois.edu/10.2/forum_tolmacheva.html (accessed July 23, 2013).

[9] See Q Nisā' 4:23 for a listing of male relations in the mahram category.

[10] See, e.g., Zaydān's summary of a minority Shāfi'ī view that one trustworthy female companion could suffice: see *Mufaṣṣal*, II: 166, and *Mufaṣṣal*, II: 169, for a discussion of the textual support from *ḥadīth* for this position.

[11] S. F. Dukhayyil, *Mawsū'at fiqh 'Ā'isha umm al-mu'minīn: ḥayātuhā wa-fiqhuhā* (Beirut: Dār al-Nafā'is, 1989), 542–546.

school, asserted that a woman who does not have a husband or mahram could travel alone to fulfill the Hajj obligation.[12] If a woman does have a male guardian, he is obligated to accompany her, and it is a sin for him to refuse. In the case of an uncooperative husband, the wife may travel without him. Finally, the Zahiris maintained that a husband may not prohibit his wife from performing the obligatory Hajj. However, if she subsequently chooses to undertake a supererogatory Hajj, he may deny her permission to do so. Thus, the Zahiris evince a concern with maintaining the centrality of the Hajj ritual for women and not rendering its fulfillment dependent on the presence or permission of a guardian (with the attendant possibility that her ability to fulfill a religious obligation would be subject to the guardian's whims).

The Imāmīs and the Zaydīs, the two main Shiʿite legal schools, articulated their own positions. The Zaydīs viewed the presence of a male guardian or the company of other women as a condition for the proper performance (*sharṭ adāʾ*) of the Hajj for women under the age of forty-five.[13] Older women could go out on their own or in the company of other trusted women. Unlike the four main Sunni schools, however, the Zaydīs do not assert that having a male guardian obligates a woman to perform the Hajj (*sharṭ wujūb*). The Imāmīs, on the other hand, do not assert that the presence of a husband or a mahram is a precondition for the Hajj.[14] Rather, they stipulate that assurance of safety is the necessary precondition for the performance of the Hajj or in determining the obligatoriness of the ritual for women.

Jurists, in requiring the presence of a male guardian for the proper performance of the Hajj, had to contemplate the right of refusal of that party to undertake the Hajj, particularly if it was only for the sake of the woman (and not in fulfillment of his own obligation). They also addressed the issue of who would bear the financial responsibility for the guardian's Hajj.[15] With respect to the latter, they agreed that when a man accompanies a woman solely as a guardian, she is financially responsible for both of their expenses. They also discussed whether a man was required to

[12] ʿA. Ibn Ḥazm, *Muḥallā*, 11 vols. (Cairo: Idārat al-Ṭibāʿa al-Munīrīya, 1929), VII: 47–52.

[13] Zaydān, *Mufaṣṣal*, II: 167.

[14] M. al-Najafī, *Jawāhir al-kalām fī sharḥ sharāʾi al-Islām*, 43 vols. (Beirut: Dār Iḥyāʾ al-Turāth al-ʿArabī, 1981), XVII: 330–332.

[15] In their discussions of this issue, jurists are concerned with the expenses of a male guardian (i.e., mahram). The question of the expenses of a female companion who is undertaking the journey solely to provide company and security for another female pilgrim is not discussed in the sources consulted.

agree to accompany the woman in question. Intriguingly, they assert that the male guardian does not have to accompany the woman even if she bears the financial burden. The Ẓāhirīs and the Imāmīs appear to be the only schools which recognize the challenges posed in the stipulation of a male guardian not only for the determination of obligatoriness of the Hajj but also for its valid performance.

Although the majority of pre-modern jurists agreed that accompaniment by a guardian was a precondition, juristic dissent created the potential for women to travel alone because they could resort to the opinions of dissenting jurists. Individual women may not have been able to actualize that potential, however, due to practical considerations, among them the expenses of the Hajj, the hazards of a solitary journey, and a woman's communal or family culture, which could limit her autonomy.

Paradoxically, in the modern period, although women's choices have expanded and the perils of the Hajj have diminished, their ability to actualize the potential of juristic dissent is severely limited. The adoption of conservative Wahhabism by the Saudi Arabian nation-state has meant that all female pilgrims have no choice now but to abide by Wahhabi ideology when planning their journey to Mecca. The website of the Saudi Consular and Travel Services mandates the following:

> All women are required to travel for Hajj with a Mahram. Proof of kinship must be submitted with the application form. Women over the age of forty-five (45) may travel without a Mahram with an organized group. They must, however submits [*sic*] a no objection letter from her husband, son or brother authorizing her to travel for Hajj with the named group. This letter should be notarized.[16]

The language of this statement starkly testifies to an unprecedented level of control over women's pilgrimage, enabled by technology and modern bureaucratic apparatuses. The ability to maintain records of birth dates, ages, kinship affiliations and to track them across international boundaries in conjunction with modern Saudi legal interpretations and inclinations to control access to the Hajj has invariably constricted women's autonomy. A recent case in which close to a thousand Nigerian women were detained, and many of them deported, for not traveling with male guardians heightened international awareness of the capriciousness of Saudi decisions, which apply rulings with varying levels of strictness from year to year and possibly on the basis of cultural or national affiliations of the pilgrims. In the

[16] Retrieved from saudiembassy.net/services/hajj_requirement.aspx (accessed February 1, 2014).

case of the Nigerian women, the Nigerian government asserted that they had been allowed to travel in a large company of women (that did not include male guardians for the pilgrims) because of a bilateral agreement between the Saudis and the Nigerians, an agreement which the Saudis were accused of not honoring.[17]

In addition to the preconditions for women's Hajj, there are a host of other gender-based legal prescriptions, including those concerning attire and individual rites.[18] Whereas the garb for men in the consecrated state (*iḥrām*) consists of two white, unadorned, unstitched pieces of cloth, women may wear their customary clothing with the caveat that their hands and faces not be covered and that they observe modesty. Women may adorn themselves with jewelry, but they may not use perfume when in ihram.[19] The following concerns are articulated in juristic discourse about the valid enactment of rites by women: modesty, the maintaining of gender boundaries to a reasonable extent in a space where the exigencies of the rituals may lead to a dissolution of such boundaries, and the defining of rituals for menstruating women, who are deemed to not be in a state of ritual purity (*ṭahāra*). In determining the proper conduct for menstruating women, jurists rely on a hadith narrated by ʿĀʾisha in which the Prophet advised her as follows when she was menstruating: "Do what other pilgrims are doing with the exception of circumambulation until you are ritually clean."[20] Some jurists also advise women to refrain from running (*al-saʿy*, one of the obligatory rites of the Hajj and ʿUmra) between the hillocks of al-Ṣafā and al-Marwa and instead to walk until they have completed their menstrual periods.[21]

HISTORICAL OVERVIEW

The first Hajj undertaken by Muslims occurred in 10 AH/632 AD. Also known as the Farewell Pilgrimage (*ḥajjat al-wadāʿ*) of the Prophet, it was

[17] For a summary description of the incident, see "Nigerian Hajj Women Held in Saudi Arabia," *BBC News*. Retrieved from bbc.co.uk/news/world-africa-19729897.

[18] There is a difference of opinion about which rites are central (*arkān*) to the Hajj. For Ḥanafīs, staying at ʿArafat and circumambulation of the Kaʿba are the central rites. The Ḥanbalīs and Mālikīs add to these two the obligations of ihram and running between the hills of al-Ṣafā and al-Marwa. The Shāfiʿīs add a fifth obligation: that of shaving or trimming the hair once the Hajj is completed. See Zaydān, *Mufaṣṣal*, II: 187.

[19] See further Zaydān, *Mufaṣṣal*, II: 303–323.

[20] Al-Bukhārī, *Ṣaḥīḥ*, I: 506, *bāb #81* "*Taqḍī al-ḥāʾiḍ al-manāsik kullahā illa al-ṭawāf biʾl-bayt.*"

[21] Zaydān, *Mufaṣṣal*, II: 223.

the first and only Hajj Muhammad performed, accompanied by numerous men and women of the first Muslim community (*umma*).[22] This occasion was therefore critical for establishing the etiquette, rituals, and even ethical guidelines for the Hajj. The female Companions' accounts of this Hajj ultimately became a part of the historical narrative of early Islam and of the authoritative corpus of Hadith, which are critical to the derivation of Islamic law. Drawing on women's reports, we can glean how early Muslims remembered this first Hajj as well as the relevance of it for setting standards specific to women.

Reports about the first Hajj are attributed to a number of female Companions. ʿĀʾisha bint Abī Bakr, a favored wife of Muḥammad and a leading narrator of hadiths in the Sunni collections, narrates more than other women on this topic. Other female Companion-narrators of reports about the Farewell Pilgrimage include Asmāʾ bint Abī Bakr, Maymūna bint al-Ḥārith, Lubāba bint al-Ḥārith, Umm Salama (Hind bint Abī Umayya), and Umm Maʿqal. Their reports cover a range of topics including the virtues of the Hajj, ritual purity (especially with respect to menstruating women), gender segregation and modesty, and accounts of how the Prophet performed various invocations or ritual acts in the course of the Hajj. In a detailed study, Aisha Geissinger analyses how female Companions contributed exegetical reports and clarified the meaning and context for a number of Qurʾanic verses about the Hajj.[23]

From a historical (rather than legal) perspective, these reports are fascinating for the details they provide about the historical memory of the Prophet's comportment and the issues that arose for women. Irrespective of the authenticity of individual reports, the reports illuminate the questions and concerns of the early Muslim community in their attempts to understand the requirements of this religious obligation. Descriptions of the Prophet's behavior with his wives during the Hajj reflect concerns about what was permitted (*ḥalāl*) with respect to conjugal relations. This was especially pertinent given the suspension of so many mundane acts when a pilgrim entered the consecrated state of ihram. Maymūna bint al-Ḥārith (d. 61/681), for example, reported that the Prophet married her when he was not in a state of ihram and when

[22] See Ibn Isḥāq, *al-Sīra al-nabawiyya*, 4 vols. (Beirut: al-Maktaba al-ʿAṣriyya), IV: 215–220.

[23] A. Geissinger, "Portrayal of the *Ḥajj* as a Context for Women's Exegesis: Textual Evidence in al-Bukhārī's (d. 870) *al-Ṣaḥīḥ*," in Sebastian Guenther (ed.), *Insights into Classical Arabic Literature and Islam* (Leiden: Brill, 2005), 153–179.

they were staying at a place called Sarif.[24] Other versions assert that the Prophet contracted the marriage in a state of ihram but did not consummate it until he was out of that state. Both variants confirm that the Prophet acted in accordance with the prohibition of sexual intercourse during the Hajj. Ritual purity and the maintenance of it were similarly central concerns of the Hajj. These guidelines presented challenges specific to menstruating women. ʿĀʾisha bint Abī Bakr is credited with hadith reports which show that the Prophet allowed her to perform the rites of pilgrimage even when she was menstruating. ʿĀʾisha's disappointment at the possibility that she might be prevented from completing the Hajj obligations is clearly conveyed in several of these reports, as is the Prophet's desire that she perform the rites of Hajj for her spiritual fulfillment. The following account is particularly evocative.

ʿĀʾisha (may God be pleased with her) reported: We went with the Messenger of God (blessings be on him) with no other aim but the Hajj. When we arrived at Sarif my menstrual period began. The Messenger of God (blessings be on him) came to me; I was weeping.

"Why are you crying?" he asked.

"By God! I wish I had not come [for Hajj] this year," I replied.

"What's the matter with you?" he asked, "has your period started?"

"Yes," I said.

And he said, "This is what has been ordained for the daughters of Adam: Do everything a pilgrim does, but do not circumambulate the House until your period is over [lit. you are purified]."

When I came to Mecca, the Messenger of God (blessings be on him) said to his Companions, "Make this the ihram for the ʿUmra."

So the people put on ihram except those who had sacrificial animals with them.

She continued: The Messenger of God (blessings be on him) had a sacrificial animal with him, as did Abū Bakr, ʿUmar and others who had the means. They [those who had taken off ihram] put on the ihram again when they began their march [toward Mina].

My period ended [lit. I was purified] on the Day of the Sacrifice [the tenth of Dhū al-Ḥijja] and I performed the circumambulation of *ifāḍa*. The meat of a cow was brought to us, and I asked, "What is this?"

They said, "The Messenger of God (blessings be on him) has offered a sacrifice on behalf of his wives."

On the night of al Ḥasba, I said, "O Messenger of God, people are coming returning (having performed) the Hajj and ʿUmra both, whereas I am returning (having performed) only the Hajj."

[24] Ibn Mājah, *Sunan*, 6 vols. (Beirut: Dār al-Jīl, 1998), III: 383, #1964. See Yāqūt al-Ḥamawī, *Muʿjam al-Buldān*, 5 vols. (Beirut: Dār Sādir, 1977) III: 212 for a brief identification of Sarif as a location several miles away from Mecca and its historical association with the Prophet's marriage to Maymūnah.

He ordered ʿAbd al-Raḥmān ibn Abī Bakr to put me on his camel behind him [so that he could accompany her to perform the rituals of ʿUmra].

I remember that I was a young girl. I was sleepy and my face reclined against the back part of the camel saddle until we arrived at al-Taʿnīm. I entered there into ihram for ʿUmra to make up for the ʿUmra which the others had performed (and in which I had not participated).[25]

This and other traditions narrated by women affirm that during this first Hajj, women strove to fulfill all the rituals of Hajj and eagerly sought the rewards of this journey alongside men. Precedents for women's Hajj were set by the actions and decisions, not just of the women accompanying the Prophet on the Farewell Pilgrimage, but also of Companions and Successors in the years after his death. In this vein, reports relate that the wives of the Prophet, with the exception of Sawda bint Zamʿa and Zaynab bint Jaḥash, obtained caliphal permission to continue to perform the Hajj. Sawda and Zaynab, on the other hand, interpreted the rulings about seclusion of the Prophet's wives to mean that they should not go out even for the Hajj after his death.[26] The early caliphs, among them ʿAbū Bakr, ʿUmar, and ʿUthmān, were instrumental in provisioning the Hajj caravans for the wives and ensuring their safe journey.

Women's participation in the Hajj continued after the earliest decades throughout Islamic history as attested by chronicles, biographical dictionaries, local histories, and bureaucratic records. Their participation was impacted by a host of variables, from personal circumstances (financial, cultural, familial) to broader events such as political transitions and turmoil, wars, famine, and plagues. For example, Ottoman juridical registers show that women used their landed property to pay their husbands to take them on the Hajj. Not all such exchanges transpired well, and some women complained of being abandoned along the way.[27]

Historical records are more detailed in their portrayals of the Hajj of elite and royal women. The retinues and lavish, heavily guarded palanquins of royal female pilgrims came to symbolize the wealth and status of their families and the largesse of their male guardians. The provisioning of

[25] Muslim, *Ṣaḥīḥ Muslim bi-sharḥ al-Nawawī*, 18 vols. (Cairo: al-Maṭbaʿa al-Miṣriyya bi-l-Azhar, 1929), VIII: 147–148. There are a number of variants of this report concerning ʿĀʾisha's desire to complete all the Hajj and ʿUmra rituals in spite of her menstruation and the Prophet's accommodation of her desires and his reassurances to her when she was distressed over the matter. See, e.g., Muslim, *Ṣaḥīḥ*: VIII, 134–160.

[26] Ibn Saʿd, *Kitāb al-Ṭabaqāt al-Kabīr*, 9 vols. (Leiden: E. J. Brill, 1904–1918), VIII: 150, also cites a report on this matter.

[27] S. Faroqhi, *Pilgrims and Sultans: The Hajj under the Ottomans, 1517–1683* (London: I. B. Tauris, 1994), 7.

the caravans of these women, their conduct on the journeys, and their reception by the general populace as well as dignitaries in the territories they traversed reveal how women's participation in the Hajj paradoxically reinforced their elite status.

From a sociological perspective, narratives depicting female pilgrimages can shed light on the position of women in their communities of origin as compared to their status in the communities they encountered along the way. The account of the Hajj of the Ilkhanid-Mongol princess El Qutlugh in 723/1323 as described by al-Ṣafadī (d. 1363), a Mamluk historian and biographer, is a case in point.[28] Her manner of traveling not just on a palanquin fastened to a camel but also astride a horse with a quiver fastened to her waist reflected her origins in the Eurasian Steppe. Also, she "led ring hunts and hunted all along the way," indicating not just that she was a skilled hunter and archer, but that she belonged to the Mongol elite wherein women were not barred from such activities.[29] The importance to the Mamluk rulers of receiving her and catering to her needs underscores that the significance of her pilgrimage extended well beyond the fulfillment of a religious obligation. Rather, it also provided an occasion for promoting stable, peaceful relations between the Mamluks and the Ilkhanid dynasty, whom El Qutlugh represented.[30] Comparing descriptions of El Qutlugh's pilgrimage with those of royal women of different provenance sheds light on the impact of local cultures on women's Hajj. The accounts of the pilgrimages of senior wives of the Mamluk sultans (*khawand al-kubra*) reveals a greater degree of seclusion of these women from the public.[31]

Unfortunately, the anecdotal information in the pre-modern sources does not give us a clear picture of the numbers or percentages of female participants and how these changed over the years. Such records of male and female participation do exist for more recent decades and confirm an increase in the number of female pilgrims. From the early 1960s to the early 1990s, the participation of women increased from 30 percent to 45 percent of the total number of pilgrims.[32] Although this is an

[28] Al-Ṣafadī's descriptions of this pilgrimage have been analyzed in detail in Y. Brack, "A Mongol Princess Making Hajj: The Biography of El Qutlugh Daughter of Abagha Ilkhan (r. 1265–82)," *Journal of Royal Asiatic Society*, ser. 3, 21, 3 (2011): 331–359.

[29] Brack, "Mongol Princess," 334, 350.

[30] Brack, "Mongol Princess," 340–352.

[31] See K. Johnson, "Royal Pilgrimage: Mamlūk Accounts of the Pilgrimages to Mecca of the Khawand al-Kubrā (Senior Wife of the Sultan)," *Studia Islamica*, 91 (2000): 107–131.

[32] R. Bianchi, *Guests of God: Pilgrimage and Politics in the Islamic World* (New York: Oxford University Press, 2004), 69.

encouraging figure overall, the picture at the local level is complex. A modern study shows vastly uneven regional participation in the mid-1970s. In Southeast Asia, the Fertile Crescent, and East Africa, women participate at higher rates than in West Asia, Southern Arabia, and Southern Europe. In some countries, such as Malaysia, Singapore, Madagascar, and Chad, women were in the majority.[33]

A closer investigation of the political and socioeconomic dynamics in Turkey reveals that rates of women's participation are closely tied to economics, though factors such as family structures also play a role. Women's financial ability as well as relative independence is higher in the Western and Central provinces, which have significantly stronger female participation in the Hajj than the Eastern ones. In Turkey, national electoral politics also impacted rates of women's participation as an electoral candidate's promotion of the Hajj became a potent symbol of his/her commitment to the more religious and conservative forces in Turkish society.[34] Finally, male and female participation in Turkey suffered during coups and periods of political unrest.

RELIGIOUS LEARNING AND CHARITY IN THE CONTEXT OF THE HAJJ

Since the earliest decades of Islam, the Hajj provided a context for religious engagement for women beyond the fulfillment of a central ritual obligation. Primary among these was the pursuit of religious learning and charitable giving.

Compelling great numbers of Muslims to travel for an extended period, the Hajj provides a natural context for cultural, social, and economic exchange. In the eras before air travel, the journey to Mecca necessitated long-term travel and sojourns in urban centers en route. This imperative created a natural matrix for the exchange of religious knowledge, which in itself became an important objective for many male and female pilgrims.[35] The following report records how these exchanges may have occurred among the earliest Muslims:

[33] Bianchi, *Guests of God*, 68.

[34] Bianchi, *Guests of God*, 159.

[35] I provide a more extensive history of women's participation in the transmission of hadith in early and classical Islam in my book *Women and the Transmission of Religious Knowledge in Islam* (New York: Cambridge University Press, 2013). The following analysis on women's hadith transmission during the Hajj draws on my book.

A certain Yaʿlā ibn Ḥakīm reported from Ṣuhayra bint Jayfar [from the generation after Muhammad]: "We performed the Hajj then went on to Medina. We went to visit Ṣafiyya bint Ḥuyyay and met a group of Kufan women in her company. They said, 'If you [i.e. the newcomers] want, you can ask [the questions] and we'll listen, or if you prefer, we'll ask and you can listen.' We said, 'You go ahead and ask.' So they asked her about matters related to women and their husbands and about menstruation. Then they asked her about a beverage made of dates in clay vessels."[36]

Ṣuhayra's account, uncommon in the narrative details it provides about the encounter between Ṣafiyya (one of Muḥammad's wives who resided in Medina), and a company of female pilgrims, confirms that the Hajj created important avenues for women's religious learning. We can easily picture Ṣuhayra and her fellow pilgrims in Medina stopping by the quarters of Ṣafiyya to inquire about practical feminine concerns. Ṣuhayra and her companions were not alone. A group of Kūfan women had the same idea, and they took turns acquiring knowledge from Ṣafiyya.

Ṣafiyya bint Shayba, a Meccan Successor (who died at end of the 90s AH) provides another example of how the pilgrimage was central to the narrative authority of some early Muslim women. Ṣafiyya was very young when Muḥammad died, and she may have only seen him during the Farewell Pilgrimage.[37] An examination of Ṣafiyya's biographies and the chains of her transmission indicate that the networks of learning in which she participated were largely connected to the Hajj. She was the daughter of Shayba ibn ʿUthmān ibn Abī Ṭalḥa (d. 59/678–679), whom Muḥammad trusted with the keys to the Kaʿba.[38] While her reputation as a narrator may have been boosted by the honor due to her father's position, she is credited with establishing her own authority as a reliable traditionist in Mecca.[39] She was one of the most prolific female Successors in terms of the number of reports in the major Sunni collections in which she is listed as an authority. Her

[36] Ibn Ḥanbal, *Musnad*, 6:380, #26857. See also Ibn Ḥanbal, *Musnad*, 6:380, #26854. For similar encounters that took place when women undertook Hajj, see M. A. Nadwi, *Al-Muḥaddithāt: The Women Scholars in Islam* (Oxford: Interface Publications, 2007), 73–74.

[37] For biographical notices about Ṣafiyya, see, e.g., Ibn Saʿd, *Al-Ṭabaqāt*, VIII: 344 and Al-Dhahabī, *Siyar Aʿlām al-Nubalāʾ*, 25 vols. (Beirut: Muʾassassat al-Risāla, 1981), III: 507–509. Ibn Ḥajar records disagreement as to whether she actually saw Muḥammad. See Ibn Ḥajar, *Al-Iṣāba fī tamyīz al-ṣaḥāba*, 13 vols. (Cairo: Maktabat al-Kulliyyāt al-Azharīya, 1977), XII: 18.

[38] Her *nisba*, "al-Ḥajabiyya," is a reference to this occupation. Ṣafiyya's son, Manṣūr ibn ʿAbd al-Raḥmān, was also entrusted with the keys to the Kaʿba. See Ibn Ḥajar, *Tahdhīb*, X: 277.

[39] Cf. Ibn Ḥibbān, who counts her among the traditionists of Medina: *Kitāb al-Thiqāt*, 5 vols. (Beirut: Dār al-Kutub al-ʿIlmiyya, 1998), II: 240–241.

residence in Mecca certainly would have contributed to the breadth of her transmission circle since pilgrims would have been likely to seek out her transmissions. One hadith explicitly refers to her reputation as an authority for ʿĀʾisha's traditions: Muḥammad ibn ʿUbayd ibn Abī Ṣāliḥ reports that he traveled to Mecca with ʿAdī ibn ʿAdī al-Kindī. There, ʿAdī sent him to Ṣafiyya bint Shayba because she was known to be an authority for ʿĀʾisha's traditions.[40] According to another report, Maymūn ibn Mihrān asserts that he went to Ṣafiyya when she was an old woman and asked her about Muḥammad's marriage to Maymūna bint al-Ḥārith and if it occurred while he was in a state of ihram (the consecrated state during Pilgrimage).[41] Ṣafiyya asserts that the marriage occurred when they were no longer in the state of ihram. Thus she is remembered as an authority for reports on issues of legal import related to the Hajj.

The complementary relationship between the Hajj and women's religious education is attested by anecdotal evidence throughout Islamic history. In the fifth/eleventh century, Karīma al-Marwaziyya (d. ca 463/1070) was known for her reliable transmission of al-Bukhārī's *Ṣaḥīḥ* through a line of transmission (*isnād*) with only two intermediaries between her and al-Bukhārī himself.[42] She traveled to Mecca with her father and took up residence there. Her reputation for piety, religious learning, and reliable transmission was such that meeting her and learning from her were important subsidiary goals for some pilgrims traveling to Mecca. Al-Dhahabī, one of Karīma's biographers, mentions that Muḥammad ibn ʿAlī al-Hamadānī set out for the Hajj in 463/1070 intending also to meet Karīma and acquire certification from her, but he received news of her death en route.[43]

The relationship between religious learning and the pilgrimage persists until today. Yet, in the modern period, it is more difficult to find records of female teachers resident in Mecca who attract male and female seekers of knowledge. This development is likely correlated to the stricter regulations regarding the mixing of men and women implemented by the conservative Saudi monarchy.

The Hajj also provided a context for women's charity. Their charitable impulses found expression in myriad ways, from the construction of

[40] Abū Dāwūd, *Sunan*, II: 258, #2193.
[41] Abū Nuʿaym al-Iṣbahānī, VI: 3379.
[42] A more detailed biography for Karīma may be found in Al-Dhahabī, *Siyar*, XVIII: 233–234.
[43] Al-Dhahabī, *Siyar* XVIII: 235.

roads, wells, or *ribāṭs* (lodges) to donations of money or provisions for individual pilgrims.[44] In form, women's charity (whether in the context of the Hajj or otherwise) resembled that of men's. But because women, especially elite women, were less often visible in the public sphere, their contributions had the added significance of rendering their presence more palpable in the public sphere.

The charity of Zubayda (d. 216/831), wife of Abbasid caliph Hārūn al-Rashīd (d. 193/809), is among the most legendary examples of elite women's charity in early Islam. A politically astute and engaged woman, and a prolific patroness of scholars, poets, and jurists, Zubayda's charity in connection with the pilgrimage reflected her outsized personality. Her projects include the following: the construction of an aqueduct along a twelve-mile route from Ḥunayn to Mecca; the digging of wells and the construction of lodges along the route from Mecca to Kufa; endowments (*waqf*, pl. *awqāf*) to pay for the maintenance of these projects; and the restoration of sacred sites in Mecca. She also distributed alms to fellow pilgrims when she herself performed the pilgrimage, an endeavor she undertook several times. The benefits and ramifications of this charity extended beyond the pilgrims who were its immediate beneficiaries as it provided the infrastructure which facilitated travel for trade, religious education, and other sundry purposes beyond the pilgrimage season. Zubayda's largesse is described in greater detail in Chapter 3 in this volume.

The charitable giving of other wealthy women is regularly mentioned in the historical sources. Paradoxically, the women themselves were often not visible as they traveled in heavily guarded, elaborately bedecked palanquins atop camels; only their charity throughout the journey, when they arrived in Mecca and Medina, and when they returned home, was public. The very juxtaposition of the lavish display of wealth alongside the invisibility of the women created a pressure on the elite for exuberant displays of charity, particularly in light of the mandate for simplicity and erasure of socioeconomic divisions during the Hajj itself. Women were thus entangled in the politics of charity, which had negative repercussions as well as positive ones. The pilgrimage of Khawand Umm Sidi Muḥammad documented in the Mamluk chronicle of Ibn Īyās is a case in point.[45] She

[44] See M. Tolmacheva, "Female Piety and Patronage in the Medieval 'Ḥajj,'" in G. R. G. Hambly (ed.), *Women in the Medieval Islamic World: Power, Patronage and Piety* (New York: St. Martin's Press, 1998) for an exploration of how the early and classical contexts of the Hajj impacted women's charity and patronage.

[45] Johnson, "Royal Pilgrims," 123–129.

undertook the Hajj in 920/1515 in one of the most flagrant displays of wealth witnessed by the Cairenes. Yet, her return was a secret affair in which she withdrew to the Citadel of Cairo without the customary distribution of sweets to those awaiting the return of the royal Hajj caravan. Ibn Īyās records the discontent of the laypeople and their profound disapproval for the miserly behavior of the Khawand as well as her son. Comparisons to the behavior of other generous khawands highlight her breach of etiquette.

MEMOIRS

For much of Islamic history, what we know of women's pilgrimages was penned by men. Beginning in the late nineteenth century, the publication of women's memoirs, in the form of travel logs, autobiographical narratives, poetry, or even advice manuals, allowed new perspectives on how women themselves experienced this powerful, transformative journey. Read in their historical contexts, these memoirs are also invaluable for understanding a host of other issues, among them gender roles and intra-Muslim relations in each author's community.[46] The perspectives of two such memoirs are discussed in the following paragraphs.

Nawab Sikandar Begum (1816–1868) commands attention as an unusual example of a female ruler: she was the *nawāb* (semi-autonomous ruler) of the central Indian province of Bhopal and was second in a dynasty of four female rulers of this province under British rule of India (1858–1947).[47] She wrote the memoir of her pilgrimage (1863–1864) in Urdu at the request of the British Major-General Sir Henry Marion Durand (d. 1871) and his wife.[48] The account was first published in 1870 as an English translation; the original manuscript has not been located. The fact that the memoir was intended for British consumption no doubt influences the tone as well as authorial decisions by Sikandar. A striking feature is the absence of spiritual ruminations. Her tone is distant. The narrative at times simply offers a dry,

[46] B. Metcalf, "Pilgrimage Remembered: South Asian Accounts of the *Hajj*," in Dale Eickelman and James Piscatori (eds.), *Muslim Travellers: Pilgrimage, Migration, and the Religious Imagination* (Berkeley: University of California Press, 1990), 85–107.

[47] See S. Khan, *Begums of Bhopal* (New York: I. B. Tauris, 2000) for the history of this female dynasty of rulers.

[48] S. Lambert-Hurley (ed.), *Princess's Pilgrimage: Nawab Sikandar Begum's "A Pilgrimage to Mecca"* (New Delhi: Women Unlimited, 2007). In her introduction (xxi), Lambert-Hurley notes that Sikandar's descendants assert that she was the first Indian ruler, male or female, to perform the Hajj as ruler.

sterile description of ritual performance intended to edify her non-Muslim readers about the pilgrimage. Further, Sikandar was privy to the secluded quarters of the women of the households of Mecca, so some of her more colorful details concern marriage, divorce, and familial relations among the political elite of Mecca. She records her frustrating interactions with the Sherif of Mecca and other Ottoman officials (the Ottoman Empire at the time of Sikandar's Hajj included central Arabia). As such, her memoir offers insights about ways in which Muslims understood the "Muslim other.[49] For example, Sikandar experienced some insults on the basis of her South Asian identity. In one instance, she was asked to vacate her quarters in Jeddah and relocate because of the arrival of an Egyptian princess who was to lodge in the same place.[50] In other cases, she was reprimanded for not understanding the customs among the Arabs and for unwittingly insulting the Sherif or his deputies.[51] After a stay of four months in Arabia, she is ultimately repulsed by the manners and appearance of Arabs. Toward the end of her memoir, she shares her impressions in rather unforgiving terms:

> The men and women have dreadfully harsh voices; their heads and shoulders are, generally speaking, handsome, but the rest of their body is not well formed . . . The people take in a great quantity of food, as much as 5 or 6 lbs. in weight in the course of the day, but their diet is gross; and their habits are dirty . . . In character, the majority of the people are miserly, violent-tempered, hard-hearted, and covetous, and they are both awkward and stupid.[52]

In spite of her large retinue and the guards traveling with her caravan, Sikandar and her advisors determined that the journey to Medina was too perilous. Consoled by juristic opinions that only the rites at Mecca were obligatory, she ended her pilgrimage at Mecca and returned to India.[53]

A second memoir of a Hajj, written six decades after that of Sikandar, provides an entirely different perspective, historically and culturally. Like Sikandar, Lady Evelyn Cobbold was observing from her position on the periphery;[54] and like Sikandar, she was writing for a Western audience. Lady Evelyn's vantage point, however, was that of an upper-class British convert, eager to share her spiritual journey and her love of Muslim

[49] For an engaging, thoughtful discussion of this point, see Lambert-Hurley's introduction to *Princess's Pilgrimage*, xli–lxii.

[50] *Princess's Pilgrimage*, 6.

[51] *Princess's Pilgrimage*, 44–54.

[52] *Princess's Pilgrimage*, 131–132.

[53] *Princess's Pilgrimage*, 133–147.

[54] Lady Evelyn Cobbold, *Pilgrimage to Mecca* (London: John Murray, 1934).

culture. She also aims to rectify misconceptions about Muslims, especially those concerning the degradation of Muslim women. The memoir dates from 1933, the first year of the establishment of the monarchy by the Saudi family led by ʿAbd al-ʿAzīz ibn Saʿūd (1876–1953). As such, it provides a fascinating view of the profound transformations in this region as Wahhabi ideology began to be implemented by the state. She herself is ambivalent about its tenets and impact. She notes, for example, that racing is among the few indulgences that Ibn Saʿūd allows himself as all other forms of amusement (singing, dancing, smoking, and music) are forbidden under Wahhabi dictates and states, "Let us hope time will lessen the scowl of the Ikhwan and soften their hearts towards their brother Moslem and teach them tolerance; at the same time we can but admire in the Wahhabi the purity of his faith and his strict adherence to his convictions."[55] A similar ambivalence marks her comments about the destruction of tombs of revered figures of early Islam, including the wives of the Prophets. While she appears to respect the desire for purity and return to the practice of the Prophet, she wisely observes the need for moderation of their message and selective adoption of European innovation, especially with respect to technological advances.[56] By Lady Evelyn's time, security for pilgrims is one area in which there appears to have been unequivocally positive advances.[57] Highway robbery and fear for one's safety, which marked Sikandar's journey and prevented her from visiting Medina, are distinctly less of a concern by the time Lady Evelyn performs her Hajj.

In marked contrast to Sikandar, who gives critical and, by turns, plaintive and emotionally distant descriptions of her sacred journey, Lady Evelyn conveys an overawed and yet deeply reflective stance. Her description of her first encounter with the Kaʿba is representative of the tone throughout, inviting readers to draw inspiration from her spiritual journey:

> It would require a master pen to describe that scene, poignant in its intensity of that great concourse of humanity of which I was one small unit, completely lost to their surroundings in a fervor of religious enthusiasm. Many of the pilgrims had tears streaming down their cheeks; others raised their faces to the starlit sky that

[55] Cobbold, *Pilgrimage to Mecca*, 26.

[56] For her comments on the destruction of graves, see, e.g., *Pilgrimage to Mecca*, 49, 65, and for comments regarding selective adaption of innovation and technology, see *Pilgrimage to Mecca*, 174–175.

[57] Cobbold, *Pilgrimage to Mecca*, 22.

had witnessed this drama so often in past centuries. The shining eyes, the passionate appeals, the pitiful hands outstretched in prayer moved me in a way that nothing had ever done before, and I felt caught up in a strong wave of spiritual exaltation. I was one with the rest of the pilgrims in a sublime act of complete surrender to the Supreme Will which is Islam ... and it was with a feeling of deepest gratitude and reverence that I joined the throng to circuit the Kaaba.[58]

Lady Evelyn edifies and corrects her audience's perceptions of Muslim culture and practice. Such is the case with her narrative detour on the topic of women and the harem, written while she had "some hours on my hands for the first time since entering Mecca." In this section, she traces the lineage of female seclusion to pre-Islamic practices and describes the rights accorded to women during Muḥammad's lifetime. She distinguishes cultural practices (e.g., the South Asian observance of *purdah* [i.e., seclusion from men]) from what she perceives as the original teachings of Muḥammad and the respect and dignity accorded to women in early Islam.[59] Finally, unlike Sikandar, who was clearly repulsed by the manners and customs of the Arabs and Turks whom she encountered, Lady Evelyn expresses admiration for the dignified bearing, good looks, and generosity of her Arab hosts (by the time Cobbold was writing her memoir, the Ottoman Turks were no longer in control of Mecca, and her recorded encounters are primarily with Arabs).

These strikingly different memoirs, written just decades apart, raise a host of questions about the variables that impacted women's experiences as well as their framing of these experiences for their audiences. Sikandar's desires as a South Asian woman, keen to assert her own elite status among her Ottoman and Arab hosts in Arabia as well as in the eyes of her British colonial readership, are profoundly inscribed in her reticent and critical narrative. Lady Evelyn's desires, similarly impacted by her race, ethnicity, and positioning in British imperial contexts, leave an indelible imprint on her casting of the journey as one which bridged cultural, racial, and even gender divides (as men of the Arab elite generously hosted and protected her throughout her journey). The dissonance between these memoirs highlights that gender cannot be isolated and analyzed apart from a broader matrix of variables, including race, class, and historical contexts,

[58] *Pilgrimage to Mecca*, 133.

[59] *Pilgrimage to Mecca*, 191–192. See also 65–68 for her sympathetic view of polygamy and her explanation for the Prophet's multiple marriages.

which impact the believer during the pilgrimage and shape her memories well after the journey has ended.

Although the British imperial context may have been critical for spurring the genre of women's Hajj memoirs, it acquired independent momentum over the course of the twentieth century. Further, it is an area in which women have increasingly recorded their spiritual transformations and voiced a host of concerns and aspirations. In a study of the Hajj in contemporary Southeast Asia, Eric Tagliacozzo notes that as the numbers of women undertaking the pilgrimage has increased in the modern period, there is a growing market of memoirs penned by housewives. This is the case particularly in Indonesia, where Muslim women have greater socio-economic autonomy and where those who have experienced the rigors and fulfillment of this journey are keen to guide other women who wish to do the same.[60] Women's recollections of the Hajj are also used to frame and reflect on contemporary challenges facing the Muslim community globally. In this vein, modern Western Muslim women, among them Asra Nomani, have deployed the Hajj memoir to call for reform of Muslim women's rights.[61]

CONCLUSION

The prophetic hadith cited at the outset of this article presented women's Hajj as a type of jihad. The physical, spiritual, and financial exigencies of this religious obligation were high for women. But the promise of ethereal reward after a fulfilling and valid Hajj drew women across time and place to undertake the journey. In the academic analysis of rituals, the Hajj exemplifies the consummate liminal space where a host of established norms are suspended or challenged and where there are ample opportunities for believers' spiritual fulfilment.[62] This potential of the Hajj to enable transformation (be it temporary or long-term) in gender relations and women's roles has been mitigated by juristic

[60] E. Tagliacozzo, *The Longest Journey: Southeast Asians and the Pilgrimage to Mecca* (New York: Oxford University Press, 2013), 261–263.

[61] Asra Nomani, *Standing Alone in Mecca* (Harper San Francisco, 2006). And see Chapter 13 in this volume.

[62] See, e.g., W. C. Young, "The Kaba, Gender, and the Rites of Pilgrimage," *International Journal of Middle East Studies*, 25, 2 (1993): 285–300, for his analysis of the inversion/suspension of gender roles during Hajj in the early twentieth century. Young applies and critiques theoretical frameworks developed by Victor Turner and Arnold Van Gennep in their analyses of liminality and rites of passage across religious traditions.

FIGURE 4 Pilgrims in the precincts of the Kaʿba, 2010

discourse as well as historical practices that invariably reproduce and reassert traditional boundaries and regulations. And yet, women's persistent, indeed increasing, participation confirms the promise of spiritual fulfillment and transformation associated with performing the Hajj.

PART TWO

JOURNEY

5

The Hajj by Land

Benjamin Claude Brower

Overland travel was and remains at the heart of every Hajj. Even the denizens of Mecca must get to ʿArafat for the vigil (*wuqūf*), a short journey outside of the holy city made by crossing over solid ground. Movement on land comprises the many rites of Hajj such as the circumambulation (*ṭawāf*) of the Kaʿba, the pilgrims' dispersal after the ʿArafat vigil (*ifāḍa*) and the back and forth traverse (*saʿy*) between al-Ṣafa and al-Marwa, two hillocks in Mecca. This last rite arguably introduces pilgrims to the essence of overland travel in this region by having them commemorate the desperate running of Ismāʿīl's mother, Hajar, as she searched the desert for water for her dying son. But while these movements of people over land are obligatory rites, the method by which pilgrims get to the Hijaz region in the first place is not subject to orthodox prescriptions.[1] In principle, people can choose their own way to travel.

The methods of travel on the Hajj have evolved significantly since the beginnings of Islam. In the early years, during the four Rāshidūn caliphs (632–661 CE), when the compact community of believers was centered in nearby Medina, pilgrims made their way to the holy places mounted or on foot, often led by the caliph himself. But when Islam expanded to the shores of the Mediterranean Sea and the Indian Ocean – the Arabian peninsula itself flanked by the "lakes of Islam," the Red Sea and Arabian/Persian Gulf[2] – water travel offered an option to landed

[1] G. Hawting, "Pilgrimage," *Encyclopaedia of the Qur'ān*, vol. 4, ed. J. D. McAuliffe (Leiden: Brill, 2004), 91.

[2] A. Miquel, *La géographie humaine du monde musulman jusqu'au milieu du 11e siècle: géographie arabe et représentation du monde, la terre et l'étranger* (Paris: Mouton, 1975), 530.

itineraries to Mecca, even if it would not be until the nineteenth century that steam ships traveling through the Suez canal (opened in 1869) partially supplanted the caravans from places to Mecca's north and west. And today, air provides what is far and away the most utilized element for Hajj travel, conveying 79 percent of people making the pilgrimage from abroad in 1994, compared to 9 percent by sea, and 12 percent by land; this shift toward air travel continues, with 94 percent of nonresident pilgrims traveling to the Hijaz by plane in 2013.[3]

The shift between these travel paradigms – land, sea, and air – is a story that can be told in many different ways. One way is to look at belief and traditions. The Qur'an implies a preference for land when it states: "Proclaim the Pilgrimage to the people. Let them come to you on foot and on every lean camel" (Q Ḥajj 22:27).[4] The example of the Prophet and the illustrious early Muslims and famous caliphs, who traveled to the pilgrimage by land, reinforced this preference. Summing up these traditions, the French scholar Maurice Gaudefroy-Demombynes, a keen student of the Hajj, observed, "[T]he land routes are those preferred by Muslim doctrine."[5] Another way to explain the changes in travel paradigms would be to tell a history of technology centered on the development of new, ever more sophisticated methods of transportation that "conquered" space.[6] But a history of the ways to Mecca is also a history to be told in terms of social and political history and their relationship to space. This approach recognizes that space is constitutive of basic institutions in its ability to give concrete expression to abstractions such as sovereignty and law.[7] In particular, the way that pilgrims have traveled has depended on their social position and their relationship to the structures of power in a given place and time.

[3] *Al-Aṭlas al-tārīkhī lil-Mamlaka al-ʿArabiyya al-Suʿūdiyya* (Riyadh: Dārat al-Malik ʿAbd al-ʿAzīz, 1999), 36; press release, Information Office of the Royal Embassy of Saudi Arabia in Washington, DC (October 13, 2013): www.saudiembassy.net/latest_news/new s10131302.aspx.

[4] *The Qur'ān,* tr. A. Jones (Cambridge: Gibb Memorial Trust, 2007), 309.

[5] M. Gaudefroy-Demombynes, *Le pèlerinage à La Mekke: étude d'histoire religieuse* (Paris: Geuthner, 1923), 315.

[6] One of the first to recognize the limits of this perspective is A. Christelow, "Political Ends and Means of Transport in the Colonial North African Pilgrimage," *The Maghreb Review*, 12, 3–4 (1987): 84–89.

[7] C. Schmitt, *The* Nomos *of the Earth in the International Law of the* Jus Publicum Europaeum, tr. G. L. Ulmen (New York: Telos, 2006 [1950]).

THE UMAYYAD- AND ABBASID-ERA ROADS, SEVENTH–THIRTEENTH CENTURIES

A spider web of beaten paths, roads, and trails have crossed the Arabian Peninsula and converged on Mecca. All said, six principal overland Hajj roads, identified by different points of departure, have taken pilgrims to the Hajj starting in the first centuries of Islam.[8] Two originated in Iraq: the Kufa/Baghdad–Mecca road, better known as the Darb Zubayda; and the Basra–Mecca route, which paralleled the Darb Zubayda to the south.[9] A third major Hajj route, known generically as the Darb al-Ḥajj al-Miṣrī (the Egyptian Hajj Road), departed from Cairo, and after crossing the Sinai Peninsula, it split, giving travelers the choice between a coastal and an inland route, with the inland route passing first to Medina before reaching Mecca. The fourth major route departed from Damascus. It was called variously the Darb al-Shāmī (Syrian Road), the Darb al-Tabūkiyya (Tabuk Road), and the Darb al-Sulṭānī (Sultan's Road, or Imperial Way), and it followed an inland route to Mecca via Medina.[10] (In the medieval era, crusaders frequently attacked both the Syrian and Egyptian routes, making these routes unreliable.) The two final routes linked Yemen to Mecca. One followed the Red Sea coast, and the other, beginning in Sanaʿa, passed inland through the mountainous ʿAsir region of southwestern Arabia.[11] There were also important feeder routes that led pilgrims to these major itineraries. They included the path traveled by pilgrims from Oman along the coast of the Arabian Sea to Yemen; and the

[8] W. C. Brice, "A New Map of the Pilgrim Roads of Arabia," *Proceedings of the Seminar for Arabian Studies*, 5 (1975): 9; S. A. Al-Rashid, *Darb Zubayda: The Pilgrim Road from Kufa to Mecca* (Riyadh University Libraries, 1980), 4–7; H. Kennedy (ed.), *An Historical Atlas of Islam/Atlas historique de l'islam*, 2nd ed. (Leiden: Brill, 2002), 19; M. Ruthven and A. Nanji, *Historical Atlas of Islam* (Cambridge, MA: Harvard University Press, 2004), 138; H. David, "Map of Pilgrimage Roads," in A. I. Al-Ghabbân et al. (eds.), *Roads of Arabia: Archaeology and History of the Kingdom of Saudi Arabia* (Paris: Louvre/Somogy, 2010), 422. An anthology of narrative accounts of these routes is in F. E. Peters, *The Hajj: The Muslim Pilgrimage to Mecca and the Holy Places* (Princeton University Press, 1994), 71–108.

[9] Al-Rashid, *Darb Zubayda.*

[10] A. Petersen, *The Medieval and Ottoman Hajj Route in Jordan: An Archaeological and Historical Study* (Oxford: Oxbow, 2012); K. K. Barbir, *Ottoman Rule in Damascus, 1708–1758* (Princeton University Press, 1980), 109.

[11] M. A. R. Thanayyan, *An Archaeological Study of the Yemeni Highland Pilgrim Route between Ṣanʿāʾ and Mecca* (Riyadh: Deputy Ministry of Antiquities and Museums, 1999); M. A. R. Al-Thenayian, "A Preliminary Evaluation of Al-Radāʿī's *Urǧūzat al-Ḥaǧǧ* as Primary Geographical Source for Surveying the Yemini Highland Pilgrim Route," *New Arabian Studies*, 4 (1997): 243–260.

FIGURE 5 Thirteenth-century manuscript illustration of a pilgrim caravan

various routes linking Persia, Khurasan, Anatolia, and other points north and east to Damascus. Finally, there have been different trails that brought pilgrims to Cairo from the African continent's northwest (al-Maghrib) and sub-Saharan regions (Bilād al-Sūdān), as well as southwest Europe (al-Andalus).[12] (Other land routes, central to the pilgrimage but not necessary to fulfill the Hajj itself, included three different Medina to Mecca routes, which, on a roughly ten-day trip, have been traveled by virtually every pilgrim making the popular "visit" or *ziyāra* to the Prophet's Mosque and his tomb, as well as Medina's al-Baqīʿ

[12] The route from Oman was especially difficult, and pilgrims often made the trip by sea to Jeddah. See Ibn Ḥawqal in Peters, *The Hajj*, 73.

Cemetery where many famous early Muslims are buried.[13]) Of these routes, many predated Islam – old routes of commerce and migration – while others were first fully developed by Muslims for the pilgrimage.[14]

The main roads achieved their status because of the patronage of powerful notables and institutions, which used the Hajj to articulate and consolidate authority. This was achieved in a number of different ways, and in this sense the landed Hajj served multiple political purposes. First the Hajj routes linked the center of Islam, Mecca, or "Umm al-Qurā" (the "Mother of Settlements") to actual political capitals such as Damascus, Baghdad, and Cairo, thus serving as vital links of communication across far-flung empires.[15] When the Hajj caravans carried symbolic markers such as the *kiswa* (the embroidered covering of the Kaʿba) and the *maḥmal* (a decorated palanquin that traveled with the various caravans from Cairo and Damascus, and, at times, Yemen and Iraq), states could use the pilgrimage to make territorial claims over the Hijaz.[16] Thus the mahmal, an empty palanquin full of political symbolism, was sent for the first time from Mamlūk Egypt in 1266, following the final collapse of the Abbasid empire, and it marked the transfer of the caliphate to Cairo. This tradition ended in 1926 when the Egyptian mahmal was refused entrance by the Saudis after their victory in western Arabia and the consolidation of the Hijaz into a new state. Beyond these direct expressions of territorial claims, the Hajj provided an occasion to express authority. Through the Hajj roads, for example, piety and power became fixed, concrete, literally written across a sacred landscape. In this sense, the "caliph could show *his* obedience to God while simultaneously showing himself as leader of the Muslim community."[17]

[13] *EI3*, s.v. "Baqīʿ al-Gharqad." The three possible routes between Mecca and Medina are described in Dr. Rifaat and Dr. Essad, *Rapport sur le voyage de retour de la caravane sacrée en l'année 1324 de l'Hégire (1907)* (Istanbul: Loeffler, [1907]), 22–24; and Evliya Çelebi, *An Ottoman Traveler: Selections from the Book of Travels of Evliya Çelebī*, tr. R. Dankoff and S. Kim (London: Eland, 2010), 346.

[14] A. Al-Wohaibi, *The Northern Hijaz in the Writings of the Arab Geographers, 800–1150* (Beirut: Al-Risala, 1973), 385; Al-Rashid, *Darb Zubayda*, 329; A. de Maigret, "La route caravanière de l'encens dans l'Arabie préislamique," *Chroniques yéménites* [online] 11 (2003): cy.revues.org/160.

[15] Ibn al-Mujāwir, *A Traveller in Thirteenth-Century Arabia: Ibn Al-Mujāwir's* Tārīkh al-Mustabṣir, tr. G. Rex Smith (London: Hakluyt Society, 2008), 32.

[16] M. Gaudefroy-Demombynes, "Le voile de la Kaʿba," *Studia Islamica*, 2 (1954), 5–21; J. Jomier, *Le maḥmal et la caravane égyptienne des pèlerins de La Mecque (XIIIe–XXe siècles)* (Cairo: Institut français d'archéologie orientale, 1953); Gaudefroy-Demombynes, *Le pèlerinage à La Mekke*, 157–166.

[17] M. E. McMillan, *The Meaning of Mecca: The Politics of Pilgrimage in Early Islam* (London: Saqi, 2011), 35.

Muslim sovereigns sponsored road-building projects that boasted water, shelter, and security. Construction first began when the second caliph, ʿUmar (634–644 CE) authorized local people to build way stations for travelers between Medina and Mecca.[18] This example guided later Muslim sovereigns and notables who displayed their political power, social status, and moral conscience by investing in the pilgrimage. The Umayyads (661–750 CE) in Damascus reputedly wavered in their commitment to the Hajj during the second civil war (680–692 CE) when the holy places passed into the hands of the opposition. Some sources even report that the caliph ʿAbd al-Malik may have proposed that Jerusalem replace Mecca as the site for the Hajj, bringing about a spacial reconfiguration of power expressing Umayyad interests.[19] Nevertheless, they recognized the Meccan pilgrimage's political significance and worked quickly to reestablish their patronage after their defeat of the Hijaz rebellion.[20]

The most important road-building project in the early history of Islam came when the Abbasid caliphs (750–1258 CE) built a 1,400 km route, the Darb Zubayda, to link their capital in Baghdad to Mecca across one of the most difficult approaches to the Hijaz. The Abbasid rise to power over their Umayyad rivals in 750 CE signaled a sizable shift in the makeup of the state and the social bases of political power. Patronage of the Hajj played a not insubstantial role in consolidating Abbasid control over a vast and diverse empire. To anchor the caliph's power, a premium was placed upon the sovereign's piety and religious authority.[21] For example, the fourth Abbasid caliph, Hārūn al-Rashīd (r. 786–809 CE) was said to make 100 units of prayer (*rakʿas*) every day, and he incarnated the ideals of Islamic leadership by personally leading the Hajj (between six and nine times during his reign) or commanding Muslim armies in

[18] Al-Ṭabari, *The History of al-Ṭabarī*, vol. 13: *The Conquest of Iraq, Southwestern Persia, and Egypt*, tr. G. H. A. Juynboll (Albany: State University of New York Press, 1989), 109.

[19] J. Wellhausen, *The Arab Kingdom and Its Fall* (London: Routledge, 2000 [1902]), 213; McMillan refutes this version in *The Meaning of Mecca*, 79–80.

[20] G. R. Hawting, "The Ḥajj in the Second Civil War," in I. R. Netton (ed.), *Golden Roads: Migration, Pilgrimage and Travel in Mediaeval and Modern Islam* (Richmond, UK: Curzon, 1993), 31–42. For Umayyad communications, see Al-Wohaibi, *The Northern Hijaz*, 373.

[21] J. Lassner, *The Shaping of ʿAbbāsid Rule* (Princeton University Press, 1979); H. Kennedy, *The Early Abbasid Caliphate: A Political History* (London: Croom Helm, 1981); M. Q. Zaman, *Religion and Politics under the Early ʿAbbāsids: The Emergence of the Proto-Sunni Elite* (Leiden: Brill, 1997).

jihad against the Byzantine Empire in alternating years.[22] A lasting monument to Abbasid devotion was the Darb Zubayda, "the most important and impressive civil engineering project undertaken in the entire early Islamic world."[23] This road used sophisticated engineering to make a safe, all-season passage across the barren plains separating Baghdad from Mecca. Where necessary, workers leveled the route and cleared obstacles. They also marked featureless sections of desert with cairns to guide pilgrims.[24] Travel across it could be made with such speed that ice was sent to Mecca in 776 CE, a true luxury this year when the pilgrimage fell at the end of summer and temperatures could be expected to have been very hot.[25] A reliable water system and police were also vital to the Zubayda road, and they were assured by a system of forts, hostels, cisterns, and wells (over 1,000 wells and points of water) placed along the route at regular intervals.[26]

Work on the road began with the first Abbasid caliph, Abū al-ʿAbbās (d. 754 CE), and intensified under the next two caliphs, al-Manṣūr (d. 775 CE) and al-Mahdī (d. 785 CE). But it claimed as its eponym Zubayda bint Jaʿfar (d. 831–832 CE). Zubayda was the wife of caliph Hārūn al-Rashīd and the mother of al-Amīn, the son who first succeeded him. She performed the Hajj at least five, maybe six times, the first in 790 CE accompanied by her husband. (They traveled part of the route this year on foot, in mourning for Khayzurān, the caliph's mother and Zubayda's maternal aunt who had recently died.[27] Their feet were cushioned, however, by rugs that servants unrolled in front of the couple.[28]) Zubayda became famous in the Abbasid chronicles for her piety and charitable works. These included spending her personal fortune to fund infrastructure projects in the Hijaz, along with building the pilgrimage road that bore her name. This deployment of a woman's economic and cultural capital charted new paths for

[22] T. El-Hibri, *Reinterpreting Islamic Historiography: Hārūn al-Rashīd and the Narrative of the ʿAbbāsid Caliphate* (Cambridge University Press, 1999), 21; M. Bonner, *Aristocratic Violence and Holy War: Studies in the Jihad and the Arab-Byzantine Frontier* (New Haven: American Oriental Society, 1996), 99–106.

[23] H. Kennedy, "Journey to Mecca: A History," in V. Porter with M. A. S. Abdel Haleem et al. (eds.), *Hajj: Journey to the Heart of Islam* (Cambridge, MA: Harvard University Press, 2012), 95.

[24] Al-Rashid, *Darb Zubayda*, 141–151.

[25] Al-Rashid, *Darb Zubayda*, 18.

[26] Al-Rashid, *Darb Zubayda*, 153–227.

[27] N. Abbott, *Two Queens of Baghdad: Mother and Wife of Hārūn al-Rashīd* (University of Chicago Press, 1946), 101, 242.

[28] Al-Rashid, *Darb Zubayda*, 20, note.

public engagement for courtly women in the changing environment of the Abbasid caliphate, when the possibility for more direct political participation may have narrowed as some scholars have argued.[29] In this respect, Zubayda exemplified "the role that a woman can have in the public sphere. Her energies must focus on pious deeds and provide comfort for Muslims – a 'Mother of the Faithful,' so to speak."[30] This strategy was successful. Patronage of the Hajj became an acceptable form of political participation for women, a tradition that lasted through the eighteenth century and earned Zubayda more than a thousand years of fame.[31]

The land routes from Iraq fell on hard times in the tenth century when the Qarmaṭī revolt made travel along the Darb Zubayda very dangerous. After the Mongol conquest of Baghdad (1258 CE), caravan travel dwindled on the Darb Zubayda.[32] But as Abbasid power waned and failed in Iraq, their rivals and later successors in Egypt, such as the Fatimids (969–1171 CE), Ayyubids (1171–1250 CE), and Mamlūks (1250–1517 CE), used the overland routes to claim territory and legitimate their rule. The important links between the Hajj and political power can be seen in the titles that linked sovereigns to the holy places, such as "Khādim al-Ḥaramayn al-Sharīfayn" ("Protector of the Two Holy Sanctuaries," i.e., Mecca and Medina) that was first claimed by Saladin in 1191 CE.[33] Other expressions included charitable efforts in the Hijaz and performing the Hajj, as did many Mamlūk sultans.[34]

[29] L. Ahmed, *Women and Gender in Islam: Historical Roots of a Modern Debate* (New Haven: Yale University Press, 1992), 79–101; D. A. Spellberg, *Politics, Gender, and the Islamic Past* (New York: Columbia University Press, 1994), 138; J. Bray "Men, Women and Slaves in Abbasid Society," in L. Brubaker and J. M. H. Smith (eds.), *Gender in the Early Medieval World: East and West, 300–900* (Cambridge University Press, 2004), 121–146.

[30] El-Hibri, *Reinterpreting Islamic Historiography*, 43.

[31] K. Johnson, "Royal Pilgrims: Mamlūk Accounts of the Pilgrimages to Mecca of the Khawand al-Kubrā (Senior Wife of the Sultan)," *Studia Islamica*, 91 (2000): 107–131; M. Tolmacheva, "Female Piety and Patronage in the Medieval 'Ḥajj,'" in G. R. G. Hambly, *Women in the Medieval Islamic World: Power, Patronage, and Piety* (New York: St. Martin's, 1998), 161–179.

[32] A. Blair and B. Ulrich, "From Iraq to the Hijaz in the Early Islamic Period," in V. Porter and L. Saif (eds.), *The Hajj: Collected Essays* (London: British Museum Press, 2013), 51.

[33] *EI2*, s.v. "Khādim al-Ḥaramayn."

[34] R. Irwin, *The Middle East in the Middle Ages: The Early Mamluk Sultanate 1250–1382* (London: Croom Helm, 1986), 95; D. Behrens-Abouseif, "Qāytbāy's Foundation in Medina, the *Madrasah*, the *Ribāṭ* and the *Dashīshah*," *Mamluk Studies Review*, 2 (1998): 61–71.

THE MAMLŪK-ERA CARAVAN (RAKB AL-ḤAJJ), THIRTEENTH–SIXTEENTH CENTURIES

Along with building and maintaining roads, overland travel depended on successfully organizing the annual Hajj caravan (*al-rakb*). In the second half of the thirteenth century, caravan activity shifted to routes originating in Mamlūk Cairo and Damascus. Defeats in Iraq were matched by victories to the northwest of Mecca where the crusaders were finally expelled from fortresses such as Karak, Shawbak, and Ayla, reopening to the Hajj routes that passed nearby.[35] Thus, the Mamlūk sultanate of Egypt and Syria became the focal point for a good part of the world's Muslims departing on the Hajj. For example, the North African Hajj caravan, called the *rakb al-Maghāriba*, brought the famous traveler Ibn Baṭṭūṭa to Cairo in 1326 CE en route for the first of as many as six pilgrimages.[36] Two years earlier, the Malian monarch Mansa Musa visited the Mamlūk capital with the West African caravan, known as the *rakb al-Takrūr*, which had crossed the Sahara to get to Egypt.[37] Both pilgrims enjoyed the security and services provided by the Mamlūks for the remainder of their journey to Mecca, and in the case of the wealthy Musa, the stopover in Cairo provided him with opportunities to spend his gold in acts of religious charity and consumption.[38] Pilgrims from Central and West Asia (Anatolia, Iraq, Persia, and Khurasan) also converged on Mamlūk territories, departing from Damascus under the Mamlūk sultan's protection.[39]

When they arrived in Mecca, the Cairo and Damascus caravans could be huge. In an era when typical commercial caravans numbered in the hundreds of camels,[40] the Hajj caravans could number in the tens of thousands of pilgrims. The 1279 CE caravan from Cairo reportedly had

[35] C. Hillenbrand, *The Crusades: Islamic Perspectives* (Edinburgh University Press, 1999), 291–293; A. Petersen, *The Medieval and Ottoman Hajj Route in Jordan*, 9.

[36] R. E. Dunn, *The Adventures of Ibn Battuta: A Muslim Traveler of the 14th Century* (Berkeley: University of California Press, 2005), 41–52, 290–295.

[37] *EI2*, s.v. "Takrūr."

[38] Musa put so much gold into circulation in the Cairene economy that its value declined 12 percent: A. 'Ankawi, "The Pilgrimage to Mecca in Mamlūk Times," *Arabian Studies*, 1 (1974), 150; see also E. W. Bovill, *The Golden Trade of the Moors* (Oxford University Press, 1970).

[39] 'Ankawi, "Pilgrimage to Mecca," 149.

[40] J. L. Meloy, "Overland Trade in the Western Islamic World (Fifth-Ninth/Eleventh-Fifteenth Centuries), in M. Fierro (ed.), *The New Cambridge History of Islam*, vol. 2: *The Western Islamic World Eleventh to Eighteenth Centuries* (Cambridge University Press, 2010), 653.

40,000 travelers.[41] Thus the caravans were literally cities on the move. The five daily prayers were called out by the caravan's muezzins, and they were led by the caravan's imam. Law was assured by qadis who presided over contracts negotiated during the journey and provided guidance concerning complex pilgrimage rites. The qadis also performed the all-important task of calculating the exact day of the ʿArafat vigil and thus establishing the calendar of the Hajj (see below). Other legal officials included probate judges who dealt with estates of people who died while on the Hajj, notaries, police, and executioners.[42] Medical care was provided by doctors, surgeons, traditional healers, and pharmacists. For those who could not be healed, corpse washers accompanied the caravan. Social services included free mounts and provisions for the poor, which were distributed according to a Qurʾanic verse outlining the duty of charity "in God's way and for the traveller" (Q Tawba 9:60).[43] The basic concerns facing any traveler, such as transportation, food, and lodging, were undertaken by a vast corps of specialized workers – cooks, firewood collectors, and water porters, carpenters and blacksmiths, donkey and camel drivers, veterinarians, guides, and grooms. Finally, pick-pockets and thieves worked among the pilgrims, however unpious their craft.[44]

Caravan society amazed pilgrims at many different levels, including its size, its organization, and also its high prices. A vivid description comes from two Ottoman doctors traveling with the Damascus caravan in 1907, the last of the great Hajj caravans. While acknowledging the many challenges the caravan faced finding sufficient water and staying healthy, these two doctors remarked upon its order and efficiency.

> "Within an hour, this movable city already has its streets, its stables, its water fountains, even its own markets and bazars with cafes, and one finds nearly everything necessary [to enjoy] relative comfort, but, it is all, very expensive ... [And] two hours after the halt, one can already see traveling shops displaying here and there their sacs of provisions. Syrian shopkeepers haggle with their clients of different languages by means of paraphrases or funny facial expressions and curious gestures. The camels, gentle and calm, are arranged in a series in the outer zones of the two leaders, grazing on grass and a special fodder prepared by the camel drivers, and the grooms care for the mounts. The rare Arab or Persian cooks prepare their national pilafs. Over on one side, sharp cries announce a few

[41] J. Loiseau, "Arabia and the Holy Cities," in Al-Ghabbân et al. (eds.), *Roads of Arabia,* 414.
[42] Johnson, "Royal Pilgrims," 110; ʻAnkawi, "Pilgrimage to Mecca," 159–160.
[43] ʻAnkawi, "Pilgrimage to Mecca," 161.
[44] Evliya Çelebi, *An Ottoman Traveler,* 365.

butchers who sell for absurd prices the meat of a sheep slaughtered on the spot, and a few bakers cook unleavened black bread that is impossible to digest . . . On the other side, the Bedouins of the nearby camps come running to take advantage of this rare occasion to sell some milk, hay, and sometimes bread or even some watermelons and other small provisions. In sum, all around the camp appears movement and activity worthy of a city."[45]

Safely crossing the desert in large groups depended on good leadership: this was not an acephalous society. At the caravan's head was the *amīr al-ḥajj*.[46] The first amir al-Hajj dated back to the time of the Prophet and was the celebrated Companion, Abū Bakr.[47] The Prophet himself fulfilled this duty in the "Farewell Pilgrimage" (*ḥajjat al-wadāʿ*) of 632, when he laid out the orthodox rites of the Hajj just prior to his death. In the ensuing centuries this prestigious office passed through the hands of caliphs and members of the various royal families. By the latter Mamlūk era, the amir al-Hajj was an official invested by the Sultan, generally from the military, who was responsible for a vast array of leadership duties. These included personally financing a good part of the caravan's expenses, a task that threatened to ruin some potential amirs.[48]

LAND VERSUS SEA IN THE MEDIEVAL ERA: THOUGHTS ON THE RELATIONSHIP OF SPACE AND TIME IN THE HAJJ

Land travel tends to be slow compared to the fastest times set by ship, but if time is money to the merchant, the essential calculation for the pilgrim is precision. Even if a Hajj voyage is counted in years, the candidate must be at the plain of ʿArafat for the vigil or "standing" (*wuqūf*) on the ninth day of the twelfth month (Dhū al-Ḥijja) or see their chance of making a successful pilgrimage disappear. Thus, "The Hajj is ʿArafah," according to a hadith. This vigil is an immutable rite, one fixed exactly in time and space: it does not have substitutes or surrogates and cannot be made up. Seen from this imperative, overland travel has historically offered advantages. Unfolding in concrete increments, it offers reliable calculations of distance and time in a way not always possible for sea travel. When the Darb Zubayda was at its peak, a pilgrim could reliably travel the 1,400 km from Kufa to Mecca in about thirty days. The trip from Cairo to Mecca was counted at about

45 Dr. Rifaat and Dr. Essad, *Rapport sur le voyage*, 13–14. Punctuation altered for clarity and flow.

46 ʿAnkawi, "Pilgrimage to Mecca," 151–153.

47 H. Djaït, *La vie de Muḥammad*, vol. 3 (Tunis: Cérès, 2012), 277.

48 Johnson, "Royal Pilgrims," 108–109.

thirty-five to forty-five days in the Mamlūk and Ottoman eras, depending on which route, coastal or inland, was taken; and there were a total of thirty-four stages between Damascus and Mecca that were covered in about forty days.[49] This precision was contingent, not exact. Weather and bandits could slow progress, just as forced marches could be used to make up time.[50] For example, scholars have found that the feeder route from Sudan, the Forty-Day Road (Darb al-Arbaʿīn) actually required up to sixty days of travel to get from the town of Al Fashir to Asyut in Egypt.[51] But in the overall scheme of things, the landed routes offered the most reliable correspondence between space and time.

Another consideration is the fact that the timing of the Hajj is determined by a lunar calendar, meaning that the month of Dhū al-Ḥijja will cycle through all of the climatic seasons, shifting ahead by ten or eleven days each year in comparison with the Gregorian solar calendar. Overland travel to Mecca is a much different experience if it takes place in winter or summer, but the roads and caravan preparations ensured that it could be undertaken in any season. When temperatures rose during a summertime Hajj, the caravan traveled by night with guides following fixed fire signals (called *manārs*) in order to keep up the same pace as in the daylight hours.[52] When these were not available, trained guides (known as *adillāʾ*) navigated by the stars and other means.[53] Nighttime travel strained order, but artificial lighting helped. When all the torches, lamps, and candles were lit, "it was as though the crescent moon had become full, and it was as bright as day," according to the seventeenth-century Ottoman pilgrim Evliya Çelebi.[54] Moreover, to ensure that people did not stray from the group, pilgrims would be assigned to a distinctively marked signal lamp, suspended from a long pole, that they were to follow.[55] By comparison, travel times and

49 Brice, "A New Map of the Pilgrim Roads," 9; Evliya Çelebi, *An Ottoman Traveler*, 346.

50 See the example of the 1671 CE Damascus caravan described in Evliya Çelebi, *An Ottoman Traveler*, 342–345.

51 *EI2*, s.v. "Darb al-Arbaʿīn."

52 Al Rashid, *Darb Zubayda*, 63.

53 ʿAnkawi, "Pilgrimage to Mecca," 161; D. A. King, *World-Maps for Finding the Direction and Distance to Mecca* (Leiden: Brill, 1999); G. Lydon, *On Trans-Saharan Trails: Islamic Law, Trade Networks, and Cross-Cultural Exchange in Nineteenth-Century Western Africa* (Cambridge University Press, 2009), 226–227.

54 Evliya Çelebi, *Evliyā Çelebī in Medina: The Relevant Sections of the Seyāhatnāme*, ed. N. Gemici, tr. R. Dankoff. (Leiden: Brill, 2012), 15.

55 J. Pitts, *A Faithful Account of the Religion and Manners of the Mahometans*, 3rd ed. (London: Osborn and Longman, 1731), 150.

conditions for ships varied greatly over the seasons.[56] Travel in the Indian Ocean was subject to the monsoons, as discussed in Chapter 6 in this volume, and sea routes were closed to sailors during these storms until the advent of heavy ship construction. In the Mediterranean Sea, wintertime travel was especially difficult, hampered by fickle, shifting winds, rough seas, and poor visibility that made reliable itineraries elusive.[57]

The Andalusian writer Ibn Jubayr (Abū al-Ḥusayn Muḥammad ibn Aḥmad ibn Jubayr al-Kinānī, d. 1217 CE) makes clear his preference for land in the accounts of the perils of Mediterranean sailing he gave in his famous twelfth-century travel account. On the outbound, month-long, March sailing from Ceuta to Alexandria, Ibn Jubayr's ship struggled with "waves like mountains [that] came upon us from every side," turning the sea into a dangerous caldron for days on end.[58] A worse trip was in store for the return sailing, made in mid-winter. Weather got the better of Ibn Jubayr's Genoese-piloted ship, and it went aground in a dramatic nighttime wreck in the Straits of Messina. In the Red Sea he again suffered the perils of sea travel.[59] When Ibn Jubayr made his Hajj, crusaders had blocked the overland route from Cairo to Mecca, and he detoured up the Nile and crossed overland to the African, Red Sea port of ʿAydhab. He was forced to layover in this miserable port for nearly a month in the summer of 1183 CE. Here his narrative reaches a low point reminiscent of the worst trials of Odysseus or like an especially bleak moment in a Cormac McCarthy novel. He found very little to eat and was repulsed by the get-rich-quick mentality of locals that reduced pilgrims to a human commodity. Ibn Jubayr met survivors of a ship that had attempted to sail from Jeddah, but had been blown off course, landing far to the south. The passengers had been forced to trek back north alongshore, arriving in ʿAydhab barely alive, "like men quickened from the [funeral] shroud."[60] When Ibn Jubayr's ship finally arrived, it took him nine days sailing to reach Jeddah, his vessel buffeted by storms through the dangerous reefs.

[56] The viability of the land versus sea routes is a subject of debate for the late pre-Islamic period: a strong case is made for the latter in P. Crone, *Meccan Trade and the Rise of Islam* (Princeton University Press, 1987), 17–26.

[57] J. Beresford, *The Ancient Sailing Season* (Leiden: Brill, 2012).

[58] Ibn Jubayr, *The Travels of Ibn Jubayr*, tr. R. J. C. Broadhurst (London: Cape, 1952), 27.

[59] G. F. Hourani, *Arab Seafaring in the Indian Ocean in Ancient and Early Medieval Times* (Princeton University Press, 1951), 5; P. Sanlaville, "Geographic Introduction to the Arabian Peninsula," in Al-Ghabbân et al. (eds.), *Roads of Arabia*, 55–69.

[60] Ibn Jubayr, *Travels*, 65.

Although he made it safely across that year, during the next Hajj in 1184 CE the Red Sea claimed the lives of 1,300 pilgrims.[61] In the end, Ibn Jubayr agreed with Ibn Rashīq al-Qayrawānī, the eleventh Maghrebi poet: "The sea is bitter of taste, intractable: No need of it have I. Is it not water, and we earth?"[62]

Eventually, sophisticated sailing technologies, capped by the steamship, and the opening of the Suez Canal in 1869 transformed pilgrimage travel for people from the Mediterranean basin who might have otherwise traveled by land. The shift toward steam-powered sea travel was marked and decisive; however, it was not immediate. Detailed figures from 1873 show that of the 124,863 pilgrims who assembled at ʿArafat for the *wuqūf* vigil, 78,100 had traveled by land and only 46,763 came by sea.[63] The fact that the largest contingent in that particular year – 53,500 – originated in the Hejaz itself somewhat confuses these figures. Nevertheless, of pilgrims coming from abroad, 24,600 arrived with the historic overland caravans (Syria, Yemen, Egypt, Iraq), compared to 34,106 people who came to Jeddah in ships from the Indian Ocean and Mediterranean Sea.

THE OTTOMAN EMPIRE AND HAJJ BY LAND, SIXTEENTH–TWENTIETH CENTURIES, THE HIJAZ RAILWAY (EST. 1908 CE)

When the Ottomans occupied Syria and Egypt in the early sixteenth century, they spent lavishly to ensure Cairo and Damascus remained Hajj gateways. Historian Suraiya Faroqhi has estimated that Ottoman Hajj expenses were roughly one-half to two-thirds that of the money budgeted to fight the Habsburgs in the early seventeenth century.[64] Ottoman sultans continued the work of previous sovereigns, building and fortifying roads, improving wells and cisterns, and constructing hostels and barracks. In spite of these efforts, however, security remained a problem. The Bedouin pastoralists who lived along the approaches to the holy places represented a constant source of concern. On the one hand, they were essential partners of pilgrims, furnishing the mounts, foodstuffs, and access to water necessary to the caravans. But on the other hand, they threatened travelers when their

[61] Jean-Claude Garcin, *Un centre musulman de la Haute-Égypte médiévale: Qūṣ* (Cairo: Institut français d'archéologie orientale du Caire, 1976), 137.

[62] Ibn Jubayr, *Travels*, 331.

[63] Calculated from É.-A. Buez, *Une Mission au Hedjaz* (Paris: Masson, 1873), 80 and 83.

[64] S. Faroqhi, *Pilgrims and Sultans: The Hajj under the Ottomans, 1517–1683* (London: I. B. Tauris, 1994), 89.

interests clashed with those of the Ottoman state. This was an old problem for the overland routes to Mecca. Avoiding state authority, Bedouin pastoralists found that they could assert their autonomy through the question of caravan security. In essence, they contested the state's monopoly of violence by claiming the right to either attack or protect pilgrims traveling through their territory. For example, during the late Abbasid period, when Baghdad's power waned, Bedouins attacked the routes from Iraq and many of them joined the Qarmaṭī revolt that devastated the Hajj, culminating in the massacre of pilgrims in 930 CE.[65] By the Ottoman era, governors adopted various tactics to manage the Bedouins, which included both military force against the recalcitrant (or the vulnerable) and largesse toward the powerful who could advance Ottoman goals.[66] The latter might be included among the recipients of the *sürre* or gifts distributed by the sultan at the time of the Hajj.[67] Until the eighteenth century, the process worked well. In the period between 1571 and 1757, there were only twenty-four recorded Bedouin attacks on the pilgrimage caravan from Damascus.[68] Security was delicate, however. Negotiations might falter on a number of factors, including the complexity of local social institutions and the fluidity of political conditions, which often eluded Ottoman authorities.[69] Bedouin migration could change the local dynamic, as when the ʿAnaza confederation moved out of Arabia into the Syrian steppes beginning in the seventeenth century, unleashing conflicts with local pastoralists and the Ottoman state over resources and authority.[70] There were struggles within the Ottoman administration as well, and these conflicts compromised Ottoman-Bedouin relations.[71] Finally, climate played a role: when drought depleted pastures, the annual caravan represented an important resource

65 H. Kennedy, "The Late ʿAbbāsid Pattern, 945–1050," in C. F. Robinson (ed.), *The New Cambridge History of Islam*, vol. 1: *The Formation of the Islamic World, Sixth to Eleventh Centuries* (Cambridge University Press, 2010), 383; C. E. Bosworth, "Ṣanawbarī's Elegy on the Pilgrims Slain in the Carmathian Attack on Mecca (317/930): A Literary-Historical Study," *Arabica*, 19, 3 (October 1972): 222–239.

66 Faroqhi, *Pilgrims and Sultans*, 54–73.

67 Faroqhi, *Pilgrims and Sultans*, 55–58.

68 Barbir, *Ottoman Rule in Damascus*, 175.

69 S. N. Faroqhi, "Rural Life," in S. N. Faroqhi (ed.), *The Cambridge History of Turkey*, vol. 3: *The Later Ottoman Empire, 1603–1839* (Cambridge University Press, 2006), 379; A. Rafeq, *The Province of Damascus, 1723–1783* (Beirut: Khayats, 1966), 198–200, 213–218.

70 K. Franz, "The Bedouin in History of Bedouin History?" *Nomadic Peoples*, 15, 1 (2011): 35–36; *EI3*, s.v. "ʿAnaza."

71 Rafeq, *Province of Damascus*, 200–222.

for Bedouins, and physical force proved to be the most efficient method of economic exchange.[72]

In this sense, the Hajj could undo strategies of political legitimation and consolidation, just as it supported them. In 1757, the Ottoman system failed dramatically when Bedouins decimated the returning caravan outside of Tabuk. Along with the robbery and murder of travelers, Bedouins carried off the mahmal and killed the sultan's sister, a catastrophe that illustrated grave failures in governance, resulting in riots in Syria and unrest in Istanbul.[73] In the following centuries, the Hajj was repeatedly threatened by Bedouins, who targeted caravans in response to declining sürre payments.[74] In the eighteenth century onward, the Ottomans struggled to project their power into the Arabian Peninsula, a struggle punctuated by stinging defeats such as the Wahhabi movement's wrestling Mecca away from Istanbul's control in 1803, and the French occupation of Egypt (1798–1801), the historic seat of suzerainty over the Hijaz.

In order to make good on their claim to the title "Servants of the Holy Places," sultans had to ensure safe overland passage to Mecca. New modes of transportation were one method by which this might be achieved, and the railway promised a way to the holy places free from Bedouins. It also offered a powerful modern symbol to support Ottoman claims to hegemony in the Muslim world.[75] In 1900, Sultan Abdulhamid II announced the construction of the Hijaz Railroad linking Damascus and the holy cities. This was an all-Muslim project, a monument to the solidarity of the Umma (the community of believers) and a tangible expression of the pan-Islamic movement that the sultan sponsored as a response to European imperialism and the corrosive force of nationalism. A call went out for Muslim donations around the world to help finance the project. In theory, "it was the property of all the world's Muslims," as historian William Ochsenwald notes.[76] The subscription drive raised about one-third of the total necessary capital, the rest coming from other investors.[77] A Syrian promoter supported

[72] Barbir, *Ottoman Rule in Damascus*, 176.

[73] Rafeq, *Province of Damascus*, 213.

[74] S. Faroqhi, "The Ottoman Empire: The Age of 'Political Households' (Eleventh–Twelfth/Seventeenth–Eighteenth Censures)," in Fierro (ed.), *New Cambridge History of Islam*, vol. 2, 385.

[75] Ş. T. Buzpinar, "Opposition to the Ottoman Caliphate in the Early Years of Abdülhamid II: 1877–1882," *Die Welt des Islams*, 36, 1 (March 1996): 61.

[76] W. Ochsenwald, *The Hijaz Railroad* (Charlottesville: University Press of Virginia, 1980), 76.

[77] Ochsenwald, *The Hijaz Railroad*, 82.

the subscription campaign with his full-throated endorsement. "The construction of this railway will assist believers in performing the pilgrimage, ʿUmra [lesser, non-obligatory pilgrimage], and visit to the tomb of the Prophet. It will also help commerce, industry, and agriculture; it will civilize the savages [*mutawaḥḥishīn*], enrich the poor, satiate the hungry, enrich the country and bring [many] Muslims to life."[78] In other words, the railway would be, like the Darb Zubayda, a concrete expression of piety, but in this case the benefits would accrue to all Muslims by advancing development projects expressed here in the distinctly modern idioms of progress and the civilizing mission.

Working under a mixed team of Ottoman and European (mainly German) engineers, thousands of laborers drawn from the army and Palestinian peasants took about six years to finish the main stretch to Medina in 1908. (Only Muslim engineers and laborers worked on the line within the Hijaz.) The planning and execution of construction was a success, with crews laying track at great speed in spite of considerable physical obstacles, which included mountains, ravines, and scarce water. The results were decidedly mixed, however. Testament to this is the fact that the planned final section linking Medina to Mecca was never completed, and most importantly, the Hijaz Railway failed to bolster Abdülhamid II, who fell from power in April 1909 after the Young Turk revolution. And while the railway allowed the Ottoman Empire to rapidly transfer troops (ferrying nearly 150,000 annually in the years leading up to 1914), it did not resolve the security problem associated with overland travel in Arabia.[79] In 1908, Bedouins near Medina staged an open revolt, and they rebelled again in 1914 in response to increased taxation and the threat of conscription with the onset of the First World War.[80] Ultimately, trains proved no easier to defend than caravans, and Bedouin attacks necessitated military escorts, fortified stations, and continued payments to local pastoralists to ensure safe passage.[81] Nevertheless, some 16,000 pilgrims a year used the railway as part of their Hajj travel,

[78] Muḥammad ʿĀrif ibn Aḥmad Munayyir, "The Book of Increasing and Eternal Happiness – the Hijaz Railway," in J. M. Landau (ed.), *The Hejaz Railway and the Muslim Pilgrimage: A Case of Ottoman Political Propaganda* (Detroit: Wayne State University Press, 1971), 148, 199 (Arabic).

[79] Landau, *The Hejaz Railway*, 16.

[80] Ochsenwald, *The Hijaz Railroad,* 124.

[81] H.-J. Philipp, "Der Beduinische Widerstand gegen die Hedschasbahn," *Die Welt des Islams*, 25 (1985): 31–83.

and a total of 213,000 civilians traveled some portion of it in the peak year of 1912–1913.[82]

Pilgrims on the Hijaz Railway came from all parts of Eastern Europe, the Middle East, and Central Asia, in and outside of the Ottoman Empire itself. Few, however, were from Muslim societies under European rule. Typically colonial states such as France, which controlled most of northern and western Africa at this time, required their subjects to travel on state-approved French shipping. The fact that the Hajj was now subject to a stringent quarantine also worked against the wider popularity of the Hijaz Railway.[83] All pilgrims were required to observe a period of quarantine at specially designated stations before they would be allowed back into their home countries. For the Hijaz Railway, a quarantine camp, which was built at Tabuk, could process 4,000 people at time and disinfect train wagons. However, the facilities in the remote camp were minimal, and the British and French refused to accept it as safe for their subjects.[84] Thus a pilgrim who did quarantine in Tabuk might be required to do another period of quarantine before returning home.[85] This effectively closed the railway for many Muslims. Ultimately, the Hijaz Railway had a short life. It opened in 1908, but the Arab Revolt beginning in 1916 made travel difficult, and the railway was effectively closed by the winter of 1917–1918.[86] After the war, King Ḥusayn, the first leader of the short-lived Hijazi monarchy (1916–1925), reopened it in a failed effort to consolidate his Hāshimid family's control in the region, and some pilgrims succeeded in traveling to Medina by rail at this time. However, disputes between local Arab sovereigns and the French and British mandatory administrations over ownership resulted in the closing of sections in the Hijaz (part of the Saudi state since 1925) before the Second World War.[87]

[82] *EI2*, s.v. "Ḥidjāz Railway."

[83] N. Ersoy, et al., "International Sanitary Conferences from the Ottoman Perspective (1851–1938)," *Hygiea Internationalis*, 10, 1 (January 2011): 53–79; V. Huber, "The Unification of the Globe by Disease? The International Sanitary Conferences on Cholera, 1851–1894," *The Historical Journal*, 49, 2 (June 2006): 453–476; W. Ochsenwald, *Religion, Society and the State in Arabia: The Hijaz under Ottoman Control, 1840–1908* (Columbus: Ohio State University Press, 1984), 58–73.

[84] F. Duguet, *Le pèlerinage de La Mecque* (Paris: Rieder, 1932), 60.

[85] Ochsenwald, *The Hijaz Railroad*, 139.

[86] Ochsenwald, *The Hijaz Railroad*, 146.

[87] W. L. Ochsenwald, "A Modern *Waqf*: The Hijaz Railway, 1900–48," *Arabian Studies*, 3 (1976): 1–12.

FRENCH COLONIALISM AND THE HAJJ ON FOOT, NINETEENTH AND TWENTIETH CENTURIES

The Hijaz Railway is a good example of the intensification of state control of Hajj travel. In the nineteenth and twentieth centuries, states moved aggressively to manage the pilgrimage. This was true of Muslim states such as the Ottoman Empire as well as non-Muslim states with Muslim subjects such as France, Britain, the Netherlands, and Russia. Driven both by risks inherent in the Hajj as well as the political capital that could be reaped from it, a global system of regulation emerged.[88] This system centered on containing dangers, and it depended upon the most advanced forms of transportation. Steamship and trains, which concentrated pilgrims into relatively compact and manageable groups, were ideal forms. If the dangers were microorganisms, like the cholera that ravaged the world in the nineteenth-century pandemics, they would be kept in check by the quarantine stations. Political dangers also had to be controlled. These might be related to religion, such as Ottoman-sponsored pan-Islamism or the Islamic reform movements feared by colonial powers, or simply the nationalism that threatened all empires.[89] Here again steamships and trains were useful. Access to them could be restricted, surveillance during the period of travel easily assured, and the time of exposure to dangerous ideas limited through tight scheduling and the speed with which the journey itself could be made. Moreover, properly deployed steam-powered transportation presented a spectacular façade upon which the ideals of the state could be drawn in bold form, ideals such as efficiency, celerity, hygiene, authority, and order.

The system of control took clear form in French territories such as Algeria in the *Arrêté* of December 10, 1894, that imposed a robust set of rules upon pilgrimage travel. In order to receive the special Hajj passport, a candidate needed 1,000 francs travel funds, assurance that family at home had ample material support, back taxes paid in full, a guarantor for debts, and round trip tickets on an approved ship.[90] To fulfill these requirements, candidates faced a confused and confusing process, one that

[88] W. R. Roff, "Sanitation and Security: The Imperial Powers and the Nineteenth Century Ḥajj," *Arabian Studies*, 6 (1982): 143–160.

[89] For an example of French views, see, "Revue de la presse musulmane pendant le mois d'août 1906." Archives nationales d'Outre Mer, 1AFFPOL/923/1.

[90] *Règlement sur le pèlerinage de La Mecque* (Algiers: Fontana, 1895). For ensuing regulations, see L. Escande, "D'Alger à La Mecque: l'administration française et le contrôle du pèlerinage (1894–1962)," *Revue d'histoire maghrébine*, 26, 95–96 (May 1999): 277–296.

required forms, documents, signatures, and stamps. The fact that applicants only had three months to complete their dossier intensified the challenges and excluded many.[91] This "work of art of bureaucratic control" effectively closed the Hajj for those without considerable economic and social capital.[92] And even those who could mobilize this capital found that hanging over the whole process was a double structural uncertainty: the often arbitrary decisions passed on individual applications and the possibility that the pilgrimage would be canceled if cholera appeared, in which case the whole process would have to be started again the next year (cancellations occurred roughly every other year between 1875 and 1915).[93]

Overland travel took place off this grid. Using only their own two feet, any able-bodied Muslim could respond to the call to perform the Hajj. For the poor, persecuted, or impulsive, this simplicity was the only way they might hope to go to Mecca. This was the case for Ahmed ben Kaddour Mehdi, who slipped out of his village in October 1904, five months before the beginning of the Hajj rites.[94] He came from Ouled Yaïche, a small settlement in the mountains of western Algeria above the Chélif river valley, a rich agricultural region heavily settled by Europeans.[95] Mehdi was about forty years old at the time; unmarried without children, land, or livestock; and thus entirely without resources and at the very bottom of what was already a poor society. He was of the subproletariat that comprised a large part of Algerian society at this time, people whose families had lost their farmlands and herds to colonization and lived day-to-day from whatever might be earned as agricultural laborers.[96] Travel was a typical response to poverty, with many people leaving rural areas during subsistence crises or epidemics to seek work and the relative security of port cities like Algiers. The pilgrimage offered another possibility. People made their way east seeking work, charity, and the many other opportunities for

[91] Si Ahmed ben Chérif, "Notes de mon voyage à La Mecque," June 23, 1914. Archives nationales d'Outre Mer, 10H54.

[92] L. Chantre, "Se rendre à La Mecque sous la Troisième République: contrôle et organisation des déplacement des pèlerins du Maghreb et du Levant entre 1880 et 1939," *Cahiers de la Méditerranée*, 78 (2009), 207.

[93] B. C. Brower, "The Colonial Hajj: France and Algeria, 1830–1962," in V. Porter and L. Saif (eds.), *The Hajj: Collected Essays* (London: British Museum Press, 2013), 109.

[94] Administrateur de la Commune Mixte d'Ammi Moussa to Préfet d'Oran, July 13, 1905, no. 2643. Archives nationales d'Outre Mer, 10G57.

[95] X. Yacono, *La colonisation des plaines du Chélif (de Lavigerie au confluent de la Mina)*, 2 vols. (Algiers: Imbert, 1952).

[96] A. Nouschi, *Enquête sur le niveau de vie des populations rurales constantinoises de la conquête jusqu'en 1919* (Paris: Presses universitaires de France, 1961).

survival that mobility opened. The Hajj doubled as economic migration, or as a proletarian analogue the prestigious *al-riḥla fi ṭalab al-ʿilm* ("travel in search of knowledge") long made by Muslim students.[97] The search for work introduced detours in itineraries as pilgrims followed labor markets. Thus the stay in the East might stretch over a long period, and many Hajjis settled permanently in places such as Syria, Egypt, or Medina and Mecca. A 1948 report shows that 2,000 people from France's North African possessions (Morocco, Algeria, Tunisia) lived permanently in the Hijaz.[98]

Although his voice is largely silent in the sources, Mehdi's itinerary speaks volumes. When he set out from his village, he did not go straight east up the Chélif valley, although he might have followed in the footsteps of such illustrious predecessors as Ibn Baṭṭūṭa.[99] Instead he went south over the mountains, and then east, going along the steppes at the northern edge of the Sahara. Previous to the French occupation, travelers used this route because the steppes offered seasonably good pastures, decent water, and flat open spaces, excellent for traveling. However, in the early twentieth century, its attraction for people like Mehdi was in the fact that the region was thinly populated and policed. Algerians needed a special permit even to travel within Algeria, let alone make an international trip like the Hajj, so the steppes and desert turned into thoroughfares for clandestine voyagers. From Algeria, Mehdi crossed into Tunisia at its southern Saharan boarder, and from there to Libya, Egypt, and the Hijaz – a trip he made entirely on foot. The itinerary was typical for the thousands of covert pilgrims from French North Africa in this period. Some crossed legally into Tunisia with work papers, which were relatively easy to come by thanks to French efforts to improve the free flow of labor between Algeria and Tunisia, which had been a French protectorate since 1881.[100] They then might continue like Mehdi overland all the way to Mecca, or board ships at Tunisian ports such as Sfax and Djerba, taking advantage of the many gaps that existed in the regime of maritime controls in territories not under full French rule.

This trip was certainly a difficult one for a poor traveler. Most nights Mehdi, traveling alone, slept under the open sky on an empty stomach.

97 H. Touati, *Islam and Travel in the Middle Ages*, tr. L G. Cochrane (University of Chicago Press, 2010).

98 Rapport de Piquet 1948. Centre des archives nationales d'Algérie, IBA/CUL-049.

99 Ben Messaïb, "Itinéraire de Tlemcen à La Mekke," tr. M. Ben Cheneb, *Revue africaine*, 44 (1900): 261–282.

100 Chef d'annexe de Tabarka to Résident Général Tunis, March 5, 1911, no. 591. Archives nationales de Tunisie, Série A, carton 276 *bis*, dossier 1.

But he successfully made the trip with the hospitality he found along his route. Ordinarily requests for charity might receive grudging replies, but Mehdi found that no one refused him food and shelter when he told them he was en route for Mecca, a destination that redoubled the injunction of hospitality for the *ibn al-sabīl* (the "son of the road," or traveler deserving of charity). Such hospitality produced something of a rough infrastructure for landed Hajj travel in the absence of state support (indeed one that was inimical to the interests of the state), marking a significant shift in the state-centered patronage system that had sustained overland Hajj travel since the beginning of Islam. Rather than finding refuge and security in an Abbasid hostel or a Mamlūk escort, Medhi found both in the hospitality offered by Muslims along the way. In such acts of generosity toward the "clandestine" overland pilgrim, Muslims overcame social cleavages and affirmed their solidarity in opposition to the state (thus giving colonial North Africa a different dynamic than that found between Bedouins and the Ottoman state in Arabia, where hospitality would be withheld from state-sponsored pilgrims). Moreover, even if the territorial integrity of the lands of Islam had been compromised by colonialism, hospitality partially constituted the Umma through the concrete performance of the Islamic ideal of social unity.[101] If being poor had always transformed the experience of being a pilgrim – making it more difficult and precarious – in this period being a pilgrim transformed the experience of being poor and upended everyday social relationships with the inversed order imposed by the sacred. This non-state infrastructure proved every bit as secure and safe as the famous early Hajj roads. For example, an Algerian named Hamida ben Slimane Helal made it back safely from an overland Hajj that he made when he was in his seventies, and another Algerian, a blind man named Mohamed ben Ali Yousfi made it to the Hijaz and back by various clandestine routes having only a young son as his escort.[102] Once the Hajj was complete, the calculus of visibility vis-à-vis the French state changed, and it became advantageous to reenter the networks controlled by the state. This was done by going to the French consulate in Jeddah, seeking food, medical care, and most of all a steamship ticket home. In February 1904, the year prior to Mehdi's pilgrimage, 1,000 destitute

[101] E. Durkheim, *The Elementary Forms of Religious Life,* tr. Karen E. Fields (New York: Free Press, 1995), 425.

[102] Helal: "Renseignements individuels," n.d. Yousfi: Préfet de Constantine to Affaires Indigènes Alger, May 31, 1906, no. 281. Both in Archives nationales d'Outre Mer, 10G41.

Algerians and Tunisians presented themselves to the consulate.[103] Diplomats tried to respond favorably to these requests, inasmuch as the humanitarian crisis on their doorstep represented a potential public relations disaster. (Medhi himself avoided this route by assuming the identity of an Algerian who had died in the Hijaz, and he returned home with the dead man's ticket.)

In the last years of colonial rule, the French brought these overland Hajj routes under state control by supporting bus travel. After the Second World War, shipping was tight and pilgrims in France's African colonies competed fiercely for the limited number of seats available for the official boats. To get around the shipping bottleneck, some proposed traveling in their own automobiles to take advantage of improved overland roads that came to link all of North Africa in the interwar years, such as the *strada litoranea* built by Mussolini across Libya.[104] After the war, there was no longer any legal reason to prevent such undertakings with the end of the indigenous codes that restricted travel for Muslims, but French authorities denied them on the grounds of safety, a decision that was supported by Saudi reluctance to see travelers from around the world descend on Mecca in private cars.[105] Commercial buses offered an alternative that was cheap and required little oversight in this era when the colonial state drew back from the heavy regulations it had imposed in 1894. Moreover, the bus was fast (the trip from Oran in western Algeria to Suez in Egypt could be made in nine days) and relatively comfortable. As one advertising brochure put it, Hajj travel by bus became a "pious promenade."[106] The volume and modest costs of bus travel made the Hajj available to a wide segment of colonial society. In particular, women enjoyed unprecedented access to the Hajj. Previously, they had been blocked from the Hajj by the individuating effects of colonial maritime travel. When families could only select one or two from their ranks to put forth as candidates, the decisions did not go favorably for mothers, daughters, sisters, and wives. Moreover, French authorities accorded few places on ships to women because they

103 Consul de France Djeddah to Résident Général Tunis, February 3, 1904, no. 1. Archives nationales de Tunisie, Série A, carton 276 *bis*, dossier 1.

104 Sous-Préfet de Tlemcen to Préfet d'Oran, August 20, 1948, no. 1879. Request of Si Moulay Ali of Zawiya Taïba in Nedroma. Centre des archives nationales d'Algérie IBA/CUL-048.

105 *Umm al-Qurā* no. 1215, June 18, 1948. Centre des archives nationales d'Algérie IBA/CUL-048.

106 Brochure "Pèlerinage à La Mecque" Centre des archives nationales d'Algérie Terr Sud, 0908.

viewed them as politically unimportant.[107] To give an idea of the new possibilities for women with busses: whereas there were only 61 women among the 958 pilgrims on the 1932 sailing of the *Floria* from North Africa to Jeddah,[108] in 1952 a bus reserved for thirty women was designated within a single, ten-bus convoy leaving from the Algerian Sahara, a case that was repeated widely across North Africa that year.[109]

CONCLUSION

Decolonization brought a series of changes to overland Hajj travel from places like Africa and the Middle East. In particular, the newly formed nation states established more robust controls of their borders, making overland travel to Mecca difficult. A dramatic precedent came during the Algerian War (1954–1962) when the French army sealed Algeria's borders with barbed wire and mine fields, and an analogous process closed borders further east in the wake of the Israeli-Arab wars. Equally prohibitive was state control of labor markets: policed by visas and work permits, the odd jobs that had sustained poor pilgrims in the past disappeared, and those without papers faced deportation. Nevertheless, postcolonial pilgrims continued to make their way by land to the holy sites. The most important examples in this era are people from west and central Africa who traveled along the Sahara's southern edge to the Red Sea. In the 1970s, some 8,500 aspiring pilgrims a year made their way by truck, camel, donkey, and on foot through Chad and Sudan.[110] Most were Hausa- and Fula-speaking people from Nigeria; they worked as seasonal laborers in Sudan's cotton farms or lived off charity in the cities. Economically, this method of travel worked well for poor people. They could depart with little to no savings and work their way across Africa, arriving in Mecca sooner than if they had tried to earn enough money at home to purchase an airline ticket.[111] Moreover, such travel could be

[107] IBA to M. Aït Ali, membre Assemblé financière de l'Algérie et M. Lechani, Conseil Général (Tizi Ouzou), September 30, 1947. Centre des archives nationales d'Algérie, IBA/CUL-047.

[108] Soubrillard, "Pèlerinage à La Mecque," June 15, 1932. Archives nationales d'Outre Mer, 16H116.

[109] Office de transport aérien to GGA 25 avril 1952. Centre des archives nationales d'Algérie Terr Sud 0908.

[110] J. S. Birks, *Across the Savannas to Mecca: The Overland Pilgrimage Route from West Africa* (London: Hurst, 1978), xii.

[111] Birks, *Across the Savannas*, 133.

done by the entire household, offsetting the individuating effects of air travel and ensuring that everyone had the opportunity to fulfill his or her Hajj obligation. This form of travel presented social risks, however. Most important was the risk that one would put down roots along the way. To prevent this, pilgrims held tenaciously to the ideal of returning home and nurtured it by maintaining "an extended state of liminality" en route.[112] They lived apart from locals in improvised shantytowns that signified a transitory status, and they shunned state education fearing their children might become acculturated to Sudanese society. On average, the round trip overland itinerary took about a decade.[113] However, for some the journey lasted a lifetime. Debts and other obstacles slowed the return, and they became what one scholar has called "permanent pilgrims."[114]

Of the five pillars of Islam, arguably it is the Hajj that most directly engages the political field. It places people in motion across political frontiers prompting questions about sovereignty; it comprises the infrastructure of trade and communication; and it has disseminated politically dangerous things ranging from ideas to germs. Finally, the Hajj is an occasion when rulers can showcase their efficiency, power, and social conscience and thereby nourish their earthly power from the great well of political capital offered by religion. All of these practices and concepts have changed over time. Contemporary conceptions of sovereignty and legitimacy and their relationships to the religious field are much different than they were in the early period of Islam, and this has impacted the journey to Mecca. The various stages of overland travel surveyed here sketches some of these changes by drawing attention to a process whereby states have used the Hajj routes to make claims on populations and territory and to project a positive image of themselves. In the first thousand years of the pilgrimage, caravans received the generous attention of the state eager to claim the political rewards of piety. This did not always have strictly hegemonic effects, however, as the history of women and patronage of the landed routes shows. Pilgrims themselves also found the land to be a favorable element in which to make their journey, relying on the inherent chronometric qualities of the solid earth (i.e., the predictable relationship between time and space) to ensure an on-time arrival. In the last two hundred years, this relationship changed, and overland travel

112 C. Bawa Yamba, *Permanent Pilgrims: The Role of Pilgrimage in the Lives of West African Muslims in Sudan* (Washington, DC: Smithsonian Institution Press, 1995), 2 and 86.

113 Birks, *Across the Savannas*, 68.

114 Yamba, *Permanent Pilgrims*.

became the realm of the politically and socially marginalized. States viewed such pilgrims with varying degrees of indifference and hostility and found that their ongoing efforts to intensify central power through the pilgrimage were best served by modern transports that exploited the sea and air.

6

The Hajj by Sea

Eric Tagliacozzo

The pilgrimage to Mecca took place on a sustained basis by land for many centuries after the time of Muhammad. This was especially so from the predominantly Arabic-speaking polities ringing the Arabian Peninsula, and stretching from Egypt and the Levant to Iraq. Yet hajjis also came in large numbers by sea, and as the centuries wore on a larger and larger percentage of religious travelers made their way to the Hijaz in this way. As we will see, by the late nineteenth and early twentieth centuries, fully half of all pilgrims en route to the holy cities of Mecca and Medina in any particular year might be coming from very distant places, and almost certainly by sea in these cases. Maritime travel was cheaper and more routinized; vast numbers of hajjis could be fit into the holds and onto the decks of vessels, especially after the steam revolution that culminated in the opening of the Suez Canal in 1869. Although the business of the pilgrimage to Mecca has been analyzed to some extent in historiographical literature about the Hajj, an analysis of the purely maritime dimensions of this historical transit has not yet been attempted.[1] We can only make a beginning toward that goal here, but it is safe to say that over time the pilgrimage to Mecca gradually became more and more of an oceanic venture, and remained thus into the middle decades of the twentieth century. It was only after this point that the Hajj began to metamorphose into new directions, whereby pilgrims began to voyage more by air than by sea, as Chapter 7 in this volume describes in some detail.

[1] See M. Miller, "Pilgrims' Progress: The Business of the Hajj," *Past and Present*, 191 (2006): 189–228.

The present chapter outlines the process of traveling by sea on the Hajj in three inter-connected parts. The first part looks at the long, outstretched coast of the Maghrib to Egypt, and travels furthest back in time, nearly one thousand years to the early second millennium CE, to show the organized beginnings of maritime Hajj transit. This section of the chapter also looks at East African and Ottoman maritime transport in the times leading up to and including the Early Modern era. The second section switches our focus to the Indian subcontinent, and examines how the Mughals directed a new volume of pilgrims toward the Hijaz, though they did so with new constraints imposed by European shipping and naval presences in the Indian Ocean. By the nineteenth and early twentieth centuries, however, Western shipping companies were helping, not hindering, the South Asian Hajj, as it became big business to move believers from the shores of the subcontinent across the Arabian Sea to the Hijaz. Finally, the third part looks at pilgrims coming from Southeast Asia to the Middle East, the most distant part of the *dār al-Islām* to send hajjis in large numbers. Although the areas that are now Malaysia and Indonesia (and scattered other parts of Southeast Asia) were the furthest Muslim-majority landscapes from the holy cities, by the fin-de-siècle period they were sending enormous numbers of Muslims to the cities of the Red Sea. Here again, as in the South Asian case, the colonial project had an ambivalent relationship with the Hajj. The pilgrimage to Mecca existed to be profited on, to be sure, but it was also often seen as a dangerous exercise in subaltern mobility, for reasons that will be made clear shortly.

THE MEDITERRANEAN AND EAST AFRICA TO THE OTTOMAN WORLD

It is clear from some of the earliest records we possess that the pilgrimage went by sea from a very early date. That this should be so in the Mediterranean should not surprise us, as this sea was relatively shallow and protected, compared to the open ocean. Still, Muslims who had designs upon performing the Hajj often had to choose how to do this, and some difficult realities presented themselves. Perhaps first among these permutations was the fact that the best-quality ships were often not in Muslim hands but rather were owned and crewed by Christians. In the western half of the Mediterranean, across the coasts of the Maghrib, many Muslims took vessels originally hailing from the Italian city-states. These ports and polities, such as Genoa, were the masters of much seaborne trade in this encircled sea, and in the first few centuries of the second millennium CE, they would have been the dominant carriers. Pilgrims from what is now Libya, Tunisia, and Algeria would have often come east across the lower stretches of the Mediterranean on these ships. In Alexandria, they likely would have docked themselves and their attendant cargoes, and then transferred to land-based caravans. These caravans would then assemble in large numbers in Cairo, and begin the journey further east and south to the holy cities.[2]

We know of the voyages of a few pilgrims in some detail. One of these men was Ibn Jubayr, a Moroccan hajji who set out from Ceuta and traveled by ship all the way to Alexandria. Like many Maghribi pilgrims, he took a Genoese ship, likely feeling it was safer from piratical attacks than indigenous Muslim ships from his own coasts. Ibn Jubayr was not impressed with many of the Muslims he met along the way on his trip, especially in some of the coastal pearling stations in Egypt; he felt these people were more animals than men, and he said so in his recorded travels. Yet some of this dyspeptic sentiment was likely colored by the kinds of receptions that pilgrims received as they made their way from North Africa all the way across the top of the continent, and down toward the Red Sea. Shippers and traders constantly extorted the would-be hajjis, fleecing them at every opportunity because they knew these travelers were so far away from home. Ibn Jubayr's descriptions of his voyage (he left Morocco in 1183 CE) give us a fairly good idea what these pilgrimage/shipping conditions would have been like, from one end of North Africa to the other. Attempting a journey such as this one, to link the ships of the Mediterranean with the caravans of Egypt (which then often made the last leg to the Hijaz), was no easy thing and was difficult to navigate for travelers even in the best of times.[3]

By the time pilgrims reached the Red Sea, many of these travelers were not in great shape. They had to possess firm constitutions, however, as the reputation of Red Sea pilgrim-brokers and carriers meant that they would have even more difficulties here than in the Mediterranean. The short hop across the northern half of the Red Sea was controlled by ship owners and brokers who made a living on getting as much as they could out of the pilgrim trade. This was so even though much of the grain that was transported from Egypt to the Hijaz, primarily for charitable purposes during the Hajj season, was actually donated, and was not coming for a

[2] P. Masson, *Histoire du commerce français dans le Levant au XVIIIè siècle* (Paris: Hachette & cie., 1911), 401.

[3] R. C. Broadhurst (tr.), *The Travels of Ibn Jubayr* (London: J. Cape, 1952), 64.

FIGURE 6 Engraved illustration of a Jeddah seascape, 1890s

business profit. This meant that the locus of searching for profit in these transactions had to shift onto the passage of the pilgrims themselves, who often took ship alongside all of that grain. Storms and hidden reefs were common in the Red Sea as well, so the practice of getting across this thin ribbon of water was almost more trouble than it was worth. At least in Ibn Jubayr's time, however (the twelfth century), crossing over the Sinai to attempt the pilgrimage by caravan via Aqaba was very difficult. There was a Christian military fortification nearby which closed the roads. Only in the seventeenth century do we know that Egyptian caravans could cross at this point, bypassing the graft and avarice of the Red Sea shipping network, as well as seasonal storms, and other maritime dangers.[4]

The Red Sea spilled out into the Arabian Sea; here the dynamics were markedly different in some respects than in the Mediterranean. The Ottomans, who had a marked naval presence in the eastern half of the Mediterranean, were much less able to project force in the approaches to the Western Indian Ocean. In the mid- to later sixteenth century, an

[4] S. Faroqhi, "Trade Controls, Provisioning Policies and Donations: The Egypt-Hijaz Connection in the Second Half of the Sixteenth Century," in H. İnalcik and C. Kafadar, (eds.), *Suleyman the Second* (Istanbul: The Isis Press, 1993): 141–143.

attempt had been made by Selim II (r. 1566–1574) to galvanize this presence, and there had even been plans on the drawing board to construct a Suez link between the two seas, primarily for the benefit of hajjis passing through. This was shelved because of the expense and seriousness of the naval wars against Venice, which left something of a political void in terms of pilgrim protection in the Arabian Sea. The Portuguese, new to the area in the sixteenth century but vigorously expanding their project east and south across the Indian Ocean, stepped (or more accurately, sailed) into this space. These mariners already had an idea of how they felt about Muslim shipping, one inherited from the religious wars of the Mediterranean. The *cartaz* system was gradually enacted, requiring vessels to possess a "passport" of sorts that allowed them free travel on the seas, under Portuguese guns. This of course destabilized and impacted the regularity of the pilgrim shipping trade in the Arabian Sea, although the Portuguese never had enough ships to be as dominant as they wished to be in this maritime arena.[5]

To the south of the Arabian Sea, the long outstretched coasts of East Africa also sent pilgrims. This part of Africa had been converted to Islam for quite some time; we know that Muslim ships had sailed south and that sailors from these ships had inter-married with Bantu East African women for at least a thousand years before our own time. The coast of "Zanj," as it came to be known, sent a steady trickle of pilgrims from what is modern-day Mozambique, Tanzania, Kenya, and Somalia up and into the Red Sea corridor. Coralite trading towns were built on the strand; the sultans of these towns and their elites inter-married with clans from the Middle East, particularly from Oman. Eventually, Hadrami wanderers came in the opposite direction, seeding the port towns of the coast. The Islam that came to dominate nearly the entirety of the East African coast was a mixture of the canonical faith and local custom, but "Swahili" came to be a term denoting both the language of this culture area (across at least four modern nation-states), and also a syncretic, mixed-race population, with its own customs and traditions. The cadence of the Swahili coasts was really more toward the Indian Ocean and the Middle East than it was geared toward its own interior in some ways, though the latter orientation was indeed important in the acquisition of ivory, gold, and slaves, in particular. But in terms of Islam generally, and the Hajj in particular, the coasts of East Africa were very much a part of this early maritime world of the Hajj. Africans would have stood side by side in the mosques

[5] S. Faroqhi, *Pilgrims and Sultans: The Hajj under the Ottomans 1517 to 1683* (London: I. B. Tauris, 1994), 133.

of the Hijaz with travelers from further east and west, and felt themselves to be very much a part of this community.[6]

Further to the west, the Arabian Sea stretched toward India. We will examine the engines and impulses of the Hajj by sea for this part of the dar al-Islam in more detail in a moment, but here suffice it to say that the Hijaz beckoned pilgrims from this part of the world, too. The Mughals saw the Ottomans as cousins, but also as competitors to a degree; this seems true from the earliest rulers of the South Asian dynasty. The emperor Akbar established a place for hajjis from his domains to stay in Mecca, but he also let it be known that his treasury would support indigent pilgrims from his lands who wished to perform the Hajj before they died. Both of these actions required a considerable amount of wealth, but also a seriousness of purpose as an act of state and of political patronage at the same time. And Akbar did not stop there. He also sent a number of high-status women from his court to perform long pilgrimages, whereby two of this company stayed in Arabia for a period of years, only returning to India in 1582 after a long residence in the Hijaz. Akbar had to negotiate their return passage with the Portuguese via the *cartaz* system, but it is notable that not only imperial favorites and those in circles of patronage went on these trips. Paradoxically, political rebels against the Mughal court also found their way to the holy cities, and used the Hijaz as a place of refuge from the wrath and vengeance of the Mughal court. This practice, too, stretched back to very early Mughal times, even to the personage of Akbar's disgraced uncle Kamran, who had his eyes put out by Akbar's father after a botched revolt. All of these Mughal pilgrims – both those protected, and those in flight – criss-crossed each other's paths by sea, moving across the Western Indian Ocean in the Early Modern era.[7]

MARITIME WORLDS OF SOUTH ASIA AND THE SUBCONTINENT

The Indian example is very important in analyzing a maritime history of the Hajj because vast numbers of the globe's maritime pilgrims did indeed

[6] See, e.g., T. Insoll, *The Archaeology of Islam in Sub-Saharan Africa* (Cambridge University Press, 2003), also Neville Chittick, *Kilwa: An Islamic Trading City on the East African Coast* (Nairobi: British Institute in Eastern Africa, 1974), and for contemporary sources, G. S. P. Freeman-Grenville, *The East African Coast: Select Documents from the First to the Earlier Nineteenth Century* (Oxford: Clarendon Press, 1962).

[7] Faroqhi, *Pilgrims and Sultans*, 131. Akbar did not go himself, judging it too dangerous to do so.

come from South Asia. We know this from a variety of sources. An anonymous exegesis dating from the late sixteenth century described three to four dozen large vessels coming to Jeddah each year from waters further east, burdened with valuable bulk cargoes, and said that these ships paid enormous custom duties to the local sultans in order to be able to practice their commerce there.[8] In the early seventeenth century, another traveler chronicled the dimensions of these vessels, to give a picture of their size. Ships en route from South Asia carried Hajj aspirants, but also large amounts of goods to pay for their trips, and these vessels were often over 50 meters long and 15 meters wide, with depth-draughts into the sea approaching 10 meters.[9] These were very big vessels, in other words, sea-worthy and capable of oceanic travel. There were large numbers of these outsized ships making the trip to the Red Sea from other port towns in the Indian Ocean as well, including ships weighing between one and two thousand tons, that were absolutely laden down with hajjis, apparently.[10] "The superstitious custom of pilgrimages to Mecca made by those who follow the infamous Koran" encouraged these trips, according to another early modern traveler, "since the ships which sailed to Juda made excellent business profits."[11] The pilgrimage to Mecca and trans-Indian Ocean trade to the subcontinent were connected, therefore. Both the Hajj and regional commerce seem to have depended on each other symbiotically.

In the later decades of the 1600s, another eyewitness traveler wrote about how inter-dependent the Muslim pilgrimage and Indian Ocean trade were becoming. This French chronicler described the working gears of these side-by-side phenomena as they pertained to commerce, politics, and Islam between Mecca and Mughal India:

[8] Anonymous, "A Description of the Yearly Voyage or Pilgrimage of the Mahumitans, Turkes and Moores unto Mecca in Arabia," in R. Hakluyt, *The Principal Navigations*, 12 vols. (Glasgow: J. MacLehose and Sons, 1903–1905), V: 340–365.

[9] See Saris quoted in S. Purchas, *Purchas, His Pilgrimes* (Glasgow: J. MacLehose and Sons, 1905–1907), III: 396.

[10] W. Foster, *Early Travels in India, 1583–1619* (Delhi: S. Chand, 1968), 301–302.

[11] J. Lobo, *The Itinerário of Jerónimo Lobo*, tr. D. M. Lockhart (London: Hakluyt Society, 1984), 89–90. He goes on to describe Jeddah as a city "which has been made so famous in these times in all of the East by the great numbers of ships that go there and the rich trade the merchants find there ... Because of the great wealth of the universal market of people and merchandise carried out in that city, they (the ships) became so famous in India that when people wanted to indicate that something was very costly and valuable they would call it a ship from Mecca."

FIGURE 7 View of the Haram, ca. 1950

"(The Mughal emperor) sends two large vessels there (to Surat), to carry pilgrims, who thus get a free passage. At the time when these vessels are ready to depart, the *fakirs* come down from all parts of India in order to embark. The vessels are laden with good articles of trade which are disposed of at Mecca, and all the profit which is made is given in charity to the poor pilgrims. The principal only is retained and this serves for another year, and this principal is at least 600,000 rupees. It is considered a small matter when only 30 or 40 per cent is made on these goods."[12]

The sheer dimension of these maritime sojourns can once more be spied via early modern sources. In the middle decades of the seventeenth century, a ship from one princely state in India arrived in Yemen with hajjis and trade goods en route to the Red Sea. The volume of commodities was so large (hundreds of individual large packages of trade items) that the bulk cargo had to be transported into Aden via an unused gate, as the urban porticos were not large enough. If this notice can be believed, there were approximately 1,500 hajjis on this one vessel, all of them on their

[12] Tavernier quoted in W. H. Coates, *The Old "Country Trade" of the East Indies* (London: Imray, Laurie, Norie, & Wilson, 1911), 124.

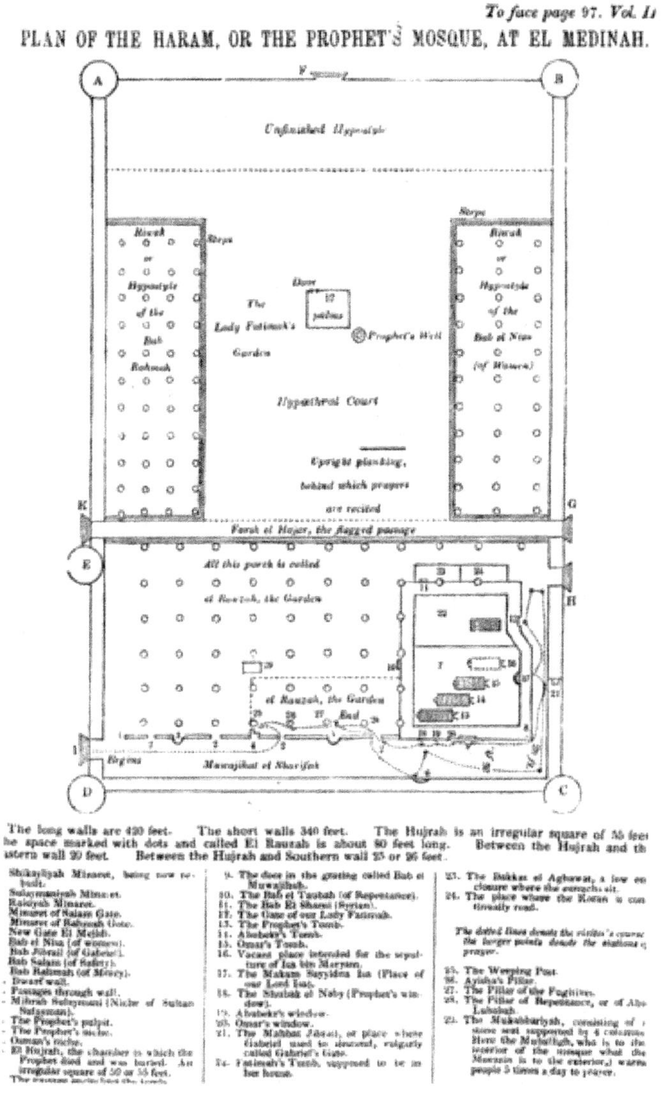

FIGURE 8 Plan of the Prophet's Mosque, Medina, 1857

way to the holy cities.[13] The commodities were to be sold in different cities of the Red Sea to assist in the payment of the trip's costs; this in fact was a normal occurrence on numerous pilgrim vessels in this era. Other craft

[13] Faroqhi, *Pilgrims and Sultans*, 159–160.

coming to Jeddah at roughly this same time, carrying both commodities and pilgrims, had values of 200,000 pounds sterling, while still others weighed in at a quarter of a million rupees.[14] Charitable gift giving, the forging of religious merit, and the social and political credibility of Islamic potentates in their relationships with their own peoples, and with other rulers in the dar al-Islam – all were part of this dialectic.

Through much of the eighteenth century, these patterns of commerce and religiosity between Mughal India and the Hijaz continued. A Danish traveler named Niebuhr commented in 1763 that Jeddah in fact connected the larger trade of India and Egypt, each of these places to the east and west of the Hijaz, respectively, precisely through the dynamics of the Hajj, and its attendant commerce. Fine shawls from Kashmir, and also coarser cloth from Gujarat and Bengal formed the majority of the value of the Indian trade goods, while Egypt sent twenty ships annually, some of these being 200–500 tons in girth, but a few of them weighing in much more ponderously at 1,000 or even 1,500 tons.[15] A French traveler named Modave, who was also observing these patterns at around this same time, stated that some of the Indian cloth traded during the Hajj wound its way even to Ottoman Turkey, via merchants who had caravans of up to 50,000 camels at one time making the trip.[16] It was clear to both the Dane and the Frenchman that the pilgrimage to Mecca by sea from Mughal territories was helped by this commerce, and in fact depended upon it. Only by the late eighteenth century did these regional patterns of trade and commerce begin to diminish, and the intertwined nature of the Hajj and regional shipping turn in new directions.

The nineteenth century saw still different factors come to the fore in the moving of pilgrims from the Indian subcontinent to the Red Sea. For much of the first two-thirds of the century, the falling off of trade described in the preceding paragraph meant that hajjis had a more difficult time moving between these two places. Ships were not as frequent as they had been prior to this time. In 1869, however, with the opening of the Suez Canal, all of this would change. Commerce picked up exponentially, and the trade in many items – among them cloth, wheat, rice, and other bulk goods – meant that more vessels were moving along this corridor of water

[14] Foster, *Early Travels*, 301–302; and M. N. Pearson, *Pious Passengers: The Hajj in Earlier Times* (Dhaka, Bangladesh: University Press Limited, 1994), 157.

[15] C. Niebuhr, *Travels through Arabia and Other Countries in the East*, tr. R. Heron, 2 vols. (Edinburgh: G. Mudie, 1792), I: 235–236.

[16] Comte de Modave, *Voyage en Inde du Comte de Modave*, 1773–1776, ed. Jean Deloche (Paris: Ecole française d'extrême-orient, 1971), 340–343, 348–350.

in the northern Indian Ocean. Indian firms that were already in the shipping business now diversified their platforms and went into the pilgrim business as well.[17] Crucial to this decision was the fact that, unlike steamship commerce between Suez and Southeast Asia, the stream-powered vessels moving between the Red Sea and the Indian subcontinent did not in fact function along set schedules. Seasonality ruled the transit here. This allowed a subset of Indian Muslim businessmen, primarily in Bombay, to start licensing older steamships for the pilgrim trade, once they were able to get the ships in question certified as seaworthy.[18] A network of brokers numbering in the 300 to 400 range then began to supply these ships with Indian pilgrims.[19] Often these brokers were accused of maximizing their profit on this clientele by "stock-piling" hajjis in Bombay, and keeping them waiting for passage so that they could wring as much money from them as possible while they waited. The British overlords of the city knew about this state of affairs. Yet they also saw in the discontent expressed by these pilgrims some of the anomie and potential disorder that they feared generally in their subject population. The fact that this expressed itself in thousands of (generally poorer) Muslims, cramped into often dismal conditions astride Bombay's port, was not lost on the surveilling anxieties of the colonial state at all.

Both in Bombay and in Calcutta, pilgrim guides (*muṭawwifs*) moved from the ports into the inland basins of Maharashtra and Bengal in search of pilgrims. In this sense, they were the terrestrial arms of processes that primarily acted upon the high seas, in finding generally poor pilgrims in the villages and transporting them to the coastal cities, and then onto ships bound for the Red Sea. The colonial authorities understood the power of these networks on this accordion-like, expanding geography, and eventually began to legislate the ties that bound these areas together. By the Second Bombay Act of 1887, the Pilgrim Department made it a requirement that these *muṭawwifs* have a license so that they could participate in the rounding-up of potential hajjis. Since the vast majority of the pilgrims were of the lower classes, they did not have reserved berths on the ships. They simply decamped wherever they could on the decks, or inside the bellies of the steamers. As such, the price of their tickets was flexible, sometimes rising

[17] W. Ochsenwald, "The Commercial History of the Hijaz Vilayet, 1840–1908," *Arabian Studies*, 6 (1982): 57–76.

[18] O. Takashi, "Friction and Rivalry over Pious Mobility: British Colonial Management of the Hajj and Reaction to It by Indian Muslims," in K. Hidemitsu (ed.), *The Influence of Human Mobility in Muslim Societies* (London: Kegan Paul, 2003), 151–175, especially 155, 163.

[19] Takashi, "Friction and Rivalry," 172.

to 200 rupees but often coming in as low as a twentieth of that, for the most indigent. Many were expected to pay in relation to their perceived station in life, with slightly better off voyagers paying significantly more than the truly poor. This was thought to be in the spirit of the Hajj. But it also meant that the brokers often overloaded the ships in order to get more and more people on board, or their own profits.[20]

Once on ship, these poor Indian pilgrims had a small space in which to put their belongings, basically twenty cubic feet, or about the size of two cotton bales' area per person.[21] That was a very limited space, considering that the hajji-aspirants needed to take with them just about everything that they might need for a journey of several months. And the fact that pilgrim-ship rules separated cargo from passengers aboard ship meant little, as both human and inanimate cargoes traveled together, for the most part. Indian hajjis usually took whatever possessions they could with them, but realistically many had to work, beg, or borrow while on their journeys, just in order to make ends meet. Statistics from the very early twentieth century suggest that anywhere between one-quarter and one-half of all hajjis from this part of the world may have paid nothing (or close to nothing) because of their indigence.[22] Brokers allowed for this, because it burnished their reputations as pious in allowing for nonpaying customers, but also because they competed vigorously for the paying clientele earlier on in the sailing season, when real profits could be made. Lower-class South Asian pilgrims often had to bide their time, though, to get home to the subcontinent, while better-off pilgrims went first. This could extend their stay in the Hijaz in difficult ways, as well as put them at risk, but it also gave them the best shot at getting home without having to pay a fortune to do so. The result of all of these factors, though, meant that the docks in ports such as Jeddah and Aden were often choked with poor Indian travelers waiting long periods of time for an opportunity to return home. This was a feature commented upon by many travelers to the Red Sea in the high colonial period, both Muslim and non-Muslim alike.[23]

[20] See generally the data and arguments put forward in N. Green, *Bombay Islam: The Religious Economy of the Western Indian Ocean, 1840–1915* (Cambridge University Press, 2011) and a forthcoming Phd dissertation by Rishad Choudhury at Cornell University.

[21] W. Ochsenwald, *Religion, Society and the State in Arabia, the Hijaz under Ottoman Control, 1840–1908* (Columbus: Ohio State University Press, 1984), 176.

[22] F. Duguet, *Le Pèlerinage de la Mecque* (Paris: Rieder, 1932), 34–35.

[23] I. Burton, *Arabia, Egypt, India, A Narrative of Travel* (London: W. Mullan and Son, 1879), 101.

A DISTANT HORIZON: PILGRIMS FROM SOUTHEAST ASIA

A last group of pilgrims who traveled primarily by sea to the holy cities came from Southeast Asia. Most of these hajjis were from the lands and seas that are today Indonesia and Malaysia. But significant numbers also came from southern Thailand and the Southern Philippines (where Muslims have been and still are a majority in places), and also from other parts of the region where Muslims form scattered minority populations. A trickle of these pilgrims likely came very early on to the Red Sea corridor, with linguistic evidence pointing to a thirteenth-century provenance for perhaps the first known Southeast Asian pilgrims, though it is indeed conceivable that some may have come earlier.[24] By the sixteenth century, we know for sure that Acehnese Muslims were in the Ottoman court representing the "lands beneath the winds," and that some of these travelers had performed the Hajj either before or after their time in Istanbul. These were diplomatic missions, but religious obligations seem to have been enacted as part of the journeys, and as a result of "being in the neighborhood."[25] A century later, in the 1600s, we start to get far better records of Southeast Asians winding their way west to Mecca. The Dutch were primarily responsible for these notices, as they began the slow process of taking over parts of the Indonesian archipelago from that time forward. Dutch records of the Hajj and hajjis begin to fill their internal correspondence in this century, telling of pilgrims either traveling to or back from the Hijaz from various scattered parts of the archipelago. Often these notices were neutral in tone. But as time went on, they often become more pointed in expression, suggesting dark or conspiratorial intent from this sort of voyaging.[26]

The VOC (Dutch East India Company) kept these records for nearly two hundred years, from the very start of the seventeenth to the very end of the eighteenth centuries. From these sources we know a good bit about a fairly steady ribbon of pilgrims heading westward across the ocean, though the numbers involved in these early centuries were never too large. By the nineteenth century, however, and particularly in its later decades, the scope of Hajj travel from this part of the world grew exponentially.

[24] R. M. Feener and M. Laffan, "Sufi Scents across the Indian Ocean: Yemeni Hagiography and the Earliest History of Southeast Asian Islam," *Archipel*, 70 (2005): 185–208.

[25] See A. Reid, "Sixteenth Century Turkish Influence in Western Indonesia," *Journal of South East Asian History*, 10, 3 (1969): 395–414.

[26] See some of the Dutch VOC-period sources laid out in E. Tagliacozzo, *The Longest Journey: Southeast Asians and the Pilgrimage to Mecca* (New York: Oxford University Press, 2013), ch. 1.

FIGURE 9 Drawing of pilgrims returning home on a Lloyd's steamer, 1876

After the opening of Suez Canal, as in the South Asia case, the sheer volume of pilgrims undertaking this trip was never even remotely the same. We know something of the costs of these voyages, which the Dutch carefully tabulated and which show us how much a trip by sea actually cost for an Indies hajji in the 1870s including, for example, a travel pass, paperwork, and the actual passage of the ship at sea.[27] We also know that pilgrims from the British dominions of Southeast Asia, just to the north of the Dutch East Indies, often traveled south to make money for their own pilgrimages, accumulating capital in order to pay for their own steamship fares across the Indian Ocean.[28] The Hajj traffic was linked across borders in this part of the world, in other words. Steamers called at ports-of-call both in the Dutch Indies and in British Malaya, before making for the open ocean to cross the vast spaces of the sea toward the Hijaz to the west. Shipping statistics from Southeast Asia were often tabulated together, in fact, in the Hajj recording offices in the Red Sea. There was seen to be a unity to the pilgrims from this part of the world (known as

[27] J. Eisenberger, "Indie en de Bedevaart naar Mekka," unpublished PhD thesis, Leiden University (1928), 32.

[28] See V. Matheson and B. W. Andaya (eds. and trs.), *The Precious Gift, Tuhfat al-Nafis* (Kuala Lumpur: Oxford University Press, 1982).

"*Jawa*") by colonial record keepers in their various inspection stations in the Red Sea.[29]

The Dutch management of the maritime Hajj was a huge endeavor and required the assistance of many kinds of people, doing many different kinds of jobs. Hajjis came from all over the archipelago, and spoke different languages; we know for certain that translation services were part of this project, as linking languages were only coming into being at this time throughout much of the Netherlands Indies.[30] Medical concerns were also a crucial part of the maritime experience, as Indonesian hajjis were on ships for weeks at a time, and crossing huge swaths of ocean where they could not expect to find any sort of help, except through the supplies provided for them by the shipping companies. These supplies were there to stop them from perishing of dehydration and overcrowding, but much more frightening dangers – such as cholera – also lurked in the holds of the ships. Passengers, after all, traveled packed against each other to maximize the profits of the companies and brokers who controlled the colonial Hajj.[31] Regulations were enacted to try to monitor and control these massive movements of people, because in any one year half of the global total of pilgrims to Mecca might indeed be coming by sea from Southeast Asia, despite the comparative distances involved.[32] At the top of the decision-making pyramid were officials who tried to see the entirety of the Hajj from a high vantage, men such as Snouck Hurgronje who wrote about this phenomenon from religious and academic vantages, but also from the point of view of civil servants. They oiled the oceanic wheels of travel, but also had their own feelings about this giant endeavor, which have come to light in their published and unpublished writings.[33]

British control over the Hajj by sea via Southeast Asia took place on a less voluminous scale, but was not less important than the Dutch dealings overall. This was because British ships ended up carrying pilgrims from

[29] See, e.g., "Report on the Quarantine Stations at Camaran for the Year 1891," in Foreign Office 195/1730, app. "A," Public Records Office (PRO), London.

[30] A good overview of this geographic diversity can be found in "De Bedevaart naar Mekka, 1909/1910," *Indische Gids* (1919): 1637.

[31] For period lists of such medical supplies, see, e.g., the *Staatsblad van Nederlandsch-Indie*, #597 (1923).

[32] For just a selection of these regulations, see *Bijblad* #5741 (1902), 5740 ff.; *Bijblad* #7130 (1909), 319 ff.; *Bijblad* #7469 (1911), 444 ff.; *Bijblad* #11689 (1928), 381 ff.; *Staatsblad* #236 (1906), 1 ff.; *Staatsblad* #531 (1912), 1 ff.; *Staatsblad* #15 (1923), 1 ff.; *Staatsblad* #44 (1931), 1 ff.; and *Staatsblad* #554 (1932), 1 ff.

[33] See Tagliacozzo, *The Longest Journey*, ch. 7.

many different colonies in the region, and not just from Malaya, Singapore, and British Burma. The Holt Line and other major British steamship firms made the pilgrim traffic a large part of their business, and local concerns sprang up alongside the major British companies to ferry pilgrims from various parts of British Southeast Asia to Penang and Singapore. These were the two main embarkation ports for travel across the Indian Ocean.[34] Here again, as in the Dutch case, we see how the shipping companies worked both hand-in-hand with the colonial government, but also outside of its wishes, at times. The companies were arms of the colonial state in many ways, but they also continually tried to maximize their profits, and often against British regulations. Because of this, the British colonial governments in both Southeast Asia and the Red Sea continually kept watch on the flood of pilgrims crossing the sea, surveilling both the politics of the pilgrims, and any links (real or imagined) that they might have to various program of "radicalism." They also watched the companies themselves, who often tried to cut corners in order to get as many bodies onto the ships as possible. Disease stalked the British vessels just as it did the Dutch ships, and with the same consequences of literally thousands of pilgrims dying over time from cholera and other maladies.[35]

Yet politics was also heavily present on the British side of the Hajj from the big-picture, geo-political angle of the sea lanes. It was not just an issue of potential colonial insurrections occurring locally in Southeast Asia, in and of itself. In the interwar years, British surveillance on pilgrim ships was constant. Both the Germans and the Japanese tried to convince Asian Muslim populations that Berlin and Tokyo had their interests at heart far more than their Western European colonial masters. The British knew that congregating Muslims by the hundreds on individual ships, and by the thousands in the holy cities in the Hijaz, provided opportunities for all of these subjects to discuss politics. In the waning years of colonialism in Southeast Asia, this became reason enough to closely monitor the maritime traffic between regions, starting in Southeast Asia and finishing in the ports of the Hijaz, where the British

[34] See Colonial Office documents CO/273/396/28656 (July 22, 1913); CO 273/402/26309 (July 30, 1913); CO 273/408/35816 (September 19, 1914); CO 273/418/34307 (September 9, 1914), and CO 273/418/38345 (October 5, 1914), as well as the *Straits Settlements Government Gazettes* for 1867 (#31); 1868 (#12), and 1890 (#7).

[35] For a harrowing period description, see an anonymous letter sent to *The Times of London*, August 17, 1880, 8, which details the periodic spread of disease on board British vessels.

also had consular representation.[36] When indigenous shipping companies began to discuss the idea of transporting their own countrymen to the Middle East, so that the Hajj could be accomplished completely under the aegis of Muslim auspices, this sent out warning signals to colonial regimes across the Straits of Melaka and beyond.[37] And by the eve of the Second World War, these concerns had only multiplied, as the traffic in pilgrims from this part of the world – with dozens of ports and multi-ethnic populations of Muslims from Burma to the distant Philippines – only grew year after year.[38] The transit of Islam across global spaces became more and more an issue for discussion, and one that was mooted not only in Singapore, Rangoon, and Batavia, but all the way back in the Hague and in Whitehall. The onset of the Second World War ended these discussions for a time, but they were eventually continued under other guises once the conflict had ended, and the beginnings of the de-colonization began.

CONCLUSION

The pilgrimage to Mecca was accomplished by sea for centuries, alongside the caravan routes that were the earliest roads to the Hijaz for Muslims wishing to fulfill an obligation of their faith.[39] While caravans – sometimes very large caravans – made their way across the deserts of the Middle East, the sea provided the field for travel by which most non-Arabic-speaking peoples arrived in the holy cities of Islam. This difference, which likely was set into practice very early on in the life of the religion, was an enduring feature of the Hajj throughout the centuries, in fact since the time of Muhammad. It would only be in the middle decades of the twentieth century that this overall paradigm would change. Only then would most religious visitors to Mecca make their way to the Red Sea by airplane, instead of through this bifurcation in surface travel. Yet the sea is still used today by pilgrims to the Hijaz, and it still plays a role in the overall numbers of hajjis showing up to pray in the sacred mosques. The maritime circuits of the present day are the legacies of travel by sail for

[36] See, e.g., India Office Records, British Consul Jeddah to Foreign Office, August 16, 1938, #1800/402/203 in IOR/L/PJ/7/789, and same to same, August 9, 1937, #E4922/201/25.

[37] See India Office Records, British Consul Batavia to Foreign Office, March 14, 1938, #75E in IOR/R/20/B/1454 and same to same, September 21, 1938, #260E, in IOR/R/20/B/1454.

[38] Tagliacozzo, *The Longest Journey*, 193 ff.

[39] For an overview of the early land-based routes and conditions, see F. E. Peters, *The Hajj: Muslim Pilgrimage to Mecca and the Holy Places* (Princeton University Press, 1994).

some thousand-plus years, and then of steam – in far larger numbers – from the mid-nineteenth century onward, to just before our own time. It is not an accident that the Hajj as an institution has such resonances with the sea, as this was by far the most convenient and also the cheapest way to get to the Hijaz for long periods in the life of Islam.[40] These voyages were accomplished first on Muslim-owned ships, and then primarily in European-owned bottoms, before reverting again in modern times to a mix of the two, as pilgrims continue to make their way to Jeddah.

The sea allowed for the pilgrimage to Mecca to take place as part of the global project of modernity, as this project was enacted and evolved in the later nineteenth century. Crucial here was the development of the steamship, a Western invention, but one that was quickly adopted both by Muslim powers and also by Muslim populations. Steamships made the long voyages of the oceans a near certainty, rather than an exercise in carefully calibrating the seasons (amidst dangerous *un*certainty), as had been the case for many centuries. Steamships also routinized Hajj-travel to a degree not known previously, as timetables were drawn up, commerce was scheduled, and religious travel fit itself to the dictates and patterns of the modern age. With the opening of the Suez Canal in 1869, the possibilities of the maritime Hajj simply exploded. Ships came out to the Indian Ocean and across the Afro-Eurasian land bridge in numbers never seen before. Pilgrims climbed aboard these ships, settling themselves amidst the cargoes that were powering a new era of human interaction across the continents. By the early twentieth century, it was normal to have tens of thousands of hajjis criss-crossing each other by sea annually, and by the middle decades of the century, the numbers climbed higher still. Only global conflagrations such as the First World War and the Second World War interrupted these upward trajectories in numbers. The Hajj became profoundly maritime in nature over these decades, and only relinquished this role in the later years of the twentieth century, when air travel (like steam travel before it) became routinized and more affordable to the masses. This would set in motion a new epoch in the history of the Hajj.

40 For the costs involved, see Miller, "Pilgrims' Progress," 189–228.

7

The Hajj by Air

Robert R. Bianchi

The current system of global Hajj management is breaking down under the combined pressures of glaring problems that have accumulated over many decades. The list of dangers and injustices is daunting – constant overcrowding, deadly stampedes, corruption, commercialization, favoritism, monopoly, political manipulation, human trafficking, pandemics, sectarian discrimination, environmental degradation, and bickering over who is to blame for the flood of protests and lawsuits in nearly every country.

Ironically, the crisis of the Hajj stems from the stunning successes of post-colonial Muslim societies in spreading economic development, technology, and political empowerment to more than a billion people. After all, the Hajj's explosive growth would have been impossible without the benefits of inexpensive air travel, disposable income, and elected governments responding to the demands of pious voters in thousands of small towns and villages throughout Asia and Africa.[1]

In view of their proven ability to mobilize such impressive resources, there is every reason to believe that Muslims can also reform the Hajj. In that case, they can turn their troubles into opportunities to demonstrate and institutionalize the ideals that Islamic pilgrimage has always sought to embody – egalitarianism, justice, and universal community. But reform requires that the leaders and citizens of the largest Islamic societies devise new methods of power sharing – both globally and locally – to accommodate the rival claims of states, interest groups, and ordinary voters that are indispensible to any workable solution.

[1] R. R. Bianchi, *Islamic Globalization: Pilgrimage, Capitalism, Democracy, and Diplomacy* (Singapore and London: World Scientific Publishers, 2013).

FIGURE 10 Hajj Terminal, Jeddah Airport, 2006

THE HAJJ GOES AIRBORNE

Jumbo jets and charter flights have revolutionized the Hajj. In just a few decades, the global diffusion of affordable air travel triggered dramatic changes in the size, composition, and organization of the pilgrimage. The number of overseas hajjis going to Mecca every year jumped rapidly from about 150,000 in the 1950s and 300,000 in the 1960s to 700,000 in the 1970s and 900,000 in the 1980s. By 1995, their number regularly exceeded one million, and throughout the twenty-first century it has climbed steadily to roughly 1.8 million.[2]

The explosion in the number of pilgrims was accompanied by a profound shift in their means of transportation. At the end of the Second World War, more than 80 percent of overseas hajjis arrived by sea, 10 percent by land,

[2] R. R. Bianchi, *Guests of God: Pilgrimage and Politics in the Islamic World* (New York: Oxford University Press, 2004), 49–55, 275, 300; Ministry of Hajj, Kingdom of Saudi Arabia, *Hajj and Umrah Statistics*, 2010; Sabir Shah, "Number of Foreign Hajis Grows by 2,824 Percent in 92 Years," *The News* (Pakistan), October 25, 2012.

and just 7 percent by air. As newly independent Muslim states supported pilgrimage with subsidized fares on national airlines, charter jets quickly took over the lion's share of the business. In the 1970s, air travel accounted for about one-half of all pilgrims compared to 30 percent for land transport and 20 percent for sea travel. Today, a handful of public and commercial airlines monopolize Hajj travel in nearly every country, and several governments have tried to prohibit pilgrimage by land and sea altogether.[3]

Even more stunning changes have occurred in hajjis' national and demographic backgrounds. What was once a semi-regional affair, dominated by men from Arabic-speaking countries, has become a truly global conclave reflecting the diversity and universal aspirations of the Islamic community as a whole. The majority of hajjis now come from the most populous non-Arab countries of the Middle East, South Asia, Southeast Asia, and West Africa. Each year, larger and larger contingents also arrive from Europe, North America, the Caribbean, Russia, Central Asia, and even China.[4]

With the growing prevalence of air travel, distance from Mecca steadily declined as an obstacle to pilgrimage. By the 1980s, it had virtually disappeared as a predictor of national rates of Hajj participation, overtaken by per capita income and other measures of economic development. Today, the major barriers to pilgrimage are man-made rather than natural – they stem from economic inequalities and bureaucratic inefficiencies instead of from mere geography.

Since the 1980s, each nation has been allotted a pilgrimage quota in which the number of hajjis is pegged to the size of the population. The current ratio permits every country to send 1,000 hajjis for each one million people enumerated in its national census. This formula guarantees that non-Arabs, who comprise about 80 percent of all Muslims, will also make up around 80 percent of every year's pilgrims. For example, more than 200,000 hajjis are sent regularly by Indonesia; followed by about 180,000 from Pakistan; 170,000 from India; 120,000 from Bangladesh; 95,000 from Nigeria; 75,000 from Iran and Egypt; and 70,000 from Turkey. These eight countries alone routinely account for about 60 percent of all overseas pilgrims and only one of them is part of the Arabic-speaking world.[5]

[3] Bianchi, *Guests of God*, 64–68, 275.

[4] R. R. Bianchi, "Hajj," in *The Encyclopedia of Global Human Migration*, ed. I. Ness and P. Bellwood (New York: Wiley, 2013); Bianchi, *Guests of God*, 55–64, 275–280.

[5] Current data and information on Hajj activity are available on the websites of the pilgrimage agencies of most countries with large Muslim populations.

The growing prominence of women hajjis is an equally impressive transformation. Before the age of air travel, female pilgrims accounted for only 30 to 35 percent of the total. Today, women comprise about 45 percent of all overseas hajjis, and in several countries they form the majority year after year. Southeast Asia was the first region where female pilgrims predominated. Indonesia, Singapore, and Malaysia led the way as early as the 1960s. Elsewhere, women majorities arose in important regions such as northeastern Pakistan, western Turkey, and southwestern Nigeria.[6] Turkey is a particularly striking example of female pilgrimage beginning as a regional trend and then quickly developing into a nationwide pattern. Twenty years ago, women majorities were limited to the Aegean and Marmara provinces in the far west. Today, female pilgrims are the majority in virtually every Turkish province except for the depressed Kurdish areas in the southeast.[7]

Women's pilgrimage flourishes in some specific environments, particularly in newly prosperous provincial capitals and towns marked by rising female literacy transmitted through popular Qur'an courses and Islamic schools for girls. Conservative townsfolk enjoying greater prosperity are often eager to send their daughters and wives to religious schools that serve as gateways to social and geographic mobility, including eventual participation in the Hajj. Furthermore, local politicians do their best to make sure that the ruling parties give generous subsidies to both the women's schools and their pilgrimages. And, as stricter Hajj quotas limit Muslims to a single Hajj in their lifetimes, pilgrimage officials encourage more "family-style" Hajjs that include mothers, wives, sisters, and daughters.[8]

Similar changes have occurred in the ages, educational levels, and occupations of hajjis from all countries. Average ages of both male and female pilgrims have fallen by five to ten years. Educational levels have risen to include greater numbers of secondary school graduates and university attendees. The proportion of civil servants and housewives have fallen in favor of private sector workers, professionals, and the self-employed. The trends toward younger, more female, and better-educated

[6] R. R. Bianchi, "Hajj, Women's Patronage of: Contemporary Practice," in *The Oxford Encyclopedia of Islam and Women*, ed. Natana Delong-Bas (New York: Oxford University Press, 2013).

[7] Türkiye İstatistik Kurumu, *Kültür İstatistikleri*, Ankara, 2009 and 2011.

[8] "Ailece hacca Diyanet'ten teşvik" (Directorate of Religious Affairs Encourages Family-Style Hajj), *samanyoluhaber*, July 10, 2006; E. Günlü and F. Okumuş, "The Hajj: Experience of Turkish Female Pilgrims," in N. Scott and J. Jafari (eds.), *Tourism in the Muslim World* (Bingley, UK: Emerald, 2010), 221–234.

hajjis reflect a thriving global Muslim citizenry that is more urban, mobile, and prosperous than ever.[9]

REGULATORY FAILURES AND POLITICAL MOTIVES

Air travel also paved the way for all-embracing government regulation of the Hajj from start to finish – and that, in turn, opened the door to countless controversies over alleged corruption and favoritism in every aspect of pilgrimage management. A lucrative and centrally controlled Hajj business provided enormous incentives for all groups to grab a share of the soaring profits and patronage in every country with a sizable Muslim population. The competition usually started with partitioning the national travel markets between state airlines and private carriers who relied on strong political connections both domestically and internationally.[10] The resulting cartels were exposed to constant criticism and renegotiation because they commonly drifted toward monopoly and collusion in setting fares and schedules.

Even when there was an effort to include both private- and public-sector firms, the most profitable terms usually went to a select group of private companies and travel agents while the biggest operating losses were absorbed by the state treasury. Politicians and Hajj managers frequently sought to lure voters with discounted ticket prices and to reward favored businesses with guaranteed profits. The formula was effective in building electoral and bureaucratic coalitions, but disastrous for public finances that were already struggling in most cases.

Controlling international air travel was just the tip of the iceberg for powerful Hajj bureaucracies that sprang up in one country after another. Before long, they ruled over a vast array of services and transactions, awarding multimillion dollar contracts and supervising huge investment funds generated by the prepaid deposits of prospective hajjis who enrolled years in advance, hoping to secure a coveted place in the ever-growing waiting lists. Recurrent scandals and regulatory lapses have drawn intense public scrutiny to all aspects of Hajj affairs, particularly when it appears that a universal religious duty is being exploited for private gain. Throughout the Islamic world, debates over Hajj policy have become one of the hottest arenas of interest group competition and diplomatic conflict.

[9] Bianchi, *Guests of God*, 162–163, 194–196.

[10] "Hajj Operations: Private Airlines Eye Larger Share," *Express Tribune* (Pakistan), October 6, 2011.

As the number of contestants in these debates proliferates, they press their demands and grievances on a wider variety of battlefields. When the quota system was proposed in the 1980s, the issue initially pitted Saudi Arabia against Iran, which was flooding Mecca with pilgrims and encouraging them to lead political demonstrators. Before long, however, the Saudis were haggling with every country that claimed to accept restricted access in principle while resisting any limits on their own contingents. Saudi Arabia has administered the quotas differently every year, carving out exceptions and temporary bonuses as they pleased and retracting them with equal abruptness.

Allocating Hajj quotas and services domestically generates even greater frictions. Each country's Hajj management is embedded in a forest of red tape running through dozens of government agencies with special powers over religion, transport, visas, health, security, education, finance, procurement, lodging, welfare, communications, and much more. These turf wars are never ending, especially when political and commercial rivals intervene to tip the balance in favor of their clients and pet projects. The newest additions to the fray are a host of citizens' groups and business associations that aggressively campaign to reshape policies on Hajj services and market shares. These groups have made the politics of pilgrimage a staple of the daily news cycle by enlisting mass media, courts, prosecutors, and legislative committees in a steady stream of exposés, trials, and investigations.[11]

These controversies have already produced a number of positive results. Demands for greater transparency and accountability have encouraged far-reaching disclosure of routine Hajj operations in the media and on the Internet. Many countries now offer online registration and payment for prospective pilgrims. Some list the names of applicants, their places in the queue, and the current status of clearance procedures. Often this personal data is broken down by province, county, and neighborhood so that everyone can see exactly how Hajj quotas are distributed geographically.

In many cases, Hajj travel agents must receive government certification and compete for customers through public auctions or lotteries. Public interest groups dedicated to protecting hajjis from fraud provide telephone hotlines to report complaints against state agencies, airlines, and private businesses. Fines, suspensions, and expulsions are regularly imposed and

[11] "Hajj Reporters Set to Monitor 2013 *Umrah* Operation," *People's Daily* (Nigeria), July 18, 2013; "ICPC to Install Free Toll Line for Information on Corruption," *Vanguard* (Nigeria), May 18, 2013; "Group Will Root Out Alleged Hajj Corruption," *Daily News* (South Africa), October 14, 2011.

publicized. Courts are increasingly willing to nullify Hajj regulations and business arrangements that are discriminatory or monopolistic. The more activist judges go so far as to rewrite the relevant codes and supervise drafting committees ordered to overhaul nationwide Hajj regimes.

At times, citizen groups voice criticisms that go far beyond efforts at reform, attacking the existing system at its core. Some human rights organizations have called for the abolition of all quota systems because they view them as violating the freedom to travel, restricting freedom of worship, and obstructing free markets.[12] Demands to abolish state subsidies for pilgrimage – especially discounted airline fares – are reverberating in more and more legislatures and high courts, throwing the future of all Hajj regimes – national and international – into serious doubt.

Meanwhile, Saudi Arabia has undertaken a number of unilateral actions that undermine the legitimacy of its Hajj policies as well as the credibility of national pilgrimage officials who are forced to cooperate in implementing them. Several waves of reconstruction around the holy sites of Mecca have demolished historic landmarks and encircled the Grand Mosque with upscale shopping centers and hotels that are beyond the means of ordinary pilgrims. New highways carrying fleets of tour buses have polluted the city air and threaten the delicate desert environment in nearby valleys. Nonetheless, Saudi authorities continue to ignore the warnings of their own experts and mounting protests from Muslims around the world who regard the holy cities as the common heritage of all humanity instead of the sovereign preserve of a single nation-state.[13]

Saudi Arabia's allocation of national Hajj quotas has always been controversial because of inconsistencies that benefited some countries and penalized others. But in June 2013, the Saudis threw the whole system into disarray. Abruptly announcing a last minute cut of 20 percent in that year's quotas, they forced Hajj officials in every country to turn away thousands of approved applicants who had already paid their expenses – often after waiting several years for permissions and visas.[14]

[12] *İnsan Hakları ve Mazlumlar için Dayanışma Derneği, Hac Raporu* (Human Rights and Victims' Support Association, *Hajj Report*), December 29, 2005.

[13] "Dr. Sami Angawi on Wahhabi Desecration of Makkah: Developers and Purists Erase Mecca's History," *Reuters*, July 12, 2005; "Mecca for the Rich: Islam's Holiest Site 'Turning into Vegas'," *The Independent*, September 24, 2011.

[14] "Haj Prices to Soar after Cut to Makkah Pilgrim Numbers," *Arabian Business*, July 16, 2013; "Haj Quota Cut to Ensure Pilgrims' Comfort: Khaled," *Saudi Gazette*, June 23, 2013.

The backlash was immediate and far ranging. Across the Islamic world, citizens demanded Saudi compensation for the lost monies and exemptions from the draconian limits.[15] The head of the Youth Section of Muhammadiya – one of Indonesia's oldest and largest religious movements – demanded that President Yudhoyono meet personally with Saudi King Abdullah to seek redress.[16] Turkey quickly announced that it would halt new Hajj selection until elderly and long-waiting applicants had their turn, even if it took several years to accomplish.[17] Istanbul city officials even organized a "virtual Hajj" near the Bosporus in sympathy with the 15,000 approved applicants who would not be able to make the real one.[18] In Nigeria, the national pilgrimage board passed the buck to its state affiliates, insisting that local officials should choose which applicants to cut and suffer the political consequences of their decisions.[19]

Many politicians and journalists doubted Saudi Arabia's contention that the cuts were necessary to protect pilgrims' safety while portions of the Great Mosque were being expanded to accommodate larger crowds in the future. They claimed that the Saudis were trying to conceal growing alarm that the sudden outbreak of a deadly SARS-like virus – Middle East Respiratory Syndrome-coronavirus, also known as MERS CoV – threatened to cause a worldwide pandemic if infected hajjis carried it back to their homelands in jam-packed charter flights.[20] Pilgrims' associations in many countries, led by South Africa and Nigeria, urged people to postpone their Hajj indefinitely until health and airline officials could guarantee safe passage, particularly for seniors, children, and pregnant women.[21]

[15] "MoRA to Suffer Rs 930.60m Losses Due to Hajj Quota Cut," *Pakistan Observer*, June 19, 2013; "Indonesia Demands Compensation over Hajj Numbers," *Arabian Business*, June 24, 2013.

[16] "Indonesia Urged to Lobby Saudi Arabia over Hajj Quota," *Antara News*, June 19, 2013; "Government Could Have Done More to Prevent Hajj Cuts, Gerindra Says," *Jakarta Globe*, July 6, 2013.

[17] "Turkey to Cancel Its Hajj Lottery Next Year," *Hürriyet-Daily News*, March 28, 2013; "Hac başvuruları 1 milyonu aştı (Hajj Applicants Exceed 1 Million)," *CNN Türk*, April 25, 2013.

[18] "Turks Find Solace in Virtual Pilgrimage as Saudi Cuts Haj Quotas," *Reuters*, July 18, 2013.

[19] "NAHCON Urges Pilgrims' Boards to Ensure Prudent Distribution of Hajj Seats," *Daily Times*, June 12, 2013; "Kaduna Screens Out All Old-timers," *Daily Trust*, June 26, 2013; "Ogun to Drop Hajj Pilgrims with Health Concerns," *Premium Times*, June 25, 2013.

[20] "As Virus Spreads, Saudi Arabia Restricts Pilgrimage Numbers," *Wall Street Journal*, June 26, 2013: "New Mideast Virus Raises Fears for Hajj," *Radio Free Europe-Radio Liberty*, June 22, 2013.

[21] "Civil Society Urges States to Stop Sponsoring Pilgrims," *Leadership* (Nigeria), June 18, 2013.

The cascading turmoil and outrage heightened long-standing demands for greater internationalization of Hajj management and for shake-ups of national pilgrimage systems. Reform proposals came from all directions. Each country and constituency vented its special grievances and advanced its own policy alternatives. Nevertheless, the common denominator in these protests was clear for all to see – the existing network of Hajj regulation had not merely failed; it had failed so often and so drastically that its flaws were predictable and, in many cases, probably intentional. Among the system's critics, there is a growing consensus that, viewing the problem in conventional terms of market failures or regulatory lapses seems naïve because the underlying causes are political rather than merely economic and administrative.[22] From this perspective, Hajj reforms can only be effective in the wider context of political and social changes that attack the inequalities and biases inherent in the current system, both nationally and globally.

INDONESIA

All eyes are on Indonesia's Hajj because its 200,000-strong contingent is the largest in the world, accounting for more than 10 percent of all overseas pilgrims year in and year out.[23] Whereas Malaysia, Pakistan, and Turkey pioneered early developments in Hajj management in the 1960s and 1970s, Indonesia has grabbed the spotlight in recent decades, primarily due to its heavy investment in air travel and its innovative practice of assembling and dismantling enormous fleets of rented charter jets during each pilgrimage season. In the late 1980s, when the quota system first went into effect, Indonesia could not mobilize enough pilgrims to meet its allotted target. Jakarta regularly donated tens of thousands of unused places to more prosperous neighbors such as Malaysia and Singapore where demand far exceeded the official allocations. However, as soon as

[22] For analyses of the political causes of repeated regulatory failures in financial markets, see V. V. Acharya, T. Cooley, M. Richardson, and I. Walter, *Market Failures and Regulatory Failures: Lessons from Past and Present Financial Crises*, Asian Development Bank Institute, February 2011; D. G. Tarr, *The Political, Regulatory and Market Failures That Caused the U.S. Financial Crisis*, World Bank, May 2010.

[23] Indonesia Direktorat Jenderal Penyelenggaraan Haji dan Umrah, *Data dan statistik Direktorat Jenderal Penyelenggaraan Haji dan Umrah*, Jakarta, 2010; Indonesia Direktorat Jenderal Penyelenggaraan Haji dan Umrah, Data dan statistik Direktorat Jenderal Penyalenggaraan Haji dan Umrah, *Haji dalam angka*, Jakarta, 2009.

Indonesia harnessed the power of tailored chartering, its Hajj contingents soared to the top of the charts and have remained there ever since.

These days, instead of pooling quotas with other Southeast Asian nations, Indonesia vigorously lobbies Saudi Arabia for special exemptions from numerical limits, arguing that its hajjis contribute so much to the Saudi economy that they deserve privileged treatment. When Saudi Arabia imposed the 20 percent cut in 2013, they unwittingly opened a Pandora's box because Indonesians responded with novel demands that challenged the very foundation of the rules that had been in place for nearly thirty years. Jakarta sent a high-level delegation to Saudi Arabia to argue that Hajj quotas should no longer be pegged to population size, but to each country's demand for Hajj travel and its capacity to transport paying customers. They noted that Indonesia's waiting list of deposit-paying applicants had already surpassed the two million mark, meaning that new aspirants would have to wait at least ten years to fulfill a basic religious obligation.[24]

When the Indonesian representatives returned home, they claimed they had extracted a Saudi pledge to increase their country's quota by 60 percent as soon as the current renovations were finished and to consider a fantastic quota of 500,000 within three years.[25] The clear implication was that the bonus would be permanent and that it would open the door for setting quotas according to economic power instead of census results. Other prospering countries would undoubtedly welcome this arrangement, particularly Turkey, where waiting lists also stretch ten years into the future. But less fortunate societies are bound to see the proposal as yet another distortion of a system that claims to strive for fairness and equality.

PAKISTAN

In Pakistan, the state has handed over about half of the Hajj business to private travel agents, and both sectors (state and non-state) regularly offer multi-tiered packages that appeal to middle-income and higher-end consumers. In recent years, this market segmentation has come under attack from dissident businesses that claim they are excluded from competition by collusive practices. Courts in Lahore and Karachi have ruled in favor of the plaintiffs in several high profile cases. In some instances, judges found

[24] "Indonesia Urged to Lobby Saudi Arabia over Hajj Quota," *Antara News*, June 19, 2013.
[25] "Saudi Arabia Pledges to Increase Hajj Quota in 3 Years," *Jakarta Globe*, June 27, 2013.

that Hajj officials regularly violated their own regulations, and a few courts struck down rules that imposed high entry barriers on new applicants offering lower prices. The Lahore High Court ordered Hajj officials to issue new business certificates through open bidding, making it clear that the government could not be trusted to vet candidates impartially.[26]

Unlike Indonesia where an economic boom is fuelling the appetite for greater Hajj spending, the Pakistani press is filled with doubts about the country's ability to afford even current levels of pilgrimage. A retired military officer recently noted that Pakistan is a habitual debtor country that must go with a begging bowl to the International Monetary Fund to cover its annual trade and fiscal deficits. He argued that because debtors are not required to perform the Hajj, Pakistan as a nation should consider foregoing the pilgrimage until its economy improves enough to justify parting with millions of dollars in foreign exchange every year. Why, he asked, should a struggling society give so much of its cash to one of the richest countries in the world? Would it not be more "Islamic" to meet the basic needs of Pakistanis at home instead of violating the well-known principle that no Muslim should make a pilgrimage that imposes hardship on herself or her family?[27]

INDIA

Even though India's Muslims comprise only about 14 percent of the nation's population, their Hajj is the third largest in the world, primarily because federal and state governments provide pilgrims with generous subsidies for air travel and lodging.[28] Unlike Pakistan where private firms control much of the Hajj market, India's party bosses keep a firm grasp on the political benefits of pilgrimage by leaving about three-quarters of the market under direct state control. Neither travel agents nor secular and Hindu opponents of state-supported Hajj have garnered much support in legislatures where pilgrimage is seen as a popular campaign draw in closely fought elections. But India's notoriously activist courts have begun to tip the balance with a series of sensational rulings against the existing arrangements.

[26] "LHC Orders Probe into 'Cartelization' of Operators," *Daily Times* (Pakistan), October 2, 2012; "Grant of Hajj Quota to New Tour Operators," *Daily Times* (Pakistan), August 25, 2012.

[27] "Hajj under Debt," *Pak Tribune*, June 20, 2013.

[28] Hajj Committee of India, *Statewise Distribution of Quota for the Pilgrims of Haj, 2012 and 2013*, New Delhi: 2012 and 2013.

High Courts in Madras and Kerala overturned restrictions on private travel agents who wanted to enter the Hajj business, claiming that they violated fundamental rights of free trade.[29] The Supreme Court of India went much further, declaring Hajj subsidies unconstitutional and ordering the government to begin phasing them out immediately and to abolish them altogether within ten years.[30] In the meantime, several state governments rushed to build new Hajj service centers to assure voters they would continue to enjoy pilgrimage support even after direct subsidies disappeared.[31]

BANGLADESH

One of the most sensational Hajj scandals unfolded in Bangladesh, where pilgrimage is still poorly regulated despite rapid increases in recent years. Just after the start of the global financial crisis of 2008, Bangladesh's Hajj skyrocketed from less than 50,000 people to nearly 130,000 – an astounding turnabout for one of South Asia's poorest countries, particularly in the midst of widespread economic turmoil.[32] Soon the Saudis started complaining that many of these so-called pilgrims were really unemployed men and women trying to circumvent new limits on foreign workers in the Persian Gulf states. The government in Dhaka agreed to investigate and eventually confirmed that private tour operators were indeed recruiting tens of thousands of would-be migrant workers who paid handsomely for assistance in entering Saudi Arabia under false pretenses. Most of them remained in Saudi Arabia long after their visas expired, swelling the already vast pool of fugitive job seekers.[33]

The humiliation triggered a wave of fines and convictions of travel agents for "human trafficking." It also prompted the government to break

[29] "Corruption, Discrimination Ousted in Hajj Quota Allotment," mylaw.net, November 18, 2010.

[30] "Indian Court Scraps Subsidy for Mecca Pilgrimage," *Radio Australia*, May 9, 2012; "Phase Out Haj Subsidy in Ten Years, Supreme Court Tells Govt," *ndtv.com*, May 8, 2012; "Hajj Subsidy: Myths and Facts," *saadut.com*, May 2012.

[31] "Three More Government Hajj Houses in Karnataka," *SahilOnline*, June 3, 2013; "Gujarat Towers over UP in Haj Applications," *Daily Pioneer*, April 24, 2013.

[32] Bangladesh Ministry of Religious Affairs, Statistics on Bangladeshi Hajj, 2009–2012, *Hajj Management Portal*, 2012; Bangladesh Ministry of Religious Affairs, Districtwise Pilgrims 2009, *Hajj Management Portal*, 2010 (in Bengali); Bangladesh Ministry of Religious Affairs, Bangladesh Pilgrim statistics, 2000–2008, *Hajj Management Portal*, 2009 (in Bengali).

[33] "Riyadh Blacklists Thirty-one Hajj Agencies for Trafficking," *Dhaka Tribune*, April 30, 2013.

up the tight cluster of private companies in the city of Dhaka that monopolized pilgrimage as well as to promote a broad-based network of competitive firms in the provincial capitals and towns. After revoking the licenses of about 100 of the 300 companies that ran the old system, Hajj officials shifted their business to more than 1,100 small and middle-sized firms, setting minimum and maximum quotas so that most agencies would survive but none could dominate the market.[34]

Although Bangladeshi bureaucrats attacked monopoly in one area, they encouraged even greater economic concentration in another. Hajj managers joined the leading association of travel agents in signing lucrative service contracts with more than a dozen banks in Bangladesh and the Persian Gulf. Government and association negotiators carefully segmented every imaginable type of Hajj-related financial service from payments and savings to ATMs, transfers, and insurance. Then they handed out the business to favored banks in all sectors – state and private, local and foreign, Islamic and conventional.[35] A few years ago, Bangladesh was a poor country with a weak and under-regulated pilgrimage. Today, it has a booming Hajj and a complex financial alliance – joining state agencies, small businesses, and international mega-banks – that penetrates towns and villages in every district.

While Bangladesh's pilgrimage managers race toward the future in banking, they are also looking to the past for solutions to chronic transportation bottlenecks. Bangladesh is one of the few countries considering a revival of sea transport long after the rest of the world has opted for air travel. The maritime proponents are centered in the southeastern port city of Chittagong – the country's fastest growing metropolis where commercial groups have long felt throttled by the politicians and bureaucrats of inland Dhaka. Travel agents complain that dilapidated roads force hajjis to spend at least thirty-seven hours to reach Jeddah via Dhaka instead of only seven hours if the government supported more direct flights to Saudi Arabia from Chittagong airport.[36] Arguing that it would be cheaper to

[34] "Private Hajj Operators Suffer Blow over Human Trafficking Claim," *Financial Express*, June 22, 2013.

[35] "Prime Bank, Al-Arafah Sign MoU with HAAB," *Financial Express*, April 11, 2012; "Shahjalal Islami Bank Signed Agreement with HAAB," *First News*, April 20, 2013; "Bank Asia Signs MoU with HAAB," *Daily Sun*, April 12, 2013; "Islamic Development Bank Signs MoU with HAAB," *TechWorld Bangladesh*, May 27, 2012.

[36] "ATAB, HAAB Semand Chittagong-Jeddah Direct Hajj Flight," *Financial Express*, September 20, 2012; "Biman Flight Debacle: Passengers Stage Rowdy Protests," *Daily Star*, September 18, 2012.

charter ships instead, Chittagong's municipal and business leaders are building special docks and service centers that will cater to economy-minded hajjis who are willing to bed down on six- or seven-day cruises.[37]

NIGERIA

Nigeria's relations with Saudi Arabia are filled with acrimony and charges of racial discrimination. Saudi police routinely detain Nigerian pilgrims on suspicion of drug dealing, prostitution, smuggling, money laundering, the carrying of infectious diseases, vagrancy, pick-pocketing, and visa overstays.[38] In 2012, Saudi authorities refused entry to more than 1,000 women hajjis from Nigeria claiming that they were traveling without male escorts. Abuja protested that the Saudis were mistaken because they did not understand that married women in Nigeria commonly use their maiden names on travel documents. Nigeria demanded that the women be allowed to complete their hajjis and the Saudis relented, but only after a row that further damaged Saudi Arabia's reputation throughout Africa.[39] Similar battles occurred in previous years when Saudi officials tried to impose a blanket ban on Nigerian pilgrims during outbreaks of meningitis and other diseases.[40]

Despite their resentment over being stigmatized in these ways, Nigerians have tried to assuage Saudi concerns by adopting strict and costly screening measures for intended pilgrims. Police reports, face-to-face interviews, means tests, and written references have become standard requirements for approving pilgrimage applications in Nigeria. These restrictions contradict the efforts of many state governments to woo voters with enhanced Hajj services.[41] The easiest way for applicants to resolve the dilemma is to pay their way through each stage of the gauntlet, but this merely undermines the integrity of the system at home and abroad.

[37] "Move to Carry Hajj Pilgrims by Sea," *Dhaka Mirror*, February 27, 2010.

[38] R. R. Bianchi, "The Hajj in Everyday Life," in D. L. Bowen, E. A. Early, and B. Schulthies (eds), *Everyday Life in the Muslim Middle East*, 3rd ed. (Bloomington: Indiana University Press, 2014).

[39] "Why Saudi Arabia Moved against Nigeria," *Nigerian Tribune*, September 29, 2012; "Nigeria Suspends Hajj Flights over Women Deportation," *BBC News*, September 27, 2012; "Hajj Imbroglio: Where the Problem Lies," *allafrica.com*, October 6, 2012.

[40] C. L. Ejembi, E. P. Renne and H. A. Adamu, "The Politics of the 1996 Cerebrospinal Meningitis Epidemic in Nigeria," *Africa*, 68, 1 (1998).

[41] Bianchi, *Guests of God*, 215–217; "Why We're Stopping Pregnant Women from Hajj," *allafrica.com*, August 18, 2012.

TURKEY

Turkey's rulers have spent decades crafting a nexus of party, state, and associational resources to boost Hajj participation from city to village in nearly every province. Year in and year out, the vote banks of the dominant party are also the hotspots of Hajj activity. The core areas stretch from the Aegean interior through Central Anatolia as far as the Black Sea coast. The only region remaining outside of the network is the depressed southeast, where the Kurdish population is most concentrated.[42]

The key links between the ruling party and its supporters are the Directorate of Religious Affairs and the thousands of local religious and cultural associations that serve as its clients and supporters. State-sponsored Qur'an courses and Islamic secondary schools have long formed the nucleus of neighborhood organizations supporting pilgrimage. Recently, the role of women has risen rapidly in these groups, and female predominance is particularly notable in Qur'an studies and in the Hajj.[43]

Hajj mobilization in Turkey is so effective that applications regularly exceed the quotas, and current waiting lists extend at least ten years into the future. Pilgrimage managers have tried to adjust to the demand overload by adopting several new policies. Each year, they lobby the Saudis to increase the national allotment, offering in return to crack down on the flow of illegal pilgrims that both countries estimate at about 30,000 annually.[44] Turkey also encourages people to make the 'Umra instead of the Hajj, particularly if they are young or if they have already completed a Hajj in the past. In the last decade, the 'Umra business has skyrocketed from 30,000 to 370,000 per year, and among the pious middle class, going on the 'Umra is regarded as an important sign of mobility and success.[45] For older citizens, the government recommends small group package tours that include several family members at once. This campaign has helped to spark a nationwide upsurge in female Hajj activity.

42 Bianchi, *Guests of God*, 154–158.

43 Türkiye İstatistik Kurumu, *Kültür İstatistikleri*, Ankara, 2009 and 2011.

44 "How Turkey Reduced Visa Overstays from 35,000 to 5,000 in One Season," *Hajj and Umrah Gazette*, June 1, 2011.

45 "Son 10 yılda umreye giden Türkler'in sayısı 25 kat arttı" (The Number of Turks Going on Umrah Has Increased 25 Times in the Last 10 Years), *Sabah*, May 20, 2012; "Marked Increase in Hajj and Umrah Demand in Turkey," *Hajj and Umrah Gazette*, January 24, 2011; "Umrah Applications from Turkey on Rise," *Hürriyet-Daily News*, July 13, 2011.

RUSSIA

Russia's endless debate over whether it is more European or Asian has taken a surprising turn. While politicians and churchgoers focus on cultural tensions between East and West, many in the government are speculating that Russia will eventually become a Muslim nation. Muslim ethnic groups and Central Asian immigrants are growing rapidly while the native Russian population is in steady decline. The demographic shift is already conspicuous in the army, which could become predominantly Muslim in another decade or two.[46] Indeed, President Putin is already declaring that "Russia is an Islamic country" in order to garner domestic and international support for his military campaigns in the Northern Caucasus.[47]

Promoting the Hajj is now a key part of Russia's effort to convince the world that it is an Islamic-friendly nation.[48] But as Moscow centralizes control over the pilgrimage business, it arouses strong resentments in local groups that feel threatened and slighted. The government's growing insistence on promoting air travel through the major cities has provoked violent resistance in two regions – Dagestan and Tatarstan – that are indispensible to Putin's Islamic policies.

Dagestani Muslims grew accustomed to enjoying the lion's share of the Russian Hajj quota when Moscow began opening the doors to Mecca. Although they still account for almost 40 percent of the national quota of 20,000, they are losing ground compared to their neighbors in Chechnya and Ingushetia and to Turkic Muslims in Tatarstan in the lower Volga region.[49] Dagestanis claim that the government wants to monopolize the Hajj by converting it to air traffic, which is more profitable and easier to control than the overland routes that hajjis prefer along the southern borders. Many of the leading religious families of Dagestan claim Syrian descent, and they are convinced that Moscow wants to disrupt their

[46] "Russia to Have Muslim Majority by 2050, Putin Advisor Says," *Window on Eurasia*, August 23, 2007; "Islam in the Russian Army," *Islam Magazine-Makhachkala*, 2005.

[47] "Russian Muslims and Foreign Policy," *Global Affairs*, October 7, 2012; "Russia Courts the Muslim World: Islam Preceded Christianity on Our Territory, Says Putin," *Le Monde Diplomatique*, December 2008; "Russia Challenges U.S. in the Islamic World," *Asia Times Online*, March 29, 2008.

[48] "Russian Council of Muftis Allocates Quotas for 2013 Hajj," *Radio Free Europe-Radio Liberty*, May 3, 2013; "Council for Hajj Reports Increase in Scale of Pilgrimages by Russian Muslims in 10 Years," *Interfax*, August 31, 2012.

[49] "Moscow Cuts Dagestan's Haj Quota, Sparking Anger There," *Window on Eurasia*, November 29, 2009; "Putin Hobbles the Hajj," *United Press International*, September 24, 2004.

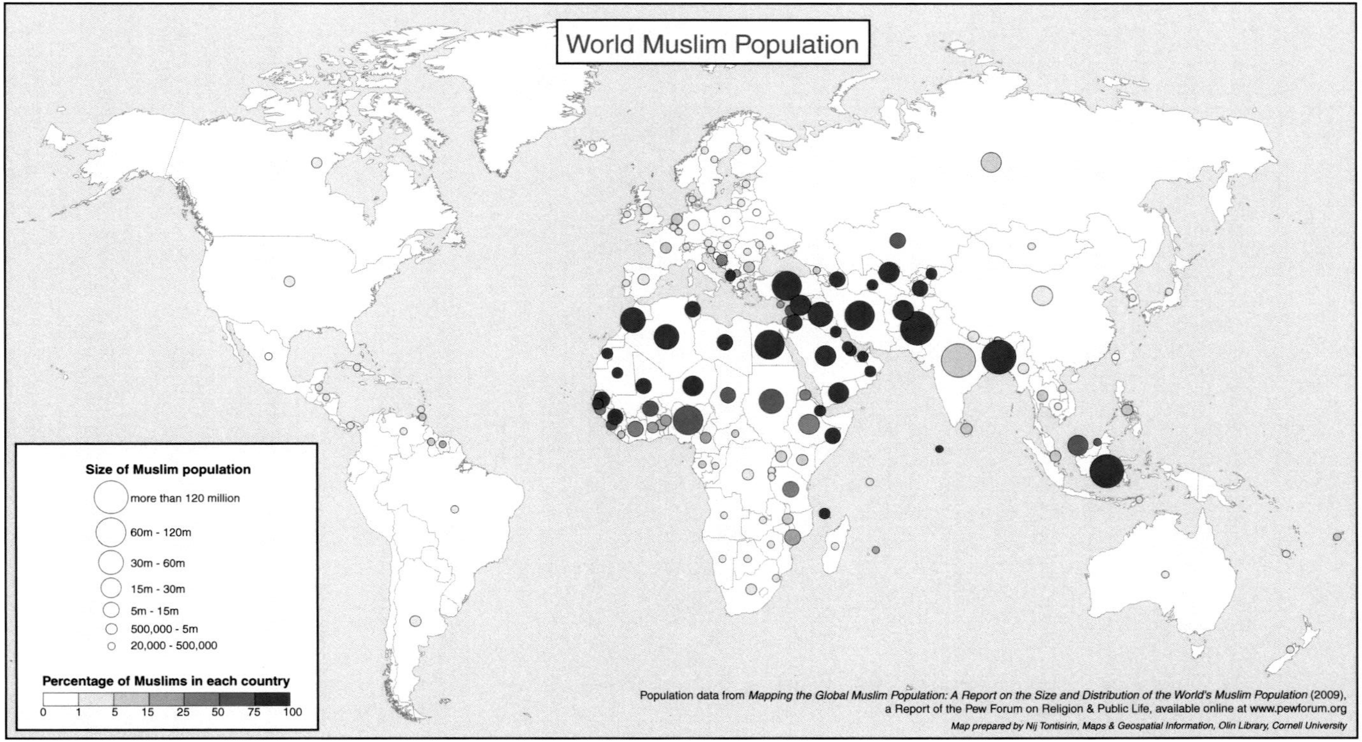
World Muslim Population
Size of Muslim population
more than 120 million
60m - 120m
30m - 60m
15m - 30m
5m - 15m
500,000 - 5m
20,000 - 500,000
Percentage of Muslims in each country
0 1 5 15 25 50 75 100
Population data from *Mapping the Global Muslim Population: A Report on the Size and Distribution of the World's Muslim Population* (2009),
a Report of the Pew Forum on Religion & Public Life, available online at www.pewforum.org
Map prepared by Nij Tontisirin, Maps & Geospatial Information, Olin Library, Cornell University

MAP 2 World Muslim population

FIGURE 18 Poster of boy praying

FIGURE 19 Ottoman ceramic depiction of Mecca

FIGURE 20 Hajj mural, Gurna, Upper Egypt

traditional links with the Arab world because of fears of Islamic radicalism.[50]

Reorganizing pilgrimage in Tatarstan triggered a turf war that might have led to the Chief Mufti's assassination. When the Mufti was kidnapped and murdered in 2011, many assumed it was the work of terrorists who were retaliating for his campaigns against Islamic radicalism. However, suspicion about the motive quickly shifted to a battle over Hajj revenues. The state-backed religious authorities in Kazan, Tatarstan's capital city, were in the midst of taking over pilgrimage management from local businesses with alleged connections to Saudi Arabian preachers. Just before the Mufti's death, his office was winding up negotiations to schedule direct flights to Jeddah and to establish a special investment fund for prepaid Hajj fees.[51]

The latest bombshell to hit Russia's pilgrimage is the cascade of scandals surrounding Akhmed Bilalov, a former Hajj official that Putin recently fired from the Russian Olympic Committee. Bilalov was accused of running an elaborate tax evasion scheme that cost the treasury $36 million. He allegedly let tour operators collect Hajj payments, convert them to dollars for a commission, and then transfer them to offshore accounts in the Middle East with no paper trail. Once the funds were laundered, they came back to "public religious groups" in Russia and on to his cronies in Dagestan and elsewhere.[52]

CHINA

Compared to Russia, China has been a model of efficiency in deploying air travel to monopolize and manipulate the Hajj. After twenty years of laying the foundation among Chinese-speaking Muslims in the central border provinces, Beijing is now expanding the network to include the long-marginalized Turkic Muslims of far western Xinjiang. China's Hajj program seeks to accomplish several goals at once – promoting mainstream

[50] "Arab Dagestanis – Direct Descendants of the Prophet Muhammad," *islam.ru*, 2011; "Syria as a Terrorism Hub – Potential Threats to Russia," *valdaiclub.com*, April 22, 2013.

[51] "Attack on Tatarstan Mufti May Have Been Due to His Control over Hajj Financing," *Interfax*, July 20, 2012; "New Rules of Distributing Hajj Tours Could Be behind Tatarstan Attacks – Russian Lawmaker," *Interfax*, July 19, 2012; "Russia's Fear of Radical Islam Drives Its Support for Assad," *Al-Monitor*, July 26, 2012.

[52] "Bilalov Suspected of Organizing Large-Scale Tax Evasion Scheme with Hajj Tours," *Interfax*, April 24, 2013.

Islamic practice, defusing ethnic and sectarian tensions, and securing vulnerable frontiers against infiltration and separatism.[53]

State-managed pilgrimage also serves broader strategic and economic interests. It strengthens trade and cultural ties with Central Asia, the Middle East, and the Caspian Basin – mineral-rich lands and transport lines that are vital to developing China's interior provinces and supporting the industrialized cities on the Pacific coast. The Chinese-speaking Hui Muslims, who benefit most from the Hajj policies, occupy pivotal locations, both geographically and socially. For centuries, they have traded and married with other communities that tend to keep their distance from one another – the Han, Mongols, Tibetans, Uyghurs, and countless smaller groups. Moreover, the provinces with the greatest concentration of Hui are also the home of China's nuclear arsenal and space program.[54]

In Mecca, the signs of Chinese workmanship shape the daily life of every hajji. Chinese Muslims provided the engineers and laborers who built the new monorail connecting the shrines in Mecca, Mina, and ʿArafat as well as the high-speed train to Medina.[55] Most of the clothing and paraphernalia of the pilgrimage is made in China, including the white robes that male hajjis don for the most sacred rituals and the ubiquitous white umbrellas that everyone uses to ward off the desert sun.

Many hajjis are surprised to discover that China not only has a large Muslim population, but that it is so intimately involved in the pilgrimage and in global Islamic affairs. Usually, Muslims find it gratifying to learn that a rising world power is a fellow member of the Islamic community. But sometimes it also produces consternation, particularly in discussing imbalances of trade. When Turkey's trade negotiators demanded a more favorable arrangement with China, one of the most sensitive issues they raised was China's takeover of what had once been a thriving local market for pilgrimage clothing and accessories. To their credit, the Chinese quickly grasped the psychological power of the grievance and resolved it by agreeing to cease exporting Hajj-related goods to Turkey.[56]

[53] R. R. Bianchi, "China-Middle East Relations in Light of Obama's Pivot to the Pacific," *China Report*, 49, 1 (2013): 103–118.

[54] R. R. Bianchi, "Travel for Religious Purposes," in J. Esposito (ed.), *The Oxford Encyclopedia of Islam* (New York: Oxford University Press, 2007); M. Rossabi (ed.), *Governing China's Multiethnic Frontiers* (Seattle: University of Washington Press, 2004).

[55] "China-built Light Rail Whisks 1 Million Hajj Pilgrims to Mecca in Saudi Arabia," *Xinhua*, November 20, 2010; "Chinese Train to Mecca?," *Wired Magazine*, September 10, 2009; "Chinese Builders Help Hajj," February 19, 2009.

[56] "Diyanet'ten Çin'e çalım: hac malzemeleri yerli olacak" (A Move on China from Religious Affairs: Hajj Equipment Will Be Locally Produced), *Sabah*, June 24, 2010.

China's Hajj is still quite modest in size – about 14,000 per year for a Muslim population of at least 20 million. Hence, there is ample room for growth in the coming decade. Most of the future increase is already targeted toward the Uyghurs of Xinjiang, who have largely shunned the official system and still engage in a lively illegal traffic of overland pilgrimage via third countries such as Pakistan and Turkey. Integrating the Uyghur Hajj into the central network of air travel is a key part of Beijing's effort to develop the western interior, pacify its most troubled borders, and broaden trade from China through Central Asia and all the way to Europe.[57]

NEW DIASPORAS AND OLD FRIENDS

Some of the most glaring disparities in allocating Hajj quotas appear in countries where Muslim minorities are influential in local politics and also have enduring overseas ties with their ancestral homelands and Saudi Arabia. Newer Muslim diasporas in France and the United Kingdom enjoy unusually generous quotas, whereas the much older communities in Singapore and South Africa are left with smaller than average and even shrinking Hajj contingents.[58] In each case, the anomaly stems from Saudi Arabia's differential assessment of political and diplomatic currents.

North Africans in France and South Asians in Britain receive government-funded Hajj services that have been included in a broad package of privileges and subsidies negotiated with officially recognized boards of Muslim representatives and preachers.[59] Over-sized quotas and funding allow Paris and London to kill two birds with one stone. They co-opt

[57] "Unfulfilled Hajj Dream for Uighur Muslims," *OnIslam.net*, October 30, 2011; "南航新疆分公司地服部: 首次独立保障"朝觐"包机" (China Southern Airline's Xinjiang Division Ground Service: The First Dedicated Hajj Charters), *cnair.com*, September 27, 2012; "China Muslims Embark on Easier Hajj," *OnIslam.net*, October 18, 2010; "The Hajj – Chinese Pilgrims Then and Now," *ummieabiworld.blogspot.com*, November 5, 2010.

[58] France sends between 25,000 and 30,000 hajjis despite an estimated Muslim population of only 5 or 6 million. The U.K.'s quota is 25,000 for a Muslim community of less than 3 million. The quota for South Africa's 2.5 million Muslims is stuck at 2,500, but applications now exceed 16,000, creating a waiting list of six years. Singapore's Muslim population has been stable at about 500,000, but since the 1980s, their quota has fallen from about 2,500 to 1,500 and most recently to only 600.

[59] "En France, les quotas de visas hajj sont déjà épuisés," *France-Hajj.fr*, September 2012; "An Academy in Paris Offers Advice and Instruction to Muslims Wishing to Make the Trip to Mecca for the Annual Hajj Pilgrimage," Reuters, *October* 3, 2012; "Bogus Hajj Tour Operators Rip-off Muslims Planning Mecca Pilgrimage out of £100,000s," *London Evening Standard*, August 16, 2012.

moderate and hand-picked religious leaders who can help manage growing social tensions, and they give their former colonies a Hajj bonus by allowing African and Asian citizens to travel with French and British passports. The Saudis cooperate with these arrangements, hoping to gain favor with European and Afro-Asian governments while taking some of the sting out of unpopular quota limits worldwide.

The older Muslim communities in South Africa and Singapore see their political clout moving in the opposite direction. South Africa's blacks and Singapore's Chinese are riding a new wave of power and prosperity that lowers their perceived need to accommodate weak Muslim minorities.[60] In both countries, previous concessions are being reviewed and reduced to reflect the growing imbalance of power between races. Local Muslims have become increasingly isolated politically despite their continuing cosmopolitanism in terms of trade and culture. For their part, the Saudis see little to gain by angering strong governments with proven influence in global commerce and finance.

THE LOOMING REFORM AGENDA

The flaws of the current Hajj regime are an open secret in the Islamic world, and the leading remedies are already being debated in government task forces, international seminars, and Internet forums. Greater internationalization of decision making is at the top of nearly every reformer's list. Saudi Arabian hegemony over the Hajj and the holy cities is under constant assault.[61] The more other Muslim countries join the mainstream of global life, the less willing they are to follow the lead of an authoritarian monarchy that rules over a closed society while championing an intolerant creed that is out of touch with the pluralism and cosmopolitanism that Muslims experience around the world. Thus, the most important change in Hajj management is likely to be a stronger role for the Organization of

60 "Row over SA's Smaller Hajj Quota," *iol news*, July 18, 2013; "Couple to Sue SA Hajj Council," *iol news*, September 28, 2012; "Fewer Places Available for Pilgrimage to Mecca," *Straits Times* (Singapore), September 12, 2012.

61 "Mecca's Mega Architecture Casts Shadow over Hajj," *Guardian*, October 23, 2012; "Black Market Thrives as Haj Missions Fail to Find Housing," *Arab News*, October 10, 2011; "Over-priced Annual Pilgrimage," *Saudi Gazette*, September 14, 2011; "The Problems of a Contemporary Hajj – Parts 1 and 2," *Muslimmatters.com*, October 10 and 16, 2011; "UAE's Faithful Say 'Luxury' Haj Is Unholy," *The National* (UAE), October 16, 2011.

Islamic Cooperation (OIC) and for the largest states of Asia and Africa that have assumed its leadership.

The toughest issue for any new regime will be deciding what to do with the quota system. There are many possibilities – quotas could be abolished, loosened, standardized, redefined, periodically renegotiated, or impartially adjudicated. However, no formula will be workable and legitimate unless it emerges from transparent and widely representative deliberations. There is little tolerance these days for the unilateral decisions of a single government that are rubber-stamped by a close-minded circle of clerical dependents.[62]

Reshaping the national Hajj systems will require great flexibility and persistence. Dominant interests are deeply entrenched and bolstered by political and social inequities far beyond the reach of any pilgrimage reformer. In addition, local tastes and practices will always resist technocratic passions for uniformity, whether they originate at home or abroad. Nonetheless, Hajj managers can learn a good deal from the success of their counterparts in the field of Islamic finance.

The OIC has already acquired considerable skill in regulating Islamic banks in widely different cultures and jurisdictions. OIC affiliates have cooperated with central banks in all Muslim countries to craft arrangements that comply with global banking standards while accommodating distinctive regional preferences in Southeast Asia, the Persian Gulf, and Europe.[63] Modern Hajj organization is increasingly intertwined with Islamic finance in all its permutations – savings, investment, insurance, and consumer lending.[64] Hajj management and Islamic finance are the leading examples of international regimes that have been tailored to the special needs of the Muslim world. Both regimes are changing rapidly and searching for greater transparency and accountability. Much of their experience can be shared and adapted by Muslim policymakers everywhere and, eventually, expanded to other transnational issues such as trade, the environment, and human rights.

[62] "Angus McDowall, Saudi Clerics Approve Fewer Hajj Pilgrims," *Reuters*, June 26, 2013.

[63] Bianchi, *Islamic Globalization*.

[64] "Pilgrim Funds Give Indonesia Banks Booster Shot," *Bloomberg*, May 2, 2013; "Indonesian Government to Put Idle Hajj Funds in Development Bonds," *Jakarta Globe*, July 23, 2012.

PART THREE

INFRASTRUCTURE

8

Economics

Agents, Pilgrims, and Profits

Sylvia Chiffoleau

In the nineteenth century, the ancient pilgrimage economy was rocked by technology and administrative rationality. Since the advent of Islam, this economy had been based on the caravan system, the support and subsidies provided by Muslim governments and individuals, and finally, the commercial role of the Hijaz, which had already begun its decline in the eighteenth century. In the Ottoman Empire and Egypt, western pattern of modernity had been widely introduced, albeit selectively, through a series of indigenous reforms (*Tanzimât*). However, with colonization, modernity penetrated even deeper into the majority of Muslim regions. The pilgrimage, which had hitherto remained a strictly Muslim affair, became a common concern of the colonial powers, which subsequently had to manage it from an administrative and economic perspective. This "European" modernity, however, affected the various economic aspects of the pilgrimage in different ways and according to a varying chronology. With the introduction of steam navigation, which was, in this case, a true *revolution*, the transportation of pilgrims proved very vulnerable to the assault of European capitalism. The internal economy of Hijaz, on the other hand, was negatively affected by the changes of this period, especially those of a political nature. The disappearance of the financial boon that came with the Ottoman Empire in particular was offset by heavier taxes on the pilgrims. Those driven by faith much more than economic rationality left for Hijaz with very modest means and sometimes in situations of real financial insecurity. On arriving in the holy places of Islam, they encountered a level of misery hardly different from their own, which the region's inhabitants sought to relieve by exploiting the pilgrims until the arrival of oil revenues propelled the pilgrimage into a new economic era.

ECONOMIC STAKES IN THE TRANSPORTATION OF PILGRIMS

European Shipping Companies' Control over the Transportation of Pilgrims

Pilgrimage caravans, which had existed since the Umayyad period, never ceased to grow and develop over the centuries, forming an annual convoy on Middle Eastern routes, which was only interrupted in the event of a major political crisis. During the Ottoman era, these caravans had become large-scale events, whose organization was based on a very elaborate economy.[1] The two principal caravans departing Cairo and Damascus for Mecca each carried 20,000 to 40,000 pilgrims, a group comprising officials and civil servants accompanied by the *amīr al-ḥajj* as well as an imposing military escort. They also transported treasure (*surra* in Arabic and *sürre* in Turkish, literally "purse") comprising gifts and money, which was intended to pacify the Bedouin tribes along the way and subsidize and maintain the holy cities, their elites, and population. This vast array of men, animals, and riches was variously financed by a tax levy on the empire's subjects, money and goods from the sultan's personal funds, and income from numerous pious foundations (*waqf*s). The caravans were also accompanied by tradesmen, who benefitted from the protection of the military escort, as well as many other pilgrims who were engaged in small-scale trade and were thus able to finance all or part of their voyage. In the departure cities, there existed a multitude of trades indispensable for manufacturing the equipment and provisioning the caravans. During the course of the journey, large markets were held in some of the stop-overs, which in turn fed the economy of these regions.

This secular organization around the pilgrimage and the intense economic activity that it generated were disrupted by the rapid development of steam navigation in the 1830s. Until the First World War, the Ottoman Empire still continued to send the traditional *sürre* to Mecca each year, although accompanied by a reduced escort, a *maḥmal*, and a handful of pilgrims. For its part, Egypt retained the privilege of sending the *kiswa* to Mecca until 1926, but the palanquin, as the symbol of the Egyptian caravan, traveled by boat like its escort from the beginning of the 1880s.

[1] See K. K. Barbir, *Ottoman Rule in Damascus, 1708–1758* (Princeton University Press, 1980); S. Faroqhi, *Pilgrims and Sultans: The Hajj under the Ottomans* (London: I. B. Tauris, 1996); J. Jomier, *Le maḥmal et la caravane égyptienne des pèlerins de La Mecque –XIIIe–XXe siècles* (Cairo: Imprimerie de l'Institut français d'archéologie orientale, 1953); R. Tresse, *Le pèlerinage syrien aux villes saintes de l'Islam* (Paris: Imprimerie Chaumette, 1937).

Thus, not only did the show of prestige fade, with its cost yet weighing heavily on the fragile finances of Egypt and the Ottoman Empire, but the economic activity on the caravans' margins all but disappeared.

For several decades, the use of steam navigation to transport the pilgrims had established a resolutely different economic system. Sailing, particularly in the Indian Ocean, but also to a lesser extent in the Mediterranean, had always contributed to the transportation of pilgrims, strongly interlinking the sacred voyage with the general movement of international trade.[2] However, the development of steam navigation in the nineteenth century substantially increased the flow of people and created a specialized and very competitive market around the pilgrimage. Steam navigation offered a faster, safer, and relatively inexpensive means of transport, allowing a much greater number of pilgrims to undertake the sacred voyage, particularly those from India and Southeast Asia, who until then had depended on the monsoon winds. Despite facilitating the pilgrimage, steam navigation nevertheless opened up the transport industry to European companies and businessmen, an industry that had previously remained the exclusive activity of Muslims. At the same time, by increasing the number of pilgrims and broadening the area of circulation, the flow of cash and wealth between the three continents likewise augmented and intensified, but this occurred in a more diffuse manner than the previous economy that was generated by caravan transport on more limited routes.

In this new market, which witnessed an extraordinary boom with the opening of the Suez Canal (1869), the British navigation companies secured the lion's share from the outset. While the pilgrim flows were henceforth largely superimposed on the colonial trade routes dominated by Great Britain, these companies could mobilize their experience and skills in trade and in the transportation of migrants and plantation workers in order to seize this new opportunity. Founded in 1877, the Bombay and Persia Steam Navigation Co., otherwise known as the Mogul Line, rapidly ascended in this market, eventually running 70 percent of all pilgrimage ships from India at the end of the 1930s. The Blue Funnel Line, whose maritime activities began in the 1850s, also played a significant role in the Indian market as well as in the transport of many Maghreb pilgrims on the scheduled shipping lines linking the metropolis to India. At the end of the nineteenth century, the Blue Funnel participated in an

[2] M. N. Pearson, *Pious Passengers: The Hajj in Earlier Times* (New Delhi: Sterling Publishers Private Limited, 1994).

Anglo-Dutch consortium involving two Dutch companies, known also as Kongsi Tiga, which had a quasi-monopoly over the transport of pilgrims from Southeast Asia (Malaya, Straits Settlements, and the Dutch East Indies).[3] In 1887, among the 135 ships transporting pilgrims to Jeddah, 53 were English and 15 were Dutch, and by 1923, British ships had taken charge of 74 percent of pilgrims arriving in Jeddah, while the Dutch transported 20 percent and the other flags shared the remainder. The economic stakes in pilgrim transportation were thus considerable for British and Dutch interests. Despite being somewhat suspicious about the political risks associated with the pilgrimage, the two colonial powers did not obstruct the freedom of movement of the pilgrims under their administration.

On the contrary, France, the third colonial power with many Muslims among its subjects, appeared rather apprehensive about entering this market and initially renounced the idea. In 1877, a report from the Marseilles Chamber of Commerce had deemed it to be unprofitable. The French policy toward the pilgrimage was most uncompromising; out of fear of a "pan-Islamist contamination," it adopted a policy of prohibition, most often justified by reasons of health safety. From 1880 to 1914, the French authorities announced twenty-three prohibitions, thus strongly reducing the pilgrimage market. In the authorized years, though often in violation of the prohibition, Maghreb pilgrims boarded British liners. Although the price of passage was relatively low, the transport conditions were extremely poor. In 1889, the General Government of Algeria issued a decree obliging Algerian pilgrims to board only French boats, which were authorized in advance by a special subcommittee. However, such a monopoly, reinforced after 1928 when the Algerian administration set about organizing the pilgrimage itself, could not apply to the protectorates (Tunisia, Morocco, and Syria), which benefited from the freedom of the flag and instead opted for a concession system following an open call for tender. Thus, strictly controlled by the colonial power, the French market for the transportation of pilgrims never managed to fully develop.

The Ottoman Empire, which had founded a national company in 1856, also participated in the transport of pilgrims, although rather modestly, as did Russia and Austrian Lloyd. Several non-European companies, notably Persian and Indian, or businesses registered in Hong Kong, such as the Nemazee Line, also took part in this operation. The Egyptians, who

[3] M. B. Miller, "Pilgrims' Progress: The Business of the Hajj," *Past & Present*, 191 (2006): 189–228.

comprised the third-largest body of pilgrims, were primarily transported by the Khedivial Mail Line, an indigenous company purchased by British interests at the end of the nineteenth century. Despite the proximity of Hijaz, which could have permitted the use of scheduled lines, the Khedivial organized a specialized transport service, because of the obligation for the pilgrim ships to stop on their return from Hijaz at the El-Tor quarantine station, located in the south of the Sinai Peninsula. From the second half of the nineteenth century until the advent of aircraft, the maritime transportation of pilgrims thus constituted a formidable international business with multiple ramifications.

A Competitive and Often Cynical Market

The majority of shipping companies operating in the pilgrim transport market, especially the British and Dutch, maintained a dense network of native agents, both in Jeddah, the port of disembarkation and embarkation of pilgrims, as well as in the Asian regions where the pilgrims were to be recruited. In Hijaz, the management of pilgrims was left to the mutawwifs (Ar. *muṭawwifin*) guides organized in guilds. These individuals, or more often, their numerous local agents, traversed the concerned areas, including the most remote villages, in order to recruit pilgrims on behalf of the shipping companies, which remunerated them on the basis of the ticket price. The mutawwifs were tasked with providing pilgrims with the necessary papers for their departure and entry into Hijaz; giving them transport tickets including, where applicable, train tickets for local travel; organizing the procedures for traveling to the ports; and so forth. This network of brokers, subject to strong internal competition, developed their own local networks (village chiefs, imams, religious teachers, etc.) to encourage recruitments. They also formed an essential and effective, though not always scrupulous, group of Muslim intermediaries between the pilgrim candidates and the European shipping companies, which maintained a good level of interpersonal relations and ensured the continuity of the economic system.[4]

At the end of the pilgrimage, Jeddah became a place of intense speculation around the sale of return tickets. With the exception of France, which made round-trip tickets compulsory in 1894, the majority of pilgrims set off with a one-way ticket, thus obliging them to buy a return

[4] J. Vredenbregt, "The Haddj: Some of Its Features and Functions in Indonesia," *Bijdragen tot de Taal-Land en Volkenkunde*, 118 (1962): 91–154; Miller, "Pilgrims' Progress."

ticket in Hijaz. This was notably the case for the great mass of Malayan and Indian pilgrims. Despite the fact that the fares were theoretically fixed by the *vali* and that the pilgrims were supposed to have the freedom to choose their own means of transport, the 1880s and 1890s witnessed the establishment of a pool. This pool grouped shipping company agents, community leaders in Hijaz, particularly the Sharif of Mecca, and employees at some of the consulates, who managed to secure a quasi-monopoly on the sale of return tickets, with the consequence that the soaring prices were prejudicial to the pilgrims' interests.[5] This illegal system of obligation only came to a stop when pilgrims were forced to purchase a round-trip ticket from the outset, which was applied to Dutch subjects in 1922, then incorporated into the 1926 International Sanitary Convention, and extended to Indian pilgrims in the 1930s.

The majority of shipping companies responsible for pilgrim transportation were hardly concerned with their passengers' comfort. They were able to profit from the financial constraints of the pilgrims, who were compensated by their tremendous desire to make the sacred voyage, by imposing harsh, even scandalous transport conditions. The anticipated profits encouraged small companies, often created ad hoc, or even simple adventurers to enter the transportation business.[6] These companies provided even fewer guarantees than the large enterprises. Cases of overloaded ships, sometimes to incredible proportions, were common, and the chronicle of the voyage to Mecca is interspersed with accidents, fires, and bankruptcies along the way, with companies unable to pay for the coal costs or the Suez Canal tolls.

The political authorities in the countries concerned by the pilgrimage did not ignore the precarious conditions under which the Muslim believers traveled. Attempting to resolve the situation, the French colonial authorities relied on the concession system to enforce restrictive contractual conditions on ship owners and brokers and demand a solid guarantee. The British, who initially refused to impose any limitations on individual pilgrims, instead tried to regulate the transport conditions on the ships, while seeking to protect the competitiveness of their navigation. The 1858 Native Passenger Ships Act, which regulated the transport of "natives" in

[5] W. L. Ochsenwald, *Religion, Society and the State in Arabia: The Hijaz under Ottoman Control, 1840–1908* (Columbus: Ohio State University Press, 1984), 101–104.

[6] In 1902, Borel estimated that an average pilgrimage with 45,000 pilgrims earned the shipping companies more than ten million francs: F. Borel, *Choléra et peste dans le pèlerinage musulman, 1860–1903* (Paris: Masson et Cie., 1904), 33.

the Empire, was in principle applicable to the pilgrim ships from 1870 onward. However, for lack of any real progress, the British reached an agreement in 1886 with the company Thomas Cook and Sons to ensure the transport of pilgrims to Hijaz with regard to governmental directives on the sanitary conditions and amenities on board. The solid reputation of the company was supposed to satisfy Muslim leaders, who demanded better treatment for the pilgrims, and prove to the international community that Bombay was no longer the "Sanitary Pariah of the East."[7] However, Cook withdrew from the market in 1893, and two years later, the General Government of India adopted new legislation, the Pilgrim Ships Act, inspired by international legislation. This indeed made it possible to control the abuses in this market. The International Sanitary Conventions, successively adopted from 1894 until 1926, included a meticulous "police regulation of the transportation of pilgrims." Forced to conform to this legislation and under pressure from the colonial powers, which had made pilgrim transport a propaganda issue since the First World War, the majority of shipping companies considerably improved their comfort and safety on board. One the eve of the Second World War, some companies made relatively comfortable and well-equipped steamships available to the pilgrims, with berths for third-class passengers who had hitherto traveled on the ground. These obligations put an end to the most shocking scandals, yet not all of the old vessels were removed from service. The improvements also entailed a loss of profitability in the market.

Entering the Competition: Nationalist Companies

In spite of these improvements, the European domination of the pilgrim transportation market was viewed as increasingly alarming with the rise of nationalism. The development of railways at the beginning of the twentieth century offered the Ottoman Empire an opportunity to counter the European quasi-monopoly. In order to reinforce Ottoman control over the turbulent Yemen still in rebellion and to relieve pilgrims of their heavy dependence on European shipping companies, the empire decided to construct the Hijaz railway, which would link Damascus to Medina. In viewing the task as having a religious nature, inscribed into the heart of Sultan Abdul Hamid II's pan-Islamic project, there was no question of financing it with foreign capital. The funds were thus raised through gifts following

[7] M. Harrison, *Public Health in British India: Anglo-Indian Preventive Medicine, 1859–1914* (Cambridge University Press, 1994), 129.

an intense propaganda campaign as well as taxes collected from the inhabitants of the empire and pilgrims. At the official inauguration on September 1, 1908, the Ottoman Empire boasted that the railway was an exclusively Muslim financial enterprise. Its aim of creating competition with European navigation was incidentally achieved: in the first few years of its operation,[8] approximately 20,000 pilgrims traveled on the railway every year, especially on the return journey, leaving certain maritime entrepreneurs in Jeddah with undercharged boats and facing bankruptcy.

During the interwar period, the overland routes in turn witnessed further development. After the arrival of motor vehicles in the Middle East, a proportion of Persian and Iraqi pilgrims, even Indians, traveled by road from Baghdad to Haifa via Transjordan, or to Beirut via Syria, where they boarded ships to continue their sacred voyage. An English company, Mesopotamia Persia Corporation Ltd., was a concessionary in trans-desert transportation along these roads. As the first state in the region to obtain independence, Iraq immediately sought to profit from the transportation of pilgrims. In 1935, Darb Zubayda, the ancient pilgrimage route from Mesopotamia, was reopened and rebuilt in collaboration with Saudi Arabia in order to accommodate motor vehicle traffic. Two native companies, created ad hoc, obtained the concession to transport pilgrims using this new road, thus contributing to the nationalization of Iraqi transport services for the Hajj.

Similarly, in Syria, the economic issue of pilgrim transportation was transformed into a nationalist issue. At the start of the 1930s, the system set up by the French Mandate was disputed on two levels. First, the concession of maritime transport had been granted to a Lebanese Christian company, which collided with the feelings of Muslims. Second, the obligation for pilgrims to use this means of transport forced them to pay a very high price on tickets, with the inclusion of numerous taxes. The financial load was especially unbearable in the years marked by the economic crisis. It quickly transpired that the overland route by motor vehicle was economically more advantageous for pilgrims, thus allowing them to escape the control of the French authorities. In 1935, the same year as the opening of the Baghdad–Medina road, an automobile expedition by Syrian traders made it possible to open, albeit with great difficulty, a road between Damascus and Mecca. However, the initiative, though welcomed by Syrian

[8] Damaged by dynamiting during the Arab Revolt of 1916–1918 and then split between three sovereignties (Great Britain, France, and Hijaz), the railway was never fully restored for the length of its route.

nationalists, only held a symbolic value in anticipation of independence, since the French authorities upheld their ban on the overland route.

Despite being an even greater distance from Hijaz, the Maghreb countries also sought to travel overland by reviving the ancient trans-Saharan trade routes. Once again, this enabled pilgrims to escape from the economic stranglehold and strict control exercised by the colonial administration over maritime transport. Only in 1951 did the first companies for vehicle transport appear, being a commercial network comprising both French companies and indigenous initiatives. Nevertheless, their success quickly spread. In 1955, in Algeria alone, 62 coaches transported 3,000 pilgrims to Suez, a figure greatly exceeding the capacities offered by the official maritime convoy.

A nationalist initiative was again at the origin of the first air service to Hijaz. The Misr Bank, the first Egyptian bank established in 1920 and a symbol of the country's economic revival, obtained the concession from the Egyptian government to organize the Egyptian pilgrimage for a period of twenty-one years. In 1935, it provided pilgrims with two steamboats with all the amenities, and the following year, Misr Airworks, the air transportation sector of the bank, enabled a group of pilgrims to undertake the first plane trip to the sacred territory. After the Second World War, and even more so from the 1960s onward, air transportation developed in the context of decolonization and the creation of nation-states, which supported their national companies at a time when the last European maritime transport companies, shaken by this competition, withdrew from the market, as they no longer yielded the handsome profits of former times.[9]

Hijaz: An Economy Heavily Dependent on Pilgrimage

Until the 1950s, the Hijaz region subsisted on the pilgrimage as well as aid given by other Muslim countries, and later England, to ensure its longevity. As long as the caravans still made the sacred journey, although admittedly reduced to a symbolic convoy transported by railway and boat, Hijaz could benefit from the official and substantial aids given by the Ottoman Empire and Egypt, on which it almost entirely depended. However, this donor economy, associated with recurrent attempts at predation toward the pilgrims, was jostled by the political movements that shook the region at the start of the twentieth century: the demise of the Ottoman Empire, followed by the short, but troubled reign of

[9] Miller, "Pilgrims' Progress."

FIGURE 11 Four early twentieth-century Hajj functionaries

Hussein, and finally the establishment of Saudi power, until the latter profoundly transformed the conditions of the pilgrimage owing to its oil windfall.

A Donor Economy Fed by the Ottoman Treasury and Waqf System

After seizing power from the Mamluks, the Ottomans endeavored to preserve the system for the exchange of goods, thus allowing the institutions and men of the two holy cities of Islam (*ḥaramayn*) to continue to be supported. To stress the religious importance of Hijaz, the Ottomans taxed the province very little and accorded it relative autonomy. Moreover, the Ottomans were viewed as being very generous, as were the other Muslim powers and many individuals of wealthy or modest means. The majority of donations and subsidies paid to Hijaz emanated directly from the Ottoman treasury and the sultan's personal funds, but a large part also came from a multitude of pious foundations (*waqfs*) established throughout the Muslim world. Waqf property, which could comprise buildings, land, or businesses (hammams, shops, etc.), were made inalienable by their owners upon their death, with the usufruct being given to the *haramayn* either immediately or after the exhaustion of heirs.

The Ottoman sultans and their families constituted influential *waqfs*, which were centrally managed in Istanbul. All of the empire's provinces, even the smallest, maintained such *waqfs*, established by individuals or ruling elites, with the profits flowing to the central fund in Istanbul.[10] Other provinces with an autonomous status, such as Algeria in the eighteenth century and Egypt in the nineteenth century, directly managed the revenues and their transfer to Hijaz. In 1830, the city of Algiers counted 1,748 properties set up as *waqf al-ḥaramayn*, "*waqf* for the two holy mosques," and the revenue, entrusted to ten notables in the form of gold coins, was sent with the pilgrimage caravan every year or two.[11] In Egypt, the *waqf al-haramayn* established since the Mamluk period were especially numerous and sizable. Between 1880 and 1924, they provided Hijaz with an average annual allowance of 54,350 Egyptian pounds.[12] Finally, Mecca and Medina possessed numerous *waqfs* of their own, particularly shops and rental properties intended for the pilgrims, with the income allowing the poor population to be partially supported.

The proportion of the budget allocated to Hijaz by the Ottoman Empire and Egypt was renegotiated each year and was regularly the subject of cost-cutting attempts. At the end of the nineteenth century, Egypt allocated an annual budget of approximately 45,000 Egyptian pounds to the pilgrimage (less than the *waqf* revenues), about half of which was dedicated to sending grains to Hijaz. On the other hand, Ottoman subsidies primarily took the form of cash transfers. The greatest part of the funds received by the province of Hijaz was devoted to internal security expenditures, notably for the police force and army, but also to paying very large, but fluctuating sums of money to pacify the tribes crossed by the flow of pilgrims. The remainder of the *sürre* was intended to supply the caravans, remunerate their officials, and subsidize the holy cities. This aid flowed primarily to the Sharif of Mecca and his family, then to the elites, particularly the religious elites, and lastly, to the poor, charity organizations, or health and educational institutions for their maintenance.[13] The money and aid in-kind intended for the Sharif were handed

[10] Faroqhi, *Pilgrims and Sultans*.
[11] H. Hoexter, *Endowments, Rulers, and Community: Waqf Al-Haramayn in Ottoman Algiers* (Leiden: Brill, 1998).
[12] I. Rifʿat Pāshā, *Mirʾāt al-ḥaramayn* (Cairo: Dār al-Kutub al-Miṣriyya, 1925), 359.
[13] W. L. Ochsenwald, "Ottoman Subsidies to the Hijaz, 1877–1886," *International Journal of Middle East Studies*, 6 (1975): 300–307.

over to him during a great ceremony in Mina at the end of the pilgrimage. Other recipients of the Ottoman *sürre* and the less significant contributions from Egypt and Algeria were inscribed in registers along with the sum to which each beneficiary was entitled. This was a lifetime privilege, although the sums varied from 1,000 to 2,000 Turkish piastres.[14] Despite such a codified organization, the distribution of funds was not free from irregularities or even corruption.

British Annuity in Lieu of Ottoman Aid

The First World War, followed by the fall of the Ottoman Empire, the principal source of Hijaz's aid, brought to an end these traditional forms of subsidies for the holy cities of Islam. The war interrupted the caravan of Damascus carrying the *sürre* and, of course, it discouraged the pilgrims, quickly threatening the economy of Hijaz. The Egyptian mahmal, however, was sent in 1915 by a British warship, with 20,000 bags of Indian flour to ensure the provision of the province despite the maritime blockade of the Arabian coastline. The beginning of the Arab Revolt in June 1916 was accompanied by a massive investment from Great Britain, as much economic as military, in order to lend support to Hussein, the Sharif of Mecca. After the initial payments to back the beginning of the Arab Revolt, the British contribution became regular, amounting to approximately £125,000 per month, with the sum increased to £225,000 in January 1918 under relentless pressure from Hussein.[15] These subsidies replaced the traditional modes of aid, thus transferring the dependence of Hijaz from the Ottoman Empire to England, all the while concentrating and privatizing these sums in the hands of the Sharif.

Although reduced after the war, the British subsidies nevertheless continued to flow into the coffers of Hijaz, notably to ensure the security of the pilgrimage, whose defense constituted a moral obligation for the English and a symbol of their domination over the region. However, Hussein's management of the pilgrimage was considered deplorable by all nations concerned. Whereas the pilgrimages at the start of the 1920s took place under particularly precarious and dangerous conditions – notably because of attacks on pilgrims, victims of the Bedouin who had not received their usual subsidies – the Sharif and his close relations openly

[14] J. L. Burckhardt, *Travels in Arabia*, 2 vols. (London: Henry Colburn, 1829).

[15] J. Teitelbaum, *The Rise and Fall of the Hashimite Kingdom of Arabia* (New York University Press, 2001).

indulged in extravagant spending, thus making them reticent to provide their English creditors with an expenditure statement. Exasperated by the situation, the English cut the Sharif's subsidies in February 1920, before renewing them in September of the same year, but at the same level as those transferred to his rival Abdulaziz Ibn Saud, the Emir of Najd, who had profited from British largesse since 1915.[16] The Sharif's stubbornness not to fulfill his obligations with regard to the pilgrimage, his opposition to the mandates, and his refusal to negotiate with Ibn Saud eventually contributed to tipping the scales in favor of the latter. In fact, Ibn Saud had judiciously used the British revenue to secure the allegiance of the tribes, which eventually enabled him to defeat his rival militarily in December 1925.

Although British aid was maintained, it was not sufficient to ensure the ambitions of the new Saudi power. By borrowing from the Indian government, merchants in the Hijaz and Najd, and private British companies, Ibn Saud victoriously succeeded in his fight against the Ikhwan, although not without running up a debt of more than £130,000 at the beginning of 1931.[17] In the years preceding the Second World War, a period marked by the effects of the economic crisis, most of the income in the new Kingdom of Saudi Arabia, which had nevertheless made great efforts to improve the pilgrimage and ensure its safety, came from alms tax (*zakāt*); from taxes on agriculture, gold, and silver; and from numerous taxes and levies imposed on the pilgrims.

Tax Levying on Pilgrims

As early as the twelfth century, Ibn Jubayr complained about the taxes levied on pilgrims and the extortion to which they were subjected from the inhabitants of Hijaz. Although the province itself was taxed very little, it benefited from diverse pilgrimage taxes, the number and amount of which greatly fluctuated according to the control exerted by the central authorities – Mamluk and then Ottoman – and the greed of the local elites, especially the Sharif. The revenue base in the province came from customs, with the Sharif and Vali splitting the profits. However, these were naturally insufficient, and if the indispensable subsidies provided by the Ottoman authorities were reduced or delayed, then the

[16] Teitelbaum, *Rise and Fall of the Hashimite Kingdom.*

[17] J. Kostiner, *The Making of Saudi Arabia, 1916–1936: From Chieftaincy to Monarchical State* (Oxford University Press, 1993).

Sharif of Mecca immediately reacted by increasing the taxation on the pilgrims. The most persistent tax in the history of the pilgrimage was the Sharif of Mecca's tax on the hire of camels used to transport pilgrims on the routes between Mecca and ʿArafat, Mecca and Medina, and Yanbu and Medina. It generally represented half of the rental fee, thus forcing the camel brokers to increase it by much more.

The organization of the system of sanitary control for pilgrims in the nineteenth century led to the introduction of sanitary taxes. The pilgrims from the south were subject to a quarantine tax at the Qamaran quarantine station, which varied according to the duration of their stay; those from the north were subjected to a fixed tax at the El-Tor quarantine station. The taxes collected in Kamaran and El-Tor went respectively to the health boards in Istanbul and Alexandria, which managed these two establishments. After arriving in Jeddah, all pilgrims had to pay an additional sanitary tax, known as the disembarkation tax, which flowed into the coffers of Hijaz province. They also paid a visa fee, and their luggage, whether their personal effects or a few goods intended to supply their modest trade, was subjected to customs duty. To these direct taxes were added indirect contributions through the taxation of foodstuffs consumed on site and charges on the money paid to the agents who organized the pilgrimage.

These taxes soared during the short reign of Hussein. Seeking to increase his income after the Ottoman aid had dried up, the king of Hijaz did not hesitate to tax the pilgrims. In addition to the usual taxes, rising to levels never before seen, the pilgrims had to pay entry and exit fees to the cities of Jeddah, Mecca, and Medina, a tax on tent hire in ʿArafat and another for slaughter in Mina, and finally, an embarkation fee at the end of their costly pilgrimage. In 1922 alone, the British Consul in Jeddah calculated that the Hashemite government collected taxes of approximately 78 rupees or £5 per pilgrim. With 56,000 pilgrims arriving by sea that year, the Sharif would have derived a substantial income amounting to £280,000.

The condemnation of this racket was unanimous and undoubtedly precipitated the fall of Hussein. When Ibn Saud welcomed the first pilgrimage of his reign in 1926, he assured not only security, but also honesty. One of Ibn Saud's main achievements at the beginning of his reign was not to lower taxes, but to rationalize and codify the tax levying on pilgrims, thus breaking with the arbitrary system that characterized the former period. From 1926 onward, all pilgrims required a passport, which was affixed with a special visa upon their entry to Hijaz, thus allowing the direct taxes to be centralized, although the sanitary and disembarkation taxes were always supplementary. Transportation within the sacred territory, from then on entrusted to automotive companies, was also taxed. However, these taxes paid directly to the government were for the most part removed in 1952 when the state treasury began to receive substantial oil revenues. In 1936, the new customs regulation authorized pilgrims to enter with fifty kilos of provisions and personal effects duty-free, but any belongings subject to customs duty were scrupulously monitored by Ibn Saud's financial advisor and his cohort of agents, who formed the core of the Ministry of Finances.[18] The perpetuation of the system of direct and indirect tax levies on the pilgrimage allowed the king to ensure the allegiance of the merchant traders living from its revenues, but unlike the period of Hussein's reign, the money collected went, at least partly, toward improving the general conditions and hygiene of the pilgrimage, a fact that was acknowledged by all observers at the time and particularly appreciated by the pilgrims themselves.

AN ECONOMIC ORDEAL FOR PILGRIMS

Economic Profile of the Pilgrims

Although wealthy individuals were never absent from the pilgrimage, the great mass of pilgrims was composed of people from the popular classes – farmers, craftsmen, tradesmen, and later civil servants – the majority being men enough old to invest their entire life's savings into the sacred voyage. For an absence of several weeks or even months in some cases, the cost of the voyage was indeed very high. In the middle of the eighteenth century, the total cost of the voyage by caravan was about 200 piastres, that is to say, more than the price of an average house in Damascus at the time, which was normally some 175 piastres.[19] While the spread of steam navigation certainly decreased the duration of the voyage, the cost of the pilgrimage continued to represent a considerable financial investment. The economic transformations associated with colonization, and more generally, with the modernization process led to the emergence of new professional categories for making money, which could partly be devoted

[18] M. Al-Rasheed, *A History of Saudi Arabia* (Cambridge University Press, 2010).

[19] A. Rafeq, "New Light on the Transportation of the Damascene Pilgrimage during the Ottoman Period," in R. Olson (ed.), *Islamic and Middle Eastern Societies* (Brattleboro, VT: Amana Books, 1987), 127–136.

to the pilgrimage. However, many pilgrims had to resort to their family or loans, or even to the sale of part of their property. Others took regional products to engage in small trade in Jeddah and Mecca, which became commercially animated during the pilgrimage and in return offered a multitude of objects and religious paraphernalia for sale. Certain pilgrims departed with only their *niyya* (pious intention), depending instead on the generosity of their co-religionists along the way. For some, especially the Africans, the pilgrimage was a matter of almost an entire lifetime. They went for many years, and their long journey was punctuated by stops lasting several years along the road, the time necessary to earn enough money before continuing.

The pilgrimage as an investment was strongly dependent on the general or local economic situation. Economic crises made the number of pilgrims plummet, as was the case in the 1930s. Overseas pilgrims, who had totaled 99,000 in 1928, numbered only 23,000 in 1933, thus strongly weakening the Hijaz economy and forcing Ibn Saud to maintain the taxation system. In every country and in every region of the Muslim world, the least disruption – drought, bad harvest, grasshopper invasion, and so forth – led to an immediate fall in departures.

Those who did make the journey were subject to different constraints according to their country of origin. In the event of their not returning from the voyage, pilgrims were required to pay their debts and put their affairs in order before departing. Drawing from the Qur'an, which states that the Hajj is a duty only "for whoever is able to find thereto a way" (Q Āl 'Imrān 3:97), the Dutch authorities imposed the obligation in 1859 for candidate pilgrims to prove that they had the means not only to make the round-trip journey, but also maintain their family for the duration of their absence.[20] In 1894, the Algerian regulations were aligned along these principles. To obtain the necessary authorization to undertake the pilgrimage, pilgrims had to present the sum required for their journey as well as a guarantee deposit to the colonial authorities. In 1903, Russia in turn required pilgrims to show their possession of sufficient funds to make the round-trip journey.[21] The British, on the other hand, always refused to impose any conditions on resources, fearing that the Muslims would perceive it as a hindrance to their religious freedom. Thus, depending on the

[20] W. R. Roff, "Sanitation and Security. The Imperial Powers and the Nineteenth Century Hajj," *Arabian Studies* 6 (1982): 143–160.

[21] P. Brower, "Russian Roads to Mecca: Religious Tolerance and Muslim Pilgrimage in the Russian Empire," *Slavic Review*, 55 (1996): 567–584.

constraints imposed by the colonial powers, the pilgrims arrived in Hijaz with more or less money. Their financial situation incidentally determined the stereotypical perception that the inhabitants of Hijaz had of them. Dutch subjects and Malayans, who tended to remain in the region for a lengthy period of time, were regarded as "good pilgrims" and considered "docile." The Maghreb pilgrims were perceived as miserly, undoubtedly because they stayed in the area for the least amount of time on account of the strict control of the French authorities. Finally, the Indians and, to a lesser extent, the Persians and Russians, often being penniless, were regarded as "bad pilgrims." It is certainly true that once in Hijaz, where the pilgrimage industry was an essential resource for its inhabitants, the pilgrims had to continuously put their hands in their pockets.

A Costly Enterprise

In addition to the taxes flowing into the province's treasury, or more often, into the Sharif's hands, the pilgrimage activities generated income for a great number of inhabitants in Hijaz, who in a few weeks could earn enough money to subsist for the rest of the year. The main pilgrim services were managed by organizations whose members had paid for the right to exercise these functions, which were often hereditary. The primary organization was that of the mutawwifs, guides who were allocated different Muslim territories: a particular country or province was thus managed by a certain number of mutawwifs, who in theory were familiar with its language and customs. These Meccan guides supervised the entire stay of the pilgrims: they were indispensable to the travelers who were all ignorant of the country, and they played a vital role in helping them perform the religious rituals, notably the numerous prayers, without committing a faux pas. They were paid a sum of money akin to a salary (*amāna*, literally "objects of trust"), but they also received plenty of baksheesh to facilitate the procedures. The principal guides had agents (*wakīl*) in Jeddah, who welcomed the pilgrims on their arrival at the port, dealt with the entry formalities, accommodated them, and then organized their departure by caravan to Mecca. The Meccan mutawwifs then took charge and accompanied their group of pilgrims for the entire duration of the pilgrimage, managing all of the material and spiritual aspects as well as guiding them in their choices and purchases. Medina likewise had its own guides (*muzawwir*) who assisted the pilgrims during their visit to the city sheltering the tomb of the Prophet. The chain of pilgrimage activities was thus tightly controlled, with the relevant agents (landlords, baggage porters, *zemzemî*, tent or camel renters, etc.) being remunerated either directly by the pilgrim or through the intermediary of the mutawwif.

The prices for these services, in theory fixed by the *vali*, were in reality highly variable according to the economic needs of the province, the arbitrariness of its leaders, or the shrewdness of its agents. The consuls in Jeddah strove to follow and bring order to this chaos as a way of updating their supervisory authorities on the situation so that the latter could calculate the approximate amount necessary to undertake the pilgrimage. After the 1908 revolution, the Young Turks tried to lower the prices, especially the remuneration of the mutawwifs, an attempt that was resumed in 1917 with Sharif Hussein, without any more success for lack of a real effort to control the situation. Once again, Ibn Saud managed to put an end to the most blatant abuses, although without succeeding in completely eradicating the exploitation of pilgrims. From 1926, an official rate was set each year for all of the proceedings conducted within the framework of the pilgrimage and then distributed across Muslim nations. It was thus possible to determine with a certain degree of precision the sum required for the pilgrimage and inform pilgrims so as to restrict the departures to those who possessed this sum, even if many continued to ignore it. However, after the Second World War, the Kingdom of Saudi Arabia held different nations responsible for respecting these "fixed pilgrim costs."[22]

The pilgrims were not only confronted with high prices, but also with the constraints of foreign exchange. Under the Ottoman Empire, the Turkish currency was in theory the only legal currency, but in practice, all existing currencies circulated in Hijaz. In the absence of banks, the currencies carried by the pilgrims were changed at a multitude of money changers at highly variable rates. The Indian rupee was the most stable currency, whereas the majority of other currencies, particularly the franc, were exchanged below the normal rate, which put further strain on the pilgrims' budget. These foreign currencies were then used to purchase the imports necessary for the province, especially during the pilgrimage. The obligation imposed by Sharif Hussein and later Ibn Saud to use only gold currency (gold pound sterling) in Hijaz, despite its instability, caused a particular difficulty for Algerian pilgrims. Indeed, as they did not have the right to export gold, France had to set up a complex system to circumvent the unfavorable exchange rate of the franc. From 1929, a French bank opened a branch in Hijaz at the time of the pilgrimage

[22] Vredenbregt, "The Haddj: Some of Its Features."

every year in order to reimburse pilgrims the gold exchange value of their checks issued in North Africa, with a credit line being granted by the French government. At the time, even for France, there was no longer any question of obstructing Muslims' religious observance. Nevertheless, all of the colonial powers still deplored the financial evasion that the pilgrimage posed to their economies.

Destitute Pilgrims during the Pilgrimage

Under the pressure of taxes, high prices, and prohibitive food costs, improvident or extravagant pilgrims found themselves without any money left at the end of the pilgrimage and sometimes unable to return home. The impetus of faith that drove pilgrims to the sacred territory was hardly encumbered by economic considerations. The Indians, who were not subjected to any conditions on resources, were the most numerous among these destitute. Each year, approximately one-quarter of the Indian quota was declared destitute at the stopover in Kamaran, where they were exempted from paying quarantine taxes. The Africans, arriving on foot from their remote region, sometimes had to live for several years in Hijaz under miserable conditions before being able to set off again. Finally, the restrictive French policy forced many Maghrebians and later Syrians to make the voyage in "clandestine," that is to say, in violation of the prohibition or outside of the official convoys. Departing without the obligatory controls and often without enough money, they then became blocked in Hijaz.

Once the pilgrimage was over, these destitute individuals crowded the streets of Jeddah while living off charity. They were vulnerable to be victims of the slave trade, especially the Africans, and they suffered a very high mortality rate. These pilgrims thus posed a constant problem, as much for the Ottoman authorities followed by the Sharif and Ibn Saud, who held the colonial powers responsible for them, as for the latter, who had a moral obligation to come to the assistance of these poor, which turned out to be a huge financial burden. The French Consulate, which did not have the funds for repatriations, had to improvise each year by drawing from its treasury or cooperating with the shipping companies, which in return accepted an overload in violation of the legislation. The British Consulate resorted to the same expedients, but it also benefited from the assistance of the Anglo-Indian government and funds collected for this purpose by Islamic associations, in particular the Jubilee Indian Pilgrim Fund Relief created in 1897. Already reduced by the increasingly common obligation to purchase a round-trip ticket, the problem was resolved once and for all with the Saudi residence regulations in 1952.

From the 1930s, ever more demanding and sophisticated Saudi regulations were added to the international sanitary regulations and colonial legislations to help regulate the pilgrimage, especially from an economic perspective. Until the 1950s, however, certain issues still endured, and the complaints, regarding embezzlements in particular, were always numerous. Even though today they have not completely disappeared, after this period, two major events profoundly altered the conditions of the pilgrimage. First, the independence of Muslim countries removed the mediation of colonial powers, thus returning the Hajj to a strictly Muslim affair. Second, the oil revenues allowed the kingdom to break its quasi-exclusive dependence on the pilgrimage, but even more so, to spend colossal sums of money on improving its conditions. Since then, the pilgrimage is no longer perceived as an exploitable resource for the country, but rather as a religious event to manage as best as possible.

9

International Bodies

The Pilgrimage to Mecca and International Health Regulations

Valeska Huber

In recent years, the Hajj has once again emerged in debates on global health. In 2009, the journey was connected to fears of H1N1, more commonly known as "swine flu," and in 2012 and 2013, there were rumors of a possibly global spread of a new disease, the Middle Eastern Respiratory Syndrome (MERS), through the annual meeting of pilgrims in Mecca. This latter affliction triggered a whole list of precautions, propagated by the World Health Organization (WHO). Pilgrims should consider at the outset if they were fit enough to travel and then take precautions such as the wearing of facial masks, frequent hand washing, good personal hygiene, and food safety practices. A publicity campaign with banners, pamphlets, and radio announcements on board planes and ships and at international points of entry should raise awareness about the disease. WHO surveillance schemes and laboratory services should be stepped up, and the health of returning pilgrims should be closely monitored with potentially ill travelers identified and transported to specific hospitals for assessment and treatment. If a diseased pilgrim was found on board a plane, a "passenger locator form" was to be used to make sure that crucial intelligence on the particular pilgrim and the outbreak of the disease could be centrally collected.[1]

These precautions – in particular, the focus on the pilgrims' bodily practices, the routes of travel, information, science, and international organizations – resonate elements of the nineteenth- and twentieth-century developments that will be teased out in the following. In this

[1] "World-Travel Advice on MERS-CoV for Pilgrimages." Retrieved from who.int/ith/updates/20130725 (accessed October 23, 2013).

chapter, I build an argument relating to the connection of the Hajj and the establishment of international health regimes. The chapter follows cycles of connection between contagious disease and the Hajj as a mass event, beginning in the 1850s and 1860s with the Conference of Constantinople and the establishment of quarantines in the Red Sea, to the introduction of new scientific measures around the turn of the century, the experiment with new international organizations in the 1920s, and the question of decolonization and self-government after the Second World War.

This chapter takes its inspiration from two approaches that are not usually juxtaposed. One is the new history of internationalism and international organizations. By looking at the different phases of sanitary internationalism from the first International Sanitary Conferences to the WHO, it will become evident that the sanitary administration of the pilgrimage took a specific role in the emergence but also in conflicts between different international (and imperial) bodies.[2] This research therefore connects with work on the history of internationalism as it has been pioneered, for instance, by Akira Iriye.[3] More recently, the period of interwar internationalism has received more attention and has been connected more explicitly with empire.[4] The emergence of postwar international organizations, particularly in the field of health, has been linked to decolonization.[5] Yet the different phases of internationalism have not often been connected, or else these connections remain on a more general level.[6]

[2] S. Chiffoleau, *Genèse de la santé publique internationale: De la peste d'Orient à l'OMS* (Presses Universitaires de Rennes, 2012); E. Tagliacozzo, *The Longest Journey: South East Asians and the Pilgrimage to Mecca* (Oxford University Press, 2013), 133–155.

[3] See, e.g., A. Iriye, *Cultural Internationalism and World Order* (Baltimore: Johns Hopkins University Press, 1997), and M. Geyer and J. Paulmann (eds.), *The Mechanics of Internationalism: Culture, Society, and Politics from the 1840s to the First World War* (Oxford University Press, 2001).

[4] See, e.g., D. Gorman, *The Emergence of International Society in the 1920s* (Cambridge University Press, 2012); S. Pedersen, *The Guardians: The League of Nations and the Crisis of Empire* (Oxford University Press, 2015).

[5] M. Mazower, *No Enchanted Palace: The End of Empire and the Ideological Origins of the United Nations* (Princeton University Press, 2006); S. S. Amrith, *Decolonizing International Health: India and Southeast Asia, 1930–65* (Basingstoke: Palgrave Macmillan, 2006).

[6] Recent broad-ranging analyses include M. Herren, *Internationale Organisationen seit 1865: Eine Globalgeschichte der internationalen Ordnung* (Darmstadt: Wissenschaftliche Buchgesellschaft, 2009); M. Mazower, *Governing the World: The History of an Idea* (London: Penguin, 2012); G. Sluga, *Internationalism in the Age of Nationalism* (Philadelphia: University of Pennsylvania Press, 2013).

As the precautions of the WHO of 2013 illuminate, questions of worldwide security, which need to be mediated through international organizations, are intimately connected to the body of the individual pilgrim as a potential disease carrier. Just like the history of international organizations, the "body on the move" has turned into a thriving field of research, connecting Foucauldian influences with reflections on technology and agency. By now classic works on the connection of the body, governmentality, and (urban) infrastructure have been complemented by work on the maritime spaces and subaltern lives.[7] More recently, health and medicine at sea has also been studied in more detail.[8]

The two bodies – international organizations and individual travelers – are however rarely brought into dialogue. Looking at the Mecca pilgrimage in the nineteenth and twentieth centuries through two tools, science and statistics, allows us to do so. Questions of laboratories, quarantine stations, disinfection, medical qualifications, and vaccinations were debated at international meetings and then applied to the pilgrims during their journey. At the same meetings, delegates moved the importance of reliable information and intelligence – that is, the statistical encapsulation of the pilgrim body – to the center. The question of the pilgrim body furthermore highlighted the competition between international, national, imperial, and religious authorities. Controlling pilgrim bodies or at least the danger of contagion that could disseminate from them, thus led to the emergence of new institutions whose interlocking was often accompanied by friction.

The chapter follows the cycles of the connection between the international and the body, but also sees the pilgrims shift between different means of transport leading to new sanitary worries and requirements. A first phase witnessed the globalization of the pilgrimage through the use of steamship and – partly as a reaction – an increased reflection on how to govern it internationally. The chapter then moves to the technologies employed to deal with this acceleration of the Hajj. A second phase after the First World War featured new forms of international and imperial

[7] See, e.g., R. Sennett, *Flesh and Stone: The Body and the City in Western Civilization* (London: Faber and Faber, 1994); P. Joyce, *The Rule of Freedom: Liberalism and the Modern City* (London: Verso, 2003); F. Steel, *Oceania under Steam: Sea Transport and the Cultures of Colonialism, c. 1870–1914* (Manchester University Press, 2011); C. Anderson, *Subaltern Lives: Biographies of Colonialism in the Indian Ocean World, 1790–1920* (Cambridge University Press, 2012).

[8] For instance, K. Foxhall, *Health, Medicine and the Sea: Australian Voyages, c.1815–1860* (Manchester University Press, 2012).

organization but also new fears connected to the pilgrims' use of the railway rather than established maritime routes. The third moment of internationalism after the Second World War, assessed in the last part of the chapter, had to face the challenge of air transportation but also of decolonization. This analysis of different moments of internationalism will be effected through a combination of international and colonial archives and the close reading of several committee, subcommittee, and conference debates.

THE EMERGENCE OF INTERNATIONALISM

In the second half of the nineteenth century, many pilgrims to Mecca changed their mode of conveyance: more and more pilgrims from different destinations traveled by steamship. Between 1868 and 1892, the number of pilgrims taking the sea route more than doubled.[9] This does not mean that all pilgrims chose this new means of conveyance of course. Pilgrims continued to travel by foot, caravan, or dhow ship, and, most of the times, they relied for their journey on more than one mode of conveyance. Multiple mobilities thus had to interlock for a successful journey to Mecca.[10]

Not only did the use of the steamship turn the Hajj into a business heavily dominated by European steamship companies, and larger numbers of pilgrims bundled together on a single ship made the pilgrims potentially more easily controllable, but the new speed of transportation also led to new fears of contagion, particularly after the 1869 opening of the Suez Canal, which established a direct link between the Red Sea and the Mediterranean. Western observers were ambivalent about the acceleration of the Hajj until it turned into a threat as it became connected with the spread of epidemic disease and the rise of anti-colonial ideas.

The cholera epidemics of the mid-nineteenth century are a first illustration of the new fear of proximity and speed and shows its intimate connection with the pilgrimage. Cholera spread from India to Europe from the 1830s onward along increasingly busy trade

[9] P. Zylberman, "Civilizing the State: Borders, Weak States and International Health in Modern Europe," in A. Bashford (ed.), *Medicine at the Border: Disease, Globalization and Security, 1850 to the Present* (Basingstoke: Palgrave Macmillan), 25. M. B. Miller, "Pilgrims' Progress: The Business of the Hajj," *Past & Present*, 191, 1 (2006): 189–228.

[10] V. Huber, "'Multiple Mobilities': Über den Umgang mit verschiedenen Mobilitätsformen um 1900," *Geschichte und Gesellschaft*, 36 (2010): 317–341.

routes.[11] The disease became the horror of the emerging European middle classes due to the rapidity with which it struck and the associations of a return to the Middle Ages. Most important for our context was cholera's association with the new global connectedness through railway and steamship. In this context, the Mecca pilgrimage moved to center stage from the 1860s onward. As the 1865 epidemic had entered the Mediterranean through the Hijaz, in the eyes of contemporaries, the whole of Europe now found itself "at the mercy of the pilgrimage to Mecca."[12] After the opening of the Suez Canal, such expressions became legion. Comments could focus on the locality of Mecca as in the case of the doctor W. H. Simpson who stated in 1892, "Mecca, I hold, is the place of danger for Europe – a perpetual menace to the Western world."[13] Other commentators coupled these spatial conceptions with the image of the pilgrim body as a breeding ground for disease: "The actual danger for Europe lies in the international Mahomedan places of pilgrimage ... Oriental squalor and the absence of any, or any serious sanitary police at the great places of pilgrimage encourage the disease whose germ finds a fertile soil in the bodies of the pilgrims, weakened by all kinds of depravations."[14]

Even though the cholera epidemics could not be traced to Mecca most of the time, but entered Europe, for instance, through Afghanistan and Russia, the pilgrim journey moved to the forefront of imperial and internationalist discussions on contagion in the second half of the nineteenth century.[15] In the case of the British and French empires, soon bacteriological contagion came to be coupled with the contagiousness of political ideas that pilgrims were exposed to while in Mecca.[16] The imperial debates thus connected three concerns related to the pilgrimage: the

[11] The cholera epidemics have yielded a huge literature. See A. Briggs, "Cholera and Society in the Nineteenth Century," *Past & Present*, 19 (1961): 76–96; R. E. McGrew, "The First Cholera Epidemic and Social History," *Bulletin of the History of Medicine*, 34 (1960): 61–73; and numerous local studies such as R. J. Evans, *Death in Hamburg: Society and Politics in the Cholera Years, 1830–1910* (Oxford University Press, 1987).

[12] Belgian Consul-General, quoted in Zylberman, "Civilizing the State," 24.

[13] W. J. Simpson, "Maritime Quarantine and Sanitation in Relation to the Cholera," *The Practitioner: A Journal of Therapeutics and Public Health*, 48 (1892): 153.

[14] Bundesarchiv, Berlin, R/901/21261: *Times of India* (no date), enclosure to a letter of the Imperial German Consulate in Bombay to Chancellor Caprivi, August 8, 1892.

[15] See A. Bashford and C. Hooker (eds.), *Contagion* (London: Routledge, 2001); M. Harrison, *Contagion: How Commerce Has Spread Disease* (New Haven and London: Yale University Press, 2013).

[16] V. Huber, *Channelling Mobilities: Migration and Globalisation in the Suez Canal Region and Beyond* (Cambridge University Press, 2013), 216–220.

spread of epidemic disease, the circulation of anti-colonial ideas, and the costs of destitute or sick pilgrims who had to be repatriated. As a reaction, both empires established new institutions to control the pilgrimage and increasingly attempted to concentrate the pilgrims on specific ships, which were accompanied by medical observers. Whereas the French Empire often resorted to the complete prohibition of the pilgrimage, the British Empire frequently adopted a more careful approach and attempted to work through so-called protectors of pilgrims in the different harbors.[17] The colonial archives not only illustrate the much broader fear of contagion shifting between the sanitary and the political realms but also that the economic side cannot be separated from sanitary issues, with different colonial regimes trying to monopolize their pilgrim traffic with specific companies.[18]

Yet, besides such imperial initiatives to bring the traveling pilgrims under tighter sanitary control – with the side effect of minimizing political risk and possible expenses – contagion and the pilgrimage were also seen as issues of an international order. As a response to the cholera epidemics, several international conferences were held from 1851 onward. They can be analyzed as prototypes of early internationalism.[19] The 1866 and 1885 conferences explicitly targeted the pilgrims. The 1866 conference was held in Constantinople after a cholera outbreak in Mecca, which had traveled at unusual speed directly into Europe. The debate at the conference led to antagonisms between Western Europeans and the delegates of Muslim countries. At the conference, an emergency measure was enacted against the heavy protest of the Muslim representatives; it was based on the French proposal of simply interrupting all maritime communication with the Hijaz and thus detaining the pilgrims without sufficient food in

[17] See material in the Archives nationales d'Outre-Mer (ANOM, for instance AFFPOL (Ministère des colonies) (Maroc) 967; Gouvernement Général d'Algerie 16H/83–90) and Centre des Archives diplomatiques de Nantes (Commission interministérielle des affaires musulmanes). There has been some new research on the British Empire's surveillance of the Hajj: M. C. Low, "Empire and the Hajj: Pilgrims, Plagues, and Pan-Islam under British Surveillance, 1865–1908," *International Journal of Middle East Studies*, 40, 2 (2008): 269–290; J. Slight, "British Imperial Rule and the Hajj," in D. Motadel (ed.), *Islam and Empire* (Oxford University Press, 2014): 53–72.

[18] M. Harrison, "Quarantine, Pilgrimage and Colonial Trade," *Indian Economic and Social History Review*, 29 (1992): 117–144; W. R. Roff, "Sanitation and Security: The Imperial Powers and the Nineteenth-Century Hajj," *Arabian Studies* VI (1982): 143–160.

[19] V. Huber, "The Unification of the Globe by Disease? The International Sanitary Conferences on Cholera, 1851–1894," *Historical Journal*, 49, 2 (2006): 453–476; see also N. Howard-Jones, *The Scientific Background of the International Sanitary Conferences 1851–1938* (Geneva: WHO, 1975).

Mecca, which was presented just after the opening speeches praising the unity of all humankind.[20] At these conferences, the Europeans more than once conceptualized their sanitary project as a civilizing mission geared toward the "Orient" and compared themselves to the Roman Empire or Christian crusaders. The focus on the pilgrims at the international conferences pointed to the different treatment of various forms of mobility and represented the possibility of keeping certain movements free from interference, while increasingly targeting other mobilities, such as those of the pilgrims.[21] The conferences also illustrate the growing weakness of the Ottoman state to implement sanitary measures with medical commissions sent to the Hijaz every year.[22] However, the close analysis of these conferences shows not only their Eurocentrism but also how Muslim delegates at times assumed agency or employed irony pointing to their subordinate role.

If at the sanitary conferences the focus was largely on contagion and on the protection of Europe, some observers took a wider perspective toward the pilgrims' health and disease. Although the pilgrimage was increasingly tightly monitored, some travelers represented Eurocentrism in a different guise, going beyond the issue of contagion and threat to Europe in their conceptualization of the pilgrims' bodies as suffering and in need of European relief. An example of someone taking this position is Isabel Burton, the wife of the famous Mecca traveler Richard Burton. In the 1870s, she traveled to India, sharing a ship with about 800 pilgrims on her journey from Jeddah to Bombay.[23] Her account of that voyage is interesting on a number of levels. Her description shows the focus on the pilgrims' suffering body. Yet suffering could take different forms, broadening definitions of well-being beyond the issues of contagion discussed at the international conferences. Suffering included old age (many pilgrims undertook the journey late in their lives), weather conditions (pilgrims

[20] Procès-verbaux de la Conférence sanitaire internationale ouverte à Constantinople le 13 février 1866, Annexe au Procès-Verbal No. 1, Proposition sur les mesures à prendre dans le cas où le choléra se manifesterait cette année parmi les pèlerins réunis à La Mecque, présentée par les Délégués du Gouvernement français.

[21] Huber, ";Multiple Mobilities": 329–333.

[22] T. M. Brown, M. Cueto, and E. Fee, "The World Health Organization and the Transition from 'International' to 'Global' Public Health," *American Journal of Public Health*, 96, 1 (2006): 62–72.

[23] *The Romance of Isabel Lady Burton. The Story of Her Life.* Told in Part by Herself and in Part by W. H. Wilkins, vol. 2, 3rd ed. (London: Hutchinson & Co, 1897), 568–572; I. Burton, *A E I Arabia Egypt India: A Narrative of Travel* (London: William Mullan and Son, 1879), 99–107.

dying of sunstroke or suffering from the notorious Red Sea heat), the quality of food and sanitary conditions on board, lack of space, or putrid air. Furthermore Burton and others described psychological aspects such as religious exhilaration and ecstasy in their reflections on the pilgrims' body and their state of health.

In her desire to help, Isabel Burton went further than others who merely observed the pilgrims' bodily conditions. Having been rejected three times as a "Nightingale nurse" during the Crimean War, in her own account, Burton tried her best to relieve the suffering of the pilgrims, of which twenty-three died during the passage. Describing a funeral at sea, she could not hide her astonishment over "their excessive facility of departing this life."[24] She observed the different "races from every part of the world," "packed like sardines," and spent whole days treating dysentery and fever, seasickness, feet covered with sores, worms, and thus diseases that were far from those debated at the international conferences: "Those who died did not die of disease so much as of privation and fatigue, hunger, thirst, and opium. They died of vermin and misery."[25] To these conditions she added psychological features such as religious fanaticism and lack of sympathy for their fellow pilgrims, going as far as advocating "Euthanasia" to alleviate their suffering. Isabel Burton's episode ends with the ship's escape from quarantine in Bombay due to her intervention, concluding: "Indeed, if we had been together a few more days, some disease must have broken out."[26]

SCIENCE AND INFORMATION, 1880–1914

While Burton applied a wider definition of health and disease, the International Sanitary Conferences continued to focus on contagion, but with a changing set of instruments at their disposal. The 1890s saw a "codification of the international procedure," which, in the case of the International Sanitary Conferences, was accompanied by scientific advances in the field of disease propagation.[27] The later conferences highlighted two themes that moved the body of the pilgrim to the center. One was the application of modern science – for instance in the form of

[24] Burton, *A E I*, 101.

[25] *The Romance of Isabel Lady Burton*, 569.

[26] Burton, *A E I*, 107.

[27] A. Rasmussen, "Jalons pour une histoire des congers internationaux au XIXe siècle: Régulation scientifique et propagande intellectuelle," *Relations internationales* 62 (1990): 120. See also C. A. Bayly, *The Birth of the Modern World 1780–1914* (Oxford: Blackwell, 2004), 239.

disinfection, bacteriological tests, and vaccination. The other was the gathering of information on individual pilgrims, the assembling of statistics, and the rapid dissemination of such information. The combination of the two, science and information, enabled the slow replacement of general quarantine by regimes of disinfection and surveillance. This shift did not mean, however, that quarantine stations became obsolete. On the contrary, the stations of al-Tur (El Tor) and Qamaran (Camaran) in the Red Sea transformed their image by highlighting the presence of scientific devices such as laboratories and disinfection apparatuses and emerged as experimental grounds with scientific access to the body, through vaccination, fumigation, disinfection, or the examination of stools. They also became places where the international regimes intersected with the individual pilgrim bodies.[28]

The debates on international health and the Hajj at the International Sanitary Conferences were closely connected to the history of changing theories of contagion and disease causation, linked for instance to the name of Robert Koch. The 1892 conference stressed chemical disinfection and bacteriological tests on the spot. However, this modern image of the quarantine stations did not mean that the problems of overcrowding, bribery, and unrest disappeared. Quarantine stations thus remained highly militarized and coercive spaces. The new focus on scientific measures also signified a new interference with religious practices, such as the sterilization of Zamzam water from the well inside Mecca's main mosque. Other methods entered the pilgrim body in the most direct sense, for instance through compulsory vaccination or obligatory stool examinations, practiced at al-Tur since 1911.

In 1894, the discussion at the International Sanitary Conferences returned more explicitly to the Mecca pilgrimage which had been avoided at the 1892 and 1893 conferences in order to facilitate agreement among the participants. The tone was still condescending. Again, the pilgrims were identified as key contaminators – to the astonishment of the British delegate who argued (in line with British geopolitical interests) that cholera had extended from the Hijaz to Europe only once, in 1865, and expressed his surprise "that not a word should have been said regarding the defence of the Russo-Afghan territory, through which cholera has penetrated Europe several times."[29]

[28] See Tagliacozzo, *The Longest Journey*, 150.

[29] Quoted in Huber, "Unification of the Globe by Disease," 469.

Besides a focus on scientific practices, the body of the individual pilgrim also appeared in the debates at the international conferences in relation to statistics and information, which was seen as a response to mere confinement. Knowing about disease outbreaks and circulating this information rapidly by means of telegraph promised to be an alternative to general quarantine. In the case of pilgrims, such knowledge should be achieved by several different measures. Large numbers of pilgrims bundled together on a single ship, of course, also meant that they were more easily controllable, and that the extraction of data was more accurate, at least in theory. Medical observers were on board to witness any outbreak and then tell the officials to disseminate this information as quickly as possible. On the initiative of the International Sanitary Conferences, in 1907 the Office International de Hygiène Publique (OIHP) was founded; the OIHP would be in charge of gathering epidemiological intelligence and reporting on cholera, plague, and yellow fever until its integration into the WHO after the Second World War. This focus on information and intelligence is reflected in the colonial archives, which also highlight the limits of these attempts, as they frequently mention pilgrims using other means of conveyance to escape medical treatment and the associated fees. The French sources even include statistical returns of those pilgrims traveling without permission.[30]

The combination of scientific devices and information practices allowed for new conceptualizations of isolation and confinement.[31] The passage in quarantine through the Suez Canal can serve as one example. Here, an elaborate system of noncontact with the shores of the canal during the passage was developed which included militarized patrols and information politics via telegrams.[32] However, pilgrim ships did not very often qualify for this scheme. Only in the interwar period were the stricter quarantine obligations of pilgrim ships slowly lifted, yet at the expense of tighter controls on the level of scientific tests, information, and documentation.

INTERNATIONALISM AND EMPIRE, 1919–1939

Many interpret the interwar period as a successful time of the expansion of national health systems and international health regimes. For instance,

[30] ANOM, GGA 16H/85.

[31] See A. Bashford and C. Strange (eds.), *Isolation: Places and Practices of Exclusion* (London: Routledge, 2003).

[32] Huber, *Channelling Mobilities*, 249–253.

the fact that no cholera epidemic struck India from 1912 to 1947 was attributed to more comprehensive inoculation. However it proved complicated to come to a solution regarding the pilgrimage on several grounds, in particular due to the changing colonial context in the region. This changing colonial context led on the one hand to stricter scientific measures and identification practices; on the other hand, non-European powers began to express their discontent more forcefully, resulting in the difficulty of establishing a more unified sanitary approach regarding the Hajj.

Right from the beginning, health was on the agenda of the League of Nations with debates on a permanent health organization beyond the existing OIHP in charge of epidemiological information.[33] In the case of the pilgrimage, this was felt to be particularly urgent, as "a very large pilgrimage of Moslems from all quarters of the globe will probably take place as soon as the war is over and transport becomes available."[34] The Italian doctor Lutrario circulated a note in 1922 pointing to the sheer volume of pilgrims from destinations "where the most dangerous countries and regions are situated, the permanent centres of the worst infections."[35] He was also concerned with the changing modes of transportation in connection with an expanded railway system, leading more and more pilgrims to abandon the "old" sea routes and to travel by train.[36] What made the situation even more dangerous in his opinion was the wide variety of pilgrims in terms of origin and social class, and his belief that the pilgrims were generally careless in regard to health matters. Although this scenario of a dangerous mass movement sounds similar to the prewar statements, there were however important changes calling for a new form of internationalism.

After the First World War, the international sanitary regime was complicated by the new political configuration of the Middle East after the

[33] J. Siddiqi, *World Health and World Politics: The World Health Organization and the UN System* (London Hurst & Company, 1995), 19. On the League of Nations more generally, see P. Clavin, *Securing the World Economy: The Reinvention of the League of Nations, 1920–1946* (Oxford University Press, 2013); S. Pedersen, "Review Essay: Back to the League of Nations," *American Historical Review*, 112, 4 (2007): 1091–1117.

[34] TNA, CO 323/800/43, sheet 296: Dr. Granville, Quarantine, December 1918.

[35] LON, Health 12B, R848, 25546: Note by Dr. Lutrario on Pilgrimages to the Holy Places, November 27, 1922, p. 5.

[36] The expansion of the railway system, of course, had already begun before the First World War: see K. Ezzerelli, "Le pèlerinage à La Mecque au temps du chemin de fer du Hedjaz (1908–1914)," in S. Chiffoleau and A. Madoeuf (eds.), *Les pèlerinages au Maghreb et au Moyen-Orient: Espaces publics, espaces du public* (Beirut: IFPO, 2005), 167–191.

demise of the Ottoman Empire. Britain and France had taken responsibility for new Muslim populations, for instance in the Mandate areas of Syria, Iraq, and Palestine. King Hussein of Saudi Arabia remained allied with Britain. As a result, several interdepartmental meetings were convened to discuss the question whether the British government should "confine themselves, as in the past, to guarding the interests of British subjects" or whether they were "to accept general responsibility for ensuring that King Hussein takes adequate precautions."[37] The interdepartmental meeting issued a report arguing that the British government had to take charge of the pilgrimage as it would be blamed if it did not proceed in a smooth manner. Others argued that King Hussein should nominally stay in control while the British government pulled all the strings: "British control was therefore desirable, but with an Arab façade."[38]

These sources illustrate that the sanitary issues connected with the Hajj directly impacted on colonial configurations, and that in this domain the international could not be separated from the imperial realm. The successful organization of the pilgrimage, meaning an orderly journey without health risks at moderate prices, was to be used as positive "propaganda" for instance in the case of Malaya and the Dutch East Indies.[39] More generally, these documents shed light on the British perception of the colonial possessions as highly unstable territories, also attributing to a slowly changing tone in which internationalism was conducted.

This perception of unclear political responsibility led to an even more diffuse situation in terms of the bodies, both international and imperial, in charge of sanitary regulations on the pilgrimage. A major debate in the interwar period focused on the multiplicity of organizations responsible for guarding the pilgrimage. The 1903 convention had charged two separate authorities, the Health Council of Constantinople and the Quarantine Board of Egypt, with the Qamaran and al-Tur stations respectively. With the Ottoman Empire unable to act, the Indian government took responsibility for Qamaran, whereas at Jeddah King Hussein was to

[37] TNA, CO 323/800/43, sheet 276: Foreign Office to Under-Secretary of State, Colonial Office, March 13, 1919. See also FO 608/93/8: Minutes of a Conference on the Pilgrimage, held at the Foreign Office on March 18, 1919, with representatives of the Foreign Office, the War Office, the Treasury, the Ministry of Shipping, the Colonial Office, the Local Government Board, and the India Office.

[38] TNA, FO 608/936: Minutes of Inter-Departmental Pilgrimage Quarantine Committee, Foreign Office on May 13, 1919, sheet 355; see also Earl Curzon of Kedleston to Sir Eyre Crowe, November 12, 1919.

[39] TNA, CO 323/800/43, sheet 281: British Consulate-General Batavia to Colonial Office, October 11, 1918.

be accounted for the quarantine arrangements at al-Tur, albeit under the supervision of the British Agent at Jeddah and acting under the orders of the High Commissioner, Cairo. What is more, the sanitation had also to be financed through taxes or otherwise, involving the British Treasury as a further agency claiming to have a say.[40]

Lutrario, in his 1922 report, dwelled on the variety of bodies in charge of sanitary issues, including the Inter-Allied Sanitary Commission, the Hedjaz Administration, and the Egyptian Quarantine Board. He called for a unification of these bodies: "Unity of control is essential if the measures required are to be effective."[41] A reform therefore had to create a uniform section, carrying out clear principles and applying the same methods everywhere.

Following Lutrario's report, a commission, established by the Health Section of the League of Nations in 1922 and composed of four European members, was therefore charged with the revision of the Sanitary Convention of 1912. The commission echoed Lutrario's proposal highlighting the new political organization of the regions necessitating a revision of the sanitary measures, the increased importance of the railway for the pilgrimage, and in consequence the need for new quarantine stations.[42]

However, despite this intervention, the creation of a uniform international regime proved problematic in the 1920s and 1930s, and the plurality of rules and regulations was not dissolved. Besides the existence of several international institutions, most importantly the OIHP and the League of Nations Health Section, imperial and international agreements often coexisted, such as the Indian Pilgrim Ship Rules of 1931, which complemented the International Sanitary Convention of 1926.[43] The different international sanitary conventions and conferences on the issue of the pilgrimage of 1926, 1929, and 1933 show how pressing the subject was for contemporaries, but also how difficult it was to come to an agreement in a charged political climate.[44] They continued the strategies

[40] TNA, T 161/1086: Arabia: Mecca Pilgrimage; sanitary control and maintenance of destitute refugees.

[41] LON, Health 12B, R848, 25546: Note by Dr. Lutrario on Pilgrimages to the Holy Places, November 27, 1922, p. 9.

[42] WHO Archives, OIHP, T27–T28: Report by the Special Commission (Health Section of the League of Nations) appointed to investigate prevailing international arrangements for the prevention of epidemic diseases in certain Middle East countries connected with the Mecca Pilgrimage (February 20–March 20, 1922).

[43] See also WHO Archives, OIHP, T29: Rules for Moroccan pilgrims.

[44] See Chiffoleau, *Genèse de la santé publique internationale*, x.

of disease containment through surveillance systems, emergency responses, and transborder regulations and still found themselves in the old tradition of sanitary internationalism, which had the objective of "isolating Europe from all dealings with the uncultivated and unhealthy habits of Oriental populations."[45] The 1929 conference in Beirut stressed the elements of information (obligatory notification of the OIHP by all the powers involved), identification (obligatory *carnets de pèlerinage* with photograph or fingerprint), and science (obligatory vaccination against cholera and smallpox).

There were many protests against these measures, for instance by Iran, which had refused the invitation to take part in the 1929 conference and which opted against the *carnet de pèlerinage*. These reactions showed how internationalism increasingly emerged as an arena in which to negotiate independence from the West.[46] As a consequence of these protests, a new meeting had to be convened in 1930. If in the nineteenth century Britain had sabotaged several international conventions, now other powers were able to assume such agency. On other occasions, some Middle Eastern countries demanded better representation in international bodies. In 1925, for instance, the Egyptian government asked for more seats in the Egyptian Quarantine Board. Its composition was still based on the 1892 conference, when the Egyptian members had been reduced from nine to four, a measure that had been accepted and later ratified by Khedivial decree despite the lively protest of the Egyptian delegate who argued that at that time, Egypt had not been an "independent country or free in his acts."[47] These examples show that the tone of the debates had changed, at least to a limited extent.

Despite this new confidence of some Middle Eastern countries, there were many continuities between early internationalist proposals and the debates of the League of Nations Health Section, for instance regarding the statistical encapsulation of the pilgrim body or the speed of information transmission.[48] The reports on the pilgrimage supplied to the British

[45] Quoted in Zylberman, "Civilizing the State," 26. See also chapter 3, "Global Health Governance in the Twentieth Century," in T. J. Keefe and M. W. Zacher, *The Politics of Global Health Governance: United by Contagion* (Basingstoke: Palgrave Macmillan, 2011),

[46] WHO, 468–2-8: Sanitary Conventions – Revision of Pilgrimage Clauses.

[47] LON, R963, 43986: Représentation du Gouvernement égyptien au sein du Conseil Sanitaire, Maritime et Quarantenaire d'Egypte.

[48] See for instance LON, R953, 42275: Proposals for a Mediterranean Epidemiological Intelligence Service.

Colonial Office also point to such continuities. Some of these reports noted increasing controls and worse treatment when comparing the pilgrimages of 1912 and 1929. At Suez pilgrims were dealt with particularly harshly. Among other procedures, all passengers had to take a bath, and their clothes were passed through a steam disinfector and returned all wet.[49]

"Scientific" actions such as disinfection remained coupled with statistics and information. The convention signed in Paris 1938 contained the Article 151 already included in the 1926 convention, which obliged the governments of Egypt and Saudi Arabia, as well as all other governments connected with the pilgrimage, to hand in reports and statistics regarding the pilgrimage.[50] Here, a broader definition of disease was adopted, and the statistics contain information on all health issues the pilgrims could encounter. The Egyptian statistics are particularly interesting because they include nationalities, passages through the Canal in quarantine, a table of stool samples to be tested for cholera, and further details. In the case of the Sudan, the procedures were exceptionally thorough due to the involvement of the government-directed Stack Medical Research Laboratories, established in the late 1920s, which was at the forefront of epidemiological, operational, and basic research projects on tropical diseases. In 1940, the laboratories tested the returning pilgrims regarding their immunity to cholera and smallpox and found that 76 percent of pilgrims were already fully immune and 14 percent at least partially immune which put the quarantine and disinfection procedures more generally in to question.[51]

In parallel with attempts to centralize the sanitary organization of the pilgrimage, local schemes were also experimented with. The African Pilgrimage Scheme can serve as an example. The ideal procedure according to this scheme included a compulsory passport and all-inclusive payments comprising visa, vaccination, and quarantine fees, a round-trip ticket for the steamer, Hijaz entry fees, fees payable to local chiefs, and

[49] TNA, CO 732/39/10: Pilgrimage to Mecca 1929: Reports and arrangements for transport and sanitation: Oral examinations of pilgrims from Karachi; see also CO 732/24/2: Pilgrimage to Mecca 1927: Reports on arrangements for transport and sanitation; CO 732/31/8-9: Pilgrimage to Mecca, 1928: Arrangements for transport and sanitation.

[50] WHO, OIHP, T16: correspondence from Member States ratifying the International Sanitary Convention of 1938.

[51] WHO, OIHP, T26: Report of the Moslem Pilgrimage for 1940 submitted by the Governments of Algeria, Egypt, Palestine and the Anglo-Egyptian Sudan in execution of Article 151 of the International Sanitary Convention of 1926 as modified by Article II of the Convention of 1938. For the history of medical research in the Sudan, see P. F. D'Arcy and D. B. Worthen, *Laboratory on the Nile: A History of the Wellcome Tropical Research Laboratories* (Binghamton: Haworth Press, 1999).

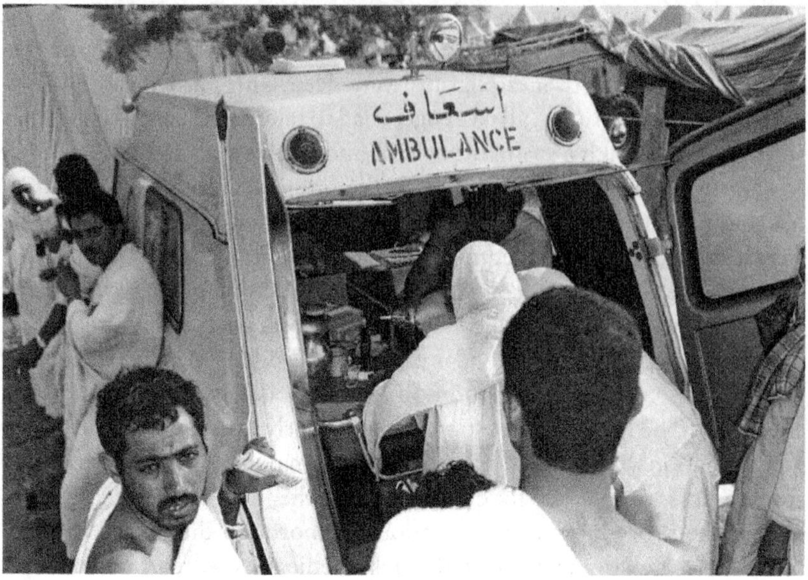

FIGURE 12 Pilgrim ambulance, ca. 1950s

so on.[52] Like earlier attempts to centralize the journey to Mecca by offering all-inclusive packages, such as Thomas Cook's attempt in India in the 1880s, it was on a voluntary basis and never implemented completely.[53] The scheme thus highlighted the weakness of such regulations as well as the continuities of surveillance measures experimented with in different colonial contexts. Similar holes in the net of the new control schemes can be seen in other contexts, for instance in the persisting traffic of sanitarily unmonitored dhows and *sambuks*, which every year carried large numbers of pilgrims across the Red Sea. Instead of the "unity of control" which Lutrario had envisaged, the interwar era thus saw the proliferation of international organizations and local schemes.

End of Empire, 1945–1960

In the years before the outbreak of the Second World War, motor and air transportation, just like steamship and railway in earlier phases, posed new

[52] M. M. Heaton, "Globalization, Health and the Hajj: The West African Pilgrimage Scheme, 1919–38," in T. Falola and M. M. Heaton (eds.), *HIV/AIDS, Illness, and African Well-Being* (University of Rochester Press, 2007), 243–267.

[53] On Thomas Cook's scheme, see Huber, *Channelling Mobilities*, 209–210.

problems of sanitary control and epidemiological information. The early material of the World Health Organization (WHO), established in 1946, shows many continuities, for instance, regarding the emphasis on statistics and information.[54] Other issues were called into question, such as the belief in science and bacteriological testing in the quarantine stations.

In 1947, a subcommittee was established and met at Alexandria and Jeddah to debate the necessary revisions of the pilgrimage clauses, particularly regarding the adequate scientific measures of protection (inoculations and vaccination, disinfection, disinsectization, biological examinations), official certification, and the sanitary measures to be taken by pilgrims traveling by land or air. In contrast to the 1922 League of Nations commission, Muslims were represented and heard in the Sub-Committee for the Revision of the Mecca Pilgrimage Clauses of the International Sanitary Conferences.

There were many connections with earlier discussions, for instance, regarding the need for rapid transmission of information using the newest technologies, including airmail, cable, and telephone, which would liberate the Hajj from other more annoying control measures.[55] Despite the emphasis on information, the quarantine station al-Tur remained the "real guarantee of Western countries."[56] The logistics of the quarantine station as a global microcosm were discussed in detail. Beyond this focus on then modern quarantine stations, scientific measures were also questioned. The obligatory stool examination, for instance, came under increasing criticism as it necessitated a "highly complicated organization, a number of highly-trained personnel – and even then the result is not likely to be reliable."[57] This measure was also seen as a problematic interference with the pilgrim body. Doubted since the 1920s in OIHP debates, Article 69 of the 1951 International Sanitary Regulations stated: "No one can be forced to submit a rectal sample."[58]

The subcommittee members voiced similar insecurities regarding the effectiveness of vaccinations and on the effective interlocking of a global market of vaccines. For instance in the Sudan, 8,000 pilgrims including

[54] WHO, 452/1/2: Mecca Pilgrimage: Various reports and circular-letters on sanitary conditions, 1946-48; see also *The First Ten Years of the WHO*.

[55] See for instance WHO, 468/2/11: Sanitary Conventions. Revision of Pilgrimage Clauses. 1st Session of Committee, Alexandria, April 1947. Documents, Reports and Minutes, April 24, 1947.

[56] WHO, 468/2/11: Twelfth Meeting, April 24, 1947, p. 8: Dr Gaud.

[57] WHO, 468/2/11: Second Meeting, April 16, 1947, p. 8: Proposal of Resolution.

[58] Zylberman, "Civilizing the State," 27.

6,000 transiting ones from West Africa had to receive vaccination. Smallpox lymph could be prepared at Khartoum, just as the cholera vaccine which was prepared at the Stack Laboratories of this city at least for those strains coming from India, while yellow fever vaccination had to be bought from the Wellcome Institute.[59] What is more, the definitions of disease were increasingly widened with the general well-being of the pilgrims, which in Isabel Burton's time had certainly not been the business of international bodies, entering the debate. The Suez Canal was still a central location for control measures, and the passage in quarantine remained a central instrument to avoid delays. While in earlier periods it had been reserved for other mobilities except the pilgrimage, it now more frequently served the pilgrims themselves.[60]

At the center of the subcommittee's debates, however, was the topic of Saudi Arabia's responsibility, and particularly the nuisance that the quarantine regulations represented for them, as expressed by "invited expert" Khalil Bey:

> The fact is that for Saudi Arabia the pilgrimage is a very important matter, perhaps more important than the oil question ... It is the opinion of the Saudi Arabian government that the measures laid down in the Convention's pilgrimage clauses, such as the isolation at El Tor, etc., have the effect of deterring people from proceeding on the pilgrimage; they are a hindrance to trade.[61]

Khalil Bey also criticized active discrimination against Muslims in terms of international sanitary controls, such as in the case of a Muslim-Christian couple where the Muslim husband was retained in quarantine while his Christian wife could travel on without hindrance: "Naturally this discrimination cannot be justified on any scientific bases."[62] The subcommittee dealt with aspects such as the damage done to the pilgrims' possessions during disinfection or the destruction of food in a less cynical manner than at earlier conferences and commission protocols.[63] Such debates on the pilgrim body also took cultural specificities into account. While Colonel Mani explained that "his note had been inspired by humanitarian considerations. Admittedly the installation of berths would involve additional expense and would increase passage costs, yet he felt that pilgrims should be treated not like cattle but be provided with berthed accommodation,"

[59] WHO, 46/2/11: Ninth Meeting, April 23, 1947, p. 2: Statement by Dr. Lorenzen.
[60] WHO, 468/2/11: Third Meeting, April 17, 1947, p. 1: Statement by Dr. Khalil Bey.
[61] WHO, 468/2/11: Third Meeting, April 17, 1947, p. 1: Statement by Dr. Khalil Bey.
[62] WHO, 468/2/11: Third Meeting, April 17, 1947, p. 1: Statement by Dr. Khalil Bey.
[63] WHO, 468/2/11: Third Meeting, April 17, 1947, p. 2: Statement by Dr. Khalil Bey.

others highlighted the cultural preferences attached to sleeping on beds or on the floor, the use of latrines, and the cooking of their own food.[64]

The composition of the subcommittee and the aspects raised in the discussion illustrate that the bulwark rhetoric of an international sanitary system aimed at safeguarding Europe from the disease-ridden "Orient" while enabling all colonial traffic was not anymore up to date, as the Dutch doctor van Loghem made explicit: "The object of an international convention was no longer the protection of Europe against 'exotic' disease but mutual aid for the participants in the convention."[65] In 1948, the WHO interim commission spoke for the integration of the convention into the general international sanitary convention for maritime and aerial navigation. When the amendments were presented to the new member states of the WHO, the responses illustrate the new postwar international organization as an arena for newly independent states practicing diplomacy and internationalism.[66]

Despite the cautions voiced by the subcommittee regarding these measures, the statistics for Sudan still gave numbers such as 4,450 examinations of stool specimen or a 100 percent successful vaccination scheme.[67] The statistics now included airplanes, even though it was not entirely clear how to deal with them. As in earlier periods, there were also many reports on the pilgrimage, mentioning all hospitalizations and at times pointing to a wider definition of the bodily and spiritual state of the pilgrims, for instance referring to their psychological condition. These reports also added new domains to the vocabulary of contagion, as when they spoke about extreme and contagious emotions.[68]

Yet the subcommittee was only partly successful in raising attention to a more careful application of scientific measures and a more inclusive approach more generally. In 1952, a new sanitary convention was drafted. An additional quarantine station for pilgrims was opened in Jeddah, sporting the most recent scientific and technological infrastructure, including an incinerator, a training school for public health assistants, equipment

[64] WHO, 468/2/11: Ninth Meeting, April 23, 1947, p. 3: Colonel Mani.

[65] WHO, 468/2/11: Fourth Meeting, April 17, 1947, p. 1: Prof. van Loghem.

[66] WHO, 468/2/12: Sanitary Conventions. Revision of Pilgrimage Clauses; WHO, EQ 9/2/9: Australian Objections.

[67] WHO, 452/1/2:Mecca Pilgrimage: Various reports and circular-letters on sanitary conditions 1946–48,

[68] WHO, 452/1/2: Gouvernement général de l'Afrique occidentale française: Direction générale de la santé publique. Rapport sur le pèlerinage de la Mecque en 1948, par le médecin africain de 3e classe Mustapha Touré, September 22–December 15, 1948.

for an operating room, electric lamps, and a refrigerating machine for post-mortem sections.[69] At the same time, delousing and disinfection with DDT represented the persistent intrusion into bodily practices.[70] The WHO documentation furthermore illustrates a standardization of information transfer.[71] The 1950s furthermore saw the liberation of Saudi Arabia from the international sanitary health regimes, now able to set its own sanitary standards, signifying in their own view an act of liberation and de-stigmatization.[72] The weakness of the Ottoman Empire to implement sanitary measures, with an international medical commission sent to the Hijaz every year, was contrasted with Saudi Arabia forcefully claiming responsibility for the Hajj.

This introduction of new chemicals in the bodily experience of the pilgrims points to the technologies interlocking in the creation of global health regimes, the treatment of pilgrims on the spot, and the dissemination of information globally. The shift in transport technologies, from steamship to railway to airplane and motorcar presented new challenges to international authorities. Yet it is important to keep in mind that pilgrims often used multiple modes of conveyance and that they sometimes used them strategically in order to escape increasing (and increasingly expensive) controls. The scientific technologies of vaccination, disinfection, and laboratory tests point to another connection of the global and the local as these technologies, chemicals, and life vaccines had to be made available in the right locations at the right time. Laboratory tests were meant to screen the pilgrim body, to make it transparent so to speak and filter disease carriers from the large numbers of traveling Muslims. Finally, information technologies carried the promise of making the pilgrim body visible wherever its location. All of these technologies were of course only partly implementable and often led to unpredictable outcomes.

These technologies could only be applied through efficient organization highlighting the question as to who had the authority to interfere with the pilgrim body in the first place. The international meetings of various sizes that have been assessed in this chapter point to the uneasy connection

69 WHO, Project files Saudi Arabia; WHO Archives, EQ 9/2: Conventions and Regulations.

70 WHO, 452/1/2.

71 WHO, I4/369/1: General Information on Pilgrimages, International Quarantine Aspects 1960–69.

72 WHO, I4/369/1: Saudi Arabia setting its own vaccination certificate requirements. On decolonization and health more generally, see Amrith, *Decolonizing International Health*.

of imperialism, internationalism, and postcolonial nationalism. Often they became a stage where very different interests and incentives could be acted out. The various international, imperial, and national bodies claiming authority over the pilgrim body in the name of global health, religious duty, imperial security, or humanitarian benevolence, of course, also adopted different definitions of disease and health which at times, as the reference to states of religious ecstasy show, could be quite fluid or even contradictory.

The combination of increasingly effective organization, growing resources through aid programs and international institutions, and the invention of more efficient vaccines and more powerful disinfection chemicals led some to the conclusion that the 1950s represented the end of epidemics. Yet the 1960s saw the return of the cholera pointing to the contradictions of globalization.[73] The emergence of new global diseases and the return of familiar ones highlighted that despite the attempt to decolonize both the pilgrim bodies and the international organizations, there were striking continuities in the effort to create global security though science and information. On different scales, the pilgrim bodies and the institutions in charge of them, thus remained testing grounds of science, global intelligence, and new languages of internationalism well into the twentieth century.

[73] K. Lee and R. Dodson, "Globalization and Cholera: Implications for Global Governance," *Global Governance*, 6, 2 (2000), 213–236.

10

The Saudis as Managers of the Hajj

Saud al-Sarhan*

> The State shall develop and maintain the Two Holy Mosques. It shall provide care and security to pilgrims to help them perform their Hajj and 'Umra and visit to the Prophet's Mosque in ease and comfort.
>
> (The Saudi Basic Law, art. 24)

This chapter discusses the history of the Saudi state's management of the Hajj, from the first Saudi state takeover of Mecca and Medina until the present day.[1] It traces the development of Saudi internal and foreign policy with regard to the Hajj, first examining the measures Imam Saud (Imām Saʿūd ibn ʿAbd al-ʿAzīz, d. 1814) took to secure Hijāz and ensuing tensions with other Muslim nations. It follows the evolution of Saudi policy on the Hajj through the reign of Ibn Saud (King ʿAbd al-ʿAzīz, r. 1926–1953) to the present time. The chapter also looks at internal and international Hajj-related conflicts, many of which involve clashes between foreign cultural practices and Salafi beliefs.

IMAM SAUD'S HAJJ POLICIES

Under the rule of Imam Saud, the first Saudi state managed the Hajj for seven seasons, from 1807–1812.[2] In previous decades, the Saudis suffered

* I want to thank Prince Turki al-Faisal, Eskandar Sadeghi-Boroujerdi, Abdulaziz al-Fahad, and Askar Al Enazy for their comments on the draft of the chapter, and to thank Bernard Haykel and ʿAbd Allāh al-Munīf for helping me to have access to some sources.

[1] Although the Kingdom of Saudi Arabia was officially established in 1932, I use the word "Saudis" to denote the people who were ruled by the Āl Saʿūd family also before this. Historians, nevertheless, usually divide the Āl Saʿūd rule into three states: the first Saudi State (1744–1818), the second Saudi State (1824–1891), and the third Saudi State (1902 to today).

[2] ʿA. Ibn ʿAbd al-Shakūr, *Tārīkh ashrāf wa-umarā' Makka al-Mukarrama* (MS, Topkapi Saray, no. 1/44), 575; ʿU. Ibn Bishr, *ʿUnwān al-majd fī tārīkh Najd*, ed. ʿA. ʿA. Āl Al-Shaykh, 4th ed. (Riyadh: Dārat al-Malik ʿAbd al-ʿAzīz, 1982), I: 291–330.

from discriminatory policy on the part of the Ottomans and the Sharīfs. In 1749 or 1750, for example, Sharif Masʿūd ibn Saʿīd (r. 1732–1752) jailed some Najdi pilgrims and ordered the judge of Mecca to pronounce them unbelievers, and Najdis were thereafter banned from performing Hajj.[3] This ban lasted until the season of 1799, when Imam Saud and Sharif Ghālib signed a treaty.[4] With the exception of a few years when their pilgrimage was contingent on the payment of heavy taxes to the Sharifs of Mecca, the Najdis were banned from performing Hajj for almost a half century.[5] After seizing Mecca and Medina, Saud performed the Hajj each year in order to personally supervise its administration. During his short period of control, Imam Saud made major changes in the management of the Hajj and the holy places. His policies were rather controversial.

Once in power, Saud ordered the destruction of all shrines in Hijaz and decided to ban the *maḥmal*, the ceremonial centerpiece of many traditional pilgrimage caravans. These dictates were based on religious objections to both traditions: to shrines because of Islamic prohibitions against tombs on graves, and to the mahmal because of its status as an "innovation," and because of the music and celebrations associated with the caravan. The mahmal also used to be accompanied by hundreds of fully armed soldiers,[6] the presence of whom Saud saw as a threat to his authority in Hijaz and a representation of the Ottoman Sultan's disrespect of his rule. Saud feared that these soldiers, given the opportunity, might join with Sharif Ghālib and drive the Saudi army out of Mecca.[7]

After banning the mahmal, Saud warned ʿAbd Allāh Pasha al-ʿAẓm that the Syrian caravan would not be allowed to bring the mahmal to Mecca. During the Hajj season of February and March 1807, Saud told his deputies in the north that the Syrian caravan would only be allowed to pass if it arrived without the mahmal and the musical band and armed guards accompanying it. ʿAbd Allāh Pasha refused to abandon these symbols of the Ottoman authority and glory and returned to Syria

3 Ibn ʿAbd al-Shakūr, *Tārīkh*, 348–349.

4 Ibn ʿAbd al-Shakūr, *Tārīkh*, 348–349, 388–389.

5 Ibn Bishr, *ʿUnwān*, I: 59–60; A. Z. Daḥlān, *Khulāṣat al-kalām fī bayān umarāʾ al-balad al-ḥarām min zaman al-Nabī ʿalayhi al-ṣalāt wa-l-salām ilā zamaninā hādhā bi-l-tamām*, 1st ed. (Cairo: al-Maṭbaʿa al-Khayriyya, 1305 AH [1888]), 228, 267–268; M. al-ʿAjlānī, *Tārīkh al-bilād al-ʿArabiyya*, 2nd ed. (Riyadh: Dār al-Shibl, 1993), I: 134–136; ʿA. al-ʿUthaymīn, *Tārīkh al-Mamlaka al-ʿArabiyya al-Suʿūdiyya*, 1st ed. (Riyaah: n.p., 1984), I: 121–129.

6 For example, in season 1806, the mahmal was accompanied by 1,500 horsemen: Ibn ʿAbd al-Shakūr, *Tārīkh*, 576.

7 Ibn Bishr, *ʿUnwān*, I: 292.

without performing the Hajj.[8] Official Syrian pilgrim caravans were halted until the end of the first Saudi state's rule in Hijaz.

Nevertheless, Saud wanted Syrian pilgrims to continue performing Hajj, and he pursued negotiations with Yūsuf Pasha, ʿAbd Allāh Pasha al-ʿAẓm's successor and the Ottoman governor of Syria from 1807 to 1810.[9] In one of his letters to Yūsuf Pasha, Saud stated that he would not allow the mahmal and army to come to Mecca, and that no pilgrim would be allowed to stay behind in Mecca or Medina after completing his pilgrimage. Even so, he asked the Ottomans to continue sending annual aid to the two Holy Mosques and the people of the two holy cities. Finally, Saud insisted that all the sinful activities (*munkarāt*) associated with the caravan should cease, concluding that if his requirements were met, he would personally guarantee the security of the pilgrims.[10] Saud gave similar warnings to the head of the Egyptian pilgrimage against bringing the mahmal, saying, "If you bring it, I will burn it."[11] The Egyptians ignored Saud's threats and brought the mahmal to the 1808 Hajj season, where it was promptly incinerated by Saud's men.[12]

Saud also reorganized the administration of prayers at the Grand Mosque in Mecca. Before his rule, each prayer was performed four times, once by an imām from each of the four Sunni schools of law. Saud restructured the system so that each prayer was performed only once a day but under an imām from a different school of law each time.[13] He also revoked all of the Sharifs' former taxations on pilgrims and residents of Mecca.[14] These actions were met with approbation by some scholars from different parts of the Islamic world, such as Aḥmad al-Ḥafaẓī from ʿAsīr (d. 1817),[15]

[8] Ibn ʿAbd al-Shakūr, *Tārīkh*, 452–452, 488; Daḥlān, *Khulāṣat al-kalām*, 294; Ali Bey, "Travels of Ali Bey," in A. de L. Rush (ed.), *Records of the Hajj: The Pilgrimage to Mecca* ([Slough]: Archive Editions, 1993), IV: 66; Ibn Bishr, *ʿUnwān*, I: 263, 291–292; Al-Jabartī, *ʿAjāʾib al-āthār fī al-tarājim wa-l-akhbār*, ed. ʿA.ʿA. ʿAbd al-Raḥīm, 1st ed. (Cairo: Dār al-Kutub al-Miṣriyya, 1998), IV: 83.

[9] For some of these letters, see Ahmet Cevdet Pasha, *Tarih-i Cevdet*, 2nd ed. (Istanbul: Matbaa-yi Osmaniye, 1892).

[10] Ottoman Archive, H.H 19550-J. Translated into Arabic in S. Ṣābān, *Al-Jazīra al-ʿArabiyya: buḥūth wa-dirāsāt min wathāʾiq al-irshīf al-ʿUthmānī wa-l-maṣādir al-Turkiyya* (Riyadh: Maktabat al-Malik Fahad al-Waṭaniyya, 2006), 140–143.

[11] ʿA. al-Jabartī, *ʿAjāʾib*, IV: 84.

[12] Daḥlān, *Khulāṣat al-kalām*, 294.

[13] Ibn ʿAbd al-Shakūr, *Tārīkh*, 454–455; Daḥlān, *Khulāṣat al-kalām*, 278.

[14] Al-Jabartī, *ʿAjāʾib*, IV: 8.

[15] ʿA. al-Muṭawwaʿ, *Idārat Makka al-Mukarrama fī ʿahd al-dawla al-Suʿūdiyya al-ūlā* (Riyadh: Maṭābiʿ al-Ḥumayḍī, 2009), 75–78.

al-Jabartī from Egypt (d. 1825),[16] and Ḥamdūn ibn al-Ḥājj from Morocco (d. 1817).[17]

In 1807, Saud opened the Prophet's tomb and seized its treasures. This move struck a major blow to the reputation of the Saudis; the Ottomans used it as evidence that Wahhābīs did not respect the Prophet.[18] The Saudis tried to limit the damage to their public image by arguing that the Ottoman Sultan's failure to send their required annual aid to the people of Medina had forced them to seize the treasure. After consulting with the scholars (*ʿulamāʾ*) from the four schools of law and receiving

FIGURE 13 Medina, outside the Prophet's Mosque, 2010

[16] Al-Jabartī, *ʿAjāʾib*, IV: 8, 84.

[17] A. al-Zayyānī, *al-Turjumāna al-kubrā fī akhbār al-maʿmūr barran wa-baḥrā*, ed. ʿA. al-Filālī, 2nd ed. (Rabat: Dār Nashr al-Maʿrifa, 1991), 388–390.

[18] Al-Jabartī, *ʿAjāʾib*, IV: 8; J. L. Burckhardt, "Notes on the Bedouins and Wahhabys," in *Records of the Hajj*, IV: 91–92. Burckhardt, who visited the region a few years later, claimed that the gold vessels had been stolen by the Ottoman military leader of Medina, Ḥasan al-Qalʿī, and his men before Saud took over the city. Also, this incident was not the first time when the treasures in the Prophet's tomb had been seized; it is evident that the Ottomans were in the habit of seizing the treasures.

their approval, he decided to spend the value of the treasures for the benefit of the people of Medina.[19]

Although Saud was driven primarily by religious motives, he also wanted to challenge Ottoman and Egyptian political authority in Hijaz. To this end, Saud commissioned his own *kiswa,* the ceremonial covering that is draped over the Kaʿba each season and which for centuries had been delivered by the Egyptians alongside their mahmal. Saud also tried to bolster his relationship with other Muslim countries, exchanging letters with the sultan of Morocco, who in 1811 sent an official Hajj caravan led by Prince Ibrāhīm. The meeting between the two dignitaries went well.[20] In addition, there were reports that Saud also exchanged gifts with the Qajar Shah of Iran.[21] Saud's major policy triumph, however, was his success in securing the safety of both pilgrims and the holy places themselves during his reign, when previously pilgrims had suffered under threat of attack every pilgrimage season.[22] Saud's campaign against the Egyptians and the Ottomans was severe: he was zealous in removing any sign of their authority in Hijaz and Hajj. His policies resulted in the halting of official caravans from Syria, Turkey, and Egypt and led to the Ottoman-Egyptian invasion and the end of the rule of the first Saudi state over Hijaz in 1812.

ʿABD AL-ʿAZĪZ'S NEW APPROACH TO ḤAJJ MANAGEMENT

After 112 years, history repeated itself: in 1919, Sharif Ḥusayn of Mecca decided to ban the Najdis from performing Hajj. In response, the Saudis

[19] ʿA. b. Ḥ. Āl al-Shaykh, *al-Itḥāf fī al-radd ʿalā al-Ṣaḥḥāf*, ed. ʿA. Āl Ḥamad (Riyadh: Dār al-ʿĀṣima, 1995), 51–52.

[20] Al-Muṭawwaʿ, *Idārat Makka*, 58–60, 84–86.

[21] H. Wahba, *Jazīrat al-ʿArab fī al-qarn al-ʿishrīn*, 3rd ed. (Cairo: Dār al-Āfāq al-ʿArabiyya, 1975), 222. In a letter to Sir Evan Nepean dated August 12, 1813, resident William Bruce writes: "I have the honor to acquaint you that during my absence to Muscat an Envoy from the Wahabee Chief named Ibrahame ibn Abdul Karim arrived at Bushire on a mission to His to His Royal Highness the Prince Hussein Ali Mirza, Governor of the Province of Fars, on his arrival he enquired if I was at Bushire .... The object of the Envoy's Mission to the ? (illegible) so far as I have been able to learn is to enter in engagements of friendship with Persia with a view to postpone her intention of launching an Army against him. Yesterday morning Shaik Ibrahim ibn Abdul Karim returned from Shiraz having been well received by His Royal Highness who on his taking his leave presented him with a number of presents for the Wahabee Chief ..." See A. Burdett, *The Expansion of Wahhabi Power in Arabia, 1798–1932: British Documentary Records* (Cambridge: Cambridge Archive Editions, 2013), I: 357–360. (I want to thank Michael Crawford for providing me with this reference.)

[22] Burckhardt, "Notes," 50; al-Zayyānī, 389.

launched an attack on Hijaz in 1924, and from the next year until the present day, the Hajj and Mecca have remained under Saudi control. ʿAbd al-ʿAzīz, then the Sultan of Najd and its dependencies, was aware of Saud's policy and had reservations about that ruler's harsh dealing with the Ottomans and the Egyptians.[23] Believing that Saud's policy had caused the Ottoman-Egyptian invasion of Arabia and resulted in the loss of Mecca and Dirʿiyya, ʿAbd al-ʿAzīz decided to take a softer approach.

Even though the Saudis entered Mecca on Thursday, October 16, 1924, ʿAbd al-ʿAzīz did not declare himself the King of Hijaz until January 14, 1926. For a year and a few months, ʿAbd al-ʿAzīz worked hard to face the propaganda campaign that the Hashemites launched against him in regional newspapers: *al-Qibla* in Hijaz, *al-Muqaṭṭam* in Egypt, and other newspapers across Iraq and Transjordan. To ease the people's concerns in Mecca and beyond, ʿAbd al-ʿAzīz issued an official statement about his program for Hijaz:

> 1. My greatest concern will be the purification of this holy area of the enemies of the faith, who hate the Islamic world, namely of Ḥusayn, his children and followers. 2. The question of the future of this holy land will be settled through consultations among the Muslims. We have already informed the Muslims and asked them to send their delegates to a pan-Islamic conference that will determine the form of government they will deem necessary to realize Allah's decisions in this sacred land. 3. The legal base of Hijaz will be the Qurʾān, the commandments sent with Allah's Messenger and those established by the ʿulamaʾ through *qiyās* [analogy]. 4. We hereby inform all ʿulamaʾ of this country and those who served the holy places earlier that they will stay here as they did before.[24]

Thereafter he made the nonofficial call for the First Islamic Congress to discuss the future of Hijaz.[25]

ʿAbd al-ʿAzīz worked hard to make the 1925 pilgrimage season successful. Jeddah, the main port for the Hajj, was under the control of Sharif ʿAlī ibn Ḥusayn, who sent messages across the Muslim world warning prospective pilgrims against performing the Hajj due to security concerns. In response, ʿAbd al-ʿAzīz took over ports, including Rābigh, al-Līth, and al-Qunfidha, prepared them to receive pilgrims, and ordered merchants in Najd to provide them with 500 camels for use in transporting pilgrims.[26]

[23] Wahba, *Jazīrat al-ʿArab*, 222.

[24] *Umm al-Qurā*, 1 (December 12, 1942): 1; translated in A. Vassiliev, *The History of Saudi Arabia* (London: Saqi Books, 1998), 262–263.

[25] See *Umm al-Qurā*, 8 (January 30, 1925): 1–2; *Umm al-Qurā*, 30 (July 24, 1925): 1.

[26] H. al-Bābaṭīn, *al-Tanẓīmāt al-idāriyya li-shuʾūn al-ḥajj fī ʿahd al-malik ʿAbd al-ʿAzīz*, (Riyadh: Maktabat al-Wafāʾ, 2003), 163.

He also commanded his son Faisal (Fayṣal) to be responsible for the safety of the Hajj.[27]

ʿAbd al-ʿAzīz sent envoys and letters to Muslim countries personally guaranteeing the safety of the Hajj, urging pilgrims to use these alternative routes instead of Jeddah's, which was blocked by the Sharif.[28] Many Muslim countries, such as Egypt, Iran, and Iraq, did not send their citizens to Hajj that year, but some did, most notably India, whose pilgrims arrived through Rābigh. Approximately 7,000 pilgrims arrived through alternate routes, mainly from India and Java with representation from Syria, Turkey, and West Africa as well.[29] The number of pilgrims that year totaled around 100,000.[30] The British traveler Eldon Rutter performed pilgrimage that year, providing later generations with an excellent description of the season.[31]

The success of the 1925 season,[32] and the end of the Hashemite rule in December 1924, encouraged many Muslims to perform the Hajj the next season. However, later developments led to political tensions between ʿAbd al-ʿAzīz and some Muslim leaders and kings.

THE KING OF HIJAZ AND SULTAN OF NAJD AND THE FIRST MUSLIM CONGRESS

Although ʿAbd al-ʿAzīz was very careful in declaring his authority over Hijaz, he never forgot that Saud's invasion of Mecca and Medina had signaled the beginning of the end for the first Saudi state. ʿAbd al-ʿAzīz announced repeatedly that he would let the worldwide Muslim community

[27] Al-Bābaṭīn, *Al-Tanẓīmāt al-idāriyya,* 160–161.

[28] *Umm al-Qurā*, 12 (February 27, 1925): 2; *Umm al-Qurā*, 13 (March 1, 1925): 3.

[29] Jeddah Report, "Supplementary notes and comments on the pilgrimage," July 21–August 10, 1925, in *Records of the Hajj*, V: 723.

[30] At *Umm al-Qurā*, 27 (June 21, 1925): 2, there is a report of the arrival of 3,248 pilgrims. Official report: 100,000 from Najd, and around 7,000 from non-Arab countries. See also *Umm al-Qurā*, 28 (July 10, 1925): 2; .Ḥ. Naṣīf, *Māḍī al-Ḥijāz wa-ḥāḍiruh* (Cairo: Maktabat wa-Maṭbaʿat Khuḍayr, 1930), 175–176.

[31] E. Rutter, *The Holy Cities of Arabia* (London & New York: G. P. Putnam's Sons Ltd., 1928), I: 104–168.

[32] M. Yaseen Khan, Indian pilgrimage officer, who performed Hajj that year, wrote a letter to the secretary of the government of India regarding the season, in which he praised its success. See *Records of the Hajj*, V: 663–665. The British vice-consul in Jeddah, S. R. Jordan, wrote a cable on September 1, 1925, which stated that "the pilgrimage has been very successful, apparently." See R. L. Jarman, *The Jedda Diaries, 1919–1940*, 4 vols. (Farnham Common: Archive Editions, 1980), II: 326.

decide the future of Hijaz,[33] calling for a Muslim Congress to be held in Mecca. On October 26, 1925, he sent official letters to the kings of Egypt and Iraq, the prince of Afghanistan, the president of Turkey, the shah of Iran, the emir of the Rif Republic, Imam Yaḥyā of Yemen, the head of the Supreme Islamic Council in Quds, and the head of the Caliphate League, and the Ahl al-Hadith and Jamiat-Ulama-i-Hind in India.[34]

Less than two months after the letters were sent, Hijaz fell completely into the hands of ʿAbd al-ʿAzīz, and the Hashemites were sent into exile. In response, the merchant elites of Mecca and Jeddah sent a letter to ʿAbd al-ʿAzīz asking him to let the people of Hijaz decide their own fate. They knew that, since Britain had declined their request for "a British protectorate or mandate over the Ḥijāz,"[35] ʿAbd al-ʿAzīz was the de facto ruler of Hijaz, and they wanted to wrest as much political power as possible.[36] In January 4, 1926, these merchants sent a letter to ʿAbd al-ʿAzīz pledging him their allegiance as a constitutional king. A few days later, ʿAbd al-ʿAzīz accepted their allegiance, and on January 8, 1926, in a ceremony in the Grand Mosque of Mecca, he became king of Hijaz and sultan of Najd and its dependencies. All across Hijaz, citizens pledged allegiance to their new king.[37] The new kingdom was soon recognized by the international powers of the time – the Soviets and the British. But recognition from Muslim countries lagged, and King ʿAbd al-ʿAzīz was aware that most Muslim countries were, at the time, under foreign colonial rule. He called again for the Islamic Congress to be held in June 1926 after the Hajj season, but with a different mission: the recognition of the Islamic world.[38] Letters of invitation to the Congress were sent in March 27, 1926, and the delegations were invited to discuss how to improve the conditions of the two holy mosques.[39] About seventy representatives took part in the Congress.[40] Three Islamic kingdoms – Egypt, Iraq, and Iran – decided to boycott the meeting. The Caliphate League, an Indian British

[33] *Umm al-Qurā*, 8 (January 30, 1925): 1–2.

[34] *Umm al-Qurā*, 29 (July 17, 1925): 3; *Umm al-Qurā*, 45 (November 6, 1925): 1; *al-Manār*, 26, 7 (January 14, 1925): 540–542.

[35] R. W. Bullard, "Consul Bullard to Mr. MacDonald," October 27, 1924, in *The Jedda Diaries*, II: 245.

[36] S. R. Jordan, "Vice-Consul Jordan to Sir Austen Chamberlain," February 4, 1926, in Jarman, *The Jedda Diaries*, II: 372–373.

[37] See *Umm al-Qurā*, 55 (January 15, 1926): 1–3; *al-Manār*, 26, 9 (February 27, 1926): 707–712; *al-Manār*, 26, 10 (March 14, 1926): 779–789.

[38] Vassiliev, *History of Saudi Arabia*, 266.

[39] *Umm al-Qurā*, 67 (April 9, 1926): 2.

[40] Vassiliev, *History of Saudi Arabia*, 266.

movement, used a different approach. Although they wanted Hijaz to become an Islamic independent republic open to all Muslims, they agreed to attend the meeting to raise their concerns regarding the new situation in the region.[41]

During the 1924–1925 war between King ʿAbd al-ʿAzīz and the Hashemites, the Caliphate League stood with the Saudis against the Sharifs, and against any involvement of the British government in the disputes over the holy places.[42] The League also played a great role in the media campaign to support King ʿAbd al-ʿAzīz against the Hashemites. Most importantly, the Caliphate League helped make the 1925 Hajj season successful by encouraging Indian Muslims to perform the Hajj,[43] and initially the Saudi newspaper *Umm al-Qurā* published articles commending the League.[44] However, good relations between the League and the Saudis soured after ʿAbd al-ʿAzīz declared himself the king of Hijaz. From the first meeting of the Congress, ʿAbd al-ʿAzīz made it clear that he would not tolerate any interference in Hijaz affairs, mandating that "[n]o international politics issues shall be discussed in the meeting."[45] The Caliphate League delegation was unhappy but powerless to change the agenda.[46] For the next two years, the Caliphate League launched a political and media campaign against King ʿAbd a-ʿAzīz. Despite their search for another Muslim king to depose Ibn Saud from Hijaz, their real bargaining chips were their threat to stop annual Indian aid to the holy places and to halt Indian pilgrimages to Mecca until Ibn Saud exited Hijaz.[47] Needless to say, their efforts resulted in nothing: Indian pilgrims continued coming each season, and King ʿAbd al-ʿAzīz used the famous and respected journal *al-Manār* to debate with the Caliphate league and to defend his rule over Hijaz.[48]

[41] J. Ḥajar, "Al-Ḥijāz fī al-fikr al-siyāsī li-muslimī al-Hind," *Majallat Kulliyyat al-Ādāb* (Alexandria), 39 (1991–92): 217–218.

[42] *Muhimmat al-wafd al-Hindī fī al-Ḥijāz*, a report by the Foreign Ministry of the Hijaz Government (Sharif ʿAlī government), January 2–30, 1925; Ṭ. Wahīm, *Mamlakat al-Ḥijāz (1916–1925): dirāsa fī al-awḍāʿ al-siyasiyya* (Basra University Press, 1982), 368–371; Ḥajar, "Al-Ḥijāz fī al-fikr al-siyāsī," 201–207.

[43] *Umm al-Qura*, 24 (June 24, 1925): 3; *Umm al-Qura*, 27 (June 26, 1925): 2.

[44] *Umm al-Qurā*, 28 (July 10, 1925): 1; *Umm al-Qurā*, 30 (July 24, 1925): 1–2.

[45] *Umm al-Qurā*, 75 (June 11, 1926): 1; M. ʿA. Ḥasan, *Ṣaḥīfa mūjaza bi-aʿmāl muʾtamar al-ʿālam al-Islāmī al-awwal bi-Makka al-Mukarrama* (Alexandria: Maṭbaʿat Nahḍat al-Sharq, 1926), 6–7, 11.

[46] Ḥajar, "al-Ḥijāz," 212–218.

[47] *Al-Manār*, 29, 3 (June 18, 1928): 165.

[48] See *al-Manār*, 29, 3 (June 18, 1928): 162–180.

ISLAMIC TOMBS

After entering Mecca and during the siege of Jeddah and Medina in 1924–1925, the Hashemites started a media campaign against the Saudis, accusing them of destroying Islamic tombs, firing cannons toward the Green Dome of the Prophet's grave, and demolishing the tomb of Ḥamza ibn ʿAbd al-Muṭṭalib. These claims appeared in the Egyptian newspaper *al-Muqaṭṭam*, in some Yemeni and Indian newspapers, and even in the *Times*.[49] The Saudis countered these accusations, releasing official statements refuting them.[50] *Al-Manār* and other journals defended the Saudis against these allegations,[51] while King ʿAbd al-ʿAzīz received envoys from Egypt and Iran to examine their validity.[52] The Egyptian delegation stayed in Mecca,[53] while the Iranian delegation visited Medina to make sure that the Prophet's tomb and the shrines of the People of the House (*Ahl al-Bayt*) in the Baqīʿ graveyard were unharmed.[54]

Many of the Islamic shrines and tombs in Mecca had, however, already been destroyed during the reign of Sharif ʿAwn (d. 1905), sometime before the Saudis took over Mecca.[55] The Saudis did not have to destroy lots of tombs in Mecca. However, one of the most important Islamic sites in Mecca, and one that survived ʿAwn's destructions, is the building marking the Prophet Muhammad's supposed birthplace (*mawlid*). The Najdis wanted to destroy it, even though doing so would play into Hashemite propaganda against Ibn Saud. ʿAbd al-ʿAzīz came up with a compromise: he destroyed the dome of the building but left its structure intact. Rutter, who was in Mecca at that time, stated that "the Wahhābīs would have

49 *Al-Manār*, 26, 5 (September 18, 1925): 396–397; Rutter, *The Holy Cities*, II: 245; S. R. Jordan, "Acting Consul Jordan to Mr. Austen Camberlain," October 19, 1925, in Jarman, *The Jedda Diaries*, II: 346–347

50 *Umm al-Qurā*, 44 (October 30, 1925): 1.

51 *Al-Manār*, 26, 5 (September 18, 1925): 396–397; *Umm al-Qurā*, 44 (October 30, 1925): 1–2.

52 *Umm al-Qurā*, 43 (October 23, 1925): 2.

53 For the Egyptian delegation's visit, see S. R. Jordan, "Acting Consul Jordan to Mr. Austen Camberlain," October 19, 1925, in Jarman, *The Jedda Diaries*, II: 346; and for their report, see *Umm al-Qurā*, 44 (October 30, 1925): 2.

54 The Iranian delegation went to Medina (which was under the Saudi siege) under King ʿAbd al-ʿAzīz's protection. See the account of eyewitness Muḥammad Zaydān in M. Zaydān, *Dhikrayāt al-ʿuhūd al-thalātha* (Riyadh: Maṭābiʿ al-Farazdaq, 1988), 120–121. For the names of the members of the Iranian delegation and on their meeting with ʿAbd al-ʿAzīz, see *Umm al-Qurā*, 43 (October 23, 1925): 2; *Umm al-Qurā*, 45 (November 6, 1925): 3.

55 M. L. al-Batanūnī, *al-Risāla al-Ḥijāziyya li-Walī al-Niʿam al-Ḥājj ʿAbbās Ḥilmī Bāshā al-Thānī Khadīw Miṣr*, 2nd ed. (Cairo: Maṭbaʿat al-Jamāliyya, 1329/1911), 56, 79–80.

entirely prohibited visitation of the Mūlid [mawlid], but the fact of its being a mosque enabled ʿAbd al-ʿAzīz to prevail upon his ʿulama to persuade the wild men that there was nothing unlawful in its being used for the purpose of prayer and meditation. Consequently, they left the gateway in the half-ruined wall unobstructed, and the Sulṭān [Ibn Saud] gained credit with them for having allowed the dome to be demolished, and credit with the foreign hājjis [ḥājjs] for protecting the place from complete demolition."[56]

After the Saudis took over Medina and Jeddah, the situation changed. The Saudis hired the Nakhāwilā (Medina's Twelver Shiʿites) to demolish the tombs in Medina that were built on the graves of the martyrs of Uḥud and the Ahl al-Bayt in the Baqīʿ Cemetery.[57] This policy accrued a great deal of anger and opposition. The Shiʿite *marājiʿ* (supreme legal authorities) issued fatwas against destroying shrines and preventing Shiʿites from visiting sacred places. They also wrote to the British government, appealing for help protecting their sacred sites from Ibn Saud.[58] Many Sunni Muslim countries, such as India, Egypt, Syria, and Yemen, had similar reactions to news of the destruction of holy sites. On the other hand, Salafi ʿulama in the Muslim world supported the Saudi decision to destroy these graves and monuments, which they regarded as reprehensible innovations. When the news of Saudi demolishment of tombs in Medina reached Shiʿite communities in Iran and Iraq and other regions, there was public outcry. To this day, the Shiʿites hold an annual gathering, called the *maʾtam*, in order to mourn the anniversary of the destruction of the tombs of the Ahl al-Bayt in Baqīʿ Cemetery in Medina. Moreover, in India, the Servants of the Haramain Committee went to great lengths to try to preserve religious sites and prevent further destruction, but without success.

THE MAHMAL

The pilgrimage season of 1926 began promisingly. The rule of the Saudis was unchallenged, Hajj routes were safe, and ʿAbd al-ʿAzīz was holding the Muslim Congress to demonstrate to all Muslims how much he had

[56] Rutter, *The Holy Cities*, I: 271.

[57] Rutter, *The Holy Cities*, II: 244–246.

[58] "Shi'a Complaints of Discrimination; Comments on Pilgrimages by Persian and Afghani Muslims; Demands Regarding Holy Shrines, 1931–32," in *Records of the Hajj*, VI: 413–432.

achieved in managing the Hajj only one year into his rule. Despite its reservations about the tradition of the mahmal, the new Saudi government sent an official letter to Egypt to ensure that the mahmal, along with its army and musical caravan, would be welcome. The Saudis did ask, however, that they leave the musical band in Jeddah and not accompany the mahmal to the holy places.[59]

King ʿAbd al-ʿAzīz was taking a risk by allowing the mahmal. The Salafis and the Najdis believed that the mahmal was innovation, and that music was sin. More importantly, King ʿAbd al-ʿAzīz had disarmed all people in the holy places. Seeing a band of well-armed Egyptian soldiers guarding a sinful, anti-Islamic caravan was not an easy thing for the Ikhwān, the ultra-religious Najdīs, to witness. Unfortunately, the mahmal caravan was led by soldiers who refused to leave their musical band in Jeddah, taking it with them to Mecca, Mina, and ʿArafat. In addition, ʿAbd al-ʿAzīz banned cars in Mecca because they would scare camels, but the Egyptian solders disobeyed and used their cars in the Mecca streets.[60] The clash was inevitable. On the eighth of Dhū al-Ḥijja (June 18, 1926), as the mahmal with its music passed by the Ikhwān camps on its way to ʿArafat, some of the Ikhwān tried, in a harsh way, to stop the music, while others threw stones at the mahmal, calling it an idol (*ṣanam*). The 400 Egyptian soldiers responded by opening fire. When the king heard the sound of guns, he sent his son Faisal and his son Saud to resolve the clash. The Egyptian army continued firing at unarmed pilgrims, and the situation deteriorated when the 90,000 Najdi pilgrims in the area heard of the clash and surrounded the mahmal. The king arrived personally with the leader of the Ikhwān and asked the Najdis to go back to their tents; he also left some of his guards to escort the mahmal and secure its safety. The incident resulted in the death of twenty-five Najdis, some of them women and children, and forty camels. On the Egyptian side, only two soldiers were injured.[61] In August 1926, King ʿAbd al-ʿAzīz sent his oldest son Saud to Cairo to ease relations with the Egyptians after the

[59] *Al-Ahrām*, 14998 (May 9, 1926): 4; *Umm al-Qurā*, 71 (May 14, 1926): 2; *Umm al-Qurā*, 72 (May 21, 1926): 3; *Umm al-Qurā*, 78 (June 29, 1926): 1; *al-Manār*, 27, 6 (September 7, 1926): 463–468; *al-Manār*, 27, 7 (October 7, 1926): 501–503; *al-Manār*, 28, 4 (May 31, 1927): 293–309.

[60] See the interview with the Mahmal's leader Major-General Maḥmūd ʿAzmī Pasha, in *al-Ahrām*, 15055 (August 1, 1926): 5; and his report in *al-Ahrām*, 15057 (August 1926): 3.

[61] See *al-Ahrām*, 15055 (August 1, 1926): 5, and *Umm al-Qurā*, 78 (June 29, 1926): 1. See also *al-Manār*, 27, 6 (September 7, 1926): 463–468.

incident.[62] Although he was largely unsuccessful, it was agreed that Egypt could continue sending the mahmal as long as it stopped in Jeddah. Since the Saudi government rejected the Egyptian kiswa in 1962, however, the mahmal has stopped coming also.

THE KISWA

For centuries, the kiswa had been made in Egypt and sent to Mecca each season along with the mahmal. However, for some years there were disputes between the Ottoman sultans, the Egyptian leadership, and the sharifs of Mecca regarding which kings and sultans should have their names written on the kiswa, and the order in which it should be done.[63]

In 1924, when the Egyptians did not perform Hajj, the Saudis made the kiswa themselves in Aḥsā.[64] The Egyptians sent the kiswa in 1925 but stopped after the mahmal incident in 1926 in order to put pressure on ʿAbd al-ʿAzīz. ʿAbd al-ʿAzīz took advantage of this move to establish a factory for the kiswa in his own country, importing well-trained workers from India.[65] The factory started making the kiswa in 1927 and stopped again in 1936, when Saudi-Egyptian relations were restored and the two countries reached a special agreement regarding the mahmal and the kiswa.[66] After 1936, the Egyptians started sending the kiswa again, but instead of writing the name of the Egyptian king, the inscription read "it is given as a gift to the great Kaʿba during the reign of his majesty King ʿAbd al-ʿAzīz Āl Saud, the King of the Kingdom of Saudi Arabia."[67] In 1962, after Saudi-Egyptian relations suffered again and Egyptian production of the kiswa ceased one more time, King Saud reopened the kiswa factory and restarted Saudi manufacture.[68]

62 *Al-Ahrām*, 15061 (August 10, 1926): 5.

63 ʿA. ʿA. Muʾadhdhin, "Kiswat al-Kaʿba wa-ṭuruzuhā al-fanniyya mundhu al-ʿahd al-ʿUthmānī," unpublished MA thesis (Umm al-Qurā University, Saudi Arabia, 1980–1981), 199–202; Wahīm, *Mamlakat al-Ḥijāz*, 263–264.

64 *Umm al-Qurā*, 29 (July 17, 1925): 3; Naṣīf, *Māḍī*, 175; Rutter, *The Holy Cities*, I: 178.

65 Y. Bā Salāma, *Tārīkh al-Kaʿba al-muʿaẓẓama: ʿimāratuhā wa-kiswatuhā wa-sadānatuhā* (Riyadh: al-Amāna al-ʿĀmma li-l-Iḥtifāl bi-Murūr Miʾat Sana ʿalā Taʾsīs al-Mamlaka al-ʿArabiyya al-Suʿūdiyya, 1999), 347–354; "Repatriation of Pilgrimage," July 1927, in *Records of the Hajj*, VI: 153–154.

66 For this agreement, see M. al-Diqin, *Kiswat al-Kaʿba al-muʿaẓẓama ʿabr al-tārīkh*, ([Cairo:] Maṭbaʿat al-Jabalāwī, 1986), 118–121.

67 Muʾadhdhin, "Kiswa," 291.

68 Muʾadhdhin, "Kiswa," 295–297.

HAJJ SECURITY

For many centuries in the history of Islam, the governments in control of Hijaz were primarily concerned with the security of Hajj roads and the pilgrimage season. Defending pilgrims from highway robbery, internecine conflict, and the hazards of travel is no easy feat, but despite periods of conflict and disruption, no government has been as successful as the Saudis in ensuring the safety of the Hajj.

After King 'Abd al-'Azīz took over Hijaz, Hajj security improved greatly in a short period of time. The improvement was noticed by pilgrims from all over the world, such as the Syrian pilgrim Shakīb Arsalān,[69] the Egyptian Ibrāhīm al-Māzinī,[70] and many Indian pilgrims.[71] The 1926 British pilgrimage report stated: "All pilgrims and visitors to the Hijaz since Ibn Saud has assumed control are loud in their praises of the perfect security of the roads to Mecca and caravan routes from Mecca, Jeddah, Rabigh and Yanbo to Medina. It is frankly stated that such a state of perfect security has never before existed in this country, and this fact has gone so far to temper the many criticisms levelled at the present Administration."[72]

'Abd al-'Azīz was very assertive in securing Hajj roads, attacking the tribes responsible for looting pilgrims.[73] After his success in the domestication of these tribes before the 1926 season, 'Abd al-'Azīz invited the chiefs of the Hijaz tribes and divided the responsibility of pilgrim security between them, warning them that the whole tribe will have to pay him back for any harm incurred by a pilgrim.[74] 'Abd al-'Azīz made the master stroke of turning the greatest threat to pilgrims' security – the Hijazi Bedouins – into their best form of insurance. The result was immediate: in a description of the build-up to the Hajj season, the British vice-consul in Jeddah explained that "the one great source of satisfaction in the Hijaz at the present is the absolute safety of the roads. Everywhere isolated groups of two or three pilgrims may be met with, who go about quite unprotected and in perfect safety."[75]

[69] S. Arsalān, *al-Irtisāmāt al-liṭāf fī khāṭir al-ḥājj ilā aqdas maṭāf*, ed. M. Rashīd Riḍā, 2nd ed. ([Cairo: Maṭba'at al-Manār], 1998), 124–125.
[70] I. al-Māzinī, *Riḥlat al-Ḥijāz* (Cairo: Maṭba'at Fu'ād, 1930), 51, 65–69.
[71] F. Anṭākī, *Al-Hind kamā ra'aytuhā* (Cairo: W. A. Fadil's Printing Press, 1933), 34–35.
[72] "Pilgrimage Report, 1926," in *Records of the Hajj*, VI: 48–49.
[73] *Umm al-Qurā*, 7 (January 23, 1924): 2.
[74] *Umm al-Qurā*, 60 (February 19, 1926): 3.
[75] S. R. Jordan, "Vice-Consul Jordan to Sir Austen Chamberlain," May 1, 1926, in Jarman, *The Jedda Diaries*, II: 385.

Nevertheless, the second half of the twentieth century saw the emergence of new security threats from other quarters. On Tuesday, November 20, 1979, which marked the beginning of the fifteenth Hijrī century, approximately 200 members of an extreme apocalyptic Salafi group managed to smuggle weapons into the Grand Mosque of Mecca; they closed the mosque doors and asked the prayers to come and pledge allegiance to one of their leaders, the Mahdī. The Saudi army succeeded in liberating the Haram after fifteen days. Although this incident took place after the Hajj season, it should be mentioned here because some pilgrims were still in Mecca and were taken hostage along with others who had been praying in the Haram at that time. In 1986, Saudi customs at the Jeddah airport found about 51 kg of plastic explosives hidden in ninety-four suitcases belonging to Iranian pilgrims.[76] In 1989, two small explosions took place just outside the Grand Mosque in Mecca, resulting in the death of a Pakistani pilgrim and wounding sixteen others. Subsequently, the Saudi government announced the arrest of sixteen Shiʿite men from Kuwait, believed to be members of Ḥizbullah Kuwayt, and accused them of committing the crime in coordination with the Iranian embassy in Kuwait.[77] However, apart from these two incidents, Saudi authorities have so far managed to keep the Hajj seasons free from terrorist attacks.

POLITICAL OR APOLITICAL HAJJ?

Although the Hajj seasons have long been the main tool for the Saudis to promote their image and counter negative press, the Saudi government insists that the Hajj season must remain an apolitical occasion. From the beginning, King ʿAbd al-ʿAzīz decided not to make Hijaz and the Hajj a place to debate political issues.[78] Although the Saudis benefit from their management of the Hajj and the services they provide to pilgrims, no groups or governments have been allowed to use the Hajj season to promote their political agenda or cause tensions and divisions among

[76] *Al-Taḍāmun al-Islāmī*, 10, 44 (November 1989): 21. Interestingly, Ahmad Khomeini admitted that there had been several and repeated attempts to smuggle arms and explosives into Saudi Arabia, which sometimes had been caught and sometimes not. He added that he disapproved of these attempts and blamed them on Mahdi Hashimi. See *Ettelaat*, 18757 (May 16, 1989): 17–20.

[77] "Media Coverage of Disorders in Mecca and Relations between the Saudi Government and Its Critics, 1986–92," in *Records of the Hajj*, VIII: 704–736. For the full Saudi official statements regarding this incident, see *al-Taḍāmun al-Islāmī*, 10, 44 (November 1989): 8–30.

[78] See his letter to the First Muslim Congress in *Umm al-Qurā*, 75 (June 11, 1926): 1.

pilgrims. However, after 1979, the new Iranian leadership has insisted on promoting its revolutionary ideology by organizing a demonstration by Iranian pilgrims in Mecca and Medina, known as 'The Demonstration of Disavowal from Polytheists' (*masīrat al-barāʾa min al-mushrikīn*). In it, pilgrims recite the revolutionary slogans.

Throughout the 1980s, there were some skirmishes between the Saudi authorities and the Iranian pilgrims who insisted on organizing revolutionary demonstrations.[79] On Friday, July 31, 1987 (Dhū al-Ḥijja 6, 1407), thousands of Iranian pilgrims began demonstrating together in Mecca. When the crowd drew close to the Grand Mosque, it started clashing with other pilgrims, especially from Pakistan and Iraq, who thought the demonstration aimed to take over the Grand Mosque. The clash turned to fighting and the Saudi police interfered. The result was a tragedy: 402 people died, including 275 Iranians, most of them women, 42 pilgrims of other nationalities, and 85 Saudis, citizens and police alike.[80] In March 23–25, 1988, the seventeenth Islamic Conference of Foreign Ministers held its meeting in Amman. Its final declaration stated:

> The Conference condemned the acts of disruption and sabotage perpetrated by Iranian pilgrims in Holy Mecca during the Hajj season of 1407 H and declared its complete solidarity with the Kingdom of Saudi Arabia and its total support of the measures the Kingdom has taken to secure a proper environment in which the pilgrims to the Holy House of God can conduct the Hajj rituals in safety and piety. The Conference confirmed the right of the Kingdom of Saudi Arabia, stemming from its responsibility to keep and maintain order and to safeguard the holy places and the security of the pilgrims, to take whatever measures it deems necessary to prevent the recurrence of the incidents of disruption and discord.[81]

Subsequently, Iranians were no longer allowed to demonstrate in the street: however, they continue to declare the *barāʾa* inside their camps each year.

CONCLUSION

Imām Saud was harsh and uncompromising in his quest to conquer Hijaz and to impose an aggressive Salafi outlook. His eventual successor King

[79] *Majallat al-Majalla*, 391 (August 11, 1978).

[80] For the Saudi version of the story, see *al-Taḍāmun al-Islāmī* (September 1987): 6–36; and for the Iranian version, see ʿA. A. H. Rafsanjānī, *Difāʿ va siyāsat: Kārnāmah va khāṭirāt-i sāl-i 1366* (Tehran: Daftar-i Nashr-i Maʿārif-i Inqilāb, 1389sh/2010), 207–212; July 31–August 3, 1987.

[81] Official website of Organization of Islamic Cooperation, available at oic-oci.org/English /conf/fm/17/17%20icfm-final-en.html (last accessed April 18, 2014).

ʿAbd al-ʿAzīz was more conciliatory. But their policies have a few key features in common, and their legacies have done much to shape the current political and religious climate of Hijaz. The most notable feature of each of their rules is their success in securing safe access to Hajj routes.

Imam Saud was preoccupied with maintaining authority in Hijaz as a route to security and the promotion of Islam. His prohibition of traditions like the mahmal was not only a symbolic assertion of Saudi power, but also a literal means of preventing the encroachment of foreign soldiers on Saudi territory. ʿAbd al-ʿAzīz followed Imam Saud's lead and experienced a revisitation of old historical conflicts: he was, however, able to build ties with Muslim nations and improve the safety and accessibility of the Hajj during his reign. During its tenure as the administrator of the Hajj and ambassador for Muslims worldwide, the Saudi state has made great strides in protecting and uniting pilgrims.

In previous centuries, the Hajj was sometimes spread out over several days (between Sunni and Shiʿite pilgrims), with some pilgrims passing through ʿArafat while others were at Mina.[82] The Saudis reorganized the administration of Hajj prayers and movements so that pilgrims could experience the Hajj in unity: many of the ʿulama across the Muslim world welcomed this development and praised the Saudis for bringing it to fruition. Despite effective management on the part of the Saudis, ill feeling persists in some parts of the Muslim world: Saudi treatment of tombs and sites sacred to many Sunnis and Shiʿites remains a source of tension between Saudi Arabia and the countries it hosts for the Hajj. Nevertheless, Mecca and Medina have been fully integrated into the Saudi state for decades, and the Hajj is more secure now than at any point in history.

[82] Arsalān, *al-Irtisāmāt*, 46–47.

PART FOUR

PERFORMANCE

11

Performing the Pilgrimage*

Shawkat M. Toorawa

INTRODUCTION

Performing the pilgrimage, circumstances permitting, is one of the so-called pillars of Islam, acts required of all Muslims.[1] As the following canonical hadith illustrates, it has a very special status:[2]

> God's Emissary was asked, "What is the best deed?" "To believe in God," he replied, "and in His Emissary."
> The questioner then asked, "What is next best?"
> "To struggle in God's cause."
> The questioner again asked, "And what is next?"
> "To perform an accepted/blessed pilgrimage," he replied.

The significance of the pilgrimage being accepted/blessed (*ḥajj mabrūr*) is echoed in a standard Hajj supplication, "God, bless/accept my pilgrimage, forgive my sins, and reward my efforts."[3] And the prophet Muhammad is reported to have said, "One ʿUmra after another is an expiation for what comes between them, and there is no reward but Paradise for an accepted Hajj."[4] Even the ʿUmra, the non-obligatory, so-called minor pilgrimage, has considerable value. The reward is nothing short of Paradise. No

* This article is affectionately dedicated to Firoz H. Toorawa.

1 See S. M. Toorawa, "Pillars," in G. Böwering (ed.), *Princeton Encyclopedia of Islamic Political Thought* (Princeton University Press, 2013), 418–420.

2 Al-Bukhārī, *Ṣaḥīḥ al-Bukhārī*, vol. 1, bk. 2, no. 26, reported by Abū Hurayra.

3 See, e.g., Anonymous, *Manāsik al-ḥajj wa-l-umra ʿalā l-madhāhib al-arbaʿa wa-adʿiyat ziyārat al-madīna al-munawwara* (Medina: Maktabat Ṭayyiba lil-Nashr wa-l-Tawzīʿ, n.d.), 11. On the phrase, see See *EI2* s.v. "Radjm."

4 Al-Bukhārī, *Ṣaḥīḥ al-Bukhārī*, vol. 3, bk. 27, no. 1, reported by Abū Hurayra.

surprise then that pilgrimage to Mecca and its precincts continues to be one of the most prestigious activities in which a Muslim can engage.

Pilgrimage to Mecca, whether the Hajj or the ʿUmra, is transformative. Even for the (probably small) percentage of pilgrims who regard the Hajj as nothing more than an obligation, and who remain spiritually unmoved by it, it is still a ritually exacting, physically demanding, and avowedly communal experience, like little else in a person's life. I can attest to this personally: I have performed the Hajj three times. I went on my first Hajj from France in 1972 at the age of nine, in the company of my parents and most of my immediate paternal relatives. Because I had not yet reached puberty in 1972, that Hajj did not discharge my obligation, did not "count" as it were, so I went again from Mauritius in 1994 at the age of thirty, with friends of the family and acquaintances. My most recent Hajj was in 2008. My wife and our two daughters (then aged eleven and fourteen) and myself, as their designated male travel companion (*maḥram*), set out from the United States. As I had already performed the Hajj in 1994, I elected to perform this one on behalf of someone else who was unable to travel: performing the Hajj is the one ritual obligation that can be proxied. I have also performed the ʿUmra several times. By virtue of being quick – it can be completed in a few hours, ʿUmra can leave less of a mark, but it is still moving. In pre-modern times, for most Muslims, performing the Hajj or ʿUmra necessitated an overland or sea journey that could last several months, sometimes even years. In modern times, the time commitment is typically only one week or several, but still involves travel to a faraway place in an otherwise rarely visited country in the company of millions of fellow Muslims.

In 2012, 3.16 million pilgrims performed the Hajj.[5] This represents a mere 0.002 percent of the world Muslim population.[6] If we exclude pilgrims based in Saudi Arabia (for whom the trip is of course much easier), the figure almost halves to 1.75 million (including repeat pilgrims[7]), or 0.001 percent of Muslims worldwide.[8] As for pilgrims performing the ʿUmra the

[5] See www.saudiembassy.net/latest_news/news10271201.aspx (accessed March 15, 2014).

[6] Using the Pew 2010 figure of 1.61 billion for the number of Muslims worldwide: www.pewforum.org/2011/01/27/the-future-of-the-global-muslim-population/ (accessed March 15, 2014).

[7] When I went on Hajj in 1994, of the eighteen people in my group, eight had performed the Hajj before.

[8] The exact figures are 1,408,641 pilgrims (from 188 countries), and 1,752,932 from Saudi Arabia: www.saudiembassy.net/latest_news/news10271201.aspx (accessed March 15, 2014).

rest of the year, they number 11 million, 1 million of whom choose to do so in Ramadan.[9] The numbers are growing – 2013 saw a reduction by one million because of health concerns, as Valeska Huber discusses in Chapter 9 in this volume – but the overall percentage of worldwide Muslims remains tiny. These figures are often cited as a reflection of the uniqueness of the Hajj, but figures for Hindu pilgrimage sites, for instance, far exceed Hajj ones.[10] Indeed, even Karbala – the site of the martyrdom of the prophet Muhammad's grandson, Husayn – attracts up to two million pilgrims on a single day.[11] Such visits are properly not a pilgrimage but a "visit" (*ziyāra*).[12]

Many Muslims are unable to go on pilgrimage because of factors beyond their control, such as the quotas assigned to each country by the Saudi Hajj authorities (currently set at a maximum of 1,000 pilgrims per 1 million), the selection procedures of national Hajj committees, and of course capacity, notably infrastructure.[13] I mention attendance figures to draw attention to the following little-considered fact: the rituals of the Hajj (*manāsik*) are experienced first-hand by a very small percentage, and very small number, of Muslims (something that was no doubt truer still in pre-modern times).[14] This means that the majority of Muslims will learn about the rituals from teachers, hear about them in the mosque,

[9] Even from relatively wealthy Western countries such as the United States and the United Kingdom, only 12,000 and 25,000 pilgrims performed the Hajj, respectively: www.huffingtonpost.com/2010/11/09/12000-american-muslims-to_n_781230.html; www.theguardian.com/world/2010/nov/15/hajj-british-pilgrims-muslims (accessed March 15, 2014).

[10] http://www.arcworld.org/projects.asp?projectID=500 (accessed March 15, 2014).

[11] http://news.bbc.co.uk/2/hi/middle_east/7197473.stm (accessed March 15, 2014).

[12] These include visits to Muhammad's grave in Medina, to those of his relatives and companions, buried in the Arabian Peninsula and elsewhere; to the tomb sites of biblical and Qur'anic prophets; and to the shrines and tomb complexes of revered Muslims all over the world. Jerusalem, as one of the three sacred precincts (together with Mecca and Medina), is also a ziyara destination. See *EI2*, s.v. Ziyāra; for a medieval guide, see, e.g., al-Harawī, *A Lonely Wayfarer's Guide to Pilgrimage*, tr. J. W. Meri (Princeton, NJ: Darwin Press, 2004).

[13] See R. R. Bianchi, *Guests of God: Pilgrimage and Politics in the Islamic World* (New York: Oxford University Press, 2004).

[14] As I have noted elsewhere, "most Muslims' actual experience of the Ḥajj is only through national discourses; sponsorship, regulation, and subsidy by governments politicizes those discourses and, in turn, the Ḥajj itself. The fact that Saudi Arabia has been in charge of the Ḥajj for the past century has meant that it, in particular, has wielded considerable political leverage." See S. M. Toorawa, "Pilgrimage," in Böwering (ed.), *Princeton Encyclopedia of Islamic Political Thought*, 417. See also Bianchi, *Guests of God*.

or listen to returning pilgrims describe them; as of several years ago, they can watch them live on television.[15]

The rituals and ceremonies that take place before the pilgrims depart on the Hajj and after they return, on the other hand, have been experienced by almost every Muslim; this is because they come from every country, every community, every town, every village, as the Qur'an seems to have anticipated:[16]

> We showed Abraham the site of the House, saying, 'Do not assign partners to Me. Purify My House for those who circle around it, those who stand to pray, and those who bow and prostrate themselves. Proclaim the pilgrimage to all people. They will come to you on foot and on every kind of swift mount, emerging from every deep mountain pass ..." (Q Ḥajj 22:26–27)

Indeed, one would be very hard pressed to find a Muslim anywhere who does not know another who has gone on the Hajj, although this is no doubt more true in some (more affluent) parts of the world than others.

In many societies, neighbors and relatives will invite pilgrims for a meal, before departure and/or after return. Doing so before provides the hosts with an occasion to ask the pilgrims to pray on their behalf; doing so after honors the pilgrims, confers social prestige on the inviter, and gives the pilgrims the opportunity to give gifts acquired in Mecca and Medina. Pilgrims often bring back prayer rugs and rosaries (typically imported to Mecca, Turkey, and Central Asia), water from the Well of Zamzam in Mecca,[17] natural perfume oils from the region, and dates from Medina. The Zamzam water is highly prized and believed by many to have curative properties. Some people will keep dried dates till the following Ramadan and use them to break the daily fast. Pieces of the *kiswa* (the ornate black brocade covering on the Kaʿba), though of no religious or spiritual value, are also treasured. The kiswa is changed every year during the Hajj, when it is temporarily garbed (some say "veiled") in a plain white covering.[18]

[15] Broadcast at www. sauditv2.tv allows for "participation" in a way that was unthinkable as recently as twenty-five years ago.

[16] Qur'an translations from *The Qur'an*, tr. M. A. S. Abdel Haleem (Oxford University Press, 2008).

[17] *EI2*, s.v. "Zamzam."

[18] See S. M. Toorawa, "Every Robe He Dons Becomes Him: Images of Clothing in the Islamic Tradition," *Parabola*, 19, 3 (1994): 23; W. C. Young, "The Kaba, Gender, and the Rites of Pilgrimage," *International Journal of Middle East Studies*, 25 (1993): 285–300.

RITUALS

Descriptions of the rites and rituals abound:[19] in legal and juridical texts,[20] pilgrimage manuals,[21] travel writing[22] (a genre, recent examples of which Michael Wolfe analyzes in Chapter 13 in this volume), in pious and spiritual reflections,[23] in autobiographical accounts,[24] and in scholarly literature.[25] Such works have been produced for well over a thousand years; and with the advent of the Internet, a formidable array of online resources is now also available, as Gary Bunt describes in Chapter 12 in this volume. I shall therefore confine my remarks here to an overview, and limit my use of Arabic terminology – in any case, the often intricate differences based on school of legal thought, rite, and custom preclude anything but a simplified account.

Preparation

When a person intends to go on the Hajj, she will start reciting the *talbiya*, the phrase "*Labbayk-Allahumma Labbayk*" ("At your service, God, we are here"), which she will intone repeatedly. She will start the lengthy application process. She must apply for a Hajj visa from the Saudi Arabian embassy, or for inclusion on a list administered by a national

[19] For a recent and beautifully illustrated account, see M. A. S. Abdel Haleem, "The Importance of Hajj: Spirit and Rituals," in V. Porter, with M. A. S. Abdel Haleem et al., *Hajj: Journey to the Heart of Islam* (Cambridge, MA: Harvard University Press, 2012), 26–67.

[20] E.g. al-Shāfiʿī, *The Epistle on Legal Theory*, ed. and tr. Joseph E. Lowry (New York University Press, 2013), 295–297.

[21] E.g., Anonymous, *Manāsik al-ḥajj wa-l-ʿumra*; Saleh Ibn Fouzan Al-Fouzan [Ṣāliḥ Āl Fawzān], *How to Perform Hajj and Umrah*, tr. M. S. Al-Muharib (Kuwait: Islamic Translation Centre, 1992); R. al-Sirjānī, *al-Ḥajj wa-l-ʿumra: aḥkām wa-khibarāt* (Cairo: Sharikat Aqlām li-l-Nashr wa-l-Tawzīʿ wa-l-Tarjamah, 2012).

[22] See, e.g., M. Wolfe, *One Thousand Roads to Mecca: Ten Centuries of Travelers Writing about the Muslim Pilgrimage* (New York: Grove Press, 2015). For a dated account, but with excellent photographs, charts, and maps, see M. L. al-Batanūnī, *al-Risāla al-Ḥijāziyya li-Walī al-Niʿam al-Ḥājj ʿAbbās Ḥilmī Bāshā al-Thānī Khadīw Miṣr*, 2nd ed. (Cairo: Maṭbaʿat al-Jamāliyya, 1329/1911).

[23] E.g., A. Shariati, *Hajj: Reflections on Its Rituals*, tr. L. Bakhtiar (Albuquerque, NM: ABJAD, 1992).

[24] E.g., K. Ellison, *My Country 'Tis of Thee: My Faith, My Family, Our Future* (New York: Gallery Books/Karen Hunter Publishing, 2014).

[25] Although dated, the following are still important: M. Gaudefroy-Demombynes, *Le pèlerinage à la Mekke* (Paris: Librairie Orientaliste Paul Geuthner, 1923); M. Hamidullah, "Le Pèlerinage à la Mecque," in *Sources Orientales III: Les Pèlerinages* (Paris: Seuil, 1960), 89–138. The relevant articles in the *Encyclopedia of Islam* are indispensable, especially "Ḥadjdj" and "ʿUmra" in *EI2*. (See also D. F. Eickelman and J. Piscatori (eds.), *Muslim Travellers: Pilgrimage, Migration and the Religious Imagination* (London: Routledge, 1990).

Hajj committee; equally important are the required vaccinations.[26] Year-round, ʿUmra pilgrims traveling by air take regularly scheduled flights to Jeddah or Medina, either directly or through other cities. In the Hajj season, the only Jeddah-bound option is flights operated by one's national carrier, all of which land at the impressive Hajj Terminal. Once the Hajj authorities have issued the visa, the pilgrim will again call or call on friends and relatives, this time to ask for forgiveness for any past offences. She will also settle any outstanding debts. The idea is to set out for Mecca having acquitted oneself of outstanding obligations and of any wrongdoing.

The Hajj can be costly. The 2014 price of a budget package offered by the US Hajj tour operator my family used in 2008 is $6,450 per person[27] – excluding standard per person transportation fees (*tanazzul*) for within Saudi Arabia, which are reimbursable if unused. Often this means one cannot afford to take one's children along. Tradition has it that parents should not worry about their children while they are away as God sends angels to look after them; the obligation on a person to perform the Hajj does not "activate" until puberty. If children do travel, schools have to be alerted: we did as much in 2008, since our daughters were going to miss school. If one is employed, one needs to request time off.

Before all these admittedly important logistics are attended to, one has to have made the intention to go on Hajj. It may be objected that one would not apply for a visa unless one intended to go. But many – lay folk and religious scholars alike – would insist that one make the *niyya*, that is, state (aloud or in one's heart) one's genuine desire to go on pilgrimage.[28] This differs from, say, applying for a visa in case one later decides to go. The prophet Muhammad is reported to have said, "Surely actions are judged by their intentions."[29] And as Amina Steinfels observes:[30]

> At their most basic, rituals are pure actions without any function beyond their definition as obligatory acts of worship. Intention (*niyya*) plays the role of demarcating and categorizing the performance of such actions as the fulfillment of a specific ritual requirement. *Niyya* also signifies the performer's conscious attention

[26] See Chapter 9 in this volume.

[27] www.caravanhajj.com/hajj-packages/ (accessed March 15, 2014)

[28] See P. R. Powers, *Intent in Islamic Law: Motive and Meaning in Medieval Sunnī* Fiqh (Leiden: Brill, 2006), chs. 2 and 3.

[29] Al-Bukhārī, *Ṣaḥīḥ al-Bukhārī*, vol. 1, bk. 2, no. 52, reported by ʿUmar ibn al-Khaṭṭāb.

[30] A. Steinfels, "Ritual," in J. Elias (ed.), *Key Themes for the Study of Islam* (Oxford: Oneworld Publications, 2010), 308.

on ritual at hand. Without such an accompanying *niyya* no performance of the basic rituals counts, that is the Muslim's obligation has not been met."

The pilgrim can therefore be thought of as being "on the Hajj" the moment he has articulated the intention. If an aspiring pilgrim dies even before leaving his home, the Hajj "counts" because of the intention, of which God is inevitably aware.[31] Ritually speaking,[32] however, the pilgrim is on the Hajj from the moment she performs the ritual washing and ritual prayer that immediately precede the putting on/entering of the Hajj clothing, puts on that clothing, and ritually recites the talbiya. Women may wear anything simple and loose fitting that covers the whole body, including the hair, but not the hands and feet, nor the face, covering which is disallowed during the five days of the Hajj. Men put on two pieces of unsewn cloth and slippers (also unsewn, usually plastic slippers). One piece is wrapped around the lower torso often held in place with an unsewn belt, the other covers the upper torso. This garb – both the women's and the men's – is known as the *iḥrām*, although many mistakenly think only the men's clothing is so-called. The confusion arises from the fact that the ritual state bears the same name as the ritual garb. Ihram is a verbal noun, meaning "making sacred/forbidden," or "sacralization." When the pilgrim is described as being "in ihram" (called in Arabic a *muḥrim*) reference is being made to this state of sacralization.[33]

Performance

The pilgrim must be in ihram before she crosses certain prescribed points, known as a *mīqāt* ("appointed place"), strategically located along seventh-century pilgrimage routes. The prophet Muhammad reportedly set five of these points; a sixth was added later.[34] When the trip to Mecca is made by sea or over land, respecting the miqat is easy. One arrives at the designated point, halts, performs the ritual prayer of sacralization, and puts on/enters ihram. Air travel has complicated matters. Most pilgrims will be able to put on/enter ihram in Jeddah, where all Hajj flights land

31 Islamic law stipulates "awareness and intention as a necessary component for the valid performance of a ritual. This validity cannot be judged by an external human audience but is only known to the actor and to God." Steinfels, "Ritual," 308.

32 I do not take up the question of what constitutes a ritual. See E. Zeusse, "Ritual," in L. Jones (ed.), *Encyclopedia of Religion*, 2nd ed. (Detroit: Macmillan Reference USA, 2005), vol. 11, 7833–7848.

33 *EI2*, s.v. "Iḥrām."

34 *EI2*, s.v. "Mīqāt."

(except for those routed through Medina first[35]). But some will cross the miqat in the air (at 800 kmh) because of their flight path: those pilgrims will put on/enter ihram when they leave their homes for the airport, while still thousands of miles away. When this is the case, the pilgrims' first leg of the Hajj is sometimes in a procession of family, friends, and well wishers, all accompanying them to the airport. In 1994, because my Jeddah-bound Air Mauritius Hajj flight was going to cross the miqat designated for pilgrims coming from the south, we put on/entered ihram at home. In 2004, because our Hajj group was going to Medina (via Amman) before Mecca, we did not put on/enter ihram until our bus crossed the designated miqat for pilgrims journeying from Medina to Mecca.

Being in ihram is demanding, not only because for men it can be quite uncomfortable but because of the strict regulations: no cutting of nails or removal of hair, no use of perfume or scented products, no sexual activity, no arguing, no hunting (i.e., no killing of any living thing). Violation of any of these must be followed by expiation, through animal sacrifice, called *dam* ("lit. blood"). The pilgrim must also be exceptionally attentive to the regular Islamic prescriptions and proscriptions: performing the ritual prayers on time, avoiding reprehensible behavior, engaging only in licit activities, eating only licit food, and so on.

There are juridical differences that govern the precise way in which one commences one's performance of the Hajj. Suffice here to say that if a pilgrim arrives in Mecca several days before the Hajj, she is likely to perform the ʿUmra (which takes a few hours), revert to a non-sacralized state, and then don the ihram again for the Hajj proper. The ʿUmra consists of (1) donning/entering ihram, (2) circumambulating the Kaʿba seven times (*ṭawāf*),[36] (3) briskly walking between the two hillocks of al-Ṣafā and al-Marwa (*saʿy*),[37] and (4) desacralizing by cutting the hair (*ḥalq*). This all takes place within the walls of the Grand Mosque or *Ḥaram*. The Hajj includes all those rituals but also involves travel away from Mecca. The Hajj always takes five days, from the eighth through the twelfth of Dhū al-Ḥijja (literally, "the (month of the) pilgrimage"). If the pilgrim arrives on the seventh or eighth, she will perform the ʿUmra and remain in the same ihram for the Hajj (see the Chart below).

On the eighth of Dhū al-Ḥijja, pilgrims recite the talbiya and set out for the town of Mina, five miles from Mecca, which they must reach before

[35] For infrastructural reasons, half the pilgrims visit Medina before Mecca.

[36] *EI2*, s.v. "Ṭawāf," *EI3*, s.v. "Circumambulation."

[37] *EI2*, s.v. "Saʿy."

Ritual	'Umra	Ḥajj		Dhū'l ijja date
Sacralization point (*mīqāt*)				
Enter state and garb of sacralization (*iḥrām*)	√	√		
→ ***Mecca***				
Circumambulation of the Ka'ba (*ṭawāf*)	√			
Walk between mounts of al-Ṣafā and Marwa (*sa'y*)	√			
	N/A	√	→ ***Minā*** *for the night*	*8*
	N/A	√	→ "Standing" on the ***Plain of 'Arafāt*** (*wuqūf 'Arafa*)	*9*
	N/A	√	→ "Halting" at ***Muzdalifa*** (*wuqūf Muzdalifa*)	
	N/A	√	→ ***Minā for 3 days*** Cast stones (*ramy*)	*10*
	N/A	√	Sacrificing an animal (*ḍaḥiyya*)	
Cutting hair	√	√		
		√	→ ***Mecca*** Circumambulation (*ṭawāf al-ifāḍa*)	
		√	Walk al-Ṣafā to al-Marwa (*sa'y*)	
		√	→ ***Minā*** Cast stones (*ramy*)	*11*
	N/A	√	→ ***Mecca*** Circumambulation of the Ka'ba (*ṭawāf al-widā'*)	*12*

The Rituals of the Hajj and the 'Umra

the post-zenith prayer and where they will spend the night. When I performed the Hajj in 1994, we were eighteen adults in a medium-sized, ill-kept rented apartment with only one bathroom, but many hundreds of thousands were either in makeshift tents or out in the open. By the time we went in 2008, the Hajj authorities had transformed Mina entirely into a city of tents. The only buildings were administrative (Hajj offices, information booths, police posts), medical (pharmacies, clinics, hospitals), restaurants, and facilities (toilets, bathrooms). Much is made of the fact that the Hajj generally is an "equalizer": everyone, irrespective of wealth or status or piousness, wears the same outfit – but this is only true of men, as women dress differently depending on their place of origin. And it is only true during the five days of the Hajj; the remaining time in Mecca and

Medina, wealth and status is evident in different ways. For example, in Mina, now consisting exclusively of accommodation in "national" tents, the American and European tents are air-conditioned and closest to facilities, whereas African and South Asian ones are distant. The placement is determined by the Hajj authorities, but is evidently a function of what money can buy. This is not to deny the fact that there is a profoundly egalitarian feeling that arises from being in austere clothing, engaging in the same rituals as everyone else, pilgrims from all over the world sharing a common purpose; this is what so struck Malcolm X.[38]

The next day, the ninth of Dhū al-Ḥijja, all pilgrims depart for the Plain of ʿArafat (or ʿArafa) after sunrise.[39] A few hundred thousand will choose to walk the nine miles, just as they walked the five miles from Mecca to Mina, and will continue to walk for the remainder to the Hajj. Men may not cover their heads when in ihram, but they may be beneath cover, such as a parasol or a covered walkway. One must arrive at ʿArafat in the daytime, remain within its prescribed boundaries (all clearly marked), and not leave till after sunset. The prophet Muhammad is reported to have said, "The ten days of the month of Dhū al-Ḥijja are the best days in the sight of God." When someone asked if they are better than ten days of pious struggle, he replied that they are and that "there is no better day in the sight of God than the Day of ʿArafa." He continued:[40]

> On this day God, the Almighty and Exalted, descends to the nearest heaven, proud of His worshippers on Earth, and says to those in Heaven, "Look at My servants. They have come from far and near, hair disheveled and faces covered in dust, to seek My mercy, even though they have not seen My punishment." Far more people are freed from Hellfire on the Day of ʿArafat than on any other day.

Consequently (and even though three days of ritual remain), pilgrims are at their most fervent at ʿArafat, without a doubt the point regarded as the apotheosis of the Hajj. Indeed, if there is one stretch during the entire Hajj when everyone is on equal footing, it is at ʿArafat and Muzdalifa. In both places, there is very little that distinguishes the different groups of pilgrims. At ʿArafat, pilgrims supplicate to God for forgiveness from all prior sins and transgressions and for the ultimate and promised reward, Paradise. It is said that an "accepted" Hajj (by God, that is) means that one leaves Mecca as sinless as a newborn child. Supplication for forgiveness for oneself and

[38] Malcolm X, with the assistance of A. Haley, *The Autobiography of Malcolm X* (New York: Grove Press, 1965), ch. 17.
[39] *EI2*, s.v. "ʿArafa," *EI3*, s.v. "ʿArafāt."
[40] *Fiqh al-Sunna*, vol. 5, Fiqh 5.094A.

others is enjoined throughout the pilgrimage. Every place and every stage has one or more set or recommended supplications or prayers to be recited by the pilgrim.[41] The pilgrim may consult these in Hajj manuals or, for the texts that need to be recited in crowded circumstances, the pilgrim can repeat the phrases shouted out by the Hajj group leader or his appointee.[42]

At ʿArafat, pilgrims combine the post-zenith and afternoon ritual prayers, rather than performing them at discrete times. At Muzdalifa, where they will head next, the sunset and nighttime prayers will be combined too. These features of the Hajj are all based on Muhammad's example. It is he who established how the ʿUmra and Hajj are to be performed, and this has evidently continued unchanged since. The Qurʾan is not silent on the rituals, but it is not very specific. Here is the Qurʾanic passage in which ʿArafat and Muzdalifa are mentioned:

> The pilgrimage takes place during the prescribed months. There should be no indecent speech, misbehavior, or quarreling for anyone undertaking the pilgrimage – whatever good you do, God is well aware of it. Provide well for yourselves: the best provision is to be mindful of God – always be mindful of Me, you who have understanding – but it is no offence to seek some bounty from your Lord. When you surge down from ʿArafāt, remember God at the sacred place [*al-mashʿar al-ḥarām*]. (Q Baqara 2:198)

The interpretation of "sacred place" as Muzdalifa is based entirely on Muhammad's practice. Like ʿArafat, it is within certain prescribed boundaries that may not be breached. At Muzdalifa, pilgrims comb the area for pebble-sized stones. Each will need forty-nine pebbles, seven to cast upon arrival in Mina, and then twenty-one each of the next two days. They leave Muzdalifa after performing the pre-dawn prayer, and before sunrise. Those who came by bus typically continue by bus, but this can be more strenuous and uncomfortable than walking. In 1994, we were delayed leaving ʿArafat because one member of our group was unwell. It took us six hours to drive five miles; and it took us fourteen hours to go the next five miles. With that memory still vivid in 2008, I suggested to my family that we walk from Muzdalifa to Mina; we did so along with a quarter of a million other pilgrims. It only took us two and a half hours. Paradoxically, this can take less time and be less tiring than going by bus.

Upon return to Mina on the tenth of Dhū al-Ḥijja, pilgrims may first regain their tents and then proceed to cast stones at the last of the three columns, or proceed directly to the stoning (*ramy*). This is the first of four

[41] Anonymous, *Manāsik al-ḥajj wa-l-ʿumra.*

[42] *EI2*, s.v. "Muṭawwif."

FIGURE 14 Jamarat (pillars representing Satan) in Mina, ca. 1911

FIGURE 15 Aerial view of the new Jamarat, 2009

rituals of de-sacralization. The pilgrim will also sacrifice an animal and cut or shave his or her hair in Mina. The casting of stones and the sacrificing of an animal can be – and often is – done by proxy, in both cases because of the crush of people. The sacrifice of the animal is also done the same day by Muslims all over the world on the tenth of Dhū al-Ḥijja, observed by non-pilgrims as the *ʿĪd al-Aḍḥā*, or the Feast of Sacrifice. Once the hair has been cut, the prohibitions of the ihram are lifted, except for sexual intercourse: that is only permitted after the pilgrim has performed the circumambulation (*ṭawāf*) of the Kaʿba and the brisk walk between the two hillocks of al-Ṣafā and al-Marwa (*saʿy*), that very same day, after having showered and put on regular clothing. The talbiya may now no longer be recited. This circumambulation of the Kaʿba as part of the Hajj ritual is therefore not done in ihram, unlike in the ʿUmra (see the preceding chart). In both cases, one must begin in line with the Black Stone, and walk counter clockwise seven times. Men are supposed to do the first three rounds at a brisk pace and the next four at a leisurely pace. Because of the crowd, the distance covered can vary between several hundred meters if one is close to the Kaʿba and ten kilometers if one is circumambulating in the outer "ring." The physically impaired used to be carried on palanquins; now they use wheelchairs. I have seen adult men carry their infirm parents on their backs; and parents routinely carry their children.

The pilgrim then does the brisk walk back and forth between al-Ṣafā, where one starts, and al-Marwa, where one ends up on the seventh crossing, a total distance of just under three kilometers. It is a straight line between the two, so here the infirm have the option of accomplishing it in wheelchairs. The entrance to the Well of Zamzam is nearby, and pilgrims flock to visit it. In 1972, I went down wide a staircase and was able to open a tap that was visibly piped into the well; in 1994, the well was behind glass, and the water was being mixed with plain water and pumped to taps located on the outside walls of the mosque. Because of the oppressive heat, the Hajj authorities also place large containers of water mixed with Zamzam every hundred feet or so in the Mosque. In 2008, access to the Well was blocked, but the mixed water was widely available throughout the mosque.

The pilgrims then return to Mina, where they stay two more days, casting stones at all three columns, seven on each, thus twenty-one on the eleventh of Dhū al-Ḥijja and twenty-one on the twelfth. Then, before sunset on the twelfth, they return to Mecca for the Farewell Circumambulation. Those who were in Medina before Mecca next go to Jeddah where they will wait for their flights in the Hajj Terminal; that wait can last up to 24 hours.

The others will go to Medina to pay respects at the tomb of the Prophet Muhammad. A ziyara to Medina is not part of the Hajj proper, but it forms an inseparable part of almost everyone's journey. Some stay a short time, others several days. Some are attracted by the possibility of visits to historical sites, including battlefields, cemeteries, and early mosques; others try to perform forty consecutive ritual prayers in Medina, said by some to guarantee Paradise, something also guaranteed to those who are able to set foot in a particular part of the mosque designated "a piece of Paradise." Because outbound Hajj flights from Jeddah all carry people back home, very few pilgrims can go elsewhere; in fact, it is disapproved to do so. One should intend to go from one's home to Mecca and return to one's home, with no side trips along the way, Medina being the one exception.

Pilgrims acquire considerable social standing upon their return home. In most communities and societies, they also acquire a special designation, *ḥājj* for men and *ḥājja* for women (or other equivalent local terms meaning "pilgrim"). In some communities, the distinction is on public display: men, clean-shaven prior to the Hajj, will afterward sport beards; women, head uncovered or face unveiled, will adopt the head covering or face veil. In some places, hajjis will now (be expected to) stand in the first row of worshippers when offering congregational prayers in the mosque.

MEANING

The Qur'an may enjoin able believers to perform the Hajj, but it provides very little guidance about how to accomplish it, confining itself to general regulations about movement and sacralization. For the rituals, Muslims have relied on Muhammad's one Hajj in 632 CE. Because the majority of the rituals that now form part of the Islamic pilgrimage were part of earlier pagan pilgrimage, modern scholars have typically tended to focus on continuity/adaptation and have ignored what these rituals might mean to Muslims.[43] One can show, for example, that circumambulating the Kaʿba is a vestige of a similar pre-Islamic practice, when the structure housed personal and tribal idols. Pilgrims care little about this. They focus instead on the fact that it is the "House of God," first built by the Prophet Adam, then periodically rebuilt as a shrine to the one true God. The Qur'an makes much of Abraham and his son Ishmael rebuilding the structure. Indeed, if anything the pre-Islamic and pagan backdrop is

[43] Cf. Shariati, *Hajj*, 158: "You must know what you are doing and why. Do not become lost in the external forms of these rituals. Do not neglect meaning. These are all allusions."

integral to the larger narrative.[44] And the history stretches back further, as the earthly Kaʿba is said to be located directly beneath an equivalent celestial one, circumambulated by angels before Earth was created.

Modern scholarly analyses of the rituals of the Hajj are very few in number,[45] part of a larger inattention to study of ritual and rituals in Islamic Studies generally,[46] and the view that the rituals have limited intrinsic meaning prevails. Marion Katz has faulted William Graham, for instance, for characterizing the Hajj as "an exercise in pure obedience to God devoid of any concept of ritual efficacy or mythic reenactment," as epitomizing semantic sparseness and exhibiting a resolutely "antimagical" quality, and for suggesting that it is nothing more than a "commemorative" ritual.[47] As Amina Steinfels puts it:[48]

> Muslims may often not perform their prayers, or fast, or go on pilgrimage; they may question, debate, replace, or modify these obligations; they may mock those who perform them assiduously; they may spend much more energy on alternative ritual activities. But, in general, *Muslims have been in agreement that these are Islamic practices with enormous symbolic value for the definition of what it means to be Muslim.* [emphasis added][49]

For me, a meaningful way – in both senses of the expression – of thinking about the Hajj (and ʿUmra) is "return."[50] Tradition has it that Adam and Eve were reunited, returned to one another, at ʿArafat. Muslims associate the Mount of Mercy on the Plain of ʿArafat with God forgiving Adam and Eve, but they also associate it with the Prophet Muhammad's return there to give his last sermon. And many Muslims hold – although there is little textual support – that Judgment Day will

[44] "The Abrahamic vision of the Kaʿba created a means of discerning an orthodox origin buried in the midst of pagan malpractices." *EI2*, s.v. Kaʿba.

[45] But see B. Wheeler, *Mecca and Eden: Ritual, Relics and Territory in Islam* (University of Chicago Press, 2006); M. H. Katz, "The Hajj and the Study of Islamic Ritual," *Studia Islamica*, 98/99 (2004): 95–129; J. E. Campo, "Authority, Ritual and Spatial Order in Islam: The Pilgrimage to Mecca," *Journal of Ritual Studies*, 5 (1991): 65–91.

[46] On this, see especially Steinfels, "Ritual," and Katz, "The Hajj."

[47] Katz, "The Hajj"; W. Graham, "Islam in the Mirror of Ritual," in R. G. Hovanissian and S. Vryonis, Jr. (eds.), *Islam's Understanding of Itself* (Malibu: Undena Publications, 1983), 53–71.

[48] Steinfels, "Ritual," 305.

[49] Cf. Powers, who argues that "actions governed by Islamic ritual law are presented as valuable and moral in and of themselves, not (just) as symbolic surfaces, signifiers, or metaphors." P. R. Powers, "Interiors, Intentions and the 'Spirituality' of Islamic Ritual Practice," *Journal of the American Academy of Religion*, 72, 2 (2004): 454.

[50] See S. M. Toorawa, "Eid and the Imagery of Return," *Le Mauricien*, September 19, 2009, 7.

take place at ʿArafat, that the "standing" during the Hajj, in unsewn white cloth, just like the plain white cloth in which dead bodies are wrapped, is a rehearsal of what is to come. ʿArafat thus represents both the beginning of the end, and the advent of return. As the Qurʾan has believers say, "We belong to God and to Him we shall return" (Q Baqara 2:156).

In the context of Abraham, return is critical. His is the return of Prophecy to the site of divine attention, Mecca. He builds the Kaʿba as a monument to the One God and another return is reenacted. When he is asked to sacrifice his son, Satan is said to have come first to him, then to Hagar, and then to Ishmael, and to have tried to deter them. Three times he tried and three times he was cast away. For pilgrims they are returning to the same spot to reenact that earlier rejection of Satan. When Abraham carries through, his son is returned to him. When pilgrims sacrifice the animals in Mina, they do not have in mind pre-Islamic, pagan rituals of sacrifice – they are thinking of Abraham.[51] The sacrificial animals assume an active role in the eschatological drama of salvation.[52] The key, however, is always Muhammad. Every ritual reenactment is ultimately the reenactment of a ritual in which Muhammad engaged, whatever its origin(s) may be, whatever its meaning(s) may be. He performed one Hajj, so Muslims must perform one Hajj. He did so in a state of ihram, so Muslims do so too. He abided by regulations, limits, and boundaries, so Muslims must too. He traveled on a set route, at set times, so Muslims do too. One need not look any further than Muhammad, who returned to Mecca to destroy the idols housed in the Kaʿba, thus returning it to right religion. He left Mecca after his one and only Hajj, never to return, but having ensured that every believer would try to return, or commemorate the return on the Feast of Sacrifice:

> Complete the pilgrimages, major and minor, for the sake of God. If you are prevented [from doing so], then [send] whatever offering for sacrifice you can afford. (Q Baqara 2:196)

[51] For a discussion of Abrahamic and Adamic paradigms, see Katz, "The Hajj," 199 ff. Cf. Shariati, *Hajj*, 184: "[God] accepts the slaughter of a sheep as a sacrifice from you. The slaughtering of a sheep instead of Ishmael is a sacrifice. The slaughter of a sheep as a sheep is butchery."

[52] Katz, "The Hajj," 102.

12

Decoding the Hajj in Cyberspace

Gary R. Bunt

ACCESSING THE HAJJ ONLINE

Understanding technological interfaces is increasingly important in developing a comprehension of contemporary Islamic issues and their dissemination. The continual evolution of interfaces, software, and hardware must be accommodated within academic interpretations. Many of these are relatively recent innovations, which have been quickly adopted by users; consider the exponential development and growth in social media since 2000, and the impact of enhanced forms of Internet access through mobile devices such as smartphones and tablets. Increased net literacy and access, with a "digital native" generation educated and brought up using the Web, has had a profound impact on Muslim individuals and communities.

The term *cyber Islamic environments* refers to a variety of contexts, perspectives, and applications of the media by those who define themselves as "Muslims."[1] Cyber Islamic environments contain elements of specific worldviews and notions of exclusivity, combined with regional and cultural understandings of the Internet and its validity, and have demonstrated the ability to transform aspects of religious understanding and expression within Muslim contexts. A complex spectrum of access, dialogue, networking, and application of the media associated with cyber Islamic environments has emerged. The term's original definition as an online Internet space with an Islamic religious orientation has evolved to

[1] I introduced the term *cyber Islamic environment* in the late 1990s. See G. R. Bunt, *Virtually Islamic: Computer-Mediated Communication and Cyber Islamic Environments* (Cardiff: University of Wales Press, 2000).

incorporate elements of so-called Web 2.0+ tools, as well as alternate interfaces such as Web-enabled smartphones and televisions with net access. It can incorporate online services such as blogs, social networking sites, media distribution channels, and interfaces in which the Internet is integrated into "traditional" media delivery, for example, media channels using online delivery in real time and storage modes.[2]

One should not separate the digital from the analogue, in terms of activities; while new networks and conceptual frameworks have emerged online, they can also connect directly at grassroots level to "real world" activities and research. Islam is "always on" technologically and through "traditional" channels, increasingly so through cell phones, with little separation for those whose online activities and levels of net literacy integrate with their everyday life. Just as there can be different levels of determining religiosity and "Islamic" activity, depending on the beholder, so the levels of Islamic activity and usage of online materials can vary. Different models could potentially be constructed, to indicate different typologies of "Islamic" Internet use.

For some, as is the case with other aspects of everyday life, it is perfectly natural to consult the Internet for a religious opinion, Islamic information, or to interact with members of a network (informal and formal). The influence of "Sheikh Google" has challenged traditional networks of authority, and raised concerns regarding influence and impact on communities and individuals.[3] As a channel of information distribution, the application of social networking tools provides immediacy in terms of connecting to followers, and a sense of identity for those participating. The reduced digital divide, particularly in relation to the expansion of cell phone networks and broadband usage, is reflected in this increasing influence of cyber Islamic environments, while recognizing that significant sectors still remain untouched – at least directly – from this discourse and participation.

[2] G. R. Bunt, *Islam in the Digital Age: E-jihad, Online Fatwas and Cyber Islamic Environments* (London and Sterling, VA: Pluto Press, 2003); G. R. Bunt, *iMuslims: Rewiring the House of Islam* (Chapel Hill: University of North Carolina Press; London: C. Hurst & Co, 2009). See also G. R. Bunt, "Surfing Islam: Ayatollahs, Shayks and Hajjis on the Superhighway," in J. K. Hadden and D. E. Cowan (eds.), *Religion on the Internet: Research Prospects and Promises* (New York: Elsevier Science, 2000), 127–151.

[3] R. Ghazal, "Grand Mufti Calls for Dialogue about the Internet," *The National*, February 20, 2012: thenational.ae/news/uae-mufti-calls-for-dialogue-about-the-internet (last accessed April 11, 2014).

The Hajj has been represented online in various ways since the emergence of the World Wide Web in the early 1990s. Over time, the text-only descriptions that appeared on early websites have been augmented with photographs, film clips, graphics, and interactive features. Social networking material discussing the Hajj can be found through Facebook and Twitter, together with film clips and personal accounts on YouTube. Some of this content is experiential, and other elements represent contemporary manifestations of pilgrimage guides with roots in the early days of Islam.

A broad range of products has been introduced for the use of pilgrims during the Hajj, which can be utilized on cell phones using a variety of operating systems, and on tablet computers such as the iPad. As software has become more sophisticated and the digital divide has reduced, the range of Hajj apps and related content has increased. This is in addition to the online marketing of Hajj packages by travel companies, which can be organized and paid for via the Internet. Advice on all aspects of pilgrimage is featured on official Saudi Arabian websites in numerous languages. Specific religious perspectives and interpretations of the pilgrimage can also be found online, aiding in the preparation and organization of pilgrimage. Mapping advice, drawing on GPS tools and technology, also facilitates effective pilgrimage.

Officially, there are still restrictions as to the use of cell phones within the precincts of Mecca. This does not seem to dissuade pilgrims from posting status updates and tweeting during the pilgrimage. It may be that the pilgrim can discreetly place a phone within the ihram, or that perspectives on the relative merits of technology during pilgrimage are changing. After all, those using digital technology can familiarize themselves with every stage of pilgrimage, in order that the ritual and practice fulfill the required obligations. This does not mean to say that every pilgrim is online or using these technologies, but for a certain age group with digital access, it would seem that the Internet and cell phone access would be natural channels for acquiring advice and information about the pilgrimage. A 3D rendering of the Kaʿba on a cell phone may not equate to the experience of being there in person during the Hajj, but it does offer a sense of location, geography, and architecture. This may be combined with observation of streaming television coverage online. It may offer a glimpse into the experience of pilgrimage, although the virtual Hajj does not confer honorific titles or status, the way the actual Hajj does (see Chapter 11 in this volume).

Some of the mystery of the pilgrimage may also be deconstructed online, by reading numerous experiential accounts, and viewing photos and film clips. Several hundred years ago, the pilgrimage would have been an event potentially full of danger along a perilous route. The relative ease of access for contemporary pilgrims, coupled with the depth of data relating to the Hajj that is now available online, is bound to have an impact on pilgrims' expectations and experiences.

SEEKING HAJJ GUIDANCE ONLINE

Those who cannot perform the Hajj may benefit from its digital manifestation, and view every pilgrimage station online. The Internet also impacts on ritualistic elements such as Eid al-Adha, where the sacrifice of animals in celebration of Abraham's sacrifice can be facilitated online: at one time, this sacrifice had to be undertaken by the pilgrims themselves. Now, technology and mass meat processing, health and safety standards, and the massive rise in pilgrim numbers have led to a modernization process. The Hajj itself has become open to wider scrutiny, from Muslims and other interested parties, through its coverage in the media. This includes satellite television, conventional print media, and Internet coverage – formal and informal, official and unofficial.

Some of this information is designed to facilitate pilgrims at specific locations. There are also very practical websites that provide a "one-stop shop" for potential pilgrims. These may have a commercial element, relating to sales of tickets, accommodations, and official mutawwif-guide services for Hajj (and ʿUmra) visits. Many factors can prevent an individual from going on the Hajj, so certain sites seek to provide a sense of an immersive experience; how close this is to attending in person is debatable.

There are other ways of approaching pilgrimage via the Internet: Google Earth offers a distant satellite view of the Kaʿba in Mecca.[4] More detailed is the 3D Kabah created by Abid S. Hussain. It represents a long-term project applying three-dimensional computer modeling to produce animated video clips, including a fly-through the Kaʿba precincts.[5] This site was developed over several years, with updated computer imagery and unique angles on the holy precincts, and files are downloadable for use on a variety of devices. The open access content introduced a new dimension and understanding of the Kaʿba, devoid of pilgrims, and

[4] "Mecca, Makka, Kaaba, Saudi Arabia" at Google Maps: goo.gl/maps/t7mG4 (last accessed April 11, 2014).

[5] 3D Kabah, youtube.com/user/3dkabah (last accessed June 26, 2015).

with a computer-enhanced aesthetic. Another site offers 360-degree panoramic 3D images of the Kaʿba.[6] The online virtual world Second Life provided a representation of the sacred precincts of Mecca, through which "cyber pilgrims" could progress through the various stages of pilgrimage. Avatars would appear in pilgrim dress. This meant that anybody, from whatever religious background (or not), could make the journey online. The avatar could perform many of the different ritual elements. This was organized by the Islam Online website in 2007 as part of their portfolio of Second Life products. A version of this experience also appeared on YouTube, incongruously accompanied by a dance music track, as the pilgrim progressed at high speed around the precincts.[7] One media account quotes one of the designers, Awatef Mohammed, as follows:

> Our first goal was to teach Muslims the correct way to make a pilgrimage. Our second goal was to introduce the Haj and Islam in general to non-Muslims. For non-Muslims, it is indeed the only way to see Mecca, which is forbidden to them.[8]

At the time of writing, this product was no longer available, which highlights the fact that Hajj materials can appear and disappear from the Internet without warning.[9]

The ephemeral nature of this material is in contrast to the enduring historical guides relating to pilgrimage practice that were originally produced in manuscript form, and reproduced by hand. These included stage-by-stage advice on the different pilgrimage stations, maps, practical information, and information based on the author's personal experiences. Examples of such guidebooks include the anonymous fifteenth-century *Kitāb Manāsik al-ḥajj wal-l-ʿumra ʿalā al-madhāhib al-arbaʿa* ("Guide to the rituals of the Hajj according to the four juridical schools") and the more poetic sixteenth-century *Futūḥ al-ḥaramayn* by Muḥyi al-Dīn Lārī.[10] Traditional Hajj materials such as these also have a place online, and in a

[6] "Masjid al-Haram – Kaaba" at 3Dmekanlar.com: 3dmekanlar/en/masjid-al-haram—kaaba.html (last accessed April 11, 2014).

[7] "Islam on Second Life – Virtual Hajj" at Islam Online: youtu.be/eNNqd2AxxyM (last accessed April 11, 2014).

[8] France 24 (November 26, 2009): 'Virtual Haj' allows Internet users to make 'pilgrimage'" at france24.com/en/20091125-virtual-haj-allows-internet-users-make-pilgrimage (last accessed April 11, 2014).

[9] K. Derrickson, "Second Life and the Sacred: Islamic Space in a Virtual World," at digitalislam.eu/article.do?articleId=1877 (last accessed April 11, 2014).

[10] V. Porter with M. A. S. Abdel Haleem et al. (eds.), *Hajj: Journey to the Heart of Islam* (Cambridge, MA: Harvard University Press, 2012); *EI2*, s.v. "Muḥyi al-dīn Lārī."

variety of locations. The *Manāsik al-ḥajj* is archived on the websites of several Muslim organizations, and the *Futūḥ al-ḥaramayn* on the websites of museums and auction houses.[11] Their contemporary equivalent is a very different experience, mediated through computer technology. It may not have the same resonance as a handwritten manuscript, or an intrinsic sacred value, but electronic guides to pilgrimage offer detail, immediacy, and personal advice. Whether they will have a future place in a museum or auction house we cannot know, but they certainly have a substantial potential audience that the authors of the historical guides might have envied.

Guidance can also come in the form of government advice, available online from a variety of official platforms: the Majlis Ugama Islam Singapura maintains a webpage including a book of ritual practice. The government of Pakistan produces webpages that include detailed information on the pilgrimage.[12] As will be seen, the Saudi Arabian Ministry of Hajj is proactive online with information for pilgrims presented in a variety of languages. This reflects an international pattern, where the Internet is the natural place for advice – whether it is ritualistic or more practical in nature. Governmental advice may also be reproduced and archived on diverse websites; for example, Aloloom English's Bulletin Board links to a set of decisions from the Saudi Arabian Permanent Committee for Scholarly Research and Ifta', on a page established by someone in the Maldives.[13]

A further location for information and advice on the Hajj, which goes beyond the traditional manuals, can be found in a variety of online forums and other sites. Particularly significant in this regard are online services providing religious opinions. These might be described as "fatwa" services, in which questions can be submitted to a religious "authority" who will answer the question online. This reflects a much wider phenomenon associated with online authority, and pilgrimage has proven to be a popular subject for discussion. Whether the providers of the information

[11] "Arts of the Islamic World: Muhyi Al-Din Lari (d.1526–7 AD), Futuh Al-Haramayn in Verse, Copied by the Scribe 'Ali, Probably Herat, Persia, Safavid, Dated 990 AH/1582 AD." At sothebys.com/en/auctions/ecatalogue/2011/arts-of-the-islamic-world/lot.96.html (last accessed April 11, 2014).

[12] Ministry of Religious Affairs and Inter Faith Harmony, Government of Pakistan: mora.gov.pk (last accessed April 11, 2014); Majlis Ugama Islam Singapura: muis.gov.sg/cms/services/haj.aspx?id=16325 (last accessed April 11, 2014).

[13] Aloloom English: "Thread: Index of important Fatwas on Hajj by Fatwa Committee," at aloloomenglish.net/vb/showthread.php?549-Index-of-important-Fatwas-on-Hajj-by-Fatwa-Committee (last accessed April 11, 2014).

are real authorities is open to question. There is a potential trend for surfers to go shopping for religious opinions in order to find information that best suits their circumstances. The range of these sites goes from those that might be classified as mainstream "orthodox Sunni," to Shiʿi and Sufi perspectives. There are also many voices on the margins of the Islamic spectrum, represented on such websites. The impact of all this might be measured by a simple Internet search, especially given that those items which appear in the top ranked section of search engines such as Google and Bing are more likely to be read than those lower down the hierarchy of results. The type of information provided goes well beyond generic advice contained in manuals, with very specific questions on particular circumstances and issues, including those from particular religious and cultural perspectives.

Guidance on the Hajj online transcends the conventional print media. Consider Google Earth, where one can "visit" Mecca (and Medina), flying into the precincts and surveying them from various angles. Hundreds of photographs offer perspectives contributed by pilgrims, uploaded for the perusal of others – including non-Muslims unable to visit Mecca. The multi-layered map on Google Earth and Google Maps also provides more practical information, relating to hotels, shops, and services in the city. Reviews of hotels (positive and negative) by pilgrims and advice for travelers can also be located. As with other areas of travel, reviews provide practical information. One should note that commercial generic sites such as Hotels.com and TripAdvisor.com offer pages of data on hotels in Mecca, including reviews from travelers – accompanied by photos.[14] It is worth considering the impact in terms of guides for pilgrims of generic information, provided by companies and organizations that do not present an explicit Muslim identity.

While there have been attempts to set up Islamic search engines, there is no doubt that the first stop for potential hajjis to get information online is likely to be a major search engine, such as Google. A basic Google search for the term *hajj fatwa* undertaken during the preparation of this chapter illustrates the diversity of content and advice available. Naturally, this advice will change depending on which search engine is used (including which version of Google), the location of the search, algorithm variables, and the time and date of the search. The top-level pages reflected advice from a variety of doctrinal perspectives, Sunni as well as Shiʿite and Sufi. Embedded within the pages were Google ads for Hajj products, such as

[14] See, e.g., tripadvisor.co.uk/HACSearch?geo=293993 (last accessed April 11, 2014).

travel agency information on flights and accommodation in Mecca. One top response came from the Fatwa-Online site, focusing on the question of permissibility of a woman traveling alone on the Hajj: the response emphasized the need for a mahram, or male companion. It cites an opinion from Shaykh Ibn Fowzaan, referring to a hadith about travel on the Hajj.[15] The commercial website Go-Makkah incorporates a listing of religious opinions on the Hajj within its pages, alongside links to travel products and advice.[16]

IslamWeb – hosted in Doha, Qatar, and offering content in Arabic, German, Spanish and French[17] – fields questions of concern to its readers, which often go beyond what is available in manuals and basic advice: "Is the man allowed to make love with his wife during Umrah or Hajj?"; "I want to go to hajj but I took some money from someone without his knowledge and I can't give it back to him. What shall I do to keep Haram money from me?"[18] There is extensive discussion on how to perform the different forms of Hajj, *ḥajj al-tamattuʿ* (combining ʿUmra and Hajj with separate ihram), *ḥajj al-ifrād* (Hajj without the animal sacrifice), and *ḥajj al-qirān* (ʿUmra and Hajj with the same ihram). IslamWeb also offers advice for children on the Hajj: this is in the form of an animated interactive manual, with links to a variety of basic advice associated with the Hajj formatted in the shape of a journal links. Information is provided for all ages and levels of knowledge and is designed accordingly: the cartoons have a degree of interactivity, and are not intense in the level of detail. By clicking on individual images, for example "No Dispute during Hajj," a cartoon image of two people facing up to fight appears; one page instructs readers to "make sure you wear a face mask during hajj" (for medical reasons).[19] This type of health advice is also found on government

[15] Fatwa-Online: "Sending a Maid for Hajj with a Group of Women or a Hajj Package Group [Shaykh Ibn Fowzaan, al-Muntaqaa min Fataawa Ibn Fowzaan – Volume 3, Page 168, Fatwa No.252]," at fatwa-online.com/fataawa/worship/hajjandumrah/haj002/000 0219_1.htm (last accessed April 11, 2014).

[16] Go Makkah: "The Hajj School: Fatwas of Hajj on Behalf of Others," at go-makkah.com /english/dossier/articles/357/Fatwas+of+Hajj+on+behalf+of+others.html (last accessed April 11, 2014).

[17] DailyWhoIs: "Domain Name: islamweb.net" at dailywhois.com/domain/islamweb.net (last accessed April 11, 2014).

[18] IslamWeb: "Hajj and Umrah: Hajj 1433 > Fataawa > General Fataawa," at islamweb.net /ehajj/index.php?page=maincategory&lang=E&vPart=1030&order=&startno=255 (last accessed April 11, 2014).

[19] IslamWeb. "Hajj for Kids" at kids.islamweb.net/english/flash.php?url=flash/hajj.swf (last accessed April 11, 2014).

sites[20] This, and the many venues that offer similar information, demonstrates that the audience is a nuanced one.

Searching for data on pilgrimage highlights the diversity of Islamic expression online too: prominent in the search was material from the Universiti Sains Islam Malaysia that reproduced a fatwa from IslamWeb as part of its Fatwa Management System.[21] Here we see the mix of governmental and other platforms competing to provide authoritative information. This was adjacent to a page of over 100 opinions presented by FatwaIslam.com, including a number from the former Grand Mufti of Saudi Arabia Shaykh ʿAbd al-ʿAziz bin Baz (1910–1999) and senior Saudi religious authority Shaykh Muḥammad bin Saalih al-ʿUthaymeen (1925–2001); the Internet is one way in which the opinions of scholars from the past can be preserved and presented, even after their death.[22]

Internet resources also enable exploration of diverse opinions on the pilgrimage: SunniForum discusses (and condemns) the opinions of Barelwi scholars on specific aspects of ritual practice. It focuses on a fatwa regarding the postponement of pilgrimage, by Moulana Mustafa Raza Khan Barelwi, which states: "The filthy Ibn-e-Saud and his associates considers all Muslims kaffir/apostate and mushrik and holds the view that their belongings are lawful (to be seized). Due to their this [sic] belief the obligation of hajj stands necessarily void and nil." Then follows a discussion on the forum of the "deviant" nature of this opinion, and those who endorse it.[23] Further discussions on this issue, from a variety of perspectives, can be found online, highlighting the controversies surrounding diverse interpretations of aspects of Islam (including pilgrimage). Barelwi Ahle Sunnat wal Jamaʿat interpretations have been at odds with other approaches to interpretation issues, and enjoy considerable support on the Indian subcontinent and in diaspora communities. While this debate is beyond the scope of this chapter, it is important to highlight

20 Kingdom of Saudi Arabia – Hajj and Umrah e-portal: "Health Tips to Be Followed During Hajj" at moh.gov.sa/en/Hajj/HealthGuidelines/Pages/DuringHajj.aspx (last accessed April 11, 2014).

21 Universiti Sains Islam Malaysia: "Fatwa Management System – Fatawa: How many times did our Prophet Muhammad (PBUH) perform Hajj and Umrah?" at infad.usim.edu.my/modules.php?op=modload&name=News&file=article&sid=8183 (last accessed April 11, 2014).

22 FatwaIslam.com: "Pilgrimage" at: fatwaislam.com/fis/index.cfm?scn=sc&sc=11&c=2 (last accessed April 11, 2014).

23 SunniForum: "Thread: Barelvi fatwa: first no prayer and now No Hajj behind Salafis?": sunniforum.com/forum/showthread.php?55916-Barelvi-fatwa-first-no-prayer-and-now-No-Hajj-behind-Salafis (last accessed April 11, 2014).

the fact that these issues emerge on the Internet, and discussed in considerable detail – often in language that condemns other parties as "unbelievers" and "deviants." The influence of Sufism on Barelwi Muslims is a significant factor here. It also raises the issue of alternatives to the Hajj that have been developed, for logistical reasons as well as spiritual ones, such as pilgrimages to other locations.

Conflicting perspectives on interpretation play out online in connection with a variety of subject matter. This incorporates conjecture and prejudice. Shiʿa Muslims also participate in the pilgrimage, and may engage in ritual practice that goes beyond the "orthodox" interpretation often presented as mainstream. Advice on these aspects can be found online in a variety of areas: the advice of Ayatollah al-Sistani on ritual and spiritual elements associated with pilgrimage is widely available online, as one prominent example of a Shiʿite perspective.[24] This advice might integrate sources that go beyond traditional hadith, for example, to include the sayings of ʿAli and the various other Shiʿite imams. Within the diversity of Shiʿism's branches and sub-branches, advice on the pilgrimage also reflects specific religious leaders and practices. Photos are also posted on pages relating to Shiʿite participation in the Hajj: for example, the Dawoodi Bohoras have an extensive collection of digital photos of pilgrimage to Mecca.[25]

From a brief survey of this initial search, based on inputting the term *hajj fatwa* into Google, it is clear that a substantial range of opinions and materials are available. Of course, greater openness is available as much to non-Muslims as to others, and can inform the way in which pilgrimage is perceived. The range of sources goes from individual websites and blogs to official governmental channels, and they are not necessarily in harmony with one another. The idea of the guide as a fixed text is perhaps redundant in the age of the Internet. Hyperlinks, animation, video, interactive features, and the opportunity to receive responses from religious authorities via question-and-answer websites are just some of the ways in which approaches to information about the pilgrimage have changed. This transition in approach, however, is not just about accessing material via a deskbound computer using a conventional Internet browser. The types of interface that are utilized for accessing information on the Internet have

[24] ziaraat.org: "Hajj Rituals by Ayatullah Ali al-Husayni al-Seestani" at: ziaraat.com/books/hajj_sistani.pdf (last accessed April 11, 2014).

[25] Mumineen.org. "Mumineen.org Photo Akhbar" at media.mumineen.org/gallery/thumbnails.php?album=12 (last accessed April 11, 2014).

changed from the formative period of website development to encompass a range of devices and software. Not only is the information marketplace becoming more crowded, with pilgrimage information providers jostling for position on search engine rankings, but the ways in which that information is conveyed are not static. Content designers have to respond and anticipate changes in access modes: the development of Web 2.0+ interfaces reflecting social media were embraced by some developers as a way of providing more accessible content. There may be a propagation motive behind this, as well as a commercial one. The digital divide has diminished, making content available on mobile phones, tablets, and cheaper computers; high-speed Internet connections have become more widely available, at least in some contexts, and using the Internet has become a natural part of day-to-day information acquisition in a variety of languages. Visual guides are a natural adjunct to more traditional guide content.[26] There may also be guides based on the special requirements of pilgrims, such as for deaf people.[27]

With this in mind, a number of different computer products have emerged in relation to the pilgrimage. These have included dedicated devices, with Qur'an recitation and prayer information. Cell phones and tablets have been a significant area for research and development of pilgrimage software and applications. Many of the products discussed are available across platforms, to include Apple iPhone and iPads, Android devices, and Windows phones. The features are similar across platforms. Their developments in relation to the pilgrimage reflects increased access levels to smartphones and related devices, together with growing 3G and 4G network access.

HAJJ AND TELECOMMUNICATIONS

Telecommunications companies have sought to promote the religious features of their devices, for example during Ramadan and the Hajj, including special packages with software features and text deals. The use of cell phones during festivals increases substantially, including during the Hajj. Pilgrims seek to celebrate their successful completion of ritual

[26] Hajj and Umra Guide at youtube.com/watch?v=CEgET1MzZ7M (last accessed April 11, 2014); Young Muslims TV: "A Visual Guide to hajj Part 1 of 3" at youngmuslims.tv /Channel5/Category42/Video709/ (last accessed 11 April, 2014).

[27] alisharahuk: "Deaf Umrah 2011 – A journey through the eyes of Deaf pilgrims" at: youtube.com/watch?v=4JGRYg6B-_g (last accessed 11 April, 2014).

practices, by sending photographs, film clips, and texts from their cell phone. Pilgrims have used cell phones while performing *ṭawāf*, in order to share their experience with relatives back home. This is in in addition to the general increase in phone use during Eid al-Adha, by pilgrims and non-pilgrims alike. 3G+ cell phones with video cameras allow for photos and clips to be posted online directly from Mecca, apparently avoiding restrictions on photography evident for the Hajj in the past. Authorities are not necessarily sympathetic to this practice.

This raises some interesting questions relating to the use of cell phones in the precincts of Mecca. The Ministry of Hajj in Saudi Arabia states that cell phones can be used to allow group members to keep in contact with one another, and recommends that special SIM cards designed for use during the Hajj are purchased: these can be put into any phone that is not locked into a network.[28] Sawa marketed a SIM card suitable for use during the Hajj and ʿUmra. One blogger suggested purchasing a phone that did not demand too much battery power, given the problems of charging on-site for battery-hungry smartphones.[29] The Communications and Information Technology Commission in Saudi Arabia surveyed the quality of phone signals during the Hajj period, noting that the average sound quality was deemed "excellent" for 55 percent all users (approximately).[30]

This has also been a question on online forums. In response to an enquiry on the SunniForum relating to whether it is permissible to use phones during pilgrimage, the answer was: "I think it is rather a necessity, there are so many people you will not be able to communicate and regroup with others without mobile, so almost everyone who can afford it will buy mobile phones; however, make sure it is on vibrate or soundless mode when you are doing salat [prayer], very important not to disturb others' salat."[31] This is a good example of ijtihad or contextual interpretation of religious principles in the light of contemporary conditions. In a more granulated discussion on Qibla.com, the view expresses is that although it

[28] Ministry of Hajj: "Can I Use My Mobile Phone/Cell Phone in Saudi Arabia?" at hajinformation.com/main/t60.htm (last accessed April 11, 2014).

[29] Masʿud Ahmed Khan, October 24, 2008: "Hajj Tips" at masudblog.com/?p=357 (last accessed April 11, 2014).

[30] Communications and Information Technology Commission, March 14, 2011: "Quality of Mobile Phone Services during the Hajj and Umrah Seasons Is within Target Limits," *CITC E-Newsletter 006* (last accessed April 11, 2014).

[31] SunniForum, March 17, 2011: "Re: Must-takes to Umrah and Hajj": sunniforum.com/forum/showthread.php?69942-Must-takes-to-Umrah-and-Hajj (last accessed April 11, 2014).

is inappropriate to use mobile phones within mosques (even during pilgrimages) using a phone on vibrate is permissible, in particular when a woman wishes to contact her guardian or vice versa. Any phone use has to be outside of the precincts of the mosque.[32]

In 2011, a Facebook campaign sought to deal with the problem of phone use in the holy places, by issuing the following statement:[33]

> By the grace of Almighty Allah you shall soon be travelling to the kingdom of Saudi Arabia for performing Hajj. Surely you shall take care of the sacredness of Harmain (Makkah Al Mukarama and Madina Al Munawara). In this regard we request you to remove Musical Ring Tones from your mobile phones before departure and during Hajj try to keep your mobile phones on Vibrators [sic]. By this you shall be avoiding any disturbance to your worship as well as to the worships of other pilgrims and furthermore the sacredness of Harmain shall not be harmed. We hope that you shall put heed to this request and shall convey this message to other pilgrims as well.

The consensus would seem to indicate a pragmatic acceptance of the presence of digital technology in the sacred precincts, reflecting an inevitably consequence of a pilgrimage process that also integrates online activity into (potentially) every aspect of a pilgrimage's organization. The commercial angle of the Hajj is well represented, with the services of pilgrimage guides, travel companies and logistical assistance providers all made accessible online. As with any other aspect of travel, the Hajj can be facilitated online; pilgrimage has a commercial edge, with varying levels of service, depending on the pilgrim's pocket. The package also incorporates the gifts and incentives for pilgrims, such as guides – which can be in digital format – as well as more traditional items. These too can be sourced online, including branded hats, umbrellas, and bags.[34]

HAJJ-PPLICATIONS

Contemporary guides have different emphases, depending on the religious orientations and interests of their authors; the marketplace is crowded, with official government resources contending with other guides, and

[32] Qibla.com: Shaykh Muhammad ibn Adam al-Kawthari: "Question ID:3176: Mobile/Cell Phones during Hajj in Mosques (2008)" at spa.qibla.com/issue_view.asp?HD=1&ID=3176&CATE=7 (last accessed April 11, 2014).

[33] Global Awareness Campaign for Hujjaj-e-Ikram: "Use of Mobile Phone (Cellular) in Harmain Shareefain for Protect the Sanctity of Harmain Shareefain" at facebook.com/muslimculturemagazine (last accessed April 11, 2014).

[34] Hajj Mabrur: hajjmabrur.net (last accessed April 11, 2014).

available in numerous languages and within diverse formats. Print versions of guides retain their value and have a market, to be sure. However, online sites, which can include versions of printed materials, no longer simply reproduce a printed work, but now design a guide specifically for use online. This is important in a number of ways: materials on the Internet tends to read very differently from the way in which a conventional printed work is read, with high levels of searchability and interactivity. There needs to be an element of navigability, together with dynamic design that suits the format of diverse electronic media. There may be an integration of printed material with multimedia, such as audiovisual content. The integration of GPS and other elements is also significant. There may be an expectation from readers that the guide is going to be user-friendly and easy to read, without any difficulties of setting up or downloading. There is also the commercial element: producing a religious guide has spiritual merits, but a number of companies have also seen this as a potentially lucrative enterprise, sometimes in conjunction with other products, such as Ramadan mobile phone offers (mentioned earlier). Apps have been designed for all major platforms; the market for iPhone apps includes several Hajj products, and a number of resources for Android, Windows, and BlackBerry phones are available. At the time of writing, Android has proven to be a more popular phone platform, offering cheaper options in general terms than iPhone and BlackBerry. Hajj apps available across platforms include various guides, wallpaper, and videos.[35]

The commercial element can be compared with some of the other products that are available, offering advice from diverse perspectives. This includes governmental agencies and organizations, which may not see it necessary to make their content dynamic or interactive, especially when they present themselves as "official" authorities and agencies of the pilgrimage. The technical data necessary for pilgrimage can be found on the official Saudi Arabian Ministry of Hajj website, a somewhat dry and technical resource, providing necessary visa, medical, and religious information. More colorful and user-friendly information can be obtained through other channels, for example on YouTube. These can present from diverse religious perspectives and offer practical information: the HajjGuide includes information on what to pack, and medical issues – as well as spiritual guidance – via YouTube videos on "Physical Aspects of

[35] Hajj Guide App at appbrain.com/app/Hajj-guide/com.v1_4.Hajjguide.com (last accessed April 11, 2014).

Hajj" by Shahin and "Medical Aspects of Hajj" by Dr. Mithani. This includes material influenced by Grand Ayatollah Sayyid ʿAli Ḥusayni al-Sistani, with its specific Shiʿite emphasis in lectures, advice, and religious language.[36]

Some sites endeavor to provide a "one-stop shop" for pilgrimage: technical information on the Kaʿba, the focus of prayer within the sacred precincts of Mecca, is contained on the Islamic Gateway.[37] Highly detailed plans relating to key areas in Mecca can be found on the site, alongside a "Glossary of Hajj Related Terms." Key concepts and places are linked to various sound and image files give further advice to assist the prospective hajji and the armchair pilgrim. The pilgrim's animal sacrifice can also be facilitated online, through the use of a credit card, while satisfying (to some) the requirements of the ritual.[38] Immersion in the Hajj experience also becomes a luxury lifestyle: IslamiCity offered deluxe and special packages for American pilgrims, complete with online booking.[39] This information was presented alongside photographs, step-by-step guides, and related commercial products such as software and videos.

Applications offer users (in many cases) a more refined and integrated online experience, with a package designed specifically for their phone's or tablet's operating system. This has proven to be an expanding area for Islamic online developments, with companies developing more granulated products on a range of themes – including for the Hajj. They are able to take advantage of elements such as global positioning satellites, multimedia streaming, and links to social media applications. Hajj apps may have a role in teaching a person how to perform their pilgrimage, through step-by-step instruction.

A prominent example of a high-tech app specifically designed for pilgrimage is Dastageeri's AMIR, a Hajj app for iPhones, incorporating location tracking and advice for each stage of the pilgrimage, and separately tailored for men and women.[40] This is facilitated through the use of GPS, which guides the pilgrim through each stage of the Hajj. The app includes an emergency button to request on-site assistance. A variety of other applications are sold via iTunes, offering different approaches and

[36] Islamic Gateway (2001): "Hajj and Eid al-Adha" retrieved August 15, 2001, from ummah.net/hajj.

[37] "Physical Aspects of Hajj – by Shahin" at tinyurl.com/ol9s3rw (last accessed April 11, 2014).

[38] qurbani.com (last accessed April 11, 2014).

[39] islamicity.com/travel/hajj/ (last accessed April 11, 2014).

[40] dastageeri.de/Dastageeri/Apps.html (last accessed April 11, 2014).

FIGURE 16 AMIR Hajj app

perspectives on the Hajj. These include apps designed for the iPad, which offers a better visual experience, but is perhaps less realistic to carry or place within the pilgrim's ihram.[41] There can be a pay wall restricting access to aspects of the apps, which may also be available in several languages; Hajj Player has been developed with material in Turkish, Arabic, English, and Urdu – taking pilgrims through all the required stages of prayer.[42]

Several apps offer basic information across different platforms, such as Hajj – Pilgrimage to Mecca by Magnicode, Inc., available on BlackBerry, Android, and iTunes (for iPad, iPhone, iPod); one user seemed to think this app focused on ʿUmra rather than the Hajj.[43] Easy Hajj n Umrah by Techlabs focuses on keeping groups of pilgrims together: "This

[41] Hajj & Umrah for iPad by AMC Apps at itunes.apple.com/us/app/Hajj-umrah/id471282657?mt=8 (last accessed April 11, 2014).

[42] Hajj Guide by ImranQureshi.com at itunes.apple.com/us/app/Hajj-guide/id473635756?mt=8 (last accessed April 11, 2014).

[43] Hajj – Pilgrimage to Mecca by Magnicode at itunes.apple.com/gb/app/hajj-pilgrimage-to-mecca/id336371771?mt=8 (last accessed April 11, 2014).

application keeps you and your group members connected through messages, current locations on map, schedule event in the Calendar and by maintaining common tasks and shopping list." The app facilitates group cohesion, which would make the pilgrimage go smoother (and potentially quicker): "It's common to get lost in the masses; with Easy Hajj n Umrah you can locate your fellow hajjis (group members) on map, send messages and call to each individual." One theory behind this would be that the app would allow more religious activity, and less in the way of logistics.[44]

BLOGGING PILGRIMS

There has been a long-standing tradition of written and circulated descriptions of the pilgrimage. Now, with the Internet, online records and accounts of the Hajj have emerged. These are interesting, especially when they are updated as the pilgrim passes through the various stages of the Hajj.[45] Such real-time accounts have been utilized by various media organizations as well, in order to present information to their readers and viewers. CNN presented a video/blog in 2005 by journalist Zain Verjee, as part of annual Hajj coverage. In 2007, CNN reporter Mohammed Jamjoom was blogging "almost live" via mobile phone from the Hajj. In 2009, Jawahrah provided a stage-by-stage account of the Hajj – which included a number of audio recordings from the Hajj, and a visit to Medina.[46] There are also accounts of the ʿUmra that have been blogged and tweeted, which can have a highly personal dimension, to include photos and acknowledgments of assistance.[47]

Accounts and representations of the Hajj have appeared on social media. On the photo-sharing site Flickr, numerous pages can be found of photos uploaded by hajjis from diverse locations and religious perspectives. Pages are also uploaded on other services, such as Facebook and Twitter.[48] Twitter features a wealth of data on the Hajj, via the #hajj hashtag. This includes photos of past pilgrimages and contemporary

[44] Easy Hajj n Umrah by Techlabs at youtube.com/watch?v=tNn99Uzyono (last accessed April 11, 2014).

[45] islamfrominside.com/Pages/Articles/AroundtheKabba.html (last accessed April 11, 2014).

[46] See, e.g., "Hajj 1425 – by Jawahrah" at hajjstories.wordpress.com/2009/06/08/hajj-1425/#more-36 (last accessed April 11, 2014).

[47] See, e.g., Mohammed Amous, "@HajjUmrahDays" at twitter.com/HajUmrahDays (last accessed April 11, 2014).

[48] See, e.g., "My Hajj" at facebook.com/pages/My-Hajj/531243706917421 (last accessed April 11, 2014).

logistical information. In 2013, it was being used to discuss possible limitations of pilgrim numbers and visas by Saudi authorities, due to construction; this information was among other data, including booking information, funding advice, and links to electronic guides.[49]

Media coverage has a role in how the Hajj is represented online. Coverage is intense on many broadcast channels, relaying live feed also available online. Awsat al-Islam links to multimedia resources on the Hajj, some drawn from external resources such as the broadcasters PBS, CNN, and ABC News.[50] Channel Four's coverage of the pilgrimage, produced by Lion Television and entitled "The Hajj: The Greatest Trip on Earth," included a "Virtual Hajj." They described this as "the closest thing to being there."[51] The site includes the prayers for every aspect of the Hajj, with recitations in English and Arabic. Scholarly opinion provided guidance on ritualistic practice. An archive of film coverage and day-by-day reports presents the perspectives of five pilgrims from different social and cultural backgrounds. These dynamic eyewitness accounts of key elements in the Hajj "experience" are presented in documentary format, with videos and interview transcripts.

CONCLUSION

It is natural for Mecca to be represented in many ways online, given that potential visitors from all over the world may "access" the precincts. This includes people who are not Muslim: had he been alive today, Richard Burton's (1821–1890) famous journey in disguise to Mecca would not have been necessary – he could have used an online avatar to immerse himself in elements of the Hajj. It may not reflect the spirituality of the analogue version, but it certainly offers unprecedented opportunities to explore Muslim pilgrimage to Mecca without the hardships, difficulties, and expense of travel.

The Internet offers a window into Mecca for those unable to travel there. There is also the potential for augmented reality, with the Hajj experience supplemented by digital tools. Personal technology and social networking offers glimpses into Hajj experiences, and will become more interactive as technology further develops. The first pilgrimage with

[49] "#hajj" at twitter.com (last accessed April 11, 2014); and Chinx786 n.d. at flickr.com /people/chinx786n.d.

[50] aswatalislam.net (last accessed April 11, 2014).

[51] channel4.com/life/microsites/H/hajj/genb_pilgrims.html (last accessed April 11, 2014).

Google Glass is awaited with interest. Through immersion in images, videos, and accounts of pilgrimage – along with detailed maps – it is possible for perceptions of the pilgrimage to change, not just for pilgrims and those aspiring to visit Mecca. Hajj guides have moved on from their traditional roots, to provide granulated, multimedia information. Participation may be more "organized" if logistic elements are engineered online: ritual may be facilitated more "appropriately" with app prompting; the recording of a pilgrimage may enable a hajji (and other viewers) to "relive" their experience. Sharing this information may become part of the process of "experience transfer." Alongside more conventional Mecca souvenirs, film clips and live feeds of activities facilitate at least part of the experience for those unable to go personally. There is no need for those staying at home to not feel part of the Hajj.

13

The Pilgrim's Complaint

Recent Accounts of the Hajj

Michael Wolfe

JALAL AL-E AHMAD'S LOST IN THE CROWD

Accounts by pilgrims traveling to Mecca date back a thousand years.[1] Although sharp criticism of the hard journey to Mecca is common, critical Muslim exposés of the actual Hajj rites and of their administration are rare and relatively recent.

In 1966, Jalal Al-e Ahmad published his diaristic account, *Lost in the Crowd*.[2] In this short work, Al-e Ahmad, one of Iran's most valued social analysts, consistently championing reason against blind orthodoxy, takes to task the sweeping, sometimes thoughtless changes of the early Saudi Hajj managers, and chastises Iranian intellectuals for slighting the importance of religion. He is, in other words, an equal opportunity critic and gadfly. Irreligious most of his life, a Marxist, then an existentialist, Al-e Ahmad's Islamic credentials nonetheless run deep. His family was closely related to a prominent ayatollah.[3] His father, an important Teheran cleric, later ran afoul of the Shah's bureaucracy. His elder brother, two brothers-in-law, and a nephew all were clerics.

1 See M. Wolfe, *One Thousand Roads to Mecca: Ten Centuries of Travelers Writing about the Muslim Pilgrimage*, rev. expanded ed. (New York: Grove Press, 2015); and the bibliographical listing in "Hajj Travel Narratives," in V. Porter and M. A. S. Abdel Haleem et al., *Hajj: Journey to the Heart of Islam* (Cambridge, MA: Harvard University Press, 2012), 282–283.

2 J. Al-e Ahmad, *Khasī dar mīqāt* (Teheran: Nil, 1345/1966). English translation: *Lost in the Crowd*, tr. John Green with Ahmad Alizadeh and Farzin Yazdanfar (Washington, DC: Three Continents Press, 1985).

3 Hajj Sayyed Mahmud Taleqani (1910–1979).

Al-e Ahmad's skepticism concerning organized religion may be traced to a series of early traumatic experiences. The most striking occurred as a schoolboy, when a traditionally minded sister died at home of breast cancer after refusing "to submit to a medical examination and treatment by a male physician, on the grounds that it would constitute a religious impropriety." One day, the young Jalal was sent to the bazaar to bring back a bucket of lead filings. He brought them home without guessing their purpose, after which a local female expert in folk remedies placed them red-hot on Jalal's sister's breasts. She died.[4]

Part of Al-e Ahmad's strength as an author is his use of such personal material, including conflicts with superstition and paternal authority. As we see in his Hajj account, Ale-Ahmad's pilgrimage was a family affair, intensely personal. He went to Mecca, he writes, to accompany several close relatives, his sister, two brothers-in-law, and an uncle.

Many of Al-e Ahmad's entries concern these relatives. He clearly saw himself as their protector, having in fact arranged the trip for them. He writes that he also went to Arabia to learn more about the mysterious death there, thirteen years before, of his older brother, a Shiʿite cleric "who had come here to the seat of Wahhabi power to keep the remnants of Shiism alive."[5]

Al-e Ahmad kept his travel journal daily, obsessively. Near the end, he reveals its intended audience: his own circle of secular intellectuals in Teheran, who by habit undervalue the importance of religion for a majority of Iranians. Concurrent with his probing observations of family and religion, we also encounter Al-e Ahmad's bruised sensibilities as an urbane, sophisticated pilgrim recoiling at the heavy-handed architecture and administrative style of the Hajj's self-styled Saudi "custodians."

In Medina, he finds the Prophet's sanctuary an architectural mishmash, "half Andalusian, half Ottoman, with a veneer of cement slabs in three or four colors":

> I always wanted to know who the architect was so I could collar him and say, "Sir! The supernatural magnificence of a building like this must be expressed with the simplest natural materials ... You, who were responsible for construction of such grandeur in Medina, did it not occur to you to seek assistance from engineers and architects from all Muslim countries?"[6]

[4] Al-e Ahmad, *Lost in the Crowd*, xxi.
[5] Al-e Ahmad, *Lost in the Crowd*, 115.
[6] Al-e Ahmad, *Lost in the Crowd*, 40.

In Mecca, he looks with disdain from the upper levels of King Saud's newly expanded Grand Mosque:[7]

The Kaaba is still the same size, but they've made the outer corridor twice as wide, and twice as high. How about destroying the Kaaba itself and making it higher and larger? Out of reinforced concrete, no doubt?

This clash of concrete modernity with a wish for something finer is mixed, in Ale-Ahmad, with a Marxist critique of petro-capitalism:[8]

In any case, something can certainly be done so that the hajji will not be such a prisoner to so many monopolies, each of which milks him in some way, controls him, and destroys his freedom.

The "something that can be a done" is a loosening of the Saudi grip on the Sacred Territories and the two holy mosques:[9]

There's no alternative but to internationalize these shrines, Mecca, Medina, Arafat and Mina, to place them under the management of a joint council of Muslim nations, and to remove them from Saudi Arab control. The revenues must come from income generated by the hajj. Instead of Saudi Arabian police there must be guides from every nation. Legitimacy must be granted to the special customs of each sect.

In a telling exchange with a pilgrim who questions why he would pray among members of a different sect, Al-e Ahmad replies with a thought that paraphrases the English title of his book: "My dear sir ... we came here to lose ourselves in the crowd. We didn't come here to reinforce our personalities and our isolation."[10] Yet by his own admission, the author hasn't prayed publicly in twenty years. Even as he performs the rites at Mecca, his inherent distaste for the literalism of much religious practice remains close to the surface. Nor does he willingly lose himself in real crowds.

If the Hajj does not transform Al-e Ahmad, it certainly clarifies his thinking, leading to "a kind of awaking," that inoculates him against ideology in general. "I mainly came on this trip looking for my brother – and all those other brothers – rather than to search for God," he writes. "In this way, I am smashing the steps of the world of certainty one by one with the pressure of experience, beneath my feet."[11] Though his pilgrimage is an act of iconoclasm, the summary emblem of this

[7] Al-e Ahmad, *Lost in the Crowd*, 58–59.
[8] Al-e Ahmad, *Lost in the Crowd*, 34.
[9] Al-e Ahmad, *Lost in the Crowd*, 30–31.
[10] Al-e Ahmad, *Lost in the Crowd*, 56.
[11] Al-e Ahmad, *Lost in the Crowd*, 123.

FIGURE 17 Pilgrims leaving ʿArafat, 2012

"smashing" is a tender image. His last visit to the Grand Mosque concludes with an arresting portrait of a woman who simultaneously evokes the maternal Hajar and flies in the face of conventional male superiority:[12]

The women must go behind the men at the time of prayer. In the row where I sat, however, ... a woman dressed in black, her child behind her, took long strides between the men in the direction of the [Kaaba] so she could greet it to her full satisfaction. The [Mosque] was full, with no room to insert a pin, row after row, but the woman seemed to be working through stone obstacles in a desert. She had neither fear of the House nor respect for the praying ranks of men. I realized that she is the master of her own house ... Why had she come here, really, to so fearlessly move her womanly presence next to the Stone? I realized that it is worthwhile that the Kaaba has served for centuries and centuries as a refuge for every weary person, for this forsaken humanity, confounded by poverty, oppression, and anomie, like a wailing wall, if it answers even one of this woman's prayers.

ABDELLAH HAMMOUDI'S SEASON IN MECCA

A professor of anthropology at Princeton University, Abdellah Hammoudi is the author of several works about his native Morocco. Born in the small town of El Kelaa des Sraghna north of Marrakesh in 1945, educated at the

[12] Al-e Ahmad, *Lost in the Crowd*, 115.

Sorbonne, Hammoudi wrote *Une Saison à la Mecque* in French. It was first published in 2005. It is both a physical account of his 1999 springtime Hajj and an emotional and theory-laden meditation. The book appeared in English translation as *A Season in Mecca* in 2006.[13]

The first quarter of the book tracks Hammoudi's encounters as a Moroccan national with the official requirements of the Hajj. These include the many stages by which an applicant then secured a place in the nation's 29,000-person annual quota. This enforced pas de deux with a late twentieth-century state bureaucracy can be disturbing. At one point, Hammoudi describes himself "going around in circles like a mule at an oil press."[14] Since visas are limited in number, there is corruption. Hammoudi flies twice from New Jersey to Morocco to turn and grease the wheels. His official file of dozens of photos, copied forms, ID cards, medical stamps, and signed validations takes on such importance that he sometimes has to remind us that the object of this bureaucratic struggle isn't a telephone line or a water meter contract, but a visa to perform the pilgrimage.

Hammoudi sets out on the pilgrim trail in early March, riding in a crowded bus from the Jeddah airport to Medina, the city "that gave the Prophet asylum, the one of his biographies, of his battles and his victories, the one where a multi-confessional constitution was invented – I had always lived in it; or perhaps it had always lived in me."[15] After arriving in this transcendently evocative first capital of Islam, he and his fellow Moroccan hajjis deposit their bags at a rented apartment and rush to the Prophet's mosque:[16]

> As I moved in immediate proximity to the tomb of the Prophet, walking in some way in his footsteps, as close as possible to his resolve, where it had melded with that of his creator, my own resolve transcended the reasons I had given myself over the years. This flash of intuition projected all around me the light and contrasts of an open clearing. I felt a joy like no joy I had felt before.

The exaltation cannot last. The moment he steps out of the mosque, Hammoudi is dragged back into an all-too-real city located in a repressive nation-state thoroughly conditioned by religious literalism, a version of Islam he typifies as a virulent "denial to Muslims of any right to live their

[13] A. Hammoudi, *A Season in Mecca: Narrative of a Pilgrimage*, tr. Pascale Ghazaleh (New York: Farrar, Straus and Giroux, 2006).
[14] Hammoudi, *A Season in Mecca*, 35.
[15] Hammoudi, *A Season in Mecca*, 70.
[16] Hammoudi, *A Season in Mecca*, 78–79.

faith differently,"[17] and as "this religion of the state, devoid of compassion and merciless to God's creatures."[18] He is speaking of Wahhabist Islam but also addressing the leveling forces of any totalitarian state. A little later he walks in the Medina markets, hoping to pass beyond their modernity and eventually reach the "old town," any piece of the original city that might link him to the Medina of his own religious imagination. Although no such place still exists, Hammoudi conjures a regenerative vision in the teeth of pervasive reality, a vision he hopes will strike down the current replacement with bolts of lightning:[19]

I searched in vain for remainders of bygones eras, something that could stand in for origins and pathways. Wahhabi Medina was doing all it could to chase away my Medina and all those Medinas that had been. But these didn't wholly disappear. They hid in a place whence their celestial irony will no doubt come and strike the new Medina with lightning ... Medina, my mythological home. It lived on in all of Islam's cities. It will find its way around the city that forbade me even from seeing the Prophet's tomb, that kept me from everything I wanted to see, touch, smell, everything that might have taken the prayer and chanting of the Qur'an and connected them physically to the miracle of a tradition's birth.

Despite all the displacement, loss, and personal conflict, Hammoudi proves occasionally capable of real religious inspiration. One day in the mosque,

I was rereading a few passages (of the Qur'an) I had selected and occasionally entire chapters, rediscovering the beauty of the text, its haunting images and sophisticated, supremely asymmetrical rhythms. I began to leave this world, walking into these stories toward horizons which pleased me with the intact freshness of all beginnings.[20]

On another day, he hears a saving grace in the multitude of praying voices:[21]

In this vast, somewhat Hollywoodesque palace, the Muslim voices rising in the air saved the place from vanity and from imitation, wresting it away from the plans of the powers who built it. The voices rose, inhabiting the building and making it theirs, intertwining as they floated toward the heavens.

At the call to prayer, the serried ranks fell silent in communal submission. The imam's clear voice brought each of us to attention. Then came the tender, dreamy

[17] Hammoudi, *A Season in Mecca*, 78–79.
[18] Hammoudi, *A Season in Mecca*, 80.
[19] Hammoudi, *A Season in Mecca*, 109–110.
[20] Hammoudi, *A Season in Mecca*, 86.
[21] Hammoudi, *A Season in Mecca*, 91.

psalmody. I thought I saw my father's white cloak open and close around the child pressed against him.

Before leaving Medina, Hammoudi visits the Baqīʿ Cemetery, a space forbidden to women by Saudi law, where many members of Islam's founding generation lie buried. He wants to visit the graves of the Prophet's companions before he leaves, "hoping to create a link with them and, despite the time separating me from them to draw moral benefits from their virtue and knowledge." Instead, he becomes embarrassed when the Saudi religious police disperse a group of Iranians mourning several Shiʿite heroes buried there:[22]

I left the cemetery, ashamed that one sect of Islam could with impunity repress other Islamic practices, could show such contempt for the religious sensibilities of other Muslims, could call them *ajam*, the Arabic equivalent of "barbarian."

Like Al-e Ahmad, Hammoudi is one of innumerable educated modern Muslims who turned in his teens from a religious practice marked by fear and superstition. His relationship to Islam, however, did not end there. He has made a life-long career of studying what he can't in conscience practice:[23]

The practitioner of old gave way to an anthropologist who wanted to understand but was divided within himself. I wanted to know what religion meant for others, but I realized I could not stop there and had to question myself on the meaning of my own views.

Throughout the book, Hammoudi is doing fieldwork, studying the pilgrimage he performs. With an opening sentence that calls to mind similar distinctions by Sir Richard Burton and other nineteenth-century pilgrim masqueraders, he claims the right to his experience, despite an intention that is very different from the crowd's:[24]

So as not to lose heart, I told myself over and over that nothing kept a pilgrim from having other objectives, beyond religious obligation, and that nobody was interested in my efforts to explain my project anyway. I was sent back repeatedly to my intention and to my relation to God, the ultimate standard by which actions were measured. And in the end, Islam was my home. No one and nothing could forbid me from inhabiting and visiting it as I saw fit.

As was true for Al-e Ahmad, the real strength of Hammoudi's account lies not in his bristling critiques of Saudi intransigence or in the flights of

[22] Hammoudi, *A Season in Mecca*, 95.
[23] Hammoudi, *A Season in Mecca*, 39.
[24] Hammoudi, *A Season in Mecca*, 40.

anthropological analysis and visionary rhetoric that every so often carry the author away. It is in his intelligent candor, his talent for giving voice to the differing views of his fellow pilgrims, in a historical imagination that sees a future beyond the present, and in his poetic evocation of the rites.

MICHAEL MUHAMMAD KNIGHT'S JOURNEY TO THE END OF ISLAM

The long second half of Michael Muhammad Knight's *Journey to the End of Islam*[25] tracks in American street-wise prose an Irish Catholic, New York convert's 2008 Hajj to Mecca. An inquisitorial author for whom heterodoxy is a welcome duty, Knight has previously written several gonzo-style memoirs and two autobiographical novels, all employing a personal voice that jumps from the hoodie of Jim Carroll's *Basketball Diaries*. His Hajj account takes its title from Céline's dyspeptic 1930s novel, *Journey to the End of the Night,* and mines a similarly humorous vein of savage misanthropy. Céline's targets were the Ford Motor Plant in Detroit, soul-murdering mechanization, and the hypocrisies of pre-Nazi France. Knight takes aim with unsparing directness at narrow-minded Muslims and the hypocritical aspects of Islam they gloss over or defend. Knight, twenty-nine at the time, casts himself as a ghetto hipster addressing the disaffected Muslims of his generation. His image of a renegade, equipped to break and enter, is balanced by a fair knowledge of his new faith:[26]

> Islam's heritage looked like a big palace to me, but most of the rooms were now locked; I just wanted to run through the halls with a crowbar, taking off the doors.

Knight reframes the pilgrimage as a stage-set, using it to dramatize the dilemma summed up in his subtitle. His narrator is "Homeless in the Umma" – even and perhaps especially in Mecca, where everyone is supposed to be coming home. To a religion claiming that all of its members belong to one community, Knight is suggesting that a large group of present-day Muslims don't fit in. How could they, he asks, when so much about the Muslim world is upside down and sideways? About to set out for Mecca, he recounts an exchange with his friend, Sadaf, who once visited there:[27]

[25] M. M. Knight, *Journey to the End of Islam* (Berkeley, CA: Soft Skull Press, 2009). The first half of the novel is titled "Book 1: Homeless in the Ummah," and the second is "Book 2: Hajji Azreal Wisdom."

[26] Knight, *Journey to the End of Islam*, 215.

[27] Knight, *Journey to the End of Islam*, 198–199.

"What was it like?" I asked her.
"A really beautiful place in the middle of a really ugly place. I wished it could have been somewhere else."
"I'm going," I said [. . .]
"Are you going to come back all crazy?" she asked.
"I don't think so. Why would I?"
"Because that's what happens."

In Mecca, Knight's Hajj, unlike Hammoudi's, is mostly a pilgrimage of one. He takes his readers through the rites, but the pulsing crowds around him rarely come into focus. Nor is he in Mecca to inform the uninitiated. Knight rarely acts as a guide or village explainer. Rather, he addresses disaffected Muslims like himself, mostly by taking them into his confidence and speaking his notion of their language. His assignment is to make space for individual spiritual engagement by questioning accepted practice, supplanting religious orthodoxy with personal reflection. To succeed at this on paper you need to be interesting, and he is:[28]

Most of the sa'ee was done at a regular walking pace, but green lights overhead signaled the parts where Hajar ran . . . We walked and ran with each lap, some pausing at the water coolers to drink Zamzam in paper cups. But there was no water for Hajar, I remembered; I'd drink when she drank, when it was done.

Whenever the green lights told us to run, I felt Hajar's grief and panic, but it stopped being about her and Ishmael, or even this city or my ritual obligations. I thought of all the mothers and babies with no choices but to run wildly between the hills, the sad ones in a world where God didn't rescue everyone, and I remembered Mom. I was just a son with the best mother in the world, who had suffered in so many ways for my sake, and she always found the water. The great pre-Sufi ascetic Hasan al-Basri even said that honoring your mother had more merit than hajj. I just cried and cried for Mom because I had hurt her with this religion, I made my beautiful Islam into something hard for her and still she never said a word against it.

As a social critic, Knight is not so tender. His preferred modes of speaking truth to power are insult and outrage. His wrath at Wahhabism and his resentment of the Saudi monarchy are as deep as Hammoudi's, but less polite. Taking a swipe at the Saudi coat of arms by associating its crossed swords with the history of polytheism, he manages to conclude that what Wahhabi society really needs is a mystical injection of the feminine, preferably from the writings of a philosopher who is anathema to the Saudi *ʿulamā* (religious scholars):[29]

[28] Knight, *Journey to the End of Islam*, 254–255.

[29] Knight, *Journey to the End of Islam*, 313. Manat (Manāt) was the idol of the Aws and Khazraj tribes in pre-Muslim Medina. According to Ibn Hishām, among other

The winners write the history, and also the religions. The Saudis were the big winners ... The carpeting at Muhammad's Mosque gave us the royal coat of arms in endless repetition ... the crest consisted of a date palm tree above two crossed swords, which some would choose to read – and I did at that moment – as remnants of the goddesses ... The swords were taken by Ali from the treasury of Manat, and the X formed by their crossing may have recalled al-Uzza. Herodotus believed Manat and al-Uzza's sister, al-Lat, to be the chief goddess of the pre-Islamic Arabs ... Saudi Arabia could have used a goddess revival; if not through Allah's daughters, at least bring back the Sakina, or Ibn 'Arabi's assertion that true divinity was female.

An impartial critic with 360-range, Knight doesn't limit himself to potshots at the Saudis. His sensibilities are equally offended by the police ("eunuchs"), Muslims who believe the Prophet's entombed body remains alive ("that freaked me out"), and mystics who view the devil as manifesting divine attributes (reminding Knight of "my grandfather, the Pentecostal preacher").

Because his seemingly off-hand paragraphs are spiced with four-letter words, some popular reviewers evoke Hunter Thompson when discussing Knight. Past the provocation, however, out of the sarcasm, humor, exaggeration, profanity, and macho rancor, a quality arises in this account that makes it unique and even enduring. Knight is capable of spiritual candor. During his visits to the mosque in Mecca, and later in Mina Valley and Medina, he adds an enriching personal element to his account. He is also occasionally humble enough to poke holes in his own inflated views. At the Hajj's high point, on the plain of 'Arafat, he digs deep and conveys real drama. On a day he calls "this ... one day when a Muslim's heart (is) the only jurisprudence," he takes readers into his own heart, where, as any Muslim will tell you, an emotional dress rehearsal occurs for the real Day of Reckoning:[30]

[G]iven one day to repent for our wasted life, you can look at the sun and watch your time running out. The day was our life, and the meaning was missed by no one. As the sun lowered towards the horizon, the intensity on those hills picked up, Arafat looking like it was supposed to: a performance of the Day of Judgment, a *pre-enactment*. The litter and makeshift shelters made it feel like I walked through the wreckage of my species; it was just like the Day, I thought.

commentators, the Prophet Muḥammad sent his cousin 'Alī to demolish the idol. 'Alī brought back two swords from the treasury there, which the Prophet gave him to keep as spoils. Here, Knight is insulting the Saudi insignia by linking it to the imagery of pre-Islamic idolatry.

[30] Knight, *Journey to the End of Islam*, 336.

Then, in case readers should miss his reference, Knight cites the 103rd Sura from the Qur'an (al-ʿAṣr):[31]

"By the Time,

Mankind is truly in loss,

Except for those who have believed and done righteous deeds, and advised each other to truth, and advised each other to patience."

He continues:[32]

I said it over and over in Arabic ... until raising my hands above my head, submitting completely to the Mercy and losing it, terrified of all the time I threw away, an insult of Allah's gifts – *What do I do, what can I do?* It wasn't that Allah asked us to be superheroes, to give away everything we owned and become monks, but he provided us with opportunities every day to do just an atom's worth of good, and I turned most of them down. The Prophet said that even a smile was charity; how many chances did I miss? Now the sun was setting for me. With every breath, the darkness came closer. By the Time, I was in loss and I knew it, everyone on this hill knew his or her loss, and we became so afraid for ourselves that we forgot each other.

Here Knight reaches into the silence of the ʿArafat plains in a sustained and creative way.

Throughout the book, Knight gleefully aligns himself with the disenfranchised outcast. His real faith is in a Big Tent Islam – a pan-gendered, post-modern all-embracing Umma without social, racial, or theological boundaries. It is a social vision as inclusive as Whitman's, as self-confident of human variety as Islam must have been at its medieval height, when it spanned the known world from Morocco to China and lit up the Dark Ages with a blaze of civilizing light.

QANTA AHMED'S IN THE LAND OF INVISIBLE WOMEN

Dr. Qanta Ahmed performed the Hajj while working as a physician in Saudi Arabia. In the opening pages of her book, *In the Land of Invisible Women*,[33] her first hospital patient while on duty in Riyadh is an elderly Bedouin woman, comatose with pneumonia and completely exposed except for a full-face veil. Ahmed writes that the patient on the gurney made for an iconic scene, with the ventilator tubing

[31] Knight, *Journey to the End of Islam*, 336.

[32] Knight, *Journey to the End of Islam*, 337.

[33] Q. Ahmed, *In the Land of Invisible Women: A Female Doctor's Journey in the Saudi Kingdom* (Naperville, IL: Sourcebooks, Inc., 2008).

disappearing into a void, as though ventilating a veil and not a woman. Even when critically ill, I learned, hiding her face was of paramount importance. I watched, entranced at the clash of technology and religion, my religion, *some version* of my religion.[34]

When Ahmed notices small scars on the patient's stomach, a colleague explains that the woman must have been treated by a Bedouin healer: "They all do that. We often see these marks on our liver patients ... The shaman uses a branding iron to treat pain."[35] Although comfortably situated in a modern hospital in 1999, the remark carried this reader back to 1930s Teheran, to Al-e Ahmad's dying sister and her local Iranian "healer's" iron filings.

So begins Dr. Ahmed's two-year encounter with Saudi Arabia, in which her upper-middle-class British-Pakistani background, professional skills, sense of humor, Manhattan style, and polish as a writer combine to deliver a brilliant clash with the world's most sex-segregated society, a modern kingdom where she notes, "I would be licensed to operate on critically ill patients – yet never to drive a motor vehicle. Only men could enjoy that privilege."[36]

At home in her judgments, aware of her human rights, she is also a relaxed and curious Muslim woman on an adventure, with a natural inclination to risk second looks and explore the actual Riyadh. We travel in chaptered layers through her cultural resistance, moving from Kentucky Fried Chicken vendors on the Riyadh airport road, to shamanism cheek-by-jowl with modern medical technology, to, of course, the clothes:[37]

Though I had spent all my life as a Muslim, my wardrobe lacked any *burqa*, or *chadhur*, or in fact any kind of veil. My family, my parents in particular, had never required me to dress anything other than modestly. I was firmly settled in the standard Western clothing of trouser suits or modest skirts. My hair was only covered when I prayed ... I would quickly find Riyadh to be much more demanding than my family.

Ahmed refers to the required *abbayah* that women must wear as "polyester incarceration," "my new armor," and "my social suicide."[38] For her the robe is symbolic of a Wahhabi-inflected Sharia law enforced in Saudi Arabia but nowhere else, "a rigid movement that (has) dismantled

[34] Ahmed, *In the Land of Invisible Women*, 2.
[35] Ahmed, *In the Land of Invisible Women*, 5.
[36] Ahmed, *In the Land of Invisible Women*, 8.
[37] Ahmed, *In the Land of Invisible Women*, 27–28.
[38] Ahmed, *In the Land of Invisible Women*, 36, 38.

centuries of careful pluralistic Islamic discourse and learned interpretations, denouncing such scholarship as 'innovative' and corrupting."[39]

Nonetheless, her first shopping trip is to buy an abaya. "My oppression had begun," she writes.[40]

Along the way, her frustration is mixed with admiration as she starts meeting local women of force and charm. She tags along on shopping sprees, at afternoon teas and dinner parties, bringing us into a world Western visitors rarely see – the distaff side of the hyper-modern Saudi Kingdom and the savvy women who daily negotiate its warren of glass ceilings, razor-wire walls, and trapdoor floors, a severely compromised social landscape as Ahmad notes, where "women cannot function as independent entities" and yet somehow remain exuberant.[41]

And then there are the men, with their "legislated male supremacy," ranging from Ahmed's stand-offish male counterparts at the hospital to the well-heeled post-adolescent bachelors in S-series Benzes and Lamborghinis cruising Tahlia Street to hip-hop blaring from their radios (and who all too often turn up in Ahmed's wards near-dead from high-speed crack-ups on desert roads), to the Wahhabi religious police – in their regulation brown gowns and white peaked scarves, their threatening canes balanced "along the tightrope of extremism," "overbearing, dangerously arrogant," "obese icons of intolerance" making certain no woman's hair is out of place, no hemline above the ankle, no one out of line or lax in prayer. It is "something to which I could never become accustomed."[42]

Ahmed turns away, befriending first the hospital nutritionist Zubaidah, an elegant woman with "flawless skin," then Zubaidah's friends, who in turn introduce her to "the lives of others inside this bell jar." Months pass. The isolation and social abrasion take their toll,

> making me very hard. There was a sharp edge to me, which wounded everyone around me. I didn't like the angry, aggressive woman I was becoming. I wanted to change.[43]

One day, a colleague's young child is killed on the street by a passing car, and Ahmed, going with others to pay her respects, receives a crash course in the salving power of faith. Soon after, she decides to perform the Hajj.

[39] Ahmed, *In the Land of Invisible Women*, 29.
[40] Ahmed, *In the Land of Invisible Women*, 31.
[41] Ahmed, *In the Land of Invisible Women*, 17.
[42] Ahmed, *In the Land of Invisible Women*, 40, 42.
[43] Ahmed, *In the Land of Invisible Women*, 93.

> As soon as I could, I went to the hospital's hajj office and booked a last minute package [tour] . . . Later that afternoon . . . I surfed the Internet for information on how to do hajj . . . At last I found a diagram explaining the stages of the journey.[44]
>
> I called my astounded parents in England. My mother sounded remote, bemused, but I could sense my father's thrill.[45]

Ahmed expresses anxiety to a friend – "How will I know what to do?" and elicits laughter: "Nearly everyone who attends hajj is going there for the first time," she is told. "No pilgrim ever knows what to do."[46] With a shrug, she sets out to shop for the right scarf.

Part of the Hajj's magic resides in its quicksilver transitions. Ahmed keeps pace. Because she is on a government contract, her Hajj visa materializes quickly, even at the eleventh hour. She makes friends quickly too, befriending a married couple on the bus to Mecca. Stopped with them on the street at the hour of prayer, she writes:

> Like a magic organism forming out of ether, the hajj crowds had become a parish. After prayer, we would again dissolve into the hajj ocean, leaving no trace of an assembly.[47]

Inside the mosque, she links her emotions and ideas to what she sees:[48]

> As I looked up and surveyed the multi-stranded circle of humanity adorning the Kaaba, a giant rich choker of pilgrim pearls, I found myself among them. In this diversity, I finally belonged. Islam was many-faceted and I was simply one.

As the political scientist Robert Bianchi has noted, "The hajj works because two million hajjis of every race and nation are determined to make it work."[49]

Nonetheless, on the desert outside Mecca in a "Women Only" tent in Mina Valley, Ahmed's Hajj turns unpleasant. As she steps into tent No. 50,007, sixty pairs of scanning eyes assess her. No one smiles in greeting. When she sheds her abaya, revealing like others a Guess T-shirt, Calvin Klein trousers, and a shiny Italian belt, a woman of forty-five glares intently. Ahmed greets her. The woman explodes:[50]

[44] Ahmed, *In the Land of Invisible Women*, 113.
[45] Ahmed, *In the Land of Invisible Women*, 115.
[46] Ahmed, *In the Land of Invisible Women*, 116.
[47] Ahmed, *In the Land of Invisible Women*, 133.
[48] Ahmed, *In the Land of Invisible Women*, 149.
[49] R. R. Bianchi, *Guests of God* (New York: Oxford University Press, 2004), 13.
[50] Ahmed, *In the Land of Invisible Women*, 156.

"You say 'Hi' to me? 'Hi?'" she snapped ... Her English was precisely enunciated. Her face flashed. She was Saudi for sure. "As a Muslim at hajj greeting another Muslim, you say 'Hi!'" She went on, practically spitting with fury.

To Ahmed's irritation, her tent mates are not mere sisters in oppression. Some prove insufferably dismissive – on religious, cultural, and racial grounds – not so different from human beings of any sex the world over. As Ahmed performs the afternoon prayer, voices behind her cluck their pursed-lipped disapproval. A Saudi woman accosts her and, touching Ahmed's exposed ear peeping from her headscarf, repeatedly says, "Forbidden!" Ahmed objects and the woman stomps off, muttering. Another woman of the same party approaches later, asking when she converted to Islam. When Ahmed replies that she has always been a Muslim, the woman insists on her question, asking whether her parents are also converts.

Late that night, circumstances conspire to win the female pilgrims over. Ahmed, awakened and led to a nearby tent, administers an injection to an elderly woman suffering from osteoarthritis. Her midnight rounds soon become common knowledge. A fellow pilgrim explains the warm reception she receives:[51]

"They are impressed with you, Qanta," she said, "because you are a doctor. Until they found out about last night, they thought you were just a Pakistani maid ... They were quite shocked to discover you are a doctor ... Now you will find they will all want to talk to you. They don't care about your race."

Ahmed concludes her encounter with an observation tailored to needle any "pure" Saudi, bringing her Hajj narrative back to its opening pages:[52]

Yet I couldn't connect this racial purity with the warmth of the toothless, lined Bedouin women who showed me such affection in the hospital ... Surely these Bedouin were the purest Saudis of all, Daughters of Arabia, born of tribal forebears who had roamed Arabia before the slick of oil wealth suffocated their culture, washing them up like half-dead seagulls into the new urban metropolis of modern Saudi Arabia. I decided it had to be wealth which made the stark difference. All I had to do was think back to the "real" Saudis I had met in Riyadh, so different than the women sharing this tent with me.

Qanta Ahmed's account is not a blanket dismissal of Saudi society, nor a naïve embrace of all-things-hajj. Her fierce resistance to social repression, gender bias, and class rejection are tempered by a genuine religious

[51] Ahmed, *In the Land of Invisible Women*, 172.
[52] Ahmed, *In the Land of Invisible Women*, 175–176.

humility, a wish to heal her "broken life," or at any rate escape from it for a while in the larger embrace of a religion where she must struggle to find her place.

ASRA NOMANI'S STANDING ALONE IN MECCA

Every year for about two weeks, a couple of million would-be pilgrims, half of them female, arrive on the outskirts of Mecca, divest themselves of distinctions, don modest look-alike cotton clothes, and blend together to stand equally before God. This egalitarian renunciation of social difference is visually stunning. Yet as Qanta Ahmed demonstrates, during the other fifty weeks each year, the same women may be treated as second-class citizens. Asra Nomani's *Standing Alone in Mecca* drives the point home.[53]

Nomani's book is less a pilgrim's account than a personal memoir that invokes the Hajj as its central metaphor. A journalist and magazine writer, Nomani first tried to perform the Hajj in 2002, when the magazine *Outside* suggested she write about it. She was then on an assignment in Pakistan, reporting on terrorism in the wake of the September 11 attacks in New York and Washington, DC and, a few months later, investigating the brutal murder in Karachi of a fellow journalist, Daniel Pearl. Nomani's initial Hajj arrangements were overtaken by these events. They were also thwarted by bureaucratic hurdles, including insistence at the Saudi consulate that as a single female applicant she must submit her passport accompanied by the passport of a guardian male relative who would travel with her. Next, within weeks of Pearl's death, Nomani learned she was pregnant and that the man in question was both unwilling to marry and frightened by the Pearl investigation swirling around her. These three catalysts – murder, pregnancy, and disavowal – accelerated a desire to make sense of her life. A year later, the Hajj became the stage where this process unfolded.

Nomani returned to her family home in West Virginia to bear her son. Then in February 2003, she set out on the Hajj. As with Ale-Ahmad, the pilgrimage detailed in her pages is a family affair – in this case one with child in arms and accompanied by her parents, a niece, and a nephew. The newborn child deepens her story's emotional and literary dimensions. He also completes the image of Nomani as Hajar, the unwed heroine of Islam,

[53] A. Q. Nomani, *Standing Alone in Mecca: An American Woman's Struggle for the Soul of Islam* (HarperSanFrancisco, 2005).

and gives form to the scarlet "Z,"[54] the stigma that Nomani suspects conventional Muslims see whenever they look at her. Her mother and father play roles in the action too, especially the latter, a devout educated man who supports his daughter's choices.

Their pilgrimage is told in 130 pages of a longer book. In Mecca, Nomani draws frequent correspondences between her experience as a single mother and Mecca's foundational story of Hajar and Ismail. Over and over she correlates her biography with the drama of the prophet Abraham's bondswoman. Hajar is never legendary for Nomani. The millennia that separate them make her more palpable. We are given a matched pair of single mothers who, escorted to Mecca, suffer trials, experience miracles, prevail by faith, find salvation in the desert, and initiate a family line.

Nomani's performance of the rites is mostly keyed to this central figuration. For that she is indebted to Ali Shari'ati, the influential Iranian sociologist and near contemporary of Jalal Al-e Ahmad, whose popular handbook on the Hajj symbolically reinterprets the pilgrim rites.[55] Attempting, in Robert Bianchi's words, to "mobilize the *umma* and redistribute power to its weakest members," Shari'ati viewed the pilgrimage as "a time for criticizing glaring injustices and protesting the exploitations of interlocking elites in political, economic and religious life." For Nomani as for Shari'ati, all blame falls on "the pyramid of clerics who treat God's word as their exclusive property and distort it to enslave others."[56]

By the time she sets foot in Mecca, the Hajj is no longer a magazine assignment. She carries her infant with her through the rites, ruminating on the timeless resonance of her situation, tracking the logic by which religion and faith underwrite her search for social justice and personal mercy. The similarity with Al-e Ahmad's energetic, independent woman striding with child toward the shrine is hard to miss. Nomani's first *ṭawāf* (circumambulation) and *sa'y* (reenacting Hajar's run between the hills for water), inspire searching narratives designed for the general reader but also addressed (in a way she shares with Knight) to an estranged and global demographic – in this case, the silenced population of young Muslim women who like Nomani have suffered or will soon suffer in "dead-end or loveless relationships" and who seek to practice their religion in ways that deliver more authentic lives.[57]

[54] For *zinā*, unlawful sexual intercourse. The allusion to Hester Prynne's "A," in Hawthorne's *The Scarlet Letter*, is Nomani's.

[55] A. Shari'ati, *Hajj* (Bedford, OH: Free Islamic Literatures, 1977).

[56] Bianchi, *Guests of God*, 24.

[57] Nomani, *Standing Alone in Mecca*, 67.

Nomani's book is less a Hajj account than a book about liberation, using the Hajj as a starting point and drawing together arguments against an oppressive religious literalism that restricts Muslim women. Her strategy to *employ* the Hajj is clearly expressed in the book's section titles, including "Bringing the Pilgrimage Home," "Asserting the Lessons of Pilgrimage," and lastly "Harvesting the Fruits of the Pilgrimage," in which Nomani describes the eighteen months after her return to the Americas, including her passionate efforts to liberalize the mosque in her hometown.

CONCLUSION

The Hajj accounts of Hammoudi, Knight, Ahmed, and Nomani are strongly conditioned by the decade in which they appeared. Well before September 11, 2001, Islam in the United States and Europe had already become "a matter of intense, sometimes vitriolic debate and polemic," a societal platform in which neither the classroom nor the media nor the street was settled territory.[58] The four authors reflect this reality, in their vocabulary, their motives, even the anecdotes they tell, whether they allude to it or not. At the same time, as they all make clear, traditional Muslim-world politics and society offered little comfort – neither to the deracinated Moroccan intellectual nor the streetwise Catholic convert, not to the acute-care physician trying hard to understand or to the modern stand-in for Hawthorne's Hester Prynne. On the contrary, they all exhibit unmistakable symptoms of feeling "homeless in the Umma." Into these uncertain lives the Hajj *erupts* (the term is Hammoudi's), shaking things up in unexpected ways. The resulting anxiety and upset, reported with candor, suggest that each of these authors' decisions to make the Hajj was at least partly inspired by impulses that the anthropologist Michael Gilsenan characterizes as "beyond the intellectual, perhaps (in) the unconscious hope of an eruption."[59]

Pilgrimage as the inspired act of a person in crisis, attempting to change the terms of individual existence, is firmly rooted in the history of the Hajj. Escape, repentance, the desperate need for fresh beginnings have always been powerful motives. Indeed, when the Prophet Muhammad undertook the first Muslim Hajj in 627, he was at a low point in his career, when all his work appeared to have come to nothing. His seemingly irrational

[58] M. Gilsenan, "And You, What Are You Doing Here?" in *The London Review of Books*, 28, 20 (October 9, 2006).

[59] Gilsenan, "And You, What Are You Doing Here?"

decision to lay down arms and march to Mecca in pilgrim dress shocked enemies and followers alike. The surprising outcome, the treaty of Hudaibiya and the rapid attraction of so many tribes and factions to his fold, including the Meccans, proved a turning point in the foundation of Islam, although many failed to understand it at the time.

Thus from the start, the Hajj has both inspired and been defined by travelers in extremis, by pilgrims driven to seek the springs of change.

14

Visualizing the Hajj

Representations of a Changing Sacred Landscape Past and Present

Juan E. Campo

Muslims have visualized the Hajj and Mecca's sacred landscape since Islam's inception. Many of these visualizations result from mediated practices of representation and re-presentation. By "mediated" I mean images produced and transmitted through pre-modern texts and manuscript illustrations, and the modern print and electronic media. The media that feature the Hajj and its changing landscapes occur in a diverse array of written, print, electronic, and digital forms: manuscripts; certificates; paintings; photographs published in books, pamphlets, periodicals, or as calendars; "framing pictures"; postcards; and signboards. They include films and videos, television broadcasts, websites, and social media. In the modern era especially, these media bring images of the Hajj and its landscapes, including the individual sacred sites and beings associated with them, to viewers on a mass scale to significant effect. In addition to being mediated, these images are also *mediating* through their capacity to connect viewers (1) as a community horizontally with each other and with actual landscapes over great distances, (2) vertically with higher beings and the cosmos, and (3) temporally with the past, present, and the future.

The Hajj, like other pilgrimages, involves flows of human beings, religious beliefs and practices, ideologies, institutions, political forces, capital, and material goods across spatiotemporal boundaries into physical connection with sacred spaces and places. Thomas Tweed has described such flows as kinetic organic-cultural processes of crossing and dwelling, linking human beings with each other and with supramundane ones.[1] Images that

[1] T. Tweed, *Crossing and Dwelling: A Theory of Religion* (Cambridge, MA: Harvard University Press, 2006).

represent and re-present the Hajj and its sacred landscapes participate in these flows through what David Morgan has called in another context "visual piety."[2] As I shall argue, mediated images of the Hajj and its landscapes, in both medieval and modern media, engage viewers by creating relationships that both *transcend* place and *put* in place – orienting them physically and perceptually. Such relational engagements of viewer and image, as posited by Morgan, situate the body of the viewer *before the image*, draw the viewer's body *into the image*, and can even lead the body *beyond the image* to a greater communal body or religious tradition.[3] In other words, images participate in the cultivation of an embodied, relational self. Moreover, although in some regards Walter Benjamin's assertion that in modernity "[mechanical] reproduction emancipates the work of art from its parasitical dependence on ritual" may hold some truth, this should not be taken to mean that reproduction completely eradicates an image's ritual value. Rather, it reproduces tradition and opens the way to possibilities that were not present when it was still "imbedded in the fabric of tradition" – even when mass produced, popular religious art still possesses its "aura."[4]

PRE-MODERN REPRESENTATIONS OF MECCA AND THE HAJJ

The genealogy of the pre-modern representation of the Hajj and its landscape consists of two main strands, one comprised of the written word, the other of figurative images. Verbal descriptions of areas where the Hajj rites occur can be found in several varieties of early Islamic literature: hadith, Qur'an commentary, biographies of Muhammad, tales of other prophets, historical chronicles, and legal texts. These verbal representations became more fully elaborated in topographical literature, travelers' accounts, and poetry. The earliest can be found in hadith and biographical

[2] D. Morgan, *Visual Piety: A History and Theory of Popular Religious Images* (Berkeley: University of California Press, 1998).

[3] D. Morgan, "The Look of the Sacred," in Robert Orsi (ed.), *Cambridge Companion to Religious Studies* (Cambridge University Press, 2012), 296–318. Morgan's work is grounded in the study of figural images in Christian art, but he proposes that his thesis is applicable to artistic expression in other religious traditions, including Islam and the Hindu religion.

[4] W. Benjamin, "The Work of Art in the Age of Mechanical Reproduction," in W. Benjamin, *Illuminations*, ed. H. Arendt, tr. H. Zohn (New York: Harcourt, Brace & World, Inc., 1968), 226, 225, 223 ff. Comparative analysis, including the work of Morgan, indicates that popular, mass-produced Islamic representations are far from unique in having a special, sacred quality and effect ascribed to them.

narratives about Muhammad's Farewell Pilgrimage (*ḥajjat al-wadāʿ*), an event that occurred in 632 CE, shortly before his death, and served as the blueprint for the obligatory pilgrimage of Islam.[5] The hadith corpus of the eighth to ninth century describes his naming of boundary points (*mīqāts*) where pilgrims must sacralize themselves (*iḥrām*) before entering Mecca, circumambulation of the house of God (the Kaʿba), arrival at the Station of Abraham next to the Kaʿba, performance of the running between the hillocks of al-Ṣafā and al-Marwa next to the Sacred Mosque, the departure for the valley of Minā, arrival at the plain of ʿArafāt and delivery of his Hajj sermon, encampment at Muzdalifa for the night, and return to Mina for the stoning of the three pillars and animal sacrifice. They conclude with mention of his noon prayer at the Kaʿba.[6] The narratives also name where Muhammad received several revelations during his pilgrimage, including his final one (Q Māʾida 5: 3), and where he performed his prayers, thereby underscoring the sacrality of the landscape. One other structure mentioned by the hadith in connection with the Hajj is the *Ḥijr* (also known as the *Ḥaṭīm*), a low, semi-circular wall that was considered to have once been part of the Kaʿba. This is where Muhammad was said to have marked the starting and ending point of the circumambulations he performed around the Kaʿba during the Farewell Pilgrimage.[7]

Such accounts establish for Muslims of future generations the temporal and spatial relations between specific Hajj rituals and the sacred landscape. As F. E. Peters has pointed out, this landscape came to be defined by a threefold zone of sanctity (*ḥaram*): the Kaʿba, the Sacred Mosque that

[5] *Encyclopedia of the Qurʾan*, s.v. "Farewell Pilgrimage." According to Muslim accounts, Mecca was an ancient cultic center and focus of pilgrimage rituals, but it was Muhammad's pilgrimage that set the example for Muslims to emulate. Modern scholars have raised questions about the original locations for Hajj rituals in Muhammad's time, noting tensions among several Qurʾanic verses. Some scholars have even suggested that ritual practices and place names from elsewhere were later transferred to Mecca. In my reading of the texts, I accept the assignation of the original Hajj ritual sites to Mecca as they have come to be understood in Islamic tradition. See further *Encyclopedia of the Qurʾan*, s.v. "Pilgrimage."

[6] See, e.g., Muslim, *Ṣaḥīḥ*, tr. A. H. Siddiqi (Lahore: Sh. Muhammad Ashraf, n.d.), 612–618; and al-Bukhārī, *al-Jāmiʿ al-Ṣaḥīḥ*. 4 vols (Cairo: al-Maṭbaʿat al-Salafiyya wa-Maktabatuhā, 1403 AH/1982–1983), *Kitāb al-Ḥajj*. The Hajj landscape receives less attention in Ibn Isḥāq's biography of Muhammad, *Sīrat rasūl Allāh*, translated as *The Life of Muhammad*, tr. A. Guillaume (Oxford University Press, 1980 [1955], 649–651).

[7] According to hadith and other sources, the *Ḥijr* is said to have been originally built by Abraham for his son Ishmael. Other sources claim that this is where Muhammad had the visionary encounter with Gabriel that led to his Night Journey and ascent to heaven. See F. E. Peters, *The Hajj: The Muslim Pilgrimage to Mecca and the Holy Places* (Princeton University Press, 1994), 15ff.

contains it, and the outer territorial limits of Mecca, as defined by the boundary points.[8] All that is lacking in the early sources are figurative representations of the ritual sites, descriptions of their appearance, and a systematic treatment of their relative locations to aid the pilgrim. These details appear not to have required mention in the opinion of these authors.

As the Islamic empire grew, and distant imperial capitals were founded and flourished, the special status of the Hajj landscape was further embellished by linking it both with cosmology and sacred ancestors, particularly Adam and Abraham. According to narratives conveyed in the tales of the prophets (*qiṣaṣ al-anbiyāʾ*), Adam was the first human being to perform the Hajj rites, as instructed by Gabriel. The prototype of the Kaʿba was sapphire sent down from heaven situated on earth under God's throne; as God's throne was circumambulated by the angels, so the prototype was circumambulated by Adam. The black stone, a focal point of ritual action located in the Kaʿba's southeastern corner, was also regarded as having a celestial origin. In the eleventh-century account of al-Thaʿlabī, Adam and Eve are reunited after their expulsion from Paradise at ʿArafat and received God's forgiveness at Mina.[9] In al-Kisāʾī's thirteenth-century version, they are placed separately on the hillocks of al-Ṣafā and al-Marwa. When Adam pronounced the *talbiya*, a short declaration pronounced by all pilgrims during the Hajj, God responded, saying, "Adam, today have I sanctified Mecca and all that surrounds it, and it shall be sacred until the day of resurrection."[10]

The Abrahamic association with the Hajj landscape is well known, as related in the Qur'an, tales of the prophets, and other sources. Al-Thaʿlabī recounts that when Abraham brought his concubine Hagar and his son Ishmael to Mecca, it was "a place of thorny shrubs, acacia, and thistles."[11] This condition changed as events in the Abrahamic narratives transpired. The story of Hagar's search for water to quench her son's thirst is linked to the discovery of the well of Zamzam next to the Kaʿba and the origin of the running ritual (*saʿy*) between al-Ṣafā and al-Marwa. Abraham and his

[8] Peters, *The Hajj*, 10 ff.

[9] Al-Thaʿlabī, *ʿArāʾis al-majālis fī qiṣaṣ al-anbiyāʾ or "Lives of the Prophets,"* tr. W. M. Brinner (Leiden: Brill, 2002), 60.

[10] Al-Kisāʾī, *The Tales of the Prophets of al-Kisa'i*, tr. W. M. Thackston, Jr. (Chicago: Kazi Publications, 1997), 63. Little is known about al-Kisāʾī, so the dates of the text are disputed. Some scholars date it as the tenth century, but a later date is more likely.

[11] Al-Thaʿlabī, *ʿArāʾis al-majālis*, 139. The Qur'an refers to the valley of Mecca as "uncultivated" (Q Ibrāhīm 14:37).

son Ishmael are credited in Islamic tradition with building the Kaʿba, proclaiming the pilgrimage to all humankind, setting the precedent for stoning the three pillars at Mina, and performing animal sacrifice at the conclusion of the Hajj. Expanding on references in the Qurʾan (Q Baqara 2:125, Q Āl ʿImrān 3:97), al-Thaʿlabī mentions the Station of Abraham (*maqām Ibrāhīm*) as a stone bearing Abraham's footprints in the vicinity of the Kaʿba that was later considered as a prayer place.[12]

The only historical topography of Mecca surviving from this period is al-Azraqī's *Kitāb akhbār Makka* ("Accounts of Mecca") which was assembled by the mid-ninth century, and updated by later editors.[13] It is the earliest work dedicated to a Muslim city, and includes abundant mythic materials from earlier sources, such as those summarized previously, as well as accounts of events that occurred after Muhammad's death. Consisting of more than six hundred pages in modern print editions, it can be divided into four parts: (1) the primordial Kaʿba, its features and rites; (2) the Kaʿba under Islam, its features and rites; (3) the Sacred Mosque under Islam, its features and rites; and (4) Mecca, its sacred boundaries and environs, including Mina, Muzdalifa, ʿArafat, residential quarters, and mountains.[14] Although it lacks the biographies of notable inhabitants that would characterize later urban histories, al-Azraqī's pious topography offers its readers remarkably detailed descriptions of Mecca's pilgrimage landscape. The Kaʿba figures prominently in the regard, as al-Azraqī guides readers around all four sides, and leads them inside, using the second person form of address ("when you enter the Kaʿba on your right there is ...").[15] But he also details the surrounding ritual landscape. For example, in a passage concerned with the rituals performed in the Sacred Mosque, he writes

Seven circumambulations of the Kaʿba is 836 cubits and thirty inches. The distance from the Station [of Abraham] to al-Ṣafā is 277 cubits, and from al-Ṣafā to al-Marwa, one circumambulation is 766 and one-half cubits, and all seven circumambulations between them amounts to 5,365 and one-half cubits. The distance from the Black Stone [in the southeast corner of the Kaʿba] to the Station [of

[12] Al-Thaʿlabī, *ʿArāʾis al-majālis*, 142, 168; cf. Peters, *The Hajj*, 16 ff. Some early Muslim commentators also speculated that the Station of Abraham meant the entire Hajj, or the sites of ʿArafat, Muzdalifa, and Mina; see al-Ṭabarī, *Tafsīr* (Cairo: al-Matbaʿa al-Kubrā al-Amīriyya, [1904] reprint edition), I: 422 ff.

[13] Al-Azraqī, *Kitāb Akhbār Makka wa-mā jāʾa fīhā min al-akhbār*, 2 vols. in 1, ed. R. al-Ṣāliḥ Malḥas (Beirut: Dar al-Andalus, [1960]). For details on what is known about al-Azraqī and the history of the text, see the editor's introduction.

[14] This is based on Oleg Grabar's division of the text, discussed in O. Grabar, "Upon Reading al-Azraqī," *Muqarnas*, 3 (1985): 2.

[15] Al-Azraqī, *Akhbār Makka*, I: 294.

Abraham], plus seven circumambulations between al-Ṣafā and al-Marwa is 6,538 and twenty-three inches.[16]

Details such as these offer al-Azraqī's readers details they can use to fashion a vision for themselves of the holy sites in the absence of figural images or floor plans. Indeed his visualizations of Mecca and its field of sacred places exemplify the spatiotemporal confluences and disjunctions we have identified as occurring in pilgrimage landscapes. As art historian Oleg Grabar has noted, in al-Azraqī

> There is a constant interplay between specific moments, usually established quite precisely with names and dates when known, and equally specific places in the sanctuary. It is as though the understanding of something seen requires its connection with a historical or a mythical event, often drawn from the lives of Abraham or Hagar, which were connected with so many places in Mecca.[17]

The spatio-temporal depiction of the Hajj landscape achieved a new mode of expression with the emergence of pilgrim travel narratives, as exemplified by that of Ibn Jubayr (d. 1217 CE) of Valencia. His account places the holy cities of Mecca and Medina at the center of a journey (*riḥla*) that took place in 1183–1185, beginning with a voyage from Ceuta to Egypt, then across the Red Sea to Arabia, Iraq, and Syria, and concluding with a hazardous sea journey to Cyprus and back home.[18] Like al-Azraqī, Ibn Jubayr enjoyed providing detailed descriptions of the pilgrimage landscape – the sacred mosque and the Kaʿba, the Station of Abraham, the hillocks of al-Ṣafā and al-Marwa, the well of Zamzam, the plain of ʿArafat, the Mount of Mercy, Muzdalifa, and the valley of Mina. The required rituals of the Hajj and ʿUmra ("minor pilgrimage") are also related by him, including sacralizing the body (*iḥrām*), encampment at Mina, standing at ʿArafat, stoning the pillars in Mina, running between al-Ṣafā and al-Marwa, and animal sacrifice. Both al-Azraqī and Ibn Jubayr participated in what Houari Touati has called "the school of the gaze," which he sees as playing counterpoint to a way of knowing the world in the Islamic Middle Ages based on audition.[19] Where Ibn Jubayr's

[16] Al-Azraqī, *Akhbār Makka*, II: 120.

[17] Grabar, "Upon Reading al-Azraqī," 2.

[18] Ibn Jubayr, *Riḥlat ibn Jubayr* (Cairo: Dār al-Maʿārif, n.d.); English translation: *The Travels of Ibn Jubayr, Being the Chronicles of a Mediaeval Spanish Moor Concerning His Journey to the Egypt of Saladin, the Holy Cities of Arabia*, tr. R. J. C. Broadhurst (London: J. Cape, 1952).

[19] H. Touati, *Islam and Travel in the Middle Ages*, tr. L. G. Cochrane (University of Chicago Press, 2010), 253. Touati's study is concerned with travel-related literature, but his understanding is more widely applicable to Islamic literature.

narrative differs from that of al-Azraqī is its framing as an observant traveler's diary, letting his readers know on what days he visited a sacred place, performed a rite, or witnessed a memorable event or activity. Unlike al-Azraqī, who had family ties to Mecca, Ibn Jubayr was highly critical of the people of the Hijaz, including their religious sectarianism. This confirmed to him that the only true Islam was that of his home in the Maghrib.[20] His was an embodied, personal vision of the pilgrimage landscape, one in which he wanted to include his readers. Although rendered through the medium of writing, both al-Azraqī's and Ibn Jubayr's portrayals of the landscape not only contribute to the iconicity of its features, but they lend to it almost filmic qualities that would only become fully realized centuries later.

At the same time that Ibn Jubayr was traveling in the Middle East, a new medium of Hajj representation was making its appearance: illustrated Hajj certificates.[21] These quasi-legal documents certified that the Hajj and/or ʿUmra had been completed by an individual or by proxy for another, living or dead.[22] Executed on paper scrolls for easy transport and storage, they combine written text with block print or hand-drawn images of the major stations of the Hajj landscape; pictures of the Prophet's Mosque in Medina and the Dome of the Rock in Jerusalem were included at the end of some of the scrolls. Individual features are labeled and shown in a schematic style, providing both simultaneous and elevation views, making possible for viewers to more easily imagine themselves on location.[23] Much of the calligraphy and all the colorations were done by hand. Although only partially preserved, there are indications that a few certificates may have been mounted for display. Not only might these be the earliest figurative representations of these Muslim pilgrimage sites, but the

[20] Ibn Jubayr, *Riḥla*, 80–81.

[21] The earliest and largest collection of certificates was rescued from the library of the Ummayad Mosque in Damascus and preserved in the Ottoman imperial archives in Istanbul in 1893. They date from 1084 to 1312, with the illustrated certificates concentrated in the years 1180-1225. See D. Sourdel and J. Sourdel-Thomine, *Certificats de pèlerinage d'époque ayyoubide: Contribution à l'histoire de l'idéologie de l'Islam au temps des Croisades* (Paris: L'Académie des Inscriptions et Belles-Lettres, 2006) and Ş. Aksoy and R. Milstein, "A Collection of Thirteenth-Century Illustrated Hajj Certificates," in İrvin Cemil Shick (ed.), *M. Uğur Derman: 65 Yaş Armağan* (Istanbul: Sabancı Universitesi, 2000), 101–134.

[22] Islamic law allows the Hajj and ʿUmra to be performed on behalf of another who is unable or deceased.

[23] D. J. Roxburgh, "Visualizing the Sites and Monuments of Islamic Pilgrimage," in Margaret S. Graves (ed.), *Architecture in Islamic Arts: Treasures of the Aga Khan Museum* (Geneva: Aga Khan Trust for Culture, 2011), 33–41.

fact that block printing technique was used suggests that Hajj certificate production was a successful craft industry in its time – especially for wealthy and influential patrons.

Rather than beginning with the Kaʿba and the Sacred Mosque, as did al-Azraqī and Ibn Jubayr, a certificate's images are organized vertically in ritual sequence, starting with ʿArafat (rendered in larger proportion than the Kaʿba), followed by Muzdalifa, Mina, and then the Sacred Mosque. Within each image, distinguishing features are also shown schematically; at the Sacred Mosque, these include the Kaʿba with its door and black covering, the Hatim, the dome of Zamzam well, the Station of Abraham, minarets, pavilions for religious and political authorities, and even the torches that illuminated the mosque by night.[24]

The inscriptions on the certificates identify which rites the pilgrims performed at each location, when they were performed, and signify the soteriological aspirations of the pilgrims and their beneficiaries. Although the images lack human figures, the words render them present and engage them both with the sacred landscape and with the transcendent. When taken together, word and image attest to an ontological transformation: the pilgrim attains God's blessing (*baraka*) and the certificate itself becomes a source of blessing. For instance, one illustrated certificate attests that pilgrim Israʾīl ibn Saʿīd ibn Abī Qāsim performed the Hajj on behalf of another man. In doing so, the document witnesses that he sacralized himself and donned the pilgrim garments at the Syrian boundary of the Hajj area, chanted the ritual formula *labbayka* ("at your service") until he reached Mecca, where he entered the Sacred Mosque, circumambulated the Kaʿba seven times, and prayed for the deceased at all four of its corners and under its rain spout (*mīzāb*), an especially blessed place. After performing two prayer prostrations, he then exited to do the seven-fold running between al-Ṣafā and al-Marwa, and proceeded to ʿArafat, "the place of mercy and blessing," for the noon and afternoon prayers. There he stood in the Place of the Prophet and prayed to him (the Prophet Muhammad) until sunset, when he left for the next station in Muzdalifa.

The certificate then confirms that the pilgrim performed prayers at the place of sacrifice near Mina, threw seven stones collected in Muzdalifa at

[24] The best-preserved certificate with images is catalogue E, no. 40. See Sourdel and Sourdel-Thoumine, *Certificats*, 228–236, with fig. 1 and pl. XLII; cf. Aksoy and Milstein, "Collection," 104–115. Ironically, even though the images related to the Hajj sites, the written testimony only concerns completion of the ʿUmra.

the ʿAqaba pillar in Mina, conducted an animal sacrifice, performed rites of descralization, and returned to Mecca for his final circumambulations, followed by completing the requisite lapidations at Mina. The document concludes with the following invocation: "May God, his angels, and the Muslims here present bear witness that the named beneficiary receive the merit of this blessed pilgrimage – may God let him benefit from it."[25] In support of the soteriological function of the certificates, it is worth noting that some conclude with a verse from the Qurʾan: "On the [Last] Day neither wealth nor sons will be of any benefit, except for those who bring to God a sound heart" (Q Shuʿarāʾ 26:88-89). In effect, the use of this verse in this context is to assure the pilgrim/beneficiary that a "sound heart" (*qalb salīm*), qualifying one for reward in the hereafter, has been attained by performance of the pilgrimage. The document also identifies God as a witness, suggesting that visualization of the pilgrimage was thought to occur from both the human and divine perspectives. In the end, even the certificate undergoes an ontological transformation – becoming a source of blessing for the bearer, the beneficiary, and anyone else who might view or touch it. In addition to their Qurʾanic content, the images, and the inventory of rites performed, the scrolls themselves were likely produced by artisans in Mecca, bearing the baraka obtained from its physical origins in the holy city. It is not surprising, therefore, to discover that amulets found together with medieval Hajj certificates recovered from the Umayyad Mosque in Damascus also contained images of the sacred Meccan landscape.[26]

Based on the available material evidence, the production of illustrated Hajj certificates appears to have waned during the thirteenth century, but it did not completely disappear. It was revived during the Ottoman era, when images of Muslim holy sites appear not only on pilgrimage certificates, but also in books and other media. The motifs employed reflect continuity with the medieval tradition, adapted to local tastes. By the sixteenth century, images of Mecca and Medina were spreading eastward from Ottoman lands to Iran and India. In 1505–1506, Muḥyī al-Dīn Lārī dedicated his Persian poetical praise of the Hajj and its sacred Arabian landscape, *Futūḥ al-ḥaramayn* (*Revelations of the Two Sanctuaries*) to the sultan of Gujarat. It was later reproduced in multiple copies that contained images of all the topographic features of Mecca mentioned by al-Azraqī and Ibn Jubayr, with additional images of the holy places in

[25] Sourdel and Sourdel-Thoumine, *Certificats*, 253–256.

[26] Aksoy and Milstein, "Illustrated Hajj Certificates," 127–130.

Medina and Jerusalem.[27] Another widely circulated work that contained images of the Sacred Mosque in Mecca and the Prophet's Mosque in Medina was a collection of devotional prayers for Muhammad, the fifteenth-century al-Jazūlī's *Dalā'il al-khayrāt* (*The Signs of Divine Benefits*).[28] By the seventeenth century, polychrome glazed tiles were being produced in the Ottoman ceramic workshops of Iznik and Kutahya that portrayed Mecca and Medina using the same combination of simultaneous and elevation views as employed in the twelfth-century Hajj certificates. Some, however, contained three-dimensional perspective. Like their predecessors, they contained Qur'an verses and labels for important locations. These ceramic images found their way into mosques, madrasas, palaces, and houses, often placed on walls facing toward Mecca. In some cases, they even inspired landscape frescoes in the mansions of elites.[29]

REPRESENTING PILGRIMAGE LANDSCAPES IN MODERN VISUAL MEDIA

The advent of modern print culture and photography brought about a revolution in the representation of pilgrimage landscapes and contributed significantly to the rise of mass pilgrimages, such as those to Mecca, involving millions of participants. Access to knowledge and information about pilgrimages and their landscapes prior to modernity was limited to oral culture and the circulation of written texts within calligraphic cultures of socioeconomic elites and traditional religious authorities. Starting in the nineteenth century, printed books and periodicals, soon combined with photography, opened the door for mass participation. While the introduction of these media in both the Middle East and South Asia occurred largely in the context of European colonial projects and fostered the formation of modern nation-states, it also created the space for alternate, at times counter-hegemonic, sovereignties and

[27] R. Milstein, "*Futuh al-Haramayn:* Sixteenth-Century Illustrations of the Hajj Route," in David J. Wasserstein and Amy Ayalon (eds.), *Mamluks and Ottomans: Studies in Honour of Michael Winter* (London, New York: Routledge, 2006), 166–194.

[28] Roxburgh, "Visualizing the Sites," 38; M. A. S. Abdel Haleem, "The Importance of Hajj: Spirit and Rituals," in V. Porter with M. A. S. Abdel Haleem et al., *Hajj: Journey to the Heart of Islam* (Cambridge, MA: Harvard University Press, 2012), 54–55.

[29] V. Porter, *The Art of Hajj* (Northampton, MA: Interlink Books, 2012), 42–43; A. Lézine, *Trois palais d'Epoque Ottomane au Caire* (Cairo: Institut Français d'Archéologie Orientale, 1972), 26, 41 and plates XXIV B and L A.

subjectivities. The "imagined communities" that arose included those framed in terms of religion and sacred landscapes, as well as those defined by secular nationalism and national territory. In the contexts of Saudi Arabia and India, these different communal currents both clashed and joined in intimate embrace.

Early photography of the Hajj rituals and their sacred Arabian landscape was done by agents of the palace, but made more widely available in the form of books and postcards.[30] The first photographs were taken in 1880 and included in albums prepared for Sultan Abdulhamid II (r. 1876–1909), who used them to project Ottoman strength to the West and promote Muslim unity in his empire and beyond.[31] They include panoramic views of Mecca and the Sacred Mosque, pilgrims at the Kaʿba, encamped at Mina, and assembling at ʿArafat. Pictures of the Sacred Mosque were taken from several positions so as to display all its features and their relative locations. Muhammad Sadiq Bey, an Egyptian officer, was one of the photographers who contributed to Abdulhamid II's albums. His photographs won international awards and were published in European and Arab magazines. In 1896, he published his own Hajj manual.[32] Although he expressed some reservations about photographing the holy sites, he composed the following verses to be included with his pictures, suggesting the affective impact of visual engagement with the Kaʿba:

> My heart has captured your presence
> In Kaʿba's grace and radiance,
> Your parting burns my heart,
> Yet aren't photographers supposed to burn in fire?
> Thee have I drawn on paper
> In friendship and recollection.[33]

[30] A history of early photography in Mecca and the Hajj is provided by C. E. S. Gavin at the beginning of F. E. Peters, *Mecca: A Literary History of the Muslim Holy Land* (Princeton University Press, 1994) and Peters, *The Hajj*.

[31] The earliest known photographs of Mecca and Medina are found in at least six of the 911 Yildiz Albums, which documented Ottoman cities and towns, and even capitals in Europe, India, and Central Asia. Fifty-one albums were sent as gifts to governments and heads of state, including England, France, and the United States; see M. B. Dorduncu, *Mecca-Medina: The Yildiz Albums of Sultan Abdulhamid II*, tr. H. Yesilova (Somerset, NJ: The Light, Inc., 2006). Abdulhamid II's appeal for Muslim unity in the face of European expansion is known as pan-Islamism.

[32] R. Irwin, "Journey to Mecca: A History (Part 2)," in Porter et al., *Hajj*, 208; J. De St. Jorre, "Pioneer Photographer of the Holy Cities," *Saudi Aramco World*, 50, 1 (1999): 36–47.

[33] Quoted in De St. Jorre, "Pioneer Photographer." Sadiq Bey's wife died in Mecca during their Hajj in 1884, so these verses may imply the sense of loss he experienced with her parting, as well as emotions evoked by his vision of the Kaʿba.

It was not long before others followed in Sadiq's path, combining photographs with personal reflections on their Hajj experience. Egyptian army officer Ibrahim Rifʿat Pasha joined four state-sponsored Hajj caravans from Cairo to Mecca between 1901 and 1908, serving as the "commander" (*amīr*) or leader of three of them. His pilgrim account, *Mirʾāt al-ḥaramayn* ("Mirror of the Two Sanctuaries"), was published in Egypt in 1925, accompanied by over 400 photographs, many of which he had taken himself.[34] Confessing that words alone would not suffice to convey the "reality" and "splendor" of what he saw, he states that his aim was "to register everything I find and photograph everything I notice so that I supplement informing you (*ikhbār*) … with visualization (*mushāhada*); it will seem as if you are seeing the holy places in person."[35] It is in this sense that Rifʿat uses the word *mirror* in the title of his book – bringing the reader/viewer into the sacred landscape virtually, if not physically. His photographs depicted the major pilgrimage sites, but unlike the pre-modern iconic representations, they also documented specific features, pilgrim crowds, and important personages.[36] In addition, Rifʿat provided statistical tables, detailed topographical maps, and floor plans, reflecting his training in engineering and modern cartography. Although he opened his book with five lengthy Qurʾan selections pertaining to pilgrimage and followed the age-old convention of praising God and the Prophet, the work is the product of new print technologies and is shaped by a modern epistemology of representation. Like many Muslim writers have done since, he saw the Hajj rites and the preservation of Islam's sacred landscape as instrumental to bridging ethnic, linguistic, and geographic divisions in the Umma and uniting all Muslims at a time when many Muslim lands were under foreign rule. He intended his book to serve this end. Like Sadiq, he was not concerned with offending Sunni Muslim norms prohibiting images, nor did these appear to be a significant issue with his publishers and readers and viewers.

Early printed Hajj accounts and guidebooks were not only produced in the Arab Middle East; they were also being published in Urdu for Indian Muslims, with the first appearing in the 1870s. While some contained printed images in the style of the pre-modern simultaneous and elevated

34 Ibrāhīm Rifʿat Pāshā, *Mirʾāt al-ḥaramayn*, 2 vols. (Beirut: Dār al-Maʿrifa, 1982 (?) [1925]).

35 Rifʿat Pāshā, *Mirʾāt al-ḥaramayn*, I, 3.

36 The author uses the Arabic term *rasm* for a photograph, which originally denotes a mark, sign, or relic. He does not use the term *ṣūra*, which is the conventional term for photograph today.

images, they soon included photographs and floor plans like those found in the accounts published by Sadiq and Rifʿat. Some featured block print pictures of pilgrims performing Hajj rites, such as the depiction of pilgrims, both men and women, standing on the plain of ʿArafat included in a 1915 pilgrim account.[37]

One of the most remarkable collections of Hajj photographs intended for Indian Muslims was that published by H. A. Mirza and Sons of Delhi. These photographs were issued in album format and as postcards in 1907. Indian artists had been involved in the production of Hajj certificates centuries before; now, with the advent of photography, Indian artisans made effective use of the new medium. Moreover, as I have argued was the case with pre-modern Hajj landscape images, these served devotional as well as descriptive ends, as pointed out in Asani and Gavin's study of them.[38] Each photo was accompanied by Urdu verse and commentary. For example, the first picture is one that looks down at Mecca, centered on the Sacred Mosque and the Kaʿba as seen from Mt. Abū Qubays on the northeast side. Verses above the picture declare,

> This is Mecca, the beloved residence of God.
> Within it is his house, the sacred house.
> All the virtues of the world are perfected in it;
> Blessings from on high descend here day and night.

The commentary then provides a list of thirteen other pilgrimage sites in Mecca, most of which are connected with Muhammad, his family, and Companions.[39] None has a direct connection with the Hajj rituals; rather, they reflect the devotional concerns of Indian Muslims. According to Asani and Gavin, "The advent of photography made available for Muslims a revolutionary way of depicting their holy places with much greater immediacy, for photographs could visually transport viewers to the actual site."[40] Revolutionary it was, yet the photos nevertheless relied upon a centuries-old tradition of visualizing Mecca's sacred landscapes to convey their meaning.

[37] B. D. Metcalf, "The Pilgrimage Remembered: South Asian Accounts of the Hajj," in Dale Eickelman and James Piscatori (eds.), *Muslim Travelers: Pilgrimage, Migration and the Religious Imagination* (London: Routledge; and Berkeley: University of California Press, 1990), 85–107, fig. 10.

[38] A. S. Asani and C. E. S. Gavin, "Through the Lens of Mirza of Delhi: The Dabbas Album of Early Twentieth-Century Photographs of Pilgrimage Sites in Mecca and Medina," *Murqarnas*, 15 (1998), 178–199.

[39] Asani and Gavin, "Through the Lens," 182–183.

[40] Asani and Gavin, "Through the Lens," 180.

In a study about the rise of Indian calendar art, Kajri Jain has argued that modern pictorial image making was a colonial project that began in the latter part of the nineteenth century. It involved vernacular counter-projects and appropriations to deploy mass cultural forms in the service of giving expression to a civilizational essence. In this project, the vernacular became conjoined with religious devotion, aesthetics, commerce, social relations, and a bureaucratic-technological infrastructure.[41] Although Jain's work is primarily concerned with modern Hindu devotional art, I contend that the early production and distribution of photographic images of the Hajj and its landscapes offer an analogous case, except that it was linked to the development of a modern globalized Islamic identity rather than a national Indian one imbued with Hindu religious iconography.

The emergence of polychrome print posters and calendars with vernacular themes does not appear to have occurred in the Middle East until the 1930s and 1940s. Inexpensive depictions of Mecca and Medina were produced and sold in Egypt, Syria, Turkey, and India-Pakistan.[42] These images, often based on early twentieth-century photographs, were usually purchased from commercial outlets during Muslim holidays and at vendors adjacent to mosques and shrines. They were subsequently mounted for display in homes, businesses, mosques, and shrines. Smaller prints could be placed in vehicles. Consumers of these products of material culture believe that they can be conveyors of blessing, talismans against evil and misfortune, or indicators of piety. The images can be divided into three groups, depending on composition of the landscape: (1) the Sacred Mosque and the Kaʿba with surrounding urban structures; (2) the Kaʿba surrounded by a circle of other prominent Muslim holy sites; and (3) the Kaʿba together with the Prophet's Mosque in Medina, as if they were in actual contiguity. In the last type, the surrounding landscape is minimized or omitted completely, suggesting that the images of Kaʿba and the Prophet's Mosque had attained full iconic status. Most posters included verses from the Qurʾan, the *shahāda* (testimony of faith), the *basmala* (the

[41] K. Jain, *Gods in the Bazaar: The Economies of Indian Calendar Art* (Durham, NC: Duke University Press, 2007), 92.

[42] Examples of Cairo posters in the 1950s can be found in R. Kriss and H. Kriss-Heinrich, *Volksglaube im Bereich des Islam*, 2 vols. (Wiesbaden: Otto Harrassowitz, 1960–1962), vol. 1. A large collection of examples, mostly from Pakistan, is available in S. Stocchi, *L'Islam nella stampe/Islam in Prints* (Milan: Be-Ma Editrice, 1988). The most complete study of Islamic poster art in India is Y. Saeed, *Muslim Devotional Art in India* (London: Routledge, 2012).

phrase "In the name of God, full of Compassion, ever Compassionate"), or the names of God and Muhammad. Human figures may be completely absent, unlike the photographs, but this is not always the case. A South Asian subgenre portrayed pious boys and attractive women at prayer or reading the Qur'an, with the Ka'ba/Prophet's Mosque displayed in the background.[43] Other religious subjects for this genre included pictures of Sufi and Shi'ite shrines and saints, and al-Burāq, the winged steed that miraculously carried Muhammad from Mecca to Jerusalem and the seven heavens.

Production of vernacular polychrome posters of such variety flourished in the Middle East until the 1970s, but dropped off significantly thereafter, to be replaced by ones featuring only Qur'anic calligraphy and arabesque designs; the Ka'ba and the Prophet's Mosque also remain ubiquitous. The decline of colorful poster art containing other vernacular devotional subjects occurred later in South Asia, around the turn of this century. This may merely reflect a change in cultural fashions, or the development of new visual technologies, but the driving force was more likely a widespread turn to Salafī-style Islam, which favors scripture over image for devotional display.

In Egypt's countryside and working class neighborhoods, local artists and family members create vernacular representations of the Hajj landscape and the Prophet's Mosque in Medina, combined with pilgrim caravans, oasis vistas, boats, airplanes, animals, calligraphy, and talismanic symbols on the walls of pilgrim houses and apartments.[44] This practice, which celebrated a family member's pilgrimage, can be dated to as early as the sixteenth century, and has roots in Egypt's ancient past. It became especially popular when the number of Egyptian pilgrims increased in the 1970s and 1980s. The murals mirror scenes that occur in print posters, but they often are more spontaneous, displaying a much wider range of motifs and styles that situate them in the Egyptian milieu. This practice, like the devotional framing posters with figural motifs, underwent retraction in the 1990s and 2000s with the resurgence of Salafī activism.

Nonetheless, figural images of the Hajj and its landscape have been used by Islamist revolutionary movements too. This is especially evident in the polemical Hajj images created in the wake of the 1978–1979 Iranian Revolution and during the long Iran–Iraq war (1980–1988). During the

[43] Saeed, *Muslim Devotional Art*, figs. 1.13 and 4.15.

[44] J. E. Campo, *The Other Sides of Paradise: Explorations into the Religious Meanings of Domestic Space in Islam* (Columbia: University of South Carolina Press, 1991), ch. 6.

early 1970s, Ali Shariati and Ayatollah Ruhollah Khomeini both identified the Hajj as a vehicle for Muslims to confront worldly forces of corruption, division, and foreign hegemony. This discourse mobilized pilgrims to participate in protests while in Saudi Arabia on the Hajj, culminating in a clash between Iranians and Saudi security forces and the death of more than 400 people (mostly Iranian pilgrims) during the 1987 Hajj.[45] Iranian artist Habib Sadeghi (b. 1957) captured this confrontation in the painting *Ramy al-jamarāt* ("Stoning the Pillars of Satan"), which depicts a pilgrim dressed in pure white Hajj garb, radiant in a heavenly light, throwing stones at evil forces depicted in the form of soldiers wearing gas masks, hooded demons, and piles of money. Evoking Sufi mystical imagery, the Kaʿba is shown in place of the pilgrim's heart.[46] Other revolutionary paintings from this time depict the Kaʿba covered in blood, or being circumambulated by bodies of pilgrim martyrs, wrapped in shrouds bearing the emblem of the Iranian flag. Such images were meant to inspire a "visual piety" that would lead the viewer not only to sympathize with the subjects depicted, but to join in the battle against Iran's enemies at the time.

PILGRIMAGE LANDSCAPES GO DIGITAL

Visualizing the Hajj and its landscapes was both embedded in and facilitated by pre-modern and modern forms of mediation: oral, written, hand-drawn painting, block printing, print, photography, and chromolithography. This repertoire of technologies expanded exponentially in the twentieth century through film, television, digital photography, the Internet, personal computers, and eventually cellular phones and minicameras. On the basis of evidence available to us, for centuries the visualization of sacred landscapes – of the spaces and places of pilgrimage – fell within the purview of elites and religious virtuosos until the late nineteenth and early twentieth century, when mass mediation and visualization became possible. In her study of South Asian Hajj accounts, historian Barbara Metcalf finds that these accounts, published in print media, have increasingly provided opportunities "for constituting a persona, a

[45] M. Kramer, "Khomeini's Messengers in Mecca," in M. Kramer, *Arab Awakening and Islamic Revival: The Politics of Ideas in the Middle East* (New Brunswick: Transaction, 1996), 161–187.

[46] See "The New Karbala," in *The Graphics of Revolution and War: Iranian Poster Arts*, lib.uchicago.edu/e/webexhibits/iranianposters/ (last accessed April 11, 2014).

representation of a self that focuses on individual experiences, perceptions, and feelings, much like autobiographies ... Authors began to present themselves not only as observers but as active participants in what they describe: the hajji and not the hajj takes center stage."[47] Although we have seen that there have been pre-modern Hajj accounts with an autobiographical perspective, Metcalf is correct in claiming that more pilgrims have the ability today to pursue a desire for individuation, self-formation, and participation through their pilgrimage narratives.

If this has been the case with print media, it is even more so with modern electronic and digital media. Pilgrims to Mecca are creating their own websites, blog spots, Facebook pages, and online photo albums featuring images of Mecca and the Hajj, as Chapter 12 in this volume describes. Would-be pilgrims and others not only have access to pilgrim narratives, but also to photographs, videos, virtual tours, and Google maps that allow them to envision themselves as participants, or at least see the sacred landscape through the eyes of pilgrims.[48] In effect, the new visual media make pilgrimage more accessible to people well beyond traditional pilgrim "catchment areas"; they create opportunities for the production of multiple representations of pilgrimage landscapes, some deeply spiritual, others very much embedded in mundane practicalities and travel trivia. Multi-visuality, together with multi-vocality, has given women, recent converts, critics, and other marginalized groups an unprecedented space for expressing their views, although these, too, are governed by conventional speech, narrative and visual tropes, and communal notions of propriety.

The new media have also provided gatekeepers – government agencies, travel companies, and local governing bodies – opportunities to control visualization, as well as to regulate and facilitate access to the holy sites. For example, photography without a permit is officially forbidden in the Sacred Mosque in Mecca, although the proliferation of cell phones and mini-cameras have made this difficult to enforce. The ban is more honored in the breach than the observance, as evidenced by the number of "selfies" taken by pilgrims in front of the Kaʿba and elsewhere in the haram area.[49] Access to the Hajj landscape is highly regulated by the Saudi government

[47] Metcalf, "The Pilgrimage Remembered," 297.

[48] For a virtual tour of the hajj, see, e.g., www.hajjinformation.com/main/v100.htm (last accessed April 11, 2014).

[49] See, e.g., the advice provided a pilgrim blogger "Chenette" at thehajj.wordpress.com (last accessed April 11, 2014).

in cooperation with other governments and international agencies, especially with regard to restricting access (hence embodied visibility) only to Muslims. The official Hajj Ministry website provides lists of services it offers to pilgrims, guidelines for obtaining Hajj visas, a simplified Hajj map, and photographs featuring pilgrims at prayer in ʿArafat and Mecca. In addition to their religious content, the photographs also provide visual confirmation of Saudi claims that they are caring for the "safety and security" of God's guests.[50]

CONCLUSION: VISUALIZATION AND THE POLITICS OF CONCEALMENT

After his return from Hajj in 2008, Mujib, a Muslim living in the UK, posted the following words on the Hajj Story blog site:

> Pictures and photographs are displayed around London, houses, Mosques etc. But the real picture is the one I saw through my eyes. The Ka'ba The House of Allah Almighty. The house that unites all hearts.
>
> Since coming back home I have seen Makkah and Madinah in my dream. It is calling me back and I really miss it. I want to see it again, touch the Ka'ba as I did, pelt the jamarat and cover my ears away from the evil whispers of the nasty shaytaan.
>
> My dear respected brothers and sisters my words are nothing compared to what your eyes will see and explain for your self.
>
> Open Your Eyes![51]

This testimony reflects the three engagements identified by Morgan that a viewer can have with a sacred image. As interpolated in relation to the present topic, the viewer stands before the image of the sacred landscape, becomes drawn into it, and is enabled to go beyond it. When those engagements become deeply experienced, as they seem to have been by Mujib, they can become the basis by which others are enjoined to emulate, to both cross and dwell as he did.

Today, the Hajj attracts some three million pilgrims annually, and the Saudis are taking steps to accommodate even more. While a number of factors combined helped to make it a modern mass pilgrimage, the effectiveness of mass mediation technologies in facilitating visualizations of its sacred landscapes has been a significant contributing factor. These technologies of representation help foster the formation of

[50] The Saudi Hajj Ministry web portal is at haj.gov.sa (last accessed April 11, 2014).

[51] hajjstories.wordpress.com/ (last accessed April 11, 2014).

subjectivities that include a disposition to cross and dwell in a sacred landscape, both physically and imaginally.

By way of a conclusion, I quote from the concluding volume of Margaret Atwood's *Oryx and Crake* trilogy: "There's the story, then there's the real story, then there's the story of how the story came to be told. Then there's what you leave out of the story. Which is part of the story, too."[52] Visualizations, too, conceal as much or more than they reveal, and that concealment must be recognized.

What has been largely left out of my rendering of the story about visualizations of the Hajj and its landscapes is the ways in which they both conceal and reflect the workings of hegemonic forces. There are hints of this in the representations I have discussed in the foregoing pages – the patrons of the Hajj certificates, the mythic narratives of prophets, the Muslim elites who participated both in the production of representations and in the construction of the represented. Detailed elucidation for this part of the story will have to be deferred to another occasion, but here I would like to highlight some salient elements. For the Hajj landscape, it is a fact that mass pilgrimage combined with Saudi control of the territory of Islam's foremost holy places has resulted both in the monstrous amplification of Mecca's architecture with constructions that have effectively erased its architectural heritage, not to mention its natural topography. Many of the features described by al-Azraqī and Ibn Jubayr and depicted on Ottoman tiles and early photographs have been eradicated to create space for more pilgrims and accommodate massive structures for air-conditioned shopping malls, five-star hotels, and hundreds of time-share apartments. Since the mid-2000s, the dominant architectural feature in Mecca's landscape is the Abraj al-Bait (*abrāj al-bayt*, the Towers of the House of God) clock tower, the tallest of its kind in the world, built by the Saudi BinLadin Group. At a height of nearly 2,000 feet, it dwarfs the Sacred Mosque, the Kaʿba, and everything in sight.

This radical transformation of the Hajj landscape has elicited criticism among Muslims in some quarters, but how it informs visualization of the Hajj and its landscape in the future is yet to be determined. It is likely, however, that the more traditional visualizations will prevail in the hearts of pilgrims and would-be pilgrims for the foreseeable future.

[52] M. Atwood, *MaddAddam: A Novel* (New York: Nan A. Talese/Doubleday, 2013), 56.

Glossary

Abbasids a dynasty that ruled as Sunni Caliphs from 750 to 1258 CE mostly from Baghdad, the capital they founded in 764 CE; they take their name from a forbear, the Prophet Muhammad's uncle, al-ʿAbbās.

Ahl al-Bayt or Āl al-Bayt, lit. "Family of the House," i.e., members of the family of the Prophet Muhammad.

ʿArafat (**Ar.** *ʿArafāt, also ʿArafa*) a plain, some twenty kilometers east of Mecca. Travel there on the ninth of Dhū al-Ḥijja for the vigil or "halting" or "standing" (*wuqūf*) is a constituent ritual of the Hajj (but not the ʿUmra). Pilgrims are either out in the open or in tents.

Ayyubids a dynasty founded by Saladin (Ṣalāh al-Dīn, d. 589/1193), based in Egypt, that ruled over Syria-Palestine, and parts of Iraq and Yemen, from 1171 to 1250 CE; they were succeeded by the Mamluks.

Darb "route, road"; term used to describe the pilgrimage route to Mecca.

Dawoodi Bohoras a small Shiʿite Indian community descended from the Fatimids, with about one million adherents worldwide.

Dhū al-Ḥijja lit. "[Month] of pilgrimage"; the twelfth month of the lunar, Islamic calendar, in which the annual Hajj pilgrimage takes place, principally from the eighth to the tenth of the month.

Fatimids a Shiʿite dynasty that ruled Egypt, North Africa, and parts of the Levant and Hijaz from 909 to 1171 CE; the Fatimids ruled from Cairo, which they founded in 969. They were succeeded by the Ayyubids.

fatwa (**Ar.** *fatwā*) a formal legal opinion, issued by a *muftī*.

hadith (**Ar.** *ḥadīth*) an orally transmitted report going back to a companion of the Prophet Muhammad that recounts Muhammad's words, actions, and tacit approvals. The entire corpus of such reports is often also referred to in English as the Hadith (capitalized).

Hajj (Ar. ***ḥajj*****)** the annual pilgrimage to Mecca, on the designated days, namely eighth–twelfth of Dhū al-Ḥijja, the pilgrimage month; as one of the "pillars" of Islam, it is an obligation on every Muslim who is able.

ḥajjat al-wadāʿ lit. "the Farewell Pilgrimage"; the name given to the Prophet Muhammad's only pilgrimage, performed in 10/632, a few months before he died.

hajji (Ar. ***ḥājj, fem. ḥājja*****)** someone who has performed the Hajj

Ḥanafī a follower of the school of legal thought of the jurist Abū Ḥanīfa (d. 150/767), one of the four such schools in Sunni Islam.

Ḥanbalī a follower of the school of legal thought of the jurist Aḥmad ibn Ḥanbal (d. 241/855), one of the four such schools in Sunni Islam.

haram (Ar. ***ḥaram*****)** lit. "sacred" or "forbidden"; term used to describe the sacred enclave, or sacred precincts around the Kaʿba.

al-Haram al-Sharif (Ar. ***al-ḥaram al-sharīf*****)** lit. "The Noble Santuary"; designation of the mosques at Mecca, Medina, and Jerusalem, and often shortened to Haram.

Hāshimī a term applied from the Abbasid period on to descendants of the Prophet Muhammad; derived from the name of his forbear Hāshim, who, like Muhammad, belonged to the tribe of Quraysh.

Ḥaṭīm a semicircular low wall at the north and west corners of the Kaʿba, said to enclose the graves of Abraham's wife Hagar and their son Ishmael (Ismāʿīl); it is also known as Ḥijr Ismāʿīl.

Hijaz (Ar. ***Ḥijāz*****)** the western part of Arabia, where Mecca and Medina are located, and including the port city of Jeddah, long a gateway to the holy cities. Also called the Hejaz.

Hijr (Ar. ***ḥijr*****)** shortened name of the *Ḥijr Ismāʿīl* (sanctum of Ishmael), another name for the Ḥaṭīm (see above).

Eid al-Adha (Ar. ***ʿĪd al-aḍḥā*****)** lit. "Festival of Sacrifice"; celebrated on the tenth of Dhū al-Ḥijja, it is a high holiday for non-pilgrims and is the third day of the Hajj for pilgrims. Animals are sacrificed on that day, both by pilgrims and by Muslims around the world.

ʿĪd al-aḍḥā *see* Eid al-Adha.

ihram (Ar. ***iḥrām*****)** lit. "entry into the sacralized or consecrated state," i.e., the state required to undertake the pilgrimage; also the name of the garb worn in that state.

Ilkhanids a breakaway khanate from the Mongol empire, based principally in Persia and neighboring territories, from 1256 to 1353 CE.

imam (Ar. ***imām*****)** any male Muslim who leads other Muslims in prayer. Sunnis also use the term as a title for revered pious figures. Shiʿites use the term especially for those descendants of the Prophet whom they regard as his spiritual and temporal successors, and also for certain very high-ranking clerics.

iman (**Ar.** ***īmān***) faith, belief.

Kaʿba lit. "cube"; a cube-shaped stone shrine in Mecca which is circumambulated during the Hajj and ʿUmra. Pilgrimage to the Kaʿba predates Islam. Muhammad oriented prayer toward the Kaʿba in ca. 624, and emptied it of the idols that were kept there when the Muslims gained control of Mecca in 631 CE.

Labbayk short form of *Labbayk Allāhumma Labbayk*, a phrase meaning "I am here, God, I am here" or "At Your service, God, at Your service." Called the talbiya, this phrase is recited by those wishing to perform Hajj, and also ritually at various points during the Hajj.

mahmal (**Ar.** ***maḥmal***) a decorated palanquin perched on a camel, initially for private use and which in the medieval period were sent by rulers, to accompany the train of pilgrims, as symbols of rulership and sovereignty.

mahram (**Ar.** ***maḥram***) legal term for a person to whom one is not marriageable because of close family or other relationship.

Mālikī a follower of the school of legal thought of the jurist Malik ibn Anas (d. 179/796), one of four such schools in Sunni Islam.

Mamluks (**Ar.** ***mamlūk***) The Mamluk Sultanate was a dynasty that ruled Egypt, the Levant, and Hijaz from the fall of the Ayyubids in 1250 CE until the Ottoman conquest of the Levant and Egypt in 1517 CE.

manāsik pilgrimage rituals.

al-Marwa see al-Ṣafā.

mīqāt the various designated locations encircling Mecca that mark the points by which pilgrims must have entered the state (and garb) of ihram.

Mina a town a few kilometers outside Mecca where pilgrims first go when performing the Hajj (on the eighth of Dhū al-Ḥijja) and to which they will return from ʿArafat and Muzdalifa (on the tenth) to stone the representations of Satan, sacrifice animals, and cut or shave their hair. Pilgrims are housed in tents.

mutawwif (**Ar.** ***muṭawwif***) lit. "guide for the tawaf"; the term is broadly applied to individuals involved in guiding pilgrims on all aspects of the Hajj. The terms *muʿallim* ("instructor"), *muzawwir* ("guide, principally used in Medina), and *shaykh* ("elder") are also common.

Muzdalifa a plain halfway between ʿArafat and Mina where pilgrims spend a night vigil, between the ninth and tenth of Dhū al-Ḥijja, and where they gather the pebbles they will use in the stoning ritual in Mina.

niyya intention, usually enunciated, before performing any act or ritual.

Ottomans an empire founded by Turks in Anatolia in 1299 CE, who then ruled large portions of the central Islamic lands, including the Hijaz. When they captured Constantinople in 1453 CE, they renamed it Istanbul and ruled from there until 1922.

Qur'an (Ar. *al-Qur'ān*) lit. "Recitation"; the scripture of Islam, believed by Muslims to have been revealed by God to the Prophet Muhammad through the Archangel Gabriel, and regarded as immutable.

al-Ṣafā a hillock several hundred meters from another hillock, al-Marwa. Hagar is said to have run between these two hills in search of water for her infant Ismāʿīl (Ishmael), Abraham's son. The brisk walking (Ar. *saʿy*) ritual is said to be a reenactment of this.

Salafi from Arabic *salaf*, "[pious] predecessors"; denotes a conservative, anti-clerical modernist strain of Islam, though it is often used uncarefully to describe any Muslim who espouses conservative religious views.

saʿy the brisk running between the hillocks of al-Ṣafā and al-Marwa in Mecca, a constituent ritual of both Hajj and ʿUmra.

Shāfiʿī a follower of the school of legal thought of the jurist al-Shāfiʿī (d. 204/820), one of four such schools in Sunni Islam.

Shiʿite from Arabic *shīʿī* ("partisan"), from *shīʿat* ("party [of ʿAlī ibn Abī Ṭālib]"); broadly any person who believes that the only legitimate successors of the Prophet Muhammad are his descendants.

siqaya (Ar. *siqāya*) the provision of water to pilgrims.

Sunni from Arabic *ahl al-sunna wal-jamāʿa*, "people of the custom [of the Prophet Muhammad] and consensus," i.e., someone who follows the exemplary practice of Muhammad and of the early Muslim community.

sürre a Turkish word, from Ar. *surra*, lit. "purse"; a term that came to designate all expenses relating to the pilgrimage caravan under the Ottomans.

talbiya *see* Labbayk.

tawaf (Ar. *ṭawāf*) a constituent ritual of the Hajj and ʿUmra involving seven counterclockwise circumambulations of the Kaʿba.

umma term used to describe the totality or entire community of Muslims.

ʿUmra the voluntary pilgrimage to Mecca, accomplished any time during the year, and taking only a few hours. Pilgrims performing the annual Hajj will also perform one ʿUmra (or more). Unlike the Hajj, its rituals are confined to the Haram.

Wahhabi an austere and conservative religious movement, revivalist when it was founded in the eighteenth century, associated with the Saudi political regime and juridical establishment. *Wahhabi* is sometimes (imprecisely) used interchangeably with *Salafi*. The term is derived from the name of Ibn ʿAbd al-Wahhāb (d. 1792), whose followers reject this label and term themselves *muwaḥḥidūn* ("strict monotheists").

waqf a pious or religious endowment, usually charitable, made by an individual; it is through waqfs that such establishments as mosques, law colleges, travelers' hostels, and way-stations are maintained.

wuqūf lit. "standing"; a term applied to the vigil at ʿArafat (and also Muzdalifa).

Zamzam the name of the wellspring, and the water that flows from it, said to have been discovered by Hagar when she searched for drink for her infant, Ismāʿīl (Ishmael).

Zaydī a Shiʿite sect, the adherents of which predominate in Yemen.

Works Cited

INTRODUCTION

Allen, R. and S. M. Toorawa. *Islam: A Short Guide to the Faith*. Grand Rapids, MI: William B. Eerdmans Pub., 2011.

Bianchi, R. R. *Guests of God: Pilgrimage and Politics in the Islamic World*. New York: Oxford University Press, 2004.

Brower, B. C. *A Desert Named Peace: The Violence of France's Empire in the Algerian Sahara*. New York: Columbia University Press, 2009.

Bunt, G. R. *iMuslims: Rewiring the House of Islam*. Chapel Hill: University of North Carolina Press; London: C. Hurst & Co, 2009.

Campo, J. *The Other Sides of Paradise: Explorations into the Religious Meanings of Domestic Space in Islam*. Columbia: University of South Carolina Press, 1991.

Chekhab-Abudaya, M. and C. Bresc (eds.). *Hajj: The Journey through Art*. Milan: Skira, 2013.

Chiffoleau, S. and A. Madoeuf (eds.). *Les pèlerinages au Maghreb et au Moyen-Orient: espaces publics, espaces de public*. Beirut: Institut français du Proche-Orient, 2005.

Gaudefroy-Demombynes, M. *Le pèlerinage à la Mekke*. Paris: P. Geuthner, 1923.

al-Ghabbân, A. I. *Les deux routes syrienne et égyptienne de pèlerinage au nord-ouest de l'Arabie Saoudite*. 2 vols. Cairo: Institut français d'archéologie orientale, 2011.

Huber, V. *Channeling Mobilities: Migration and Globalisation in the Suez Canal Region and Beyond, 1869–1914*. Cambridge University Press, 2013.

McMillan, M. E. *The Meaning of Mecca: The Politics of Pilgrimage in Early Islam*. London: Saqi Books, 2011.

Mols, L. and M. Buitelaar (eds.). *Hajj: Global Interactions through Pilgrimage*. Leiden: Sidestone Press, 2014.

Munt, H. *The Holy City of Medina: Sacred Space in Early Arabia*. Cambridge University Press, 2014.

Peters, F. E. *The Hajj: The Muslim Pilgrimage to Mecca and the Holy Places*. Princeton University Press, 1994.

Peters, F. E. *A Literary History of the Muslim Holy Land*. Princeton University Press, 1994.
Petersen, A. *The Medieval and Ottoman Hajj Route in Jordan: An Archaeological and Historical Study*. Oxford: Oxbow, 2012.
Porter, V. *The Art of Hajj*. Northampton, MA: Interlink Books, 2012.
Porter, V. (ed.). *Hajj: Journey to the Heart of Islam*. Cambridge, MA: Harvard University Press, 2012.
Rush, A. (ed.). *Records of the Hajj*. 10 vols. Slough: Archive Editions, 1993.
al-Sarhan, S. "Early Muslim Traditionalism: A Critical Study of the Works and Political Theology of Ahmad Ibn Hanbal." Unpublished PhD thesis. University of Exeter, 2011.
Sayeed, A. *Women and the Transmission of Religious Knowledge in Islam*. Cambridge University Press, 2013.
Tagliacozzo, E. *The Longest Journey: Southeast Asians and the Pilgrimage to Mecca*. New York: Oxford University Press, 2013.
Wolfe, M. *One Thousand Roads to Mecca: Ten Centuries of Travelers Writing about the Muslim Pilgrimage*. rev. expanded ed. New York: Grove Press, 2015.
Zadeh, T. *Mapping Frontiers Across Medieval Islam: Geography, Translation and the ʿAbbāsid Empire*. London and New York: I. B. Tauris, 2011.

CHAPTER 1

Classical Sources

al-Azraqī. *Akhbār Makka wa-mā jāʾa fīhā min al-āthār*. Ed. R. Malḥas. 2 vols. Beirut: Dār al-Andalus, n.d.
Diodorus Siculus. *Bibliotheca Historica*. Ed. and trans. C. H. Oldfather et al. 12 vols. London: William Heinemann, 1933–1967.
Epiphanius, *Panarion*. Trans. F. Williams. 2 vols. Leiden: Brill, 1987–1994.
al-Hamdānī. *Al-Iklīl*. Ed. N. A. Faris. Book 8. Beirut: Dār al-ʿAwda, n.d.
al-Hamdānī. *Al-Iklīl*. Ed. M.-D. al-Khaṭīb. Book 10. Cairo: al-Maṭbaʿa al-Salafiyya, 1368/1949.
Jerome. *Life of Hilarion*. Trans. C. White. *Early Christian Lives*. Ed. C. White. London: Penguin, 1998.
Photius. *Bibliotheca*. Ed. and trans. R. Henry. 9 vols. Paris: Société d'Édition « Les Belles Lettres », 1959–1991.
Photius. *Bibliotheca: A Selection*. Trans. N. G. Wilson. London: Duckworth, 1994.
Pliny. *Naturalis Historia*. Ed. and trans. H. Rackham et al. 10 vols. London: William Heinemann, 1938–1963.
Procopius. *History of the Wars*. Ed. and trans. H. B. Dewing. 5 vols. London: William Heinemann, 1914–1928.
Strabo. *Geography*. Ed. and trans. H. L. Jones. 8 vols. London: William Heinemann, 1917–1932.
Wilkinson, J. *Egeria's Travels*. 3rd ed. Oxford: Aris & Phillips, 1999.
Wilkinson, J. *Jerusalem Pilgrims before the Crusades*. Warminster: Aris & Phillips, 1977.

Secondary Literature

Alpass, P. *The Religious Life of Nabataea*. Leiden: Brill, 2013.
Beeston, A. F. L. et al. *Sabaic Dictionary (English-French-Arabic)*. Leuven: Peeters, 1982.
Biella, J. C. *Dictionary of Old South Arabic: Sabaean Dialect*. Chico, CA: Scholars Press, 1982.
Bitton-Ashkelony, B. *Encountering the Sacred: The Debate on Christian Pilgrimage in Late Antiquity*. Berkeley: University of California Press, 2005.
Bowersock, G. W. "Nonnosus and Byzantine Diplomacy in Arabia." *Rivista storica italiana* 124 (2012): 282–290.
Breton, J.-F. "Shabwa, capitale antique du Ḥaḍramawt." *Journal Asiatique* 275 (1987): 13–34.
Brown, W. L. and A. F. L. Beeston. "Sculptures and Inscriptions from Shabwa." *Journal of the Royal Asiatic Society* 86, 1–2 (1954): 43–62.
Crone, P. *Meccan Trade and the Rise of Islam*. Oxford: Blackwell, 1987.
Dentzer, J.-M. "Développement et culture de la Syrie du sud dans la période préprovinciale (ier s. avant J.-C. – ier s. après J.-C.)." In J.-M. Dentzer (ed.), *Hauran i: recherches archéologiques sur la Syrie du sud à l'époque hellénistique et romaine*. Paris: Paul Geuthner, 1986: 387–420.
Dentzer-Feydy, J. et al. (eds.). *Hauran ii. Les installations de Sīʿ 8: du sanctuaire à l'établissement viticole*. Beirut: Institut Français d'Archéologie du Proche-Orient, 2003.
Elsner, J. "The Itinerarium Burdigalense: Politics and Salvation in the Geography of Constantine's Empire." *Journal of Roman Studies* 90 (2000): 181–195.
Fisher, G. *Between Empires: Arabs, Romans, and Sasanians in Late Antiquity*. Oxford University Press, 2011.
al-Ghabbân, A. I. *Les deux routes syrienne et égyptienne de pèlerinage au nord-ouest de l'Arabie Saoudite*. 2 vols. Cairo: Institut français d'archéologie orientale, 2011.
Ghul M. A. and A. F. L. Beeston. "The Pilgrimage at Itwat." *Proceedings of the Seminar for Arabian Studies* 14 (1984): 33–39.
Goodman, M. "The Pilgrimage Economy of Jerusalem in the Second Temple period." In L. I. Levine (ed.), *Jerusalem: Its Sanctity and Centrality to Judaism, Christianity, and Islam*. New York: Continuum, 1999: 69–76.
Harding, G. L. "The Cairn of Haniʾ." *Annual of the Department of Antiquities of Jordan* 2 (1953): 8–56.
al-Hawas, F. et al. "Taqrīr awwalī ʿan aʿmāl al-tanqībāt al-athariyya bi-madīnat Fayd al-taʾrīkhiyya bi-minṭaqat Ḥāʾil (al-mawsim al-awwal 1427h. – 2006 m.)." *al-Aṭlāl* 20 (1431/2010): 31–53.
Hawting, G. R. *The Idea of Idolatry and the Emergence of Islam: From Polemic to History*. Cambridge University Press, 1999.
Hawting, G. R. "The 'Sacred Offices' of Mecca from Jāhiliyya to Islam." *Jerusalem Studies in Arabic and Islam* 13 (1990): 62–84.
Healey, J. F. *The Religion of the Nabataeans: A Conspectus*. Leiden: Brill, 2001.
Hoyland, R. G. *Arabia and the Arabs from the Bronze Age to the Coming of Islam*. London: Routledge, 2001.
al-Iryānī, M. ʿA. *Fī taʾrīkh al-Yaman*. Cairo: Dār al-Hanā, 1973.

Kaizer, T. *The Religious Life of Palmyra: A Study of the Social Patterns of Worship in the Roman Period*. Stuttgart: Franz Steiner, 2002.
Kister, M. J. "'Rajab Is the Month of God ... ' A Study in the Persistence of an Early Tradition." *Israel Oriental Studies* 1 (1971): 192–223.
Kitchen, K. A. *Documentation for Ancient Arabia*. 2 vols. Liverpool University Press, 1994–2000.
Knauf, E. A. "More Notes on Ǧabal Qurma, Minaeans and Safaites." *Zeitschrift des deutschen Palästina-Vereins* 107 (1991): 92–101.
Korotayev, A. "Religion and Society in Southern Arabia and among the Arabs." *Arabia* 1 (2003): 65–76.
Korotayev [Korotaev], A., V. Kilmenko, and D. Proussakov. "Origins of Islam: Political-Anthropological and Environmental Context." *Acta Orientalia Academiae Scientiarum Hungaricae* 52 (1999): 243–276.
Littmann, E. *Syria: Publications of the Princeton University Archaeological Expeditions to Syria in 1904–5 and 1909, Division IV, Semitic Inscriptions, Section C, Safaïtic Inscriptions*. Leiden: Brill, 1943.
Macdonald, M. C. A. "Arabs, Arabias, and Arabic before Late Antiquity." *Topoi* 16 (2009): 277–332.
Macdonald, M. C. A. "Nomads and the Ḥawrān in the Late Hellenistic and Roman Periods: A Reassessment of the Epigraphic Evidence." *Syria* 70 (1993): 303–403.
Macdonald, M. C. A. "References to Sīʿ in the Safaitic Inscriptions." In J. Dentzer-Feydy et al. (eds.), *Hauran ii. Les installations de Sīʿ 8: du sanctuaire à l'établissement viticole*. Beirut: Institut Français d'Archéologie du Proche-Orient, 2003: 278–280.
Macdonald, M. C. A. "Reflections on the Linguistic Map of Pre-Islamic Arabia." *Arabian Archaeology and Epigraphy* 11 (2000): 28–79.
McCorriston, J. *Pilgrimage and Household in the Ancient Near East*. Cambridge: Cambridge University Press, 2011.
Millar, F. *The Roman Near East, 31 BC – AD 337*. Cambridge, MA: Harvard University Press, 1993.
Niehr, H. *Baʿalšamen: Studien zu Herkunft, Geschichte und Rezeptionsgeschichte eines phönizischen Gottes*. Leuven: Peeters, 2003.
Peters, F. E. *The Hajj: The Muslim Pilgrimage to Mecca and the Holy Places*. Princeton University Press, 1994.
Peters, F. E. *Mecca: A Literary History of the Muslim Holy Land*. Princeton University Press, 1994.
Pirenne, J. *Les témoins écrits de la région de Shabwa et l'histoire*. Paris: Paul Geuthner, 1990.
Robin, C. *Inventaire des inscriptions sudarabiques, tome 1: Inabbaʾ, Haram, al-Kāfir, Kamna et al-Ḥarāshif*. Paris: De Boccard, 1992.
Robin, C.-J. "Arabia and Ethiopia." In S. F. Johnson (ed.), *The Oxford Handbook of Late Antiquity*. Oxford University Press, 2012: 297–306.
Robin, C. J. "Ḥimyar et Israël." *Comptes rendus des séances de l'année: académie des inscriptions et belles-lettres* (2004): 831–906.

Robin, C.-J. and J.-F. Breton. "Le sanctuaire préislamique du Ǧabal al-Lawḏ (Nord-Yémen)." *Comptes rendus des séances de l'année: académie des inscriptions et belles-lettres* (1982): 610–616.
Roche, M.-J. "Remarques sur les Nabatéens en Méditerranée." *Semitica* 45 (1996): 73–99.
Ryckmans, J. "Himyaritica (5)." *Le muséon* 88 (1975): 199–219.
Ryckmans, J. "Les inscriptions sud-arabes anciennes et les études arabes." *Annali dell'Istituto Orientale di Napoli* 35 (1975): 443–463.
Ryckmans, J. "Le repas rituel dans la religion sud-arabe." In M. A. Beek et al. (eds.), *Symbolae biblicae et mesopotamicae Francisco Mario Theodoro de Liagre Böhl dedicatae*. Leiden: Brill, 1973: 327–334.
Serjeant, R. B. "Haram and Hawtah: The Sacred Enclave in Arabia." In A. Badawi (ed.), *Mélanges Taha Husain: offerts par ses amis et disciples à l'occasion de son 70ième anniversaire*. Cairo: Dār al-Ma'ārif, 1962: 41–58.
Shahîd, I. *Byzantium and the Arabs in the Sixth Century*. 2 vols. Washington, DC: Dumbarton Oaks, 1995–2009.
Solá Solé, J. M. *Sammlung Eduard Glaser iv: Inschriften aus Riyām*. Vienna: Harmann Böhlaus, 1964.
Tarrier, D. "Banquets rituels en Palmyrène et en Nabatène." *ARAM* 7 (1995): 165–182
Turner, V. "The Center out There: Pilgrims' Goals." *History of Religions* 12 (1973): 191–230.
Wheeler, B. "Models of Pilgrimage: From Communitas to Confluence." *Journal of Ritual Studies* 13 (1999): 26–41.
Winnett, F. V. and G. L. Harding. *Inscriptions from Fifty Safaitic Cairns*. University of Toronto Press, 1978.

CHAPTER 2

Print sources

Aḥmad, S. *Mu'allim al-ḥujjāj*. Karachi: Maktaba al-Bushra, 2011.
al-Ālūsī, *Rūḥ al-ma'ānī*. 30 vols. Beirut: Dār Iḥyā' al-Turāth al-'Arabī, 1999.
al-Būṭī. *Fiqh al-sīra al-nabawiyya*. Damascus: Dār al-Fikr, 1996.
al-Ghazālī. *Inner Dimensions of Islamic Worship*. Trans. Muhtar Holland. Leicester: The Islamic Foundation, 1983.
Ibn al-Naqīb. *Reliance of the Traveller: The Classic Manual of Islamic Sacred Law*. Trans. N. H. Keller. Beltsville, MD: Amana Publications, 1994.
Kandahlawi, M. Z. *Faḍā'il-e Hajj*. Karachi: Maktaba al-Bushra, 2011.
al-Kharkūshī, *Sharaf al-Muṣṭafā*. Mecca: Dār al-Bashā'ir al-Islāmiyya, 2003.
Lings, M. *Muhammad: His Life Based on the Earliest Sources*. Rochester, VT: Inner Traditions International, 1983.
al-Qurṭubī. *Tafsīr al-Qurṭubī al-jāmi' li-aḥkām al-Qur'ān*. 4 vols. Cairo: Dār al-Sha'b, 1961.
Reinhart, R. K. "Haram." In J. L. Esposito (gen. ed.), *Oxford Encyclopedia of the Islamic World*. 6 vols. New York: Oxford University Press, 2009: II, 379.

Thānawī, B. Z. A. *Taskīn-i Hajj-o 'Umra ma'a khawātin ke khususi masa'il.* Karachi: Kutub Khana Mazhari, n.d.
Thānawī, A. A. *Zād al-Sa'īd.* Lahore: Ummi Press, n.d.
Usmānī, M. M. Shafi' *Ma'āriful-Qur'ān.* Trans. M. H. Askari and M. Shamim. Rev. M. Taqi Usmani. 6 vols. Karachi: Maktaba-e Darul-Uloom, 1996–2005.
Zāyid, S. *Mukhtaṣar al-Jāmi' fī al-sīra al-nabawiyya.* 6 vols. Damascus: al-Maṭba'a al-'Ilmiyya, 1995.

Online sources

Genesis, New International Version. 17:20 (NIV). Retrieved from biblegateway.com/passage/?search=Genesis+17
Ibn 'Āshūr, *al-Taḥrīr wa-l-tanwīr.* Retrieved from www.library.islamweb.net/newlibrary/display_book.php?idfrom=1746&idto=1746&bk_no=61&ID=1763
Yusuf Ali (trans.). *The Holy Qur'ān.* Retrieved from www.islamicity.com/quransearch/

CHAPTER 3

Primary Sources

'Abd al-Razzāq. *Al-Muṣannaf.* Ed. Ḥ. al-A'ẓamī. 11 vols. Beirut: al-Maktab al-Islāmī, 1970–1972.
Abū Yūsuf. *Kitāb al-Āthār.* Ed. A. al-Afghānī. Hyderabad: Lajnat Iḥyā' al-Ma'ārif al-Nu'māniyya, 1355/1936–1937.
Akhbār al-dawla al-'Abbāsiyya. Ed. 'A. al-Dūrī and 'A. al-Muṭṭalibī. Beirut: Dār al-Ṭalī'a, 1971.
al-Azraqī. *Akhbār Makka.* Ed. 'A. b. 'A. b. Duhaysh. 2 vols. Mecca: Maktabat al-Asadī, 2003.
al-Bakjarī. *Al-Zahr al-bāsim fī siyar Abī l-Qāsim.* Ed. A. A. 'Abd al-Shakūr. 2 vols. Beirut: Dār al-Salām, 2012.
al-Balādhurī. *Ansāb al-ashrāf.* Ed. S. Zakkār and R. Ziriklī. 13 vols. Beirut: Dār al-Fikr, 1996.
Bashshār ibn Bwd, *Dīwān*, ed. M. T. B. 'Āshūr, 4 Vols. Cairo: Lajnat al-Ta'līf wa-l-Tarjama wa-l-Nashr, 1950.
al-Bayhaqī. *Ma'rifat al-sunan wa-l-āthār.* Ed. 'A. A. Qal'ajī. 15 vols. Cairo: Dār al-Wa'ī, 1991.
al-Dīnawarī. *Akhbār al-ṭiwāl.* Ed. 'U. F. al-Ṭabbā'. Beirut: Dār al-Arqam ibn al-Arqam, 1995.
al-Fākihī. *Akhbār Makka.* Ed. 'A. b. 'A. b. Duhaysh. 6 vols. Beirut: Dār Khiḍr, 1994.
al-Ḥasan al-Baṣrī (attributed). *Faḍā'il Makka.* Ed. M. Z, M. 'Azab. Cairo: Maktabat al-Thaqāfa al-Dīniyya, 1995.
Ibn 'Abd Rabbih. *Al-'Iqd al-farīd.* Ed. M. M. Qumayḥa. 9 vols. Beirut: Dār al-Kutub al-'Ilmiyya, 1983.

Ibn al-Faqīh. *Kitāb al-Buldān*. Ed. Y. Hādī. Beirut: ʿĀlam al-Kutub, 1996.
Ibn Ḥabīb. *Kitāb al-Muḥabbar*. Ed. I. Lichtenstadter. Hyderabad: Dāʾirat al-Maʿārif al-ʿUthmāniyya, 1942.
Ibn Ḥajar al-ʿAsqalānī. *Tahdhīb al-tahdhīb*. Ed. I. al-Zaybaq and ʿĀ. Murshid. 4 vols. Beirut: Muʾassasat al-Risāla, 1996.
Ibn Ḥanbal. *Al-Musnad*. Ed. S. al-Arnāʾūṭ and ʿĀ. Murshid. 52 vols. Beirut: Muʾassasat al-Risāla, 1993–2001.
Ibn Hishām. *Al-Sīra al-nabawiyya*. Ed. M. al-Saqqā, I. al-Ibyārī, and ʿA. Shalabī. 2nd ed. Cairo: Maṭbaʿat al-Bābī al-Ḥalabī, 1955.
Ibn Khurdādhbih. *Al-Masālik wa-l-mamālik*. Ed. M. J. de Goeje. Leiden: E.J. Brill, 1889.
Ibn al-Nadīm. *Al-Fihrist*. Ed. Ayman Fuʾād Sayyid. 2 vols in 4. London: Al-Furqan Islamic Heritage Foundation, 2009.
Ibn Qutayba (ps.). *Kitāb al-Imāma wa-l-siyāsa*. Ed. ʿA. Shayrī. 2 vols. Beirut: Dār al-Aḍwāʾ, 1990.
Ibn Rusta. *Al-Aʿlāq al-nafīsa*. Ed. M. J. de Goeje. Leiden: E. J. Brill, 1882.
Ibn Saʿd. *Kitāb al-Ṭabaqāt al-kabīr*. Ed. ʿA. M. ʿUmar. 11 vols. Cairo: Maktabat al-Khānjī, 2001.
Ibn al-Sāʿī. *Nisāʾ al-khulafāʾ*. Ed. M. Jawād. Cairo: Dār al-Maʿārif, 1968.
al-Iṣfahānī, Abū al-Faraj. *Kitāb al-Aghānī*. 24 vols. Cairo: Dār al-Kutub al-Miṣriyya, 1927–1961.
al-Jaṣṣāṣ. *Aḥkām al-Qurʾān*. Ed. ʿA. M. ʿA. Shāhīn. 3 vols. Beirut: Dār al-Kutub al-ʿIlmiyya, 1415/1994.
Khalīfa ibn al-Khayyāṭ. *Kitāb al-Ṭabaqāt*. Ed. A. Ḍ. al-ʿUmarī. Baghdad: Maṭbaʿat al-ʿĀnī, 1967.
al-Khalīl ibn Aḥmad. *Kitāb al-ʿAyn*. Ed. M. al-Makhzūmī and I. al-Sāmarrāʾī. 8 vols. Baghdad: Dār al-Rashīd, 1980–1985.
Kitāb al-Manāsik wa-amākin ṭuruq al-ḥajj. Ed. Ḥ. al-Jāsir. Riyadh: Dār al-Yamāma 1969.
al-Maqrīzī. *Al-Dhahab al-masbūk fī dhikr man ḥajja min al-khulafāʾ wa-l-mulūk*. Ed. J. al-Shayyāl. Cairo: Maktabat al-Thaqāfa al-Dīniyya, 2000.
al-Masʿūdī. *Murūj al-dhahab wa-maʿādin al-jawhar*. Ed. C. Pellat. 7 vols. Beirut: al-Jāmiʿa al-Lubnāniyya, 1966–1979.
al-Shāfiʿī. *Kitāb al-Umm*. Ed. R. F. ʿAbd al-Muṭṭalib. 11 vols. Mansura: Dār al-Wafāʾ li-l-Ṭibāʿa, 2001.
al-Ṭabarī. *Tārīkh al-rusul wa-l-mulūk = Annales quos scripsit Abu Djafar Mohammed ibn Djarir at-Tabari*. Ed. M. J. de Goeje et al. 15 vols. in 3 series. Leiden: E. J. Brill, 1879–1901.
al-Thaʿlabī. *Al-Kashf wa-l-bayān*. Ed. A. M. b. ʿĀshūr. 10 vols. Beirut: Dār Iḥyāʾ al-Turāth al-ʿArabī, 2002.
al-Wāqidī. *Kitāb al-Maghāzī*. Ed. M. Jones. 3 vols. Oxford University Press, 1966.
al-Yaʿqūbī. *Kitāb al-Buldān*. Ed. M. J. de Goeje. Leiden: E. J. Brill, 1892.
al-Yaʿqūbī. *Tārīkh*. Ed. M. Th. Houstma. 2 vols. Leiden: E. J. Brill, 1883.
Yāqūt. *Muʿjam al-Buldān*. 5 vols. Beirut: Dār al-Ṣādir, 1955–1957.
al-Zubayr ibn Bakkār. *Al-Akhbār al-muwaffaqiyyāt*. Ed. S. M. al-ʿĀnī. Baghdad: Maṭbaʿat al-ʿĀnī, 1972.

Secondary Literature

Abbott, N. *Two Queens of Baghdad: Mother and Wife of Hārūn al-Rashīd.* University of Chicago Press, 1942.

Avinoam, S. "Made for the Show: The Medieval Treasury of the Kaʿba in Mecca." In B. O'Kane (ed.), *The Iconography of Islamic Art, Studies in Honour of Robert Hillenbrand.* Edinburgh University Press, 2005: 269–283.

El-Hibri, T. "Harun al-Rashid and the Mecca Protocol of 802: A Plan for Division or Succession?" *International Journal of Middle Eastern Studies* 24, 3 (1992): 461–480.

Firestone, R. *Journeys in Holy Lands: The Evolution of the Abraham-Ishmael Legends in Islamic Exegesis.* Albany: State University of New York Press, 1990.

Gaudefroy-Demombynes, M. *Le pèlerinage à la Mekke.* Paris: P. Geuthner, 1923.

Goldziher, I. *Muslim Studies.* Trans. C. R. Barber and S. M. Stern. 2 vols. Chicago: Aldine, 1966–1971.

Hawting, G. "The Disappearance and Rediscovery of Zamzam and the 'Well of the Kaʿba'." *Bulletin of the School of Oriental and African Studies* 43, 1 (1980): 44–54.

Hawting, G. "The Origins of the Muslim Sanctuary at Meccan." In G. H. A. Juynboll (ed.), *Studies on the First Century of Islamic Society.* Carbondale: Southern Illinois University Press, 1982: 23–48.

Hawting, G. "The 'Sacred Offices' of Mecca, from Jahiliyya to Islam." *Jerusalem Studies in Arabic and Islam* 13 (1990): 62–84.

Heinrichs, W. "Al-Sharqī b. al-Quṭāmī and his Etiologies of Proverbs." In S. Leder (ed.), *Story-telling in the Framework of Non-Fictional Arabic Literature.* Wiesbaden: Harrassowitz Verlag, 1998: 282–308.

Hodgson, M. G. S. *The Venture of Islam: Conscience and History in a World Civilization.* 3 vols. University of Chicago Press, 1974.

Ilisch, L. "Münzgeschenke und Geschenkmünzen in der mittelalterlichen islamischen Welt." *Münstersche Numismatische Zeitung*, 14 (1984): 7–12, 15–34, and 15 (1985): 5–12.

Katz, M. "The Ḥajj and the Study of Islamic Ritual." *Studia Islamica* 98/99 (2004): 95–129.

al-Kilābi, Ḥ. *Al-Nuqūsh al-Islāmiyya ʿalā ṭarīq al-ḥajj al-shāmī min al-qarn al-awwal ilā l-qarn al-khamīs al-hijrī* Riyadh: Maktabat al-Malik Fahd al-Waṭaniyya, 2009.

Kimber, R.A. "Hārūn al-Rashīd's Meccan Settlement of AH 186/AD 802." *School of ʿAbbāsid Studies, Occasional Papers* 1 (1986): 55–79.

Latham, J. D. "The Beginnings of Arabic Prose Literature: The Epistolary Genre." In A. F. L. Beeston et al. (eds.), *Arabic Literature to the End of the Umayyad Period.* Cambridge University Press, 1983: 154–179.

Marlow, L. *Hierarchy and Egalitarianism in Islamic Thought.* Cambridge University Press, 1997.

McMillan, M. E. *The Meaning of Mecca: The Politics of Pilgrimage in Early Islam.* London: Saqi Books, 2011.

Mottahedeh, R. "The Shuʿūbiyya Controversy and the Social History of Early Islamic Iran." *International Journal of Middle East Studies* 7, 2 (1976): 161–182.

Mourad, S. A. *Early Islam between Myth and History: Al-Ḥasan al-Baṣrī (d. 110H/728CE) and the Formation of His Legacy in Classical Islamic Scholarship*. Leiden: Brill, 2006.
Rāshid, S. b. ʿA. *Darb Zubaydah: The Pilgrim Road from Kufa to Mecca*. Riyadh University Libraries, 1980.
Rāshid, S. b. ʿA. et al. *Silsilat Āthār al-Mamlaka al-ʿArabīya al-Saʿūdiyya*. 13 vols. Riyadh: Wizārat al-Maʿārif, 2003.
Rihaoui, A. "Découverte de deux inscriptions arabes." *Annales archéologiques de syrie*, 11/12 (1961–1962): 207–211.
Rubin, U. "Ḥanīfiyya and Kaʿba: An Inquiry into the Arabian Pre-Islamic Background of Dīn Ibrāhīm." *Jerusalem Studies in Arabic and Islam* 13 (1990): 85–112.
Savant, S. "Isaac as the Persians' Ishmael: Pride and the Pre-Islamic Past in Ninth and Tenth-Century Islam." *Comparative Islamic Studies* 2, 1 (2006): 5–25.
Sharon, M. "Ahl al-Bayt, People of the House: A Study of the Transformation of a Term from *Jāhiliyyah* to Islam." *Jerusalem Studies in Arabic and Islam* 8 (1986): 169–184.
Sharon, M. *Black Banners from the East, the Establishment of the ʿAbbāsid State, Incubation of a Revolt*. Leiden: Brill, 1983.
Sharon, M. "The Umayyads as *Ahl al-Bayt*." *Jerusalem Studies in Arabic and Islam* 14 (1991): 115–149.
Silverstein, A. *Postal Systems in the Pre-Modern Islamic World*. Cambridge University Press, 2007.
al-Wuhaybī, ʿA. b. N. "Hal huwa *al-Manāsik* am *Manāzil al-ṭarīq*? Wa-hal huwa li-Imām al-Ḥarbī am li-l-Qāḍī Wakīʿ?" *Majallat al-ʿArab* 7–8, s. 23 (1409/1988): 433–441.
Zadeh, T. "Of Mummies, Poets, and Water Nymphs: Tracing the Codicological Limits of Ibn Khurradādhbih's Geography." In M. Bernards (ed.), *ʿAbbāsid Studies IV*. Warminster: Gibb Memorial Trust, 2013: 8–75.

CHAPTER 4

Primary Sources

Abū Dāwūd. *Sunan Abī Dāwūd*, 3 vols. Beirut: Dār al-Kutub al-ʿIlmiyya, 1996.
Abū Nuʿaym al-Iṣbahānī. *Ḥilyat al-awliyāʾ*. 10 vols. Beirut: Dār al-Kitāb al-ʿArabī, 1967–1968.
al-Bukhārī. *Al-Jāmiʿ al-Ṣaḥīḥ*. 4 vols. Cairo: al-Maṭbaʿat al-Salafiyya wa-Maktabatuhā, 1403 AH/1982–1983.
al-Dhahabī. *Siyar Aʿlām al-Nubalāʾ*, 25 vols. Beirut: Muʾassassat al-Risāla, 1981.
Ibn Ḥajar. *Al-Iṣāba fī tamyīz al-ṣaḥāba*. 13 vols. Cairo: Maktabat al-Kulliyyāt al-Azharīya, 1977.
Ibn Ḥajar. *Tahdhīb al-tahdhīb*, 12 vols. Beirut: Dār al-Kutub al-ʿIlmiyya, 1994.
Ibn Ḥibbān. *Kitāb al-Thiqāt*, 5 vols. Beirut: Dār al-Kutub al-ʿIlmiyya, 1998.
Ibn Isḥāq. *Al-Sīra al-nabawiyya*. 4 vols. Beirut: al-Maktaba al-ʿAṣriyya, n.d.
Ibn Mājah. *Sunan*. 6 vols. Beirut: Dār al-Jīl, 1998.

Ibn Qudāma. *Al-Mughnī*. 9 vols. Beirut: Dār al-Kutub al-ʿIlmiyya, 1996.
Ibn Saʿd. *Kitāb al-Ṭabaqāt al-Kabīr*. 9 vols. Leiden: E.J. Brill, 1904–1918.
Ibn Ḥanbal. *Ibn Ḥanbal, al-Musnad*. Ed. Sh. al-Arnāʾūṭ and ʿĀ. Murshid. 52 vols. Beirut: Muʾassasat al-Risāla, 1993–2001.
Muslim. Ṣaḥīḥ *Muslim bi-sharḥ al-Nawawī*. 18 vols. Cairo: al-Maṭbaʿa al-Miṣriyya bi-l-Azhar, 1929.
al-Nasāʾī. *Sunan al-Kubrā*. 12 vols. Beirut: Muʾassasat al-Risālah, 2001.
Yāqūt. *Muʿjam al-Buldān*. 5 vols. Beirut: Dār Sādir, 1977.

Secondary Literature

Bianchi, R. R. *Guests of God: Pilgrimage and Politics in the Islamic World*. New York: Oxford University Press, 2004.
Brack, Y. "A Mongol Princess Making Hajj: The Biography of El Qutlugh Daughter of Abagha Ilkhan (r. 1265–82)." *Journal of Royal Asiatic Society*, ser. 3, 21, 3 (2011): 331–359.
Cobbold, E. *Pilgrimage to Mecca*. London: John Murray, 1934.
Dukhayyil, S. F. *Mawsūʿat fiqh ʿĀʾisha umm al-muʾminīn: ḥayātuhā wa-fiqhuhā*. Beirut: Dār al-Nafāʾis, 1989.
Faroqhi, S. *Pilgrims and Sultans: The Hajj under the Ottomans, 1517–1683*. London: I. B. Tauris, 1994.
Geissinger, A. "Portrayal of the *Ḥajj* as a Context for Women's Exegesis: Textual Evidence in al-Bukhārī' *al-Ṣaḥīḥ*. " In S. Guenther (ed.), *Insights into Classical Arabic Literature and Islam*. Leiden: Brill, 2005: 153–179.
Johnson, K. "Royal Pilgrimage: Mamlūk Accounts of the Pilgrimages to Mecca of the Khawand al-Kubrā (Senior Wife of the Sultan)." *Studia Islamica* 91 (2000): 107–131.
Khan, S. *Begums of Bhopal*. New York: I. B. Tauris, 2000.
Lambert-Hurley, S. (ed.). *Princess's Pilgrimage: Nawab Sikandar Begum's "A Pilgrimage to Mecca."* New Delhi: Women Unlimited, 2007.
Metcalf, B. "Pilgrimage Remembered: South Asian Accounts of the *Hajj*. " In Dale Eickelman and James Piscatori (eds.), *Muslim Travellers: Pilgrimage, Migration, and the Religious Imagination*. Berkeley: University of California Press, 1990: 85–107.
Nadwi, M. A. *Al-Muḥaddithāt: The Women Scholars in Islam*. Oxford: Interface Publications, 2007.
Nomani, A. *Standing Alone in Mecca*. San Francisco: Harper San Francisco, 2006.
Sayeed, A. *Women and the Transmission of Religious Knowledge in Islam*. New York: Cambridge University Press, 2013.
Tagliacozzo, E. *The Longest Journey: Southeast Asians and the Pilgrimage to Mecca*. New York: Oxford University Press, 2013.
Tolmacheva, M. "Female Piety and Patronage in the Medieval 'Ḥajj'." In G. R. G. Hambly (ed.), *Women in the Medieval Islamic World: Power, Patronage and Piety*. New York: St. Martin's Press, 1998: 161–179.
Tolmacheva, M. "Medieval Muslim Women's Travel: Defying Distance and Danger." *World History Connected* (June 2013) at worldhistoryconnected.press.illinois.edu (last accessed April, 11, 2014).

Zaydān, ʿA. *Mufaṣṣal fī aḥkām al-marʾa wa-l-bayt al-muslim.* 11 vols. Beirut: Muʾassasat al-Risāla, 1993.

Online Resources

British Broadcasting Corporation at bbc.co.uk
Royal Embassy of Saudi Arabia, Washington, DC at saudiembassy.net

CHAPTER 5

Primary Sources

Çelebi., Evliya. *Evliyā Çelebī in Medina: The Relevant Sections of the Seyāhatnāme.* Ed. N. Gemici. Trans. R. Dankoff. Leiden: Brill, 2012.
Çelebi., Evliya. *An Ottoman Traveler: Selections from the Book of Travels of Evliya Çelebī.* Trans. R. Dankoff and S. Kim. London: Eland, 2010.
al-Ḥusaynī al-Dimashqī. "The Book of Increasing and Eternal Happiness – the Hejaz Railway" = In J. M. Landau (trans.), *The Hejaz Railway and the Muslim Pilgrimage: A Case of Ottoman Political Propaganda.* Detroit: Wayne State University Press, 1971.
Ibn Jubayr. *The Travels of Ibn Jubayr.* Trans. R. J. C. Broadhurst. London: Cape, 1952.
Ibn al-Mujāwir. *A Traveller in Thirteenth-Century Arabia: Ibn Al-Mujāwir's Tārīkh al-Mustabṣir.* Trans. G. R. Smith. London: Hakluyt Society, 2008.
The Qurʾān. Trans. Alan Jones. Cambridge: Gibb Memorial Trust, 2007.
al-Ṭabarī. *The History of al-Tabari. XIII: The Conquest of Iraq, Southwestern Persia, and Egypt.* Trans. G. H. A. Juynboll. Albany: State University of New York Press, 1989.

Secondary Literature

Abbott, N. *Two Queens of Baghdad: Mother and Wife of Hārūn al-Rashīd.* University of Chicago Press, 1946.
Ahmed, L. *Women and Gender in Islam: Historical Roots of a Modern Debate.* New Haven, CT: Yale University Press, 1992.
'Ankawi, A. "The Pilgrimage to Mecca in Mamlūk Times." *Arabian Studies* 1 (1974): 146–170.
Al-Aṭlas al-Tārīkhī lil-Mamlaka al-ʿArabiyya al-Suʿūdiyya. Riyadh: Dārat al-Malik ʿAbd al-ʿAzīz, 1999.
Barbir, K. K. *Ottoman Rule in Damascus, 1708–1758.* Princeton University Press, 1980.
Behrens-Abouseif, D. "Qāytbāy's Foundation in Medina, the Madrasah, the Ribāṭ and the Dashīshah. " *Mamluk Studies Review* 2 (1998): 61–71.
Ben Messaïb. "Itinéraire de Tlemcen a la Mekke." Trans. M. Ben Cheneb. *Revue africaine* 44 (1900): 261–282.
Beresford, J. *The Ancient Sailing Season.* Leiden: Brill, 2012.

Birks, J. S. *Across the Savannas to Mecca: The Overland Pilgrimage Route from West Africa*. London: Hurst, 1978.
Blair, A. and B. Ulrich. "From Iraq to the Hijaz in the Early Islamic Period." In V. Porter and L. Saif (eds.), *The Hajj: Collected Essays*. London: British Museum Press, 2013: 44–51.
Bonner, M. *Aristocratic Violence and Holy War: Studies in the Jihad and the Arab-Byzantine Frontier*. New Haven, CT: American Oriental Society, 1996.
Bosworth, C. E. "Ṣanawbarī's Elegy on the Pilgrims Slain in the Carmathian Attack on Mecca (317/930): A Literary-Historical Study." *Arabica* 19, 3 (1972): 222–239.
Bovill, E. W. *The Golden Trade of the Moors*. Oxford University Press, 1970.
Bray, J. "Men, Women and Slaves in Abbasid Society." In L. Brubaker and J. M. H. Smith (eds.), *Gender in the Early Medieval World: East and West, 300–900*. Cambridge University Press, 2004: 121–146.
Brice, W. C. "A New Map of the Pilgrim Roads of Arabia." *Proceedings of the Seminar for Arabian Studies* 5 (1975): 8–11.
Brower, B. C. "The Colonial Hajj: France and Algeria, 1830–1962." In V. Porter and L. Saif (eds.), *The Hajj: Collected Essays*. London: British Museum Press, 2013: 106–112.
Buez, E-A. *Une mission au Hedjaz*. Paris: Masson, 1873.
Buzpinar, Ş. T. "Opposition to the Ottoman Caliphate in the Early Years of Abdülhamid II: 1877–1882." *Die Welt des Islams* 36 (1996): 59–89.
Chantre, L. "Se rendre à La Mecque sous la Troisième République: contrôle et organisation des déplacement des pèlerins du Maghreb et du Levant entre 1880 et 1939." *Cahiers de la Méditerranée* 78 (2009): 202–227.
Christelow, A. "Political Ends and Means of Transport in the Colonial North African Pilgrimage." *The Maghreb Review* 12, 3–4 (1987): 84–89.
Crone, P. *Meccan Trade and the Rise of Islam*. Princeton University Press, 1987.
David, H. "Map of Pilgrimage Roads" In A. I. Al-Ghabban et al. (eds.), *Roads of Arabia: Archaeology and History of the Kingdom of Saudi Arabia*. Paris: Louvre/Somogy, 2010: 422.
Duguet, F. *Le pèlerinage de La Mecque*. Paris: Rieder, 1932.
Dunn, R. E. *The Adventures of Ibn Battuta: A Muslim Traveler of the 14th Century*. Berkeley: University of California Press, 2005.
Durkheim, E. *The Elementary Forms of Religious Life*. Trans. K. E. Fields. New York: Free Press, 1995.
El-Hibri, T. *Reinterpreting Islamic Historiography: Hārūn al-Rashīd and the Narrative of the ʿAbbāsid Caliphate*. Cambridge University Press, 1999.
Ersoy, N. et al. "International Sanitary Conferences from the Ottoman Perspective (1851–1938)." *Hygiea Internationalis* 10, 1 (2011): 53–79.
Escande, L. "D'Alger à La Mecque: l'administration française et le contrôle du pèlerinage (1894–1962)." *Revue d'histoire maghrébine* 26, 95–96 (1999): 277–296.
Faroqhi, S. "The Ottoman Empire: The Age of 'Political Households' (Eleventh-Twelfth/Seventeenth-Eighteenth Centuries)." In M. Fierro (ed.), *The New Cambridge History of Islam, II: The Western Islamic World Eleventh to Eighteenth Centuries*. Cambridge University Press, 2010: 366–410.

Faroqhi, S. *Pilgrims and Sultans: The Hajj under the Ottomans, 1517–1683*. London: I. B. Tauris, 1994.
Faroqhi, S. N. "Rural Life." In S. N. Faroqhi (ed.), *The Cambridge History of Turkey, III: The Later Ottoman Empire, 1603–1839*. Cambridge University Press, 2006: 376–390.
Franz, K. "The Bedouin in History or Bedouin History?" *Nomadic Peoples* 15, 1 (2011): 11–53.
Garcin, J.-C. *Un centre musulman de la Haute-Égypte médiévale: Qūṣ*. Cairo: Institut français d'archéologie orientale du Caire, 1976.
Gaudefroy-Demombynes, M. *Le pélerinage à La Mekke: étude d'histoire religieuse*. Paris: Geuthner, 1923.
Gaudefroy-Demombynes, M. "Le voile de la Ka'ba." *Studia Islamica* 2 (1954): 5–21.
Al-Ghabban, A. I. et al. (eds.), *Roads of Arabia: Archaeology and History of the Kingdom of Saudi Arabia*. Paris: Louvre/Somogy, 2010.
Hawting, G. R. "The Ḥajj in the Second Civil War." In I. R. Netton (ed.), *Golden Roads: Migration, Pilgrimage and Travel in Mediaeval and Modern Islam*. Richmond, UK: Curzon, 1993: 31–42.
Hillenbrand, C. *The Crusades: Islamic Perspectives*. Edinburgh University Press, 1999.
Hourani, G. F. *Arab Seafaring in the Indian Ocean in Ancient and Early Medieval Times*. Princeton University Press, 1951.
Huber, V. "The Unification of the Globe by Disease? The International Sanitary Conferences on Cholera, 1851–1894." *The Historical Journal* 49, 2 (2006): 453–476.
Irwin, R. *The Middle East in the Middle Ages: The Early Mamluk Sultanate 1250–1382*. London: Croom Helm, 1986.
Johnson, K. "Royal Pilgrims: Mamlūk Accounts of the Pilgrimages to Mecca of the Khawand al-Kubrā (Senior Wife of the Sultan)." *Studia Islamica* 91 (2000): 107–131.
Jomier, J. *Le maḥmal et la caravane égyptienne des pèlerins de La Mecque (XIIIe–XXe siècles)*. Cairo: Imprimerie de l'institut français d'archéologie orientale, 1953.
Kennedy, H. *The Early Abbasid Caliphate: A Political History*. London: Croom Helm, 1981.
Kennedy, H. (ed.). *An Historical Atlas of Islam/Atlas historique de l'islam*. 2nd ed. Leiden: Brill, 2002.
Kennedy, H. "Journey to Mecca: A History." In V. Porter, with M. A. S. Abdel Haleem et al. (ed.) *Hajj: Journey to the Heart of Islam*. Cambridge, MA: Harvard University Press, 2012: 68–135.
Kennedy, H. "The Late 'Abbāsid Pattern, 945–1050." In C. F. Robinson (ed.), *The New Cambridge History of Islam, I: The Formation of the Islamic World Sixth to Eleventh Centuries*. Cambridge University Press, 2010: 360–394.
King, D. A. *World-Maps for Finding the Direction and Distance to Mecca*. Leiden: Brill, 1999.
Lassner, J. *The Shaping of 'Abbāsid Rule*. Princeton University Press, 1979.
Loiseau, J. "Arabia and the Holy Cities." In A. I. Al-Ghabbān et al. (eds.), *Roads of Arabia: Archaeology and History of the Kingdom of Saudi Arabia*. Paris: Louvre/Somogy, 2010: 406–419.

Lydon, G. *On Trans-Saharan Trails: Islamic Law, Trade Networks, and Cross-Cultural Exchange in Nineteenth-Century Western Africa*. Cambridge University Press, 2009.
de Maigret, A. "La route caravanière de l'encens dans l'Arabie préislamique." *Chroniques yémenites* 11 (2003) at cy.revues.org/160.
McMillan, M. E. *The Meaning of Mecca: The Politics of Pilgrimage in Early Islam*. London: Saqi, 2011.
Meloy, J. L. "Overland Trade in the Western Islamic World (Fifth-Ninth/Eleventh-Fifteenth Centuries)." In M. Fierro (ed.), *The New Cambridge History of Islam vol. 2: The Western Islamic World Eleventh to Eighteenth Centuries*. Cambridge University Press, 2010: 648–664.
Miquel, A. *La géographie humaine du monde musulman jusqu'au milieu du 11è siècle: géographie arabe et représentation du monde, la terre et l'étranger*. Paris: Mouton, 1975.
Nouschi, A. *Enquête sur le niveau de vie des populations rurales constantinoises de la conquête jusqu'en 1919*. Paris: Presses universitaires de France, 1961.
Ochsenwald, W. W. L. "A Modern Waqf: the Hijaz Railway, 1900–48." *Arabian Studies* 3 (1976): 1–12.
Ochsenwald, W. *The Hijaz Railroad*. Charlottesville: University Press of Virginia, 1980.
Ochsenwald, W. *Religion, Society and the State in Arabia: The Hijaz under Ottoman Control, 1840–1908*. Columbus: Ohio State University Press, 1984.
Peters, F. E. *The Hajj: The Muslim Pilgrimage to Mecca and the Holy Places*. Princeton University Press, 1994.
Petersen, A. *The Medieval and Ottoman Hajj Route in Jordan: An Archaeological and Historical Study*. Oxford: Oxbow, 2012.
Philipp, H.-J. "Der Beduinische widerstand gegen die Hedschasbahn." *Die Welt des Islams* 25 (1985): 31–83.
Pitts, J. *A Faithful Account of the Religion and Manners of the Mahometans*. 3rd ed. London: Osborn and Longman, 1731.
Rafeq, A. *The Province of Damascus, 1723–1783*. Beirut: Khayats, 1966.
Al-Rashid, S. A. *Darb Zubayda: The Pilgrim Road from Kufa to Mecca*. Riyadh University Libraries, 1980.
Règlement sur le pèlerinage de La Mecque. Algiers: Fontana, 1895.
[Dr.] Rifaat and Dr. Essad. *Rapport sur le voyage de retour de la caravane sacrée en l'année 1324 de l'Hégire (1907)*. Istanbul: Loeffler, [1907].
Roff, W. R. "Sanitation and Security: The Imperial Powers and the Nineteenth Century Ḥajj." *Arabian Studies* 6 (1982): 143–160.
Ruthven, M. and A. Nanji. *Historical Atlas of Islam*. Cambridge, MA: Harvard University Press, 2004.
Sanlaville, P. "Geographic Introduction to the Arabian Peninsula." In A. I. Al-Ghabbān et al. (eds.), *Roads of Arabia: Archaeology and History of the Kingdom of Saudi Arabia*. Paris: Louvre/Somogy, 2010: 55–69.
Schmitt, C. *The Nomos of the Earth in the International Law of the Jus Publicum Europaeum*. Trans. G. L. Ulmen. New York: Telos, 2006 [1950].
Spellberg, D. A. *Politics, Gender, and the Islamic Past*. New York: Columbia University Press, 1994.

Al-Thanayyan, M. A. R. *An Archaeological Study of the Yemeni Highland Pilgrim Route between Ṣan'ā' and Mecca*. Riyadh: Deputy Ministry of Antiquities and Museums, 1999.
Al-Thenayian [Al-Thanayyan], M. A. R. "A Preliminary Evaluation of Al-Radā'ī's Urǧūzat al-Ḥaǧǧ as Primary Geographical Source for Surveying the Yemini Highland Pilgrim Route." *New Arabian Studies* 4 (1997): 243–260.
Tolmacheva, M. "Female Piety and Patronage in the Medieval 'Ḥajj.'" In G. R. G. Hambly (ed.), *Women in the Medieval Islamic World: Power, Patronage, and Piety*. New York: St. Martin's, 1998: 161–179.
Touati, H. *Islam and Travel in the Middle Ages*. Trans. L. G. Cochrane. University of Chicago Press, 2010.
Wellhausen, J. *The Arab Kingdom and its Fall*. London: Routledge, 2000 [1902].
Al-Wohaibi, A. *The Northern Hijaz in the Writings of the Arab Geographers, 800–1150*. Beirut: Al-Risāla, 1973.
Yacono, X. *La colonisation des plaines du Chélif (de Lavigerie au confluent de la Mina)*. 2 vols. Algiers: Imbert, 1952.
Yamba, C. B. *Permanent Pilgrims: The Role of Pilgrimage in the Lives of West African Muslims in Sudan*. Washington, DC: Smithsonian Institution Press, 1995.
Zaman, M. Q. *Religion and Politics under the Early 'Abbāsids: The Emergence of the Proto-Sunni Elite*. Leiden: Brill, 1997.

Archival Sources

Administrateur de la Commune Mixte d'Ammi Moussa to Préfet d'Oran, July 13, 1905, no. 2643. Archives nationales d'Outre Mer, 10G57.
Brochure "Pèlerinage à La Mecque." Centre des archives nationales d'Algérie, Terr Sud 0908.
Chef d'annexe de Tabarka to Résident Général Tunis, March 5, 1911, no. 591. Archives nationales de Tunisie, Série A, carton 276 *bis*, dossier 1.
Consul de France Djeddah to Résident Général Tunis, February 3, 1904, no. 1. Archives nationales de Tunisie, Série A, carton 276 *bis*, dossier 1.
Helal: "Renseignements individuels," n.d. Yousfi: Préfet de Constantine to Affaires Indigènes Algiers, May 31, 1906, no. 281. Both in Archives nationales d'Outre Mer, 10G41.
IBA to M. Aït Ali, membre Assemblé financière de l'Algérie et M. Lechani, Conseil Général (Tizi Ouzou), September 30, 1947. Centre des archives nationales d'Algérie, IBA/CUL-047.
Umm al-Qurā no. 1215, June 18, 1948. Centre des archives nationales d'Algérie, IBA/CUL-048.
Rapport de Piquet 1948. Centre des archives nationales d'Algérie, IBA/CUL-049.
"Revue de la presse musulmane pendant le mois d'Août 1906." Archives nationales d'Outre Mer, 1AFFPOL/923/1.
Si Ahmed ben Chérif, "Notes de mon voyage à La Mecque," June 23, 1914. Archives nationales d'Outre Mer, 10H54.
Soubrillard, "Pèlerinage à La Mecque," June 15, 1932. Archives nationales d'Outre Mer, 16H116.

Sous-Préfet de Tlemcen to Préfet d'Oran, August 20, 1948, no. 1879. Request of Si Moulay Ali of Zawiya Taïba in Nedroma. Centre des archives nationales d'Algérie, IBA/CUL-048.

Online Source

Royal Embassy of Saudi Arabia, Washington, DC, at saudiembassy.net

CHAPTER 6

Print Sources

Burton, I. *Arabia, Egypt, India, A Narrative of Travel*. London: W. Mullan and Son, 1879.

Coates, W. H. *The Old "Country Trade" of the East Indies*. London: Imray, Laurie, Norie, & Wilson, 1911.

Chittick, N. *Kilwa: An Islamic Trading City on the East African Coast*. Nairobi: British Institute in Eastern Africa, 1974.

"De Bedevaart naar Mekka, 1909/1910," *Indische Gids* (1919): 1637.

"A Description of the Yeerly Voyage or Pilgrimage of the Mahumitans, Turkes and Moores unto Mecca in Arabia." In R. Hakluyt, (ed.), *The Principal Navigations*. 12 vols. Glasgow: J. MacLehose and Sons, 1903–1905, V: 340–65.

Duguet, F. *Le Pèlerinage de la Mecque*. Paris: Rieder, 1932.

Eisenberger, J. "Indie en de Bedevaart naar Mekka." Unpublished PhD thesis. Leiden University, 1928.

Faroqhi, S. "Trade Controls, Provisioning Policies and Donations: The Egypt-Hijaz Connection in the Second Half of the Sixteenth Century." In H. İnalcik and C. Kafadar (eds.), *Suleyman the Second [sic] and His Time*. Istanbul: The Isis Press, 1993: 131–143.

Faroqhi, S. *Pilgrims and Sultans: The Hajj under the Ottomans 1517 to 1683*. London: I. B. Tauris, 1994.

Feener R. M. and M. Laffan. "Sufi Scents across the Indian Ocean: Yemeni Hagiography and the Earliest History of Southeast Asian Islam." *Archipel* 70 (2005): 185–208.

Foster, W. *Early Travels in India, 1583–1619*. Delhi: S. Chand, 1968.

Freeman-Grenville, G. S. P. *The East African Coast: Select Documents from the First to the Earlier Nineteenth Century*. Oxford: Clarendon Press, 1962.

Green, N. *Bombay Islam: The Religious Economy of the Western Indian Ocean, 1840–1915*. Cambridge University Press, 2011.

Ibn Jubayr. *The Travels of Ibn Jubayr*. Trans. R. C. Broadhurst. London: J. Cape, 1952.

Insoll, T. *The Archaeology of Islam in Sub-Saharan Africa*. Cambridge University Press, 2003.

Lobo, J. *The Itinerário of Jerónimo Lobo*. Trans. D. M. Lockhart. London: Hakluyt Society, 1984.

Masson, P. *Histoire du commerce français dans le Levant au XVIIIè siècle*. Paris: Hachette & Cie., 1911.
Matheson, V. and B. W. Andaya (eds. and trans.). *The Precious Gift, Tuhfat al-Nafis*. Kuala Lumpur: Oxford University Press, 1982.
de Modave, Comte. *Voyage en Inde du Comte de Modave, 1773–1776*. Ed. J. Deloche. Paris: Ecole française d'extrême-orient, 1971.
Miller, M. "Pilgrims' Progress: The Business of the Hajj." *Past and Present* 191 (2006): 189–228.
Niebuhr, C. Travels through Arabia and Other Countries in the East. 2 *vols*. Trans. R. Heron. Edinburgh: G. Mudie, 1792.
Ochsenwald, W. *Religion, Society and the State in Arabia, the Hijaz under Ottoman Control. 1840–1908*. Columbus: Ohio State University Press, 1984.
Ochsenwald, W. "The Commercial History of the Hijaz Vilayet, 1840–1908." *Arabian Studies* 6 (1982): 57–76.
Pearson, M. N. *Pious Passengers: The Hajj in Earlier Times*. Dhaka, Bangladesh: University Press Limited, 1994.
Peters, F. E. *The Hajj: Muslim Pilgrimage to Mecca and the Holy Places*. Princeton University Press, 1994.
Purchas, S. *Purchas, His Pilgrimes*. Glasgow: J. MacLehose and sons, 1905–1907.
Reid, A. "Sixteenth Century Turkish Influence in Western Indonesia." *Journal of South East Asian History* 10, 3 (1969): 395–414.
Tagliacozzo, E. *The Longest Journey: Southeast Asians and the Pilgrimage to Mecca*. New York: Oxford University Press, 2013.
Takashi, O. "Friction and Rivalry over Pious Mobility: British Colonial Management of the Hajj and Reaction to It by Indian Muslims." In K. Hidemitsu (ed.), *The Influence of Human Mobility in Muslim Societies*. London: Kegan Paul, 2003: 151–175.

Archival Sources

Bijblad #5741 (1902); *Bijblad* #7130 (1909); *Bijblad* #7469 (1911); *Bijblad* #11689 (1928).
Colonial Office documents CO/273/396/28656 (July 22, 1913); CO 273/402/26309 (July 30, 1913); CO 273/408/35816 (September 19, 1914); CO 273/418/34307 (September 9, 1914), and CO 273/418/38345 (October 5, 1914).
India Office Records, British Consul, Jeddah, to Foreign Office, August 16, 1938, #1800/402/203 in IOR/L/PJ/7/789, and same to same, August 9, 1937, #E4922/201/25.
India Office Records, British Consul, Batavia, to Foreign Office, March 14, 1938, #75E in IOR/R/20/B/1454 and same to same, September 21, 1938, #260E, in IOR/R/20/B/1454.
"Report on the Quarantine Stations at Camaran for the Year 1891," in Foreign Office 195/1730, Appendix "A," Public Records Office (PRO), London.
Staatsblad #236 (1906); *Staatstblad* #531 (1912); *Staatsblad* #15 (1923); *Staatsblad* #44 (1931); and *Staatsblad* #554 (1932).
Staatsblad van Nederlandsch-Indie, #597 (1923).

Straits Settlements Government Gazettes for 1867 (#31); 1868 (#12), and 1890 (#7).
Times of London, August 17, 1880.

CHAPTER 7

Scholarly Literature

Bianchi, R. R. "China-Middle East Relations in Light of Obama's Pivot to the Pacific." *China Report* 49, 1 (2013): 103–118.
Bianchi, R. R. *Guests of God: Pilgrimage and Politics in the Islamic World*. New York: Oxford University Press, 2004.
Bianchi, R. R. "Hajj." In I. Ness and P. Bellwood (eds.). *The Encyclopedia of Global Human Migration*. New York: Wiley, 2013.
Bianchi, R. R. "The Hajj in Everyday Life." In D. L. Bowen, E. A. Early, and B. Schulthies (eds.), *Everyday Life in the Muslim Middle East*. 3rd ed. Bloomington: Indiana University Press, 2013: 319–328.
Bianchi, R. R. "Hajj, Women's Patronage of: Contemporary Practice." In N. Delong-Bas (ed.), *The Oxford Encyclopedia of Islam and Women*. New York: Oxford University Press, 2013.
Bianchi, R. R. *Islamic Globalization: Pilgrimage, Capitalism, Democracy, and Diplomacy*. Singapore and London: World Scientific Publishers, 2013.
Bianchi, R. R. "Travel for Religious Purposes." In J. Esposito (ed.), *The Oxford Encyclopedia of Islam*. New York: Oxford University Press, 2007. Accessed at www.islamicstudies.com/article/opr/t236/e1270
Ejembi, C. L., E. P. Renne, and H. A. Adamu, "The Politics of the 1996 Cerebrospinal Meningitis Epidemic in Nigeria." *Africa* 68, 1 (1998): 118–134.
Günlü, E. and F. Okumu☒. "The Hajj: Experience of Turkish Female Pilgrims." In N. Scott and J. Jafari (eds.), *Tourism in the Muslim World*. Bingley, UK: Emerald, 2010: 221–234.
Rossabi, M. (ed.). *Governing China's Multiethnic Frontiers*. University of Washington Press, 2004.

Media Sources

"Ailece hacca Diyanet'ten teşvik (Directorate of Religious Affairs Encourages Family-Style Hajj)," *samanyoluhaber*, July 10, 2006 [M. Albayrak,].
"An Academy in Paris Offers Advice and Instruction to Muslims Wishing to Make the Trip to Mecca for the Annual Hajj Pilgrimage," *Reuters*, October 3, 2012.
"Arab Dagestanis – Direct Descendants of the Prophet Muhammad," *islam.ru*, 2011 [H. Radjabov].
"As Virus Spreads, Saudi Arabia Restricts Pilgrimage Numbers," *Wall Street Journal*, June 26, 2013 [E. Knickmeyer].
"ATAB, HAAB Demand Chittagong-Jeddah Direct Hajj Flight," *Financial Express*, September 20, 2012.

"Attack on Tatarstan Mufti May Have Been Due to His Control over Hajj Financing," *Interfax*, July 20, 2012.

"Bank Asia Sings MoU with HAAB," *Daily Sun*, April 12, 2013.

"Bilalov Suspected of Organizing Large-Scale Tax Evasion Scheme with Hajj Tours," *Interfax*, April 24, 2013.

"Biman Flight Debacle: Passengers Stage Rowdy Protests," *Daily Star*, September 18, 2012.

"Black Market Thrives as Haj Missions Fail to Find Housing," *Arab News*, October 10, 2011 [B. Abu al-Naja].

"Bogus Hajj Tour Operators Rip-off Muslims Planning Mecca Pilgrimage out of £100,000s," *London Evening Standard,* August 16, 2012.

"China-Built Light Rail Whisks 1 Million Hajj Pilgrims to Mecca in Saudi Arabia," *Xinhua*, November 20, 2010.

"China Muslims Embark on Easier Hajj," *OnIslam.net*, October 18, 2010.

"南航新疆分公司地服部: 首次独立保障"朝覲"包机" (China Southern Airline's Xinjiang Division Grounds Service: The First Dedicated Hajj Charters), *cnair.com*, September 27, 2012.

"Chinese Builders Help Hajj," *Wired Magazine*, February 19, 2009.

"Chinese Train to Mecca?" *Wired Magazine*, September 10, 2009 [K. Barry].

"Civil Society Urges States to Stop Sponsoring Pilgrims," *Leadership* (Nigeria), June 18, 2013 [I. Bunmi].

"Corruption, Discrimination Ousted in Hajj Quota Allotment," *mylaw.net*, November 18, 2010 [P. T. Geeverghese].

"Council for Hajj Reports Increase in Scale of Pilgrimages by Russian Muslims in 10 Years," *Interfax*, August 31, 2012.

"Couple to Sue SA Hajj Council," *iol news*, September 28, 2012 [L. Johns].

"Dr. Sami Angawi on Wahhabi Desecration of Makkah: Developers and Purists Erase Mecca's History," *Reuters*, July 12, 2005 [L. Abou-Ragheb].

"En France, les quotas de visas hajj sont déjà épuisés," *France-Hajj.fr*, September 2012.

"Fewer Places Available for Pilgrimage to Mecca," *Straits Times* (Singapore), September 12, 2012 [M. Almenoar].

"Government Could Have Done More to Prevent Hajj Cuts, Gerindra Says," *Jakarta Globe*, July 6, 2013[Markus J. Sihaloho].

"Grant of Hajj Quota to New Tour Operators," *Daily Times* (Pakistan), August 25, 2012.

"Group Will Root out Alleged Hajj Corruption," *Daily News* (South Africa), October 14, 2011 [R. Sheik Umar].

"Gujarat Towers over UP in Haj Applications," *Daily Pioneer,* April 24, 2013 [H. Raza].

"Hac başvuruları 1 milyonu aştı" (Hajj Applicants Exceed 1 Million), *CNN Türk*, April 25, 2013.

"Haj Prices to Soar after Cut to Makkah Pilgrim Numbers," *Arabian Business*, July 16, 2013 [C. Trenwith].

"Haj Quota Cut to Ensure Pilgrims' Comfort: Khaled," *Saudi Gazette*, June 23, 2013.

"Hajj Imbroglio: Where the Problem Lies," *allafrica.com*, October 6, 2012 [A. M. Alfa].
"Hajj Operations: Private Airlines Eye Larger Share," *Express Tribune* (Pakistan), October 6, 2011 [F. Zaheer].
"Hajj Reporters Set to Monitor 2013 Umrah Operation," *People's Daily* (Nigeria), July 18, 2013.
"Hajj Subsidy: Myths and Facts," *saadut.com*, May 2012 [Saadut].
"Hajj under Debt," *Pak Tribune*, June 20, 2013 [Col. Riaz Jafri].
"How Turkey Reduced Visa Overstays from 35,000 to 5,000 in One Season," *Hajj and Umrah Gazette*, June 1, 2011 [M. Balji].
"ICPC to Install Free Toll Line for Information on Corruption," *Vanguard* (Nigeria), May 18, 2013.
"Indian Court Scraps Subsidy for Mecca Pilgrimage," *Radio Australia*, May 9, 2012.
"Indonesia Demands Compensation over Hajj Numbers," *Arabian Business*, June 24, 2013 [D. Shane].
"Indonesia Urged to Lobby Saudi Arabia over Hajj Quota," *Antara News*, June 19, 2013 [A. Abdussalam].
"Indonesian Government to Put Idle Hajj Funds in Development Bonds," *Jakarta Globe*, July 23, 2012.
"Islam in the Russian Army," *Islam Magazine-Makhachkala*," 2005 [I. Nasirov].
"Islamic Development Bank Signs MoU with HAAB," *TechWorld Bangladesh*, May 27, 2012.
"Kaduna Screens Out All Old-Timers," *Daily Trust*, June 26, 2013 [I. Mudashir].
"LHC Orders Probe into 'Cartelisation' of Operators," *Daily Times* (Pakistan), October 2, 2012.
"Marked Increase in Hajj and Umrah Demand in Turkey," *Hajj and Umrah Gazette*, January 24, 2011 [O. Assaf].
"Mecca for the Rich: Islam's Holiest Site 'Turning into Vegas'," *The Independent*, September 24, 2011 [J. Taylor].
"Mecca's Mega Architecture Casts Shadow over Hajj," *Guardian*, October 23, 2012 [R. Butt].
"MoRA to Suffer Rs 930.60 m Losses Due to Hajj Quota Cut," *Pakistan Observer*, June 19, 2013.
"Moscow Cuts Dagestan's Haj Quota, Sparking Anger There," *Window on Eurasia*, November 29, 2009 [P. Goble].
"Move to Carry Hajj Pilgrims by Sea," *Dhaka Mirror*, February 27, 2010.
"NAHCON Urges Pilgrims' Boards to Ensure Prudent Distribution of Hajj Seats," *Daily Times*, June 12, 2013 [A. Aminu].
"New Mideast Virus Raises Fears for Hajj," *Radio Free Europe-Radio Liberty*, June 22, 2013 [C. Recknagel].
"New Rules of Distributing Hajj Tours Could Be behind Tatarstan Attacks—Russian Lawmaker," *Interfax*, July 19, 2012.
"Nigeria Suspends Hajj Flights over Women Deportation," *BBC News*, September 27, 2012.
"Number of Foreign Hajis Grows by 2,824 Percent in 92 Years," *The News* (Pakistan), October 25, 2012 [S. Shah].

"Ogun to Drop Hajj Pilgrims with Health Concerns," *Premium Times*, June 25, 2013 [D. Kayode-Adedeji].
"Over-priced Annual Pilgrimage," *Saudi Gazette*, September 14, 2011 [A. Al-Sibai].
"Phase Out Haj Subsidy in Ten Years, Supreme Court Tells Govt," *ndtv.com*, May 8, 2012 [A. Vaidyanathan].
"Pilgrim Funds Give Indonesia Banks Booster Shot," *Bloomberg*, May 2, 2013.
"Prime Bank, Al-Arafah Sign MoU with HAAB," *Financial Express*, April 11, 2012.
"Private Hajj Operators Suffer Blow over Human Trafficking Claim," *Financial Express*, June 22, 2013 [J. Hasan].
"The Problems of a Contemporary Hajj – Parts 1 and 2," *Muslimmatters.com*, October 10 and 16, 2011 [Dr. M. Ali].
"Putin Hobbles the Hajj," *United Press International*, September 24, 2004 [P. Goble].
"Riyadh Blacklists 31 Hajj Agencies for Trafficking," *Dhaka Tribune*, April 30, 2013 [S. S. Zaman].
"Row over SA's Smaller Hajj Quota," *iol news*, July 18, 2013 [K. Legg].
"Russia Challenges U.S. in the Islamic World," *Asia Times Online*, March 29, 2008 [M. K. Bhadrakumar].
"Russia Courts the Muslim World: Islam Preceded Christianity on Our Territory, Says Putin, *Le Monde Diplomatique*, December 2008 [J. Lévesque].
"Russia to Have Muslim Majority by 2050, Putin Advisor Says," *Window on Eurasia*, August 23, 2007 [P. Goble].
"Russian Council of Muftis Allocates Quotas for 2013 Hajj," *Radio Free Europe–Radio Liberty*, May 3, 2013.
"Russian Muslims and Foreign Policy," *Global Affairs*, October 7, 2012 [R. Mukhametov].
"Russia's Fear of Radical Islam Drives Its Support for Assad," *Al-Monitor*, July 26, 2012 [A. Mudallali].
Saudi Arabia Pledges to Increase Hajj Quota in 3 Years, *Jakarta Globe*, June 27, 2013 [Suara Pembaruan].
"Saudi Clerics Approve Fewer Hajj Pilgrims," *Reuters*, June 26, 2013 [A. McDowall].
"Shahjalal Islami Bank Singed Agreement with HAAB," *First News*, April 20, 2013 [N. Ahmedi].
"Son 10 yılda umreye giden Türkler'in sayısı 25 kat arttı" (The Number of Turks Going on Umrah Has Increased 25 Times in the Last 10 Years), *Sabah*, May 20, 2012.
"Syria as a Terrorism Hub – Potential Threats to Russia," *valdaiclub.com*, April 22, 2013 [A. Baklanov].
"Three More Government Hajj Houses in Karnataka," *SahilOnline*, June 3, 2013.
"Turkey to Cancel Its Hajj Lottery Next Year," *Hürriyet-Daily News*, March 28, 2013.
"Turks Find Solace in Virtual Pilgrimage as Saudi Cuts Haj Quotas," *Reuters*, July 18, 2013 [E. Toksabay].
"UAE's Faithful Aay 'Luxury' Haj Is Unholy," *The National* (UAE), October 16, 2011 [Y. Kakande].

"Uğur Becerikli, Diyanet'ten Çin'e çalım: hac malzemeleri yerli olacak" (A Move on China from Religious Affairs: Hajj Equipment Will Be Locally Produced), *Sabah*, June 24, 2010.
"Umrah Applications from Turkey on Rise," *Hürriyet-Daily News*, July 13, 2011.
"Ummie, The Hajj – Chinese Pilgrims Then and Now, *ummieabiworld.blogspot.com*, November 5, 2010.
"Unfulfilled Hajj Dream for Uighur Muslims," *OnIslam.net*, October 30, 2011;
"Why Saudi Arabia Moved against Nigeria," *Nigerian Tribune*, September 29, 2012 [H. Ibrahim].
"Why We're Stopping Pregnant Women from Hajj," *allafrica.com*, August 18, 2012 [I. Sa'idu].

Reports

Acharya, V. V., T. Cooley, M. Richardson, and I. Walter. *Market Failures and Regulatory Failures: Lessons from Past and Present Financial Crises*. Asian Development Bank Institute, February 2011.
Bangladesh Ministry of Religious Affairs. Bangladesh Pilgrim Statistics, 2000–2008, *Hajj Management Portal*, 2009 (in Bengali).
Bangladesh Ministry of Religious Affairs. Districtwise Pilgrims, 2009, *Hajj Management Portal*, 2010 (in Bengali).
Bangladesh Ministry of Religious Affairs. Statistics on Bangladeshi Hajj, 2009–2012, *Hajj Management Portal*, 2012.
Hajj Committee of India. *Statewise Distribution of Quota for the Pilgrims of Haj, 2012 and 2013*. New Delhi, 2012 and 2013.
Indonesia Direktorat Jenderal Penyelenggaraan Haji dan Umrah. *Data dan statistik Direktorat Jenderal Penyelenggaraan Haji dan Umrah*, Jakarta, 2010.
Indonesia Direktorat Jenderal Penyelenggaraan Haji dan Umrah. *Data dan statistik Direktorat Jenderal Penyalenggaraan Haji dan Umrah, Haji dalam angka*, Jakarta, 2009.
Insan Hakları ve Mazlumlar için Dayanışma Derneği, Hac Raporu (Human Rights and Victims' Support Association, Hajj Report), December 29, 2005.
Ministry of Hajj, Kingdom of Saudi Arabia. *Hajj and Umrah Statistics*, 2010.
Tarr, D. G. *The Political, Regulatory and Market Failures That Caused the U.S. Financial Crisis*. World Bank, May 2010.
Türkiye İstatistik Kurumu, *Kültür İstatistikleri*, Ankara, 2009 and 2011.

CHAPTER 8

Barbir, K. K. *Ottoman Rule in Damascus, 1708–1758*. Princeton University Press, 1980.
Borel, F. *Choléra et peste dans le pèlerinage musulman, 1860–1903*. Paris: Masson et Cie., 1904.

Brower, P. "Russian Roads to Mecca: Religious Tolerance and Muslim Pilgrimage in the Russian Empire." *Slavic Review* 55, 3 (1996): 567–584.
Burckhardt, J. L. *Travels in Arabia*. 2 vols. London: Henry Colburn, 1829.
Faroqhi, S. *Pilgrims and Sultans: The Hajj under the Ottomans*. London: I. B. Tauris, 1996.
Harrison, M., *Public Health in British India: Anglo-Indian Preventive Medicine, 1859–1914*. Cambridge University Press, 1994.
Hoexter, H. *Endowments, Rulers, and Community: Waqf Al-Haramayn in Ottoman Algiers*. Leiden: Brill, 1998.
Jomier, J. Le maḥmal et la caravane égyptienne des pèlerins de La Mecque –XIIIᵉ–XXᵉ siècles. Cairo: Imprimerie de l'Institut français d'archéologie orientale, 1953.
Kostiner, J. *The Making of Saudi Arabia, 1916–1936: From Chieftaincy to Monarchical State*. Oxford University Press, 1993.
Miller, M. B. "Pilgrims' Progress: The Business of the Hajj." *Past & Present*, 191 (2006): 189–228.
Ochsenwald, W. L. "Ottoman Subsidies to the Hijaz, 1877–1886." *International Journal of Middle East Studies* 6 (1975): 300–307.
Ochsenwald, W. L. *Religion, Society and the State in Arabia: The Hijaz under Ottoman Control, 1840–1908*. Columbus: Ohio State University Press, 1984.
Pearson, M. N. *Pious Passengers: The Hajj in Earlier Times*. New Delhi: Sterling Publishers Private Limited, 1994.
Al-Rasheed, M. *A History of Saudi Arabia*. Cambridge University Press, 2010.
Rafeq, A. "New Light on the Transportation of the Damascene Pilgrimage during the Ottoman Period." In R. Olson (ed.), *Islamic and Middle Eastern Societies*. Brattleboro, VT: Amana Books, 1987: 127–136.
Rifʿat Pāshā, I. *Mirʾāt al-ḥaramayn*. Cairo: Dar al-Kutub al-Miṣriyya, 1925.
Roff, W. R. "Sanitation and Security. The Imperial Powers and the Nineteenth Century Hajj." *Arabian Studies* 6 (1982): 143–160.
Teitelbaum, J. *The Rise and Fall of the Hashimite Kingdom of Arabia*. New York University Press, 2001.
Tresse, R. *Le pèlerinage syrien aux villes saintes de l'Islam*. Paris: Imprimerie Chaumette, 1937.
Vredenbregt, J. "The Haddj: Some of Its Features and Functions in Indonesia." *Bijdragen tot de Taal-Land en Volkenkunde* 118 (1962): 91–154.

CHAPTER 9

Scholarly Literature and Sources

Amrith, S. S. *Decolonizing International Health: India and Southeast Asia, 1930–65*. Basingstoke: Palgrave Macmillan, 2006.
Anderson, C. *Subaltern Lives: Biographies of Colonialism in the Indian Ocean World, 1790–1920*. Cambridge University Press, 2012.
Bashford, A. and C. Hooker (eds.). *Contagion*. London: Routledge, 2001.

Bashford, A. and C. Strange (eds.). *Isolation: Places and Practices of Exclusion*. London: Routledge, 2003).

Bayly, C. A. *The Birth of the Modern World 1780–1914*. Oxford: Blackwell, 2004.

Briggs, A. "Cholera and Society in the Nineteenth Century." *Past & Present* 19 (1961): 76–96.

Brown, T.M., M. Cuento, and E. Fee "The World Health Organization and the Transition from 'International' to 'Global' Public Health," *American Journal of Public Health*, 96, 1(2006), 62–72.

Burton, I. *AEI Arabia Egypt India: A Narrative of Travel*. London: Wiliam Mullan and son, 1879.

Burton, I. *The Romance of Isabel Lady Burton. The Story of her Life*. 2 vols. Told in Part by Herself and in Part by W. H. Wilkins. 3rd ed. London: Hutchinson & Co, 1897.

Chiffoleau, S. *Genèse de la santé publique internationale: De la peste d'Orient à l'OMS*. Presses Universitaires de Rennes, 2012.

Clavin, P. *Securing the World Economy: The Reinvention of the League of Nations, 1920–1946*. Oxford University Press, 2013.

D'Arcy, P. F. and D. B. Worthen. *Laboratory on the Nile: A History of the Wellcome Tropical Research Laboratories*. Binghamton, NY: Haworth Press, 1999.

Evans, R. J. *Death in Hamburg: Society and Politics in the Cholera Years, 1830–1910*. Oxford University Press, 1987.

Ezzerelli, K. "Le pèlerinage à La Mecque au temps du chemin de fer du Hedjaz (1908–1914)." In S. Chiffoleau and A. Madoeuf (eds.), *Les pèlerinages au Maghreb et au Moyen-Orient: Espaces publics, espaces du public*. Beirut: Institut français du Proche-orient, 2005: 167–191.

Foxhall, K. *Health, Medicine, and the Sea: Australian Voyages, c. 1815–1860*. Manchester University Press, 2012.

Geyer, M. and J Paulmann (eds.), *The Mechanics of Internationalism: Culture, Society, and Politics from the 1840s to the First World War*. Oxford University Press, 2001.

Gorman, D. *The Emergence of International Society in the 1920s*. Cambridge University Press, 2012.

Harrison, M. *Contagion: How Commerce Has Spread Disease*. New Haven and London: Yale University Press, 2013.

Harrison, M. "Quarantine, Pilgrimage and Colonial Trade." *Indian Economic and Social History Review* 29 (1992): 117–144.

Heaton, M. M. "Globalization, Health and the Hajj: The West African Pilgrimage Scheme, 1919–38." In T. Falola and M. M. Heaton (eds.), *HIV/AIDS, Illness, and African Well-being*. University of Rochester Press, 2007: 243–270.

Herren, M. *Internationale Organisationen seit 1865: Eine Globalgeschichte der internationalen Ordnung*. Darmstadt: Wissenschaftliche Buchgesellschaft, 2009.

Howard-Jones, N. *The Scientific Background of the International Sanitary Conferences 1851–1938*, Geneva (WHO), 1975.

Huber, V. *Channelling Mobilities: Migration and Globalisation in the Suez Canal Region and Beyond*. Cambridge University Press, 2013.

Huber, V. "'Multiple Mobilities': Über den Umgang mit verschiedenen Mobilitätsformen um 1900." *Geschichte und Gesellschaft* 36 (2010): 317–341.
Huber, V. "The Unification of the Globe by Disease? The International Sanitary Conferences on Cholera, 1851–1894." *Historical Journal* 49, 2 (2006): 453–476.
Iriye, A. *Cultural Internationalism and World Order*. Baltimore: Johns Hopkins University Press, 1997.
Joyce, P. *The Rule of Freedom: Liberalism and the Modern City*. London and New York: Verso, 2003.
Lee, K. and R. Dodson, "Globalization and Cholera: Implications for Global Governance." *Global Governance* 6, 2 (2000): 213–236.
Low, C. "Empire and the Hajj: Pilgrims, Plagues, and Pan-Islam under British Surveillance, 1865–1908." *International Journal of Middle East Studies* 40, 2 (2008): 269–290.
Mazower, M. *Governing the World: The History of an Idea*. London: Penguin, 2012.
Mazower, M. *No Enchanted Palace: The End of Empire and the Ideological Origins of the United Nations*. Princeton University Press, 2006.
McGrew, R. E. "The First Cholera Epidemic and Social History." *Bulletin of the History of Medicine* 34 (1960): 61–73.
Miller, M. B. "Pilgrims' Progress: The Business of the Hajj." *Past & Present* 191, 1 (2006): 189–228.
Pedersen, S. *The Guardians: The League of Nations and the Crisis of Empire*. Oxford University Press, 2015.
Pedersen, S. "Review Essay: Back to the League of Nations." *American Historical Review* 112, 4 (2007): 1091–1117.
Rasmussen, A. "Jalons pour une histoire des congers internationaux au XIXe siècle: Régulation scientifique et propagande intellectuelle." *Relations internationales* 62 (1990): 115–133.
Roff, W. R. "Sanitation and Security: The Imperial Powers and the Nineteenth-Century Hajj." *Arabian Studies* 6 (1982): 143–160.
Sennett, R. *Flesh and Stone: The Body and the City in Western Civilization*. London: Faber and Faber, 1994.
Siddiqi, J. *World Health and World Politics: The World Health Organization and the UN System*. London: Hurst & Company, 1995.
Simpson, W. J. "Maritime Quarantine and Sanitation in Relation to the Cholera." *The Practitioner: A Journal of Therapeutics and Public Health* 48 (1892): 148–160.
Slight, J. "British Imperial Rule and the Hajj." In David Motadel (ed.), *Islam and the European Empires*. Oxford University Press, 2014: 53–72.
Sluga, G. *Internationalism in the Age of Nationalism*. Philadelphia: University of Pennsylvania Press, 2013.
Steel, F. *Oceania under Steam: Sea Transport and the Cultures of Colonialism, c. 1870–1914*. Manchester University Press, 2011.
Tagliacozzo, E. *The Longest Journey: South East Asians and the Pilgrimage to Mecca*. Oxford University Press, 2013.
Zylberman, P. "Civilizing the State: Borders, Weak States and International Health in Modern Europe." In A. Bashford (ed.), *Medicine at the Border: Disease, Globalization and Security, 1850 to the Present*. Basingstoke: Palgrave Macmillan, 2006: 21–40.

Archival Sources

Archives nationales d'Outre-Mer, Aix-en-Provence (ANOM) *Bundesarchiv, Berlin Centre des Archives diplomatiques, Nantes League of Nations Archives, Geneva (LON) The National Archives, Kew (TNA) World Health Organization* Archives, Geneva (WHO)

CHAPTER 10

Secondary Literature

Ahmet Cevdet Pasha. *Tarih-i Cevdet*. 2nd ed. 12 vols. in 6. Istanbul: Matbaa-yi Osmaniye, 1892.

al-ʿAjlānī, M. *Tārīkh al-bilād al-ʿArabiyya*. 2nd ed. Riyadh: Dār al-Shibl, 1993.

Āl al-Shaykh, ʿA. b. ʿA. *Al-Ithḥāf fī al-radd ʿalā al-ṣaḥḥāf*. Ed. ʿA. al-Zīr Āl Ḥamad. Riyadh: Dār al-ʿĀṣima, 1995.

Anṭākī, F. *Al-Hind kamā raʾaytuhā*. Cairo: W. A. Fadil's Printing Press, 1933.

Arsalān, S. *Al-Irtisāmāt al-liṭāf fī khāṭir al-ḥājj ilā aqdas maṭāf*. Ed. M. R. Riḍā. 2nd ed. [Cairo: Maṭbaʿat al-Manār], 1998.

Bābaṭīn, H. *Al-Tanẓīmāt al-idāriyya li-shuʾūn al-ḥajj fī ʿahd al-malik ʿAbd al-ʿAzīz*. [Riyadh]: Maktabat al-Wafāʾ, 2003.

Bā Salāma, Y. *Tārīkh al-Kaʿba al-muʿaẓẓama: ʿimāratuhā wa-kiswatuhā wa-sadānatuhā*. Riyadh: al-Amāna al-ʿĀmma li-l-Iḥtifāl bi-Murūr Miʾat Sana ʿalā Taʾsīs al-Mamlaka al-ʿArabiyya al-Suʿūdiyya, 1999.

al-Batanūnī, M. L. *Al-Risāla al-Ḥijāziyya li-Walī al-Niʿam al-Ḥājj ʿAbbās Ḥilmī Bāshā al-Thānī Khadīw Miṣr*. 2nd ed. Cairo: Maṭbaʿat al-Jamāliyya, 1329/1911.

Burdett, A. *The Expansion of Wahhabi Power in Arabia, 1798–1932: British Documentary Records*. Cambridge: Cambridge Archive Editions, 2013.

Daḥlān, A. Z. *Khulāṣat al-kalām fī bayān umarāʾ al-balad al-ḥarām min zaman al-Nabī ʿalayhi al-ṣalāt wa-l-salām ilā zamaninā hādhā bi-l-tamām*. Cairo: al-Maṭbaʿa al-Khayriyya, 1305/[1888].

al-Diqin, M. *Kiswat al-Kaʿba al-muʿaẓẓama ʿabr al-tārīkh*. [Cairo]: Maṭbaʿat al-Jabalāwī, 1986.

Ḥajar, J. "Al-Ḥijāz fī al-fikr al-siyāsī li-muslimī al-Hind." *Majallat Kulliyyat al-Ādāb* (Alexandria), 39 (1991–1992): 179–228.

Ibn ʿAbd al-Shakūrʿ A. *Tārīkh ashrāf wa-umarāʾ Makka al-Mukarrama*. MS Topkapi Saray, 1/44.

Ibn Bishr, ʿU. *ʿUnwān al-majd fī tārīkh Najd*. Ed. ʿA. ʿA. Āl Al-Shaykh. 4th ed. Riyadh: Darat al-Malik 'Abd al-'Azız, 1982.

al-Jabartī, ʿA. *ʿAjāʾib al-āthār fī al-tarājim wa-l-akhbār*. Ed. ʿA. ʿA. ʿAbd al-Raḥīm. 4 vols. Cairo: Dār al-Kutub al-Miṣriyya, 1997–1998.

al-Māzinī, I. *Riḥlat al-Ḥijāz*. Cairo: Maṭbaʿat Fuʾād, 1930.

Muʾadhdhin, ʿA. ʿA. "Kiswat al-Kaʿba wa-ṭuruzuha al-fanniyya mundh al-ʿahd al-ʿUthmānī." Unpublished MA thesis. Umm al-Qurā University, Saudi Arabia, 1980–1981.

al-Muṭawwaʿ, ʿA. *Idārat Makka al-Mukarrama fī ʿahd al-dawla al-Suʿūdiyya al-ūlā*. Riyadh: Maṭābiʿ al-Ḥumayḍī, 2009.
Naṣīf, Ḥ. *Māḍī al-Ḥijāz wa-ḥāḍiruh*. Cairo: Maktabat wa-Maṭbaʿat Khuḍayr, 1349/1930.
Rafsanjānī, ʿA. A. H. *Difāʿ va siyāsat: Kārnāmah va khāṭirāt-i sāl-i 1366*. Tehran: Daftar-i Nashr-i Maʿārif-i Inqilāb, 1389sh/2010.
Rutter, E. *The Holy Cities of Arabia*. London & New York: G. P. Putnam's Sons Ltd., 1928.
Ṣābān, S. *Al-Jazīra al-ʿArabiyya: buḥūth wa-dirāsāt min wathāʾiq al-irshīf al-ʿUthmānī wa-l-maṣādir al-Turkiyya*. Riyadh: Maktabat al-Malik Fahad al-Waṭaniyya, 2006.
al-ʿUthaymīn, ʿA. *Tārīkh al-Mamlaka al-ʿArabiyya al-Suʿūdiyya*. Riyadh: n.p., 1984.
Vassiliev, Alexei. *The History of Saudi Arabia*. London: Saqi Books, 1998.
Wahba, Ḥ. *Jazīrat al-ʿArab fī al-qarn al-ʿishrīn*. 3rd ed. Cairo: Dār al-Āfāq al-ʿArabiyya, 1975.
Wahīm, Ṭ. *Mamlakat al-Ḥijāz (1916–1925): dirāsa fī al-awḍāʿ al-siyasiyya*. Basra University Press, 1982.
Zaydān, M. *Dhikrayāt al-ʿuhūd al-thalātha: al-ʿuthmānī, al-sharīfī, al-saʿūdī*. Riyadh: Maṭābiʿ al-Farazdaq, 1988.
al-Zayyānī. *Al-Tarjumāna al-kubrā fī akhbār al-maʿmūr barran wa-baḥrā*. Ed. ʿA. al-Fīlālī. 2nd ed. Rabat: Dār Nashr al-Maʿrifa, 1991.

Documents

Ḥasan, M. ʿA. *Ṣaḥīfa mūjaza bi-aʿmāl muʾtamar al-ʿālam al-Islāmī al-awwal bi-Makka al-Mukarrama*. Alexandria: Maṭbaʿat Nahḍat al-Sharq, 1926.
Jarman, R. L. *The Jedda Diaries, 1919–1940*. 4 vols. [Farnham Common]: Archive Editions, 1980.
Muhimmat al-wafd al-Hindī fī al-Ḥijāz. Report by the Foreign Ministry of the Hijaz Government (Sharif ʿAlī government), January 2–30, 1925.
Records of the Hajj. Ed. A. Rush. 10 vols. [Slough]: Archive Editions, 1993. I: Pilgrim Prayers, Invocations and Rites. II: The Early Caliphal, Mamluk and Ottoman Periods, 630–1814. III: The Ottoman Period, 1814–1887. IV: The Ottoman Period, 1888–1915. V: The Hashimite Period, 1916–1925. VI: The Saudi Period, 1926–1935. VII: The Saudi Period, 1935–1951. VIII: The Saudi Period, 1951–. IX: Health Affairs and the Hajj. X: Documents and Maps.

Archival Sources

Ottoman Archive, H.H 19550-J.

Newspapers

al-Ahrām

al-Manār
Majallat al-Majalla
al-Taḍāmun al-Islāmī
Umm al-Qurā

CHAPTER 11

Primary Sources

Al-Fouzan, S. [Ṣ. Āl Fawzān]. *How to Perform Hajj and Umrah*. Trans. M. S. Al-Muharib. Kuwait: Islamic Translation Centre, 1992.

al-Batanūnī, M. L. *Al-Risāla al-Ḥijāziyya li-Walī al-Niʿam al-Ḥājj ʿAbbās Ḥilmī Bāshā al-Thānī Khadīw Miṣr*. 2nd ed. Cairo: Maṭbaʿat al-Jamāliyya, 1329/1911.

al-Bukhārī. *Al-Jāmiʿ al-Ṣaḥīḥ*. 4 vols. Cairo: al-Maṭbaʿat al-Salafiyya wa-Maktabatuhā, 1403/1982–1983.

al-Harawī. *A Lonely Wayfarer's Guide to Pilgrimage*. Trans. J. W. Meri. Princeton, NJ: Darwin Press, 2004.

Malcolm X, with the assistance of A. Haley. *The Autobiography of Malcolm X*. New York: Grove Press, 1965.

Manāsik al-ḥajj wa-l-umra ʿalā l-madhāhib al-arbaʿa wa-adʿiyat ziyārat al-Madīna al-munawwara. Medina: Maktabat Ṭayyiba li-l-Nashr wal-Tawzīʿ, n.d.

The Qur'an. Trans. M. A. S. Abdel Haleem. Oxford University Press, 2008.

al-Shāfiʿī. *The Epistle on Legal Theory*. Ed. and trans. J. E. Lowry. New York University Press, 2013.

Shariati, A. *Hajj: Reflections on Its Rituals*. Trans. L. Bakhtiar. Albuquerque, NM: ABJAD, 1992.

Secondary Literature

Abdel Haleem, M. A. S. "The Importance of Hajj: Spirit and Rituals." In V. Porter et al. (eds.), *Hajj: Journey to the Heart of Islam*. Cambridge, MA: Harvard University Press, 2012: 26–67.

Bianchi, R. R. *Guests of God: Pilgrimage and Politics in the Islamic World*. New York: Oxford University Press, 2004.

Campo, J. E. "Authority, Ritual and Spatial Order in Islam: The Pilgrimage to Mecca." *Journal of Ritual Studies* 5 (1991): 65–91.

Eickelman D. F. and J. Piscatori (eds.). *Muslim Travellers: Pilgrimage, Migration and the Religious Imagination*. London: Routledge, 1990.

Ellison, K. *My Country 'Tis of Thee: My Faith, My Family, Our Future*. New York: Gallery Books/Karen Hunter Publishing, 2014.

Gaudefroy-Demombynes, M. *Le pèlerinage à la Mekke*. Paris: Librairie Orientaliste Paul Geuthner, 1923.

Graham, W. "Islam in the Mirror of Ritual." In R. G. Hovanissian and S. Vryonis, Jr. (eds.), *Islam's Understanding of Itself*. Malibu: Undena Publications, 1983: 53–71.

Hamidullah, M. "Le Pèlerinage à la Mecque." In *Sources Orientales III: Les Pèlerinages*. Paris: Seuil, 1960: 89–138.

Katz, M. H. "The Hajj and the Study of Islamic Ritual." *Studia Islamica* 98/99 (2004): 95–129.

Porter, V. with M. A. S. Abdel Haleem et al. (eds.) *Hajj: Journey to the Heart of Islam*. Cambridge, MA: Harvard University Press, 2012.

Powers, P. R. *Intent in Islamic Law: Motive and Meaning in Medieval Sunnī Fiqh*. Leiden: Brill, 2006.

Powers, P. R. "Interiors, Intentions and the 'Spirituality' of Islamic Ritual Practice." *Journal of the American Academy of Religion* 72, 2 (2004): 426–454.

al-Sirjānī, R. *Al-Ḥajj wa-l-ʿumra: aḥkām wa-khibarāt*. Cairo: Sharikat Aqlām lil-Nashr wa-l-Tawzīʿ wa-l-Tarjama, 2012.

Steinfels, A. "Ritual." In J. Elias (ed.), *Key Themes for the Study of Islam*. Oxford: Oneworld Publications, 2010: 304–320.

Toorawa, S. M. "Eid and the Imagery of Return." *Le Mauricien*. September 19, 2009: 7.

Toorawa, S. M. "Every Robe He Dons Becomes Him: Images of Clothing in the Islamic Tradition." *Parabola* 19, 3 (1994): 23–28.

Toorawa, S. M. "Pilgrimage." In G. Böwering (ed.), *Princeton Encyclopedia of Islamic Political Thought*. Princeton University Press, 2013: 417–418.

Toorawa, S. M. "Pillars." In G. Böwering (ed.), *Princeton Encyclopedia of Islamic Political Thought*. Princeton University Press, 2013: 418–420.

Wheeler, B. *Mecca and Eden: Ritual, Relics and Territory in Islam*. University of Chicago Press, 2006.

Wolfe, M. *One Thousand Roads to Mecca: Ten Centuries of Travelers Writing about the Muslim Pilgrimage*. New York: Grove Press, 2015.

Young, W. C. "The Kaba, Gender, and the Rites of Pilgrimage." *International Journal of Middle East Studies* 25 (1993): 285–300.

Zeusse, E. "Ritual." In L. Jones (ed.), *Encyclopedia of Religion*. 2nd ed. Detroit: Macmillan Reference USA, 2005. XI: 7833–7848.

Web Sources

ARC (Alliance of Religions and Conservation) at arcworld.org

British Broadcasting Corporation at bbc.co.uk

The Guardian (London) at theguardian.com

The Huffington Post at huffingtonpost.com

Pew Forum on Religion & Public Life at pewforum.org

Royal Embassy of Saudi Arabia (Washington, DC) at saudiembassy.net

Saudi Television Channel Two at sauditv2.tv

CHAPTER 12

Print Sources

Bunt, G. R. *iMuslims: Rewiring the House of Islam*. Chapel Hill: University of North Carolina Press; London: C. Hurst & Co, 2009.

Bunt, G. R. *Islam in the Digital Age: E-jihad, Online Fatwas and Cyber Islamic Environments*. London and Sterling, VA: Pluto Press, 2003.

Bunt, G. R. "Surfing Islam: Ayatollahs, Shayks and Hajjis on the Superhighway." In J. K. Hadden and D. E. Cowan (eds), *Religion on the Internet: Research Prospects and Promises*. New York: Elsevier Science, 2000: 127–151.

Bunt, G. R. *Virtually Islamic: Computer-Mediated Communication and Cyber Islamic Environments*. Cardiff: University of Wales Press, 2000.

Porter, V. with M. A. S. Abdel Haleem et al. (eds.). *Hajj: Journey to the Heart of Islam*. Cambridge, MA: Harvard University Press, 2012.

Online Sources

(all last accessed April 11, 2014, except where indicated)

3D Kabah 3D Kabah, youtube.com/user/3dkabah

Alisharahuk. "Deaf Umrah 2011 – A Journey through the Eyes of Deaf Pilgrims," at youtube.com/watch?v=4JGRYg6B-_g

Aloloom. "Thread: Index of Important Fatwas on Hajj by Fatwa Committee," at aloloomenglish.net/vb/showthread.php?549-Index-of-important-Fatwas-on-Hajj-by-Fatwa-Committee

aswatalislam.net

Channel 4. channel4.com/life/microsites/H/hajj/genb_pilgrims.html

Communications and Information Technology Commission. "Quality of Mobile Phone Services during the Hajj and Umrah Seasons Is within Target Limits," *CITC E-Newsletter* 006 (March 14, 2011).

DailyWhoIs. "Domain Name: islamweb.net," at dailywhois.com/domain/islam web.ne

Dastageeri. dastageeri.de/Dastageeri/Apps.htm

Derrickson, K. "Second Life and the Sacred: Islamic Space in a Virtual World," at digitalislam.eu/article.do?articleId=1877

Easy Hajj n Umrah by Techlabs. youtube.com/watch?v=tNn99Uzyono

Facebook. "My Hajj," at facebook.com/pages/My-Hajj/53124370691742

FatwaIslam.com. "Pilgrimage," at fatwaislam.com/fis/index.cfm?scn=scš11&c=2

Fatwa-Online. "Sending a maid for Hajj with a group of women or a Hajj package group [Shaykh Ibn Fowzaan, al-Muntaqaa min Fataawa Ibn Fowzaan – Volume 3, Page 168, Fatwa No.252]," at fatwa-online.com/fataawa/worship/hajjandumrah/haj002/0000219_1.htm

Flickr. Chinx786 n.d., at flickr.com/people/chinx786 n.d.

Global Awareness Campaign for Hujjaj-e-Ikram. "Use of Mobile Phone (Cellular) in Harmain Shareefain for Protect the Sanctity of Harmain Shareefain," at facebook.com/muslimculturemagazine
Go Makkah. "The Hajj School: Fatwas of Hajj on Behalf of Others," at go-makkah.com/english/dossier/articles/357/Fatwas+of+Hajj+on+behalf+of+others.html
Google Maps. "Mecca, Makka, Kaaba, Saudi Arabia," at goo.gl/maps/t7mG4
"Hajj 1425 – by Jawahrah," at hajjstories.wordpress.com/2009/06/08/hajj-1425/#more-36
Hajj and Umra Guide. youtube.com/watch?v=CEgET1MzZ7 M (last accessed April 11, 2014)
Hajj & Umrah for iPad by AMC Apps. itunes. apple.com/us/app/Hajj-umrah/id471282657?mt=8
Hajj Guide App. appbrain.com/app/Hajj-guide/com.v1_4.Hajjguide.com
Hajj Guide By ImranQureshi.com. itunes.apple.com/us/app/Hajj-guide/id473635756?mt=8
Hajj Mabrur. hajjmabrur.net
Hajj – Pilgrimage to Mecca by Magnicode. itunes.apple.com/gb/app/hajj-pilgrimage-to-mecca/id336371771?mt=
Islamfrominside. islamfrominside.com/Pages/Articles/AroundtheKabba.html
Islamicity. islamicity.com/travel/hajj
Islam Online. "Islam on Second Life – Virtual Hajj," at youtu.be/eNNqd2AxxyM
Islamic Gateway. "Hajj and Eid al-Adha," at ummah.net/hajj (retrieved August 15, 2001)
IslamWeb. "Hajj and Umrah: Hajj 1433 > Fataawa > General Fataawa," at islamweb.net/ehajj/index.php?page=maincategory&lang=E&vPart=1030&order=&startno=255
IslamWeb. "Hajj for Kids," at kids.islamweb.net/english/flash.php?url=flash/hajj.swf
Kingdom of Saudi Arabia – Hajj and Umrah e-portal. "Health Tips to Be Followed during Hajj," at moh.gov.sa/en/Hajj/HealthGuidelines/Pages/DuringHajj.aspx
Majlis Ugama Islam Singapura. muis.gov.sg/cms/services/haj.aspx?id=16325
"Masjid al-Haram – Kaaba." 3Dmekanlar.com:3dmekanlar/en/masjid-al-haram—kaaba.html
Mas'ud Ahmed Khan. "Hajj Tips" at: masudblog.com/?p=357 (October 24, 2008)
Ministry of Hajj. "Can I Use My Mobile Phone/Cell Phone in Saudi Arabia?" at hajinformation.com/main/t60.htm
Ministry of Religious Affairs and Inter Faith Harmony, Government of Pakistan. mora.gov.pk
momin.org. "Introduction of Manasik-e-Haj," at momin. org
Mumineen.org. "Mumineen.org Photo Akhbar," at media.mumineen.org/gallery/thumbnails.php?album=12
"Physical Aspects of Hajj – by Shahin," at tinyurl.com/ol9s3rw
Qibla.com/Shaykh Muhammad ibn Adam al-Kawthari. "Question ID:3176: Mobile/Cell Phones during Hajj in Mosques (2008)," at spa.qibla.com/issue_view.asp?HD=1&ID=3176&CATE=7
qurbani.com

The National (Abu Dhabi)/Ghazal, G. "Grand Mufti Calls for Dialogue about the Internet," at thenational.ae/news/uae-mufti-calls-for-dialogue-about-the-internet (February 20, 2012)
Sotheby's. "Arts of the Islamic World: Muhyi Al-Din Lari (d.1526–7 Ad), Futuh Al-Haramayn in Verse, Copied by the Scribe 'Ali, Probably Herat, Persia, Safavid, Dated 990 AH/1582 AD." At sothebys.com/en/auctions/ecatalogue/2011/arts-of-the-islamic-world/lot.96.html (last accessed April 11, 2014)
SunniForum. "Re: Must-Takes to Umrah and Hajj," at sunniforum.com/forum/showthread.php?69942-Must-takes-to-Umrah-and-Hajj (March 17, 2011)
SunniForum. "Thread: Barelvi Fatwa: First No Prayer and Now No Hajj behind Salafis?" at sunniforum.com/forum/showthread.php?55916-Barelvi-fatwa-first-no-prayer-and-now-No-Hajj-behind-Salafis
TripAdvisor. tripadvisor.co.uk/HACSearch?geo=29399
Twitter. "#hajj" at: twitter.com
Twitter. Mohammed Amous, "@HajjUmrahDays" at: twitter.com/HajUmrahDays
Universiti Sains Islam Malaysia. "Fatwa Management System – Fatawa: How Many Times Did Our Prophet Muhammad (PBUH) Perform Hajj and Umrah?" at infad.usim.edu.my/modules.php?op=modload&name=News&file=article&sid=8183
Young Muslims TV. "A Visual Guide to hajj Part 1 of 3," at youngmuslims.tv/Channel5/Category42/Video709/
ziaraat.org. "Hajj Rituals by Ayatullah Ali al-Husayni al-Seestani," at ziaraat.com/books/hajj_sistani.pdf

CHAPTER 13

Āl-e Ahmad, J. *Khasī dar mīqāt*. Tehran: Nil, 1345/1966.
Āl-e Ahmad, J. *Lost in the Crowd*. Trans. J. Green. Washington DC: Three Continents Press, 1985.
Ahmed, Q. A. *In the Land of Invisible Women: A Female Doctor's Journey in the Saudi Kingdom*. Naperville, IL: Sourcebooks, Inc., 2008.
Bianchi, R. R. *Guests of God*. New York: Oxford University Press, 2004.
Gilsenan, M. "And You, What Are You Doing Here?" *The London Review of Books* 28 (October 9, 2006), 20.
"Hajj Travel Narratives." In V. Porter with M. A. S. Abdel Haleem et al. (eds.), *Hajj: Journey to the Heart of Islam*. Cambridge, MA: Harvard University Press, 2012: 282–283.
Hammoudi, A. *A Season in Mecca: Narrative of a Pilgrimage*. Trans. P. Ghazaleh. New York: Farrar, Straus and Giroux, 2006.
Knight, M. M. *Journey to the End of Islam*. New York: Soft Skull Press, 2009.
Nomani, A. Q. *Standing Alone in Mecca: An American Woman's Struggle for the Soul of Islam*. HarperSanFrancisco, 2005.
Shari'ati, A. *Hajj*. Trans. A. A. Behzadnia and N. Denny. Houston, TX: Free Islamic Literatures, 1977.

Wolfe, M. *One Thousand Roads to Mecca: Ten Centuries of Travelers Writing about the Muslim Pilgrimage*, rev. expanded ed. New York: Grove Press, 2015.

CHAPTER 14

Classical Sources

al-Azraqī. *Kitāb Akhbār Makka wa-mā jā'a fihā min al-akhbār*. 2 vols. in 1. Ed. R. al-Ṣāliḥ Malḥas. Beirut: Dar al-Andalus, 1960.

al-Bukhārī. *Al-Jamiʿ al-Ṣaḥīḥ*. 9 vols. Trans. M. M. Khan. Medina: Dār al-Fikr, 1981.

Ibn Isḥāq [/Ibn Hishām]. *The Life of Muhammad*. Trans. A. Guillaume. Oxford University Press, 1980 [1955].

Ibn Jubayr. *Riḥlat ibn Jubayr*. Cairo: Dār al-Maʿārif, n.d.

Ibn Jubayr. *The Travels of Ibn Jubayr, Being the Chronicles of a Mediaeval Spanish Moor Concerning His Journey to the Egypt of Saladin, the Holy Cities of Arabia*. Trans. R. J. C. Broadhurst. London: J. Cape, 1952.

al-Kisā'ī. *The Tales of the Prophets of al-Kisa'i*. Trans. W. M. Thackston, Jr. Chicago: Kazi Publications, 1997.

Muslim. *Ṣaḥīḥ*. Trans. Abdul Hamid Siddiqi. Lahore: Sh. Muhammad Ashraf, n.d.

Rifʿat Pāshā, I. *Mir'āt al-ḥaramayn*, 2 vols. Beirut: Dār al-Maʿrifa, 1982 (?) [1925].

al-Ṭabarī, *Tafsīr*. Cairo: al-Matbaʿa al-Kubrā al-Amīriyya, 1904.

al-Thaʿlabī. *ʿArā'is al-majālis fi qiṣaṣ al-anbiyā'* or *"Lives of the Prophets"*. Trans. W. M. Brinner. Leiden: Brill, 2002.

Secondary Literature

Abdel Haleem, M. A. S. "The Importance of Hajj: Spirit and Rituals." In V. Porter with M. A. S. Abdel Haleem et al. (eds.), *Hajj: Journey to the Heart of Islam*. Cambridge, MA: Harvard University Press, 2012: 26–67.

Aksoy, Ş and R. Milstein. "A Collection of Thirteenth-Century Illustrated Hajj Certificates." In İ. C. Shick (ed.), *M. Uğur Derman: 65 Yaş Armağan*. Istanbul: Sabancı Universitesi, 2000: 101–134.

Asani, A. S. and C. E. S. Gavin. "Through the Lens of Mirza of Delhi: The Dabbas Album of Early Twentieth-Century Photographs of Pilgrimage Sites in Mecca and Medina." *Murqarnas* 15 (1998): 178–199.

Atwood, M. *MaddAddam: A Novel*. New York: Nan A. Talese/Doubleday, 2013.

Benjamin, W. "The Work of Art in the Age of Mechanical Reproduction." In W. Benjamin. *Illuminations*. Ed. H. Arendt. Trans. H. Zohn. New York: Harcourt, Brace & World, Inc., 1968: 219–253.

Campo, J. E. *The Other Sides of Paradise: Explorations into the Religious Meanings of Domestic Space in Islam*. Columbia: University of South Carolina Press, 1991.

De St. Jorre, J. "Pioneer Photographer of the Holy Cities." *Saudi Aramco World* 50, 1 (1999): 36–47.

Dorduncu, M. B. *Mecca-Medina: The Yildiz Albums of Sultan Abdulhamid II*. Trans. H. Yesilova. Somerset, NJ: The Light, Inc., 2006.
Grabar, O. "Upon Reading al-Azraqī." *Muqarnas* 3 (1985): 1–7.
Irwin, R. "Journey to Mecca: A History (Part 2)." In V. Porter with M. A. S. Abdel Haleem et al. (eds.), *Hajj: Journey to the Heart of Islam*. Cambridge, MA: Harvard University Press, 2012: 136–219.
Jain, K. *Gods in the Bazaar: The Economies of Indian Calendar Art*. Durham, NC: Duke University Press, 2007.
Kramer, M. "Khomeini's Messengers in Mecca." In M. Kramer (ed.), *Arab Awakening and Islamic Revival: The Politics of Ideas in the Middle East*. New Brunswick, NJ: Transaction, 1996: 161–187.
Kriss, R. and H. Kriss-Heinrich. *Volksglaube im Bereich des Islam*, 2 vols. Wiesbaden: Otto Harrassowitz, 1960–1962.
Lézine, A. *Trois palais d'Epoque Ottomane au Caire*. Cairo: Institut français d'archéologie orientale, 1972.
Metcalf, B. D. "The Pilgrimage Remembered: South Asian Accounts of the Hajj." In D. Eickelman and J. Piscatori (eds.), *Muslim Travelers: Pilgrimage, Migration and the Religious Imagination*. London: Routledge; and Berkeley: University of California Press, 1990: 85–107.
Milstein, R. "*Futuh al-Haramayn*: Sixteenth-Century Illustrations of the Hajj Route." In D. J. Wasserstein and A. Ayalon (eds.), *Mamluks and Ottomans: Studies in Honour of Michael Winter*. London, New York: Routledge, 2006: 166–194.
Morgan, D. "The Look of the Sacred." In R. Orsi (ed.), *Cambridge Companion to Religious Studies*. Cambridge University Press, 2012: 296–318.
Morgan, D. *Visual Piety: A History and Theory of Popular Religious Images*. Berkeley: University of California Press, 1998.
Peters, F. E. *The Hajj: The Muslim Pilgrimage to Mecca and the Holy Places*. Princeton University Press, 1994.
Peters, F. E. *Mecca: A Literary History of the Muslim Holy Land*. Princeton University Press, 1994.
Porter, V. *The Art of Hajj*. Northampton, MA: Interlink Books, 2012.
Roxburgh, D. J. "Visualizing the Sites and Monuments of Islamic Pilgrimage." In M. S. Graves (ed.), *Architecture in Islamic Arts: Treasures of the Aga Khan Museum*. Geneva: Aga Khan Trust for Culture, 2011: 33–41.
Saeed, Y. *Muslim Devotional Art in India*. London: Routledge, 2012.
Stocchi, S. *L'Islam nella stampe/Islam in Prints*. Milan: Be-Ma Editrice, 1988.
Sourdel, D. and J. Sourdel-Thomine. *Certificats de pèlerinage d'époque ayyoubide: Contribution à l'histoire de l'idéologie de l'Islam au temps des Croisades*. Paris: L'Académie des Inscriptions et Belles-Lettres, 2006.
Touati, H. *Islam and Travel in the Middle Ages*. Trans. L. G. Cochrane. University of Chicago Press, 2010.
Tweed, T. *Crossing and Dwelling: A Theory of Religion*. Cambridge, MA: Harvard University Press, 2006.

ONLINE SOURCES

Hajj 1425 by Jawahrah. hajjstories.wordpress.com
Kingdom of Saudi Arabia, Ministry of Hajj Portal. haj.gov.sa
Lilandra and Chennette make Hajj. thehajj.wordpress.com
Ministry of Hajj, Kingdom of Saudi Arabia. www. hajinformation.com/main/v1 00.htm
"The New Karbala," in *The Graphics of Revolution and War: Iranian Poster Arts*, at lib.uchicago.edu/e/webexhibits/iranianposters/

Videography (chronologically)

Sacred Journeys with Bruce Feiler. United States: PBS Distribution, 2014. DVD, 360 mins.
Al-Hajj: Le Guide du Pèlerin et du Visiteur de La Mosquée Sacrée de La Mecque. Paris: Orientica [éd., distrib.], 2012. DVD, 40 mins.
Davies, T., et al. *Roads to Mecca*. United States: King Abdulaziz Public Library, 2011. DVD, 60 mins.
Neibaur, B., et al. *Journey to Mecca*. United States: National Geographic, 2011. DVD, 45 mins.
Ramadan, H. *Le Pélerinage Al Hadj: Objectif et Rites*. Lyon: Éd. Tawhid [éd., distrib.], 2010. DVD, 120 mins.
Lings, M., and O. Salazar. *Circling the House of God: Reflections on the Hajj*. N.p.: Matmedia Productions, 2009. DVD, 35 mins.
Kermani, F., et al. *Seven Wonders of the Muslim World*. Alexandria, VA: PBS, 2009. DVD, 60 mins.
Misch, G., et al. *A Road to Mecca: The Journey of Muhammad Asad*. Brooklyn, NY: Icarus Films, 2008. DVD, 92 mins.
Akhtar, N. and K. Chaudry. *Hajj: The Greatest Trip on Earth*. Hindmarsh, S. Australia: Tape Services, 2007. DVD, 98 mins.
Side by Side: From Mecca to Morgantown [featuring Asra Nomani]. New York: ABC News Productions, 2007. DVD, 21 mins.
Sim, K., R. Dobbs, and D. Dhaliwal. *Pilgrimage to Karbala*. Princeton, NJ: Films for the Humanities & Sciences, 2007. DVD, 86 mins.
Cazalé, N., et al. *Le Grand Voyage: Al-riḥlah Al-Kubrá*. Fair Lawn, NJ: Film Movement, 2006. DVD, 102 mins + 5.
Salazar, O., et al. *The Furthest Mosque*. London: Matmedia Productions, 2006. DVD, 25 mins.

Harrison, T. *Islam*. Princeton, NJ: Films for the Humanities & Sciences, 2006. DVD, 24 mins.
Mohan, T. N., et al. *Role of the Prophet*. Princeton, NJ: Films for the Humanities & Sciences, 2005. DVD, 27 mins.
Hata, S., et al. *Hajj: The Pilgrimage*. Princeton, NJ: Films for the Humanities & Sciences, 2004. DVD, 52 mins.
Wolfe, M., and T. Koppel. *ABC News Nightline: One American's Pilgrimage to Mecca*. United States: MPI Home Video, 2004. DVD, 22 mins.
Callebaut, P.-J., and N. Saey. *Today – Sunnis and the Prohibited Mecca*. Falls Church, VA: Landmark Media, 2004. DVD, 27 mins.
Mehdi, A., et al. *Inside Mecca*. Washington DC: National Geographic Television & Film, 2003. DVD, 60 mins.
Kronemer, A., et al. *Muhammad: Legacy of a Prophet*. Potomac Falls, VA: Unity Productions Foundation, 2003. DVD, 116 mins.
Bakhtaoui, S., and T. Oiron. *The Secret Mecca*. Princeton, NJ: Films for the Humanities & Sciences, 2003. DVD, 54 mins.
Saudi Arabia: The Hajj. Derry, NH: Chip Taylor Communications, 2002. DVD, 30 mins.
Shakir, Z., and H. Yusuf. *Reflections on the Pilgrimage of Malcolm X*. Hayward, CA: Alhambra Productions, 2002. DVD, 70 mins.
Küng, H. *World Religions: Le Grandes Religions Universelles. L'Islam = Religiones Del Mundo. Islam*. Princeton, NJ: Films for the Humanities & Sciences, 2002. DVD, 56 mins.
Arnaud, M., and M. Bakewell. *The Five Pillars of Islam*. Princeton, NJ: Films for the Humanities & Sciences, 2002. DVD, 30 mins.
Saudi Arabia: The Hajj. Derry, NH: Chip Taylor Communications, 2002. DVD, 30 mins.
Malik, A., and O. A. Salazar. *Hajj: The Journey of a Lifetime*. London: BBC, 2001. DVD, 59 mins.
Doyle, M. W. *Religions of the Book: Holy Places and Pilgrimage*. Princeton, NJ: Films for the Humanities & Sciences, 1991. DVD, 29 mins.

Index